FINLEY PETER DUNNE
& MR. DOOLEY

Charles Fanning

FINLEY PETER DUNNE
& MR. DOOLEY

The Chicago Years

The University Press
of Kentucky

Front endpaper: Bridgeport Area in the 1890s
Back endpaper: Chicago in the 1890s

Frontispiece: Finley Peter Dunne, about 1900.
Courtesy of the Chicago Historical Society.

The quotations on pp. 91, 139, and 172 from *The Collected Poems of W. B. Yeats* are reprinted with the kind permission of Macmillan Publishing Company.
The quotation on p. 105 from *Hogan's Goat* by William Alfred, copyright © 1958, 1966 by William Alfred, is reprinted with the permission of Farrar, Straus and Giroux, Inc.

ISBN: 0-8131-1365-2

Library of Congress Catalog Card Number: 77-75483

Copyright © 1978 by The University Press of Kentucky

A statewide cooperative scholarly publishing agency serving Berea College, Centre College of Kentucky, Eastern Kentucky University, The Filson Club, Georgetown College, Kentucky Historical Society, Kentucky State University, Morehead State University, Murray State University, Northern Kentucky University, Transylvania University, University of Kentucky, University of Louisville, and Western Kentucky University.

Editorial and Sales Offices: Lexington, Kentucky 40506

for Jane Frances

CONTENTS

References to Chicago newspapers in both text and notes use the following abbreviations and shortened forms:

EP: Chicago Evening Post
Herald: Chicago Herald
Journal: Chicago Evening Journal
News: Chicago Daily News

SP: Chicago Sunday Post
Times: Chicago Times
T-H: Chicago Times-Herald
Tribune: Chicago Tribune

PREFACE

EVERY four years editorial writers remember that Finley Peter Dunne created a bartender-philosopher named Martin Dooley, whose comments on national politics remain fresh enough for resurrection and application to the current presidential campaign. Historians and students of history remember further that this same Dooley delivered trenchant observations on a great variety of national and international topics to a large and enthusiastic American audience around the turn of the century. Some may even recall that it was Dooley's commentary on the Spanish-American War of 1898 that catapulted him into the prominent public position that was his until World War I. But few devotees of Mr. Dooley know anything about his origin in Chicago or about what he was like before he became a national celebrity.

I have looked back over the early years—the Chicago years—of Mr. Dooley and his creator, Finley Peter Dunne, and have found a body of literature of sufficient extent and quality to warrant study. Dunne wrote well over 300 dialect pieces in Chicago in the 1890s, from which he selected 100 for his first two published collections, *Mr. Dooley in Peace and in War* (1898) and *Mr. Dooley in the Hearts of His Countrymen* (1899). As he never again returned to these pieces, all the rest remained buried in Chicago newspaper files for nearly eighty years. Happily, the best of these pieces have now been resurrected in two recent collections.[1]

I have read all of Dunne's Chicago pieces in their original form and have dealt with them thematically here to illustrate the range and depth of his treatment of four subjects: the daily life of Chicago's working-class Irish community, the impact on that community of the process of assimilation into American life, the strange phenomenon of Irish nationalism as it affected the American Irish, and the view from an Irish ward of American city politics in the 1890s. In none of these areas has Dunne's contribution been sufficiently appreciated, and my hope is that he will now be reckoned a pioneer social historian and literary realist.

In addition, I have tried to place the Dooley pieces, including the more familiar utterances about the Spanish-American War and American imperialism, as products of Dunne's peculiar combination of backgrounds—his Irish inheritance, his life in a vibrant, expanding American city, and his place in the world of Chicago journalism.

My comparison of Dunne's editorials and Dooley pieces on similar subjects is meant to establish the often radical divergence of opinion between Editor Dunne and his cantankerous creation, a divergence that I see as another example of the self-destructive contradictions in the lives of so many successful American writers.

I quote extensively from the dialect pieces themselves because, to paraphrase Robert Frost on poetry, the flavor of Mr. Dooley is what gets lost in translation.

My greatest debt in writing this book is to Thomas N. Brown, who introduced me to Mr. Dooley and gave so generously of his time and knowledge through the various stages of this project. In addition, his own writing about the American Irish provided an unapproachable model of combined scholarship and grace. I am grateful also to Daniel Hoffman of the University of Pennsylvania for his considerate direction of the dissertation on Finley Peter Dunne that constituted the earliest form of this book.

Most of my research consisted of examination of a number of Chicago newspapers and periodicals, on microfilm or in bound form at the Chicago Historical Society, the Chicago Public Library, the Newberry Library in Chicago, and the Illinois State Historical Library at Springfield. Special thanks are due to the librarians at these institutions. For the illustrations, I am indebted to the Graphics Division staff of the Chicago Historical Society and to Mary Ann Johnson and Sheilamae O'Hara of Jane Addams' Hull-House, all of whom were extremely helpful. Also, I want to thank Ellen Skerrett for sharing her knowledge of Chicago geography and parish history.

For their heartening encouragement of my work, I am grateful to Lawrence J. McCaffrey and Andrew M. Greeley, two Chicago inheritors of Mr. Dooley's wit and passion for truth. Most of all, heartfelt thanks to my wife Jane Frances for her textual criticism, mapmaking, encouragement, and understanding.

1

CHICAGO BACKGROUNDS

The Genesis of Mr. Dooley

Other cities have produced other humorists, but Chicago appears to be the right atmosphere for a humorist to grow up in. After he has grown up, has suffered enough from his environment, so to speak, he may go elsewhere with personal safety, but it is doubtful if he will ever do anything better than what Chicago has given him to do.

THOMAS L. MASSON [1]

On FEBRUARY 24, 1890, the United States Congress crowned Chicago the archetypal American city by appointing her hostess for the national celebration of the four-hundredth anniversary of the discovery of America by Christopher Columbus. On April 30, 1893, one year behind schedule, President Grover Cleveland and Chicago Mayor Carter H. Harrison officially opened the World's Columbian Exposition, a fairyland extravaganza of plaster and whitewash in Jackson Park on the shores of Lake Michigan. Unfortunately, that sunny spring of self-congratulation was followed by the worst winter of poverty, homelessness, and starvation in the city's history—the "Black Winter" of 1893–1894, when thousands froze on the streets and fought for sleeping space in the corridors of city hall.

This wrenching contrast was typical of Chicago in the 1890s, a stormy, sprawling monster of a place, stuffed to bursting with unconscionable extremes. The sparkling lake was fed by typhoid-breeding backwater sloughs. Michigan Avenue mansions backed up against miles of squalid, cold-water tenements. Pioneer skyscrapers of the heralded Chicago School of architecture looked down over grim, utilitarian steel mills and stockyards. In 1893 the city boasted two hundred millionaires while thousands lived below the subsistence level. She also had a university, an opera house, an art institute, a symphony orchestra, several research libraries, and an academy of sciences—all brand new since 1885, all attempts to lay a veneer of instant culture over the bloody butcher's block that was her real defining symbol. Of course, these gestures failed to fool anyone, for they were forced to compete for newspaper coverage with labor disputes about sweatshop conditions and working children, with seasonal starvation and poverty crises, periodic typhoid epidemics and a soaring infant mortality rate, and abundant examples of citywide corruption from stinking back alleys to the city council chamber.

Most of these powerful ironies were traceable to incredible explosions of population, economics, and industry. Between her two defining spectacles, the Chicago Fire of 1871 and the World's Fair of 1893, Chicago grew from 300,000 to 1.3 million souls, many of them new immigrants. In the same years she became a world leader in grain, lumber, and meat-packing, banking, investments, and finance, manufacture and merchandising. Because city planning was unheard of in this, the heyday of laissez-faire sociology and economics, she soon became impossible to govern or to serve; the council served mostly itself, and social services were inadequate or nonexistent. In addition, this sticky mess of suffering and exploitation was aggravated by divisions within the city: there were as many Chicagos as problems to solve. The South Side stockyards were the city's belly and guts; the midtown business section, the Loop, was her calculating brain; the miles of railroad tracks and waterways were the arteries through which her lifeblood churned. But the human analogy did not hold, for Chicago's people had no cooperative base on which to build. The city's heart—the places where her people lived—was hopelessly fragmented, divided against itself. Chicagoans lived on a confused checkerboard of mutually distrustful ethnic and economic enclaves, whose boundaries were constantly shifting with the tides of immigration and fortune.

In the 1890s two of these enclaves were identifiably Irish. On the South Side, below the Chicago River's South Branch and above the stockyards, stretching from the crossing of Archer Avenue and Halsted Street, was Bridgeport. The Irish had first settled in numbers there, to build the Illinois and Michigan Canal, in the late 1830s and 1840s, and it had remained a working-class community. On the near West Side, just west of the Loop and radiating from St. Patrick's Church at the corner of West Adams and Desplaines streets, was the Irish middle-class neighborhood, the place one went when moving out of Bridgeport and up to respectability.

Here, on July 10, 1867, Peter Dunne was born, on West Adams Street, literally in the shadow of St. Patrick's, where his uncle, Dennis Dunne, had been the first pastor. One of twin sons born to Peter and Ellen Finley Dunne, young Peter added his mother's name to his own in 1886 and reversed his first and second names two years later. His twin brother died in infancy, but Peter grew up with four sisters and two other brothers. Dunne's father had come with his parents from Queens County, Ireland, to New Brunswick at the age of six. There he was raised and learned the craft of ship's carpenter. He moved to Chicago along with several of his brothers and settled on the West Side, where he built a successful business in carpentry and lumber. He seems to have been a rather typical Chicago Irishman, a lifelong Democrat and supporter of Irish nationalism with no great intellectual bent. His wife, born in County Kilkenny, was a lover of Dickens, Scott, and Thackeray who encouraged her children in reading and the life of the mind. The most precocious child was Peter, the only son to be sent to high school. Not much interested in the unimaginative classical curriculum, he allowed his studies to lapse after his mother's death and graduated last in his class of fifty. He took a job immediately as an office boy and novice reporter for the *Telegram,* one of the least popular of Chicago's thirty-odd daily papers. This was in June 1884, shortly before his seventeenth birthday. The date marks the real beginning of his education.[2]

There was no better place to be educated into the realities of American life in 1884 than the staff of a Chicago newspaper. The city was inexhaustibly various and stood at the vortex of a hurricane of political, social, and economic forces that were changing the face of America overnight. To be sure, reporters could not often write the whole truth of what they were seeing, trammeled as they were by conservative owners and publishers, but they were at least witnessing all of it, and from a vantage point at the eye of the storm.[3] Nor was their exposure merely negative, to the geometrically mounting problems of urban life; reporters were also privy to the special vitality of the city, manifested in the customs and speech patterns of the different neighborhoods and ethnic groups. To capture all this they brought the techniques of local-color writing to the feature pages of their newspapers. Articles began to appear illustrating that a walk through the Halsted Street Italian ghetto was every bit as idiosyncratic and colorful as one of Sarah Orne Jewett's rambles in Maine.

Not surprisingly, this new urban journalism was crucially important to the development of the generation of novelists who spearheaded the realistic movement in American literature in the nineties. The young Theodore Dreiser, fresh from his year at the University of Indiana, saw newspaper work as the most direct and exciting way of coming to grips with his fascination for city life. After more than a year's exposure to every corner of Chicago through work for a real estate office and as the driver of a laundry wagon, he took a job in the spring of 1892 with the struggling *Chicago Globe.* For this paper he wrote his first sketches of the slums, which were authentic enough to be praised by *Globe* city editor John T. McEnnis. Certainly his knowledge of Chicago was to inspire Dreiser's vision of a young downstate girl, Carrie Meeber, on her way north by train to make her fortune.[4] Stephen Crane's apprenticeship in New York journalism and Frank Norris's work for the San Francisco *Wave* are equally well known. Newspaper coverage of the city sharpened Crane's eye, and his fascination with the Bowery provided material for his trail-blazing novel, *Maggie: A Girl of the Streets* (1893). Norris's sketches of San Francisco's Chinese and Spanish communities prepared him to create the teeming Polk Street setting of *McTeague* (1899).[5]

By the same token, the most important influences on the genesis of Martin Dooley, bartender and resident philosopher of Archey Road, Chicago, were the examples of dialect and local-color writing about city life to which Peter Dunne was exposed (and ostensibly contributed) during his journalistic apprenticeship. Thus, we must examine in detail his education on six different Chicago newspapers between 1884 and 1893.

As in the city generally, there was plenty of opportunity for advancement in the world of Chicago journalism. Talent was rewarded regardless of age, and many young men gained responsible positions rapidly. Dunne's own career is a case in point. Chicago newspapermen had pride and spirit; they were conscious of belonging to a tradition of able response to the characteristic state of crisis inherent in reporting life as lived in their city. Also, and predictably, in a city where twenty-five or thirty papers were fighting it out for the daily penny or two of the reading public, competition was fierce. Insults and accusations of stolen scoops or imitated ideas buzzed around like bullets. The result of this warlike atmosphere, however, was a creditable product: Lincoln Steffens, while on his muckraking round, had found the Chicago press "the best in any of our large cities. There are several newspapers in Chicago which have served always the public interest, and their advice is taken by their readers." An 1895 observer for *The Review of Reviews* praised them as "well-printed, cleanly edited and dignified. They are pre-eminently *news* papers. The range of their telegraphic reports is vastly greater than that of any other newspapers in America. They 'cover' New York news as the New York dailies 'cover' the happenings in Jersey City—or better." And a study in 1888 showed that the Chicago papers carried a higher ratio of editorial comment to news and other features than the press of Boston, New York, Philadelphia, Cincinnati, or St. Louis.[6]

Peter Dunne's first significant newspaper training came on the *Chicago Daily News,* to which he was recruited while still in his seventeenth year by that newspaper's managing editor, Henry Ten Eyck White, who had been impressed by one of his police reports for the *Telegram.* The *News* was by far the most successful newspaper in Chicago. The product of the partnership of Chicagoans Melville Stone and Victor Lawson, it had begun as a penny paper specializing in brief, local items in 1876, when most reputable publishers were charging two cents. Keen judges of talent and masters of the art of self-advertising, Stone and Lawson attracted top-notch journalists like White and Eugene Field from other papers and ran imaginative campaigns and contests to boost circulation. (One year they flooded the Midwest with postcards carrying the cryptic message "One a Day," explained in a second mailing to be the price in pennies of the *News.*) In 1886, after ten years of sound management, including a split into morning and evening editions, the *News* was selling 160,000 copies daily, in Lawson's estimate "the largest daily circulation figure in America," and "probably 40,000 greater than the circulation of all other Chicago daily papers combined."[7]

"Butch" White, so called for his ruthless cutting of reporters' copy, instructed Dunne in his unique personal style of editorial writing: short, pointed, often satirical paragraphs, as opposed to the lengthy and labored polemics characteristic of many of his contemporaries.[8] White was himself a humorist of some local reputation, having published a collection of his newspaper pieces as *The Lakeside Musings* in 1884. Both the style and the subject matter of these may have influenced Dunne, for White's major creation is a Dooleyesque dispenser of wisdom, "the horse reporter," who uses realism and racing slang (White was an avid horse fancier) to undercut the pretensions of visitors to the city room of a Chicago newspaper. The reporter specializes in composing properly solemn and truthless obituaries for leading Chicagoans, and in giving hard-headed advice to love-sick maidens who appear at his door swimming in their own sentimental rhetoric.[9] White also included a series of sketches about "The Loves of the Mulcaheys," a large Irish family whose adventures center around their "ancestral home on Archer Avenue." He mocks the tradition of genteel romance by juxtaposing highfalutin language and earthy situations set on Chicago's South Side, as in the love story of "Reginald Mulcahey" and the daughter of "Ethelbert McMurty, eighth Duke of Blue Island Avenue." Dunne may have noted the lobbying for realism here, as well as the recognition of Bridgeport life as legitimate subject matter for literature, albeit satire. Certainly "Butch" White's concern over abuses of language was not lost on his young pupil.[10]

Dunne must also have noted the example of Eugene Field, whose *News* column, "Sharps and Flats," made him the most popular and best paid journalist without editorial rank in Chicago between 1883 and his death in 1895. Lured from Denver by *News* publisher Melville Stone, Field was best at light, occasional satire, and he filled his six-a-week column with inoffensive one-liners, snippets of dialect, and sentimental verse. Field always played it safe, eschewing controversy in favor of entertainment, and was therefore a less than adequate model for Dunne to follow; but his personal popularity and that of his 1887 collection, *Culture's Garland,* demonstrated that newspaper humor was a marketable commodity.[11]

It was also "Butch" White who selected Dunne to report on the Chicago White Stockings in the summer of 1887. Championship teams in 1885 and 1886 had spurred public interest in baseball to the extent that the *News* management decided to cover the games with full-dress articles instead of merely printing the box scores. Elmer Ellis, Dunne's biographer, explains the importance of the assignment for Dunne: "Here was the twenty-year-old boy, whose only experience outside of Chicago had been one summer on an uncle's farm, now traveling for half the long baseball season to Detroit, New York, Boston, Philadelphia, Washington, and the other cities with clubs in the old National League." [12] Dunne performed the assignment enthusiastically and was credited, along with Charles Seymour of the *Herald,* with bringing exciting baseball coverage to Chicago. His stories were spiced with colorful, detailed descriptions of the setting and with dramatic focus on important plays. They were well enough received to be run on the front page most of the time.

These pieces also reveal that Dunne's interests were steadily broadening. Larger issues intrude regularly, as, for example, when he interrupts the report of a road trip to Philadelphia with a satiric comparison of the quality of justice in two local court cases. In one, a woman has been indicted by the grand jury for "listening about houses and under windows, bearing tattle, and repeating the same, all of which is against the peace and dignity of the state." In the other, a "W. H. Kemble, one of the millionaire Gas-Trust syndicate, was convicted of bribery but escaped with a five-hour service in prison" because "he had the board of pardons with him, who were politicians of his own sort" (*News,* July 9, 1887). A flickering of interest in dialect also comes through occasionally, as in the story of a Chicago-Indianapolis game, in which Dunne describes the crowd as "staid old pumpkin-huskers whose only sport had been pitching horseshoes on Sunday while the 'wimmen folks wuz off to meetin'.' " He goes on to quote one farmer, "an old rustic wearing the tie he bought when Jackson was elected, with hair to match," who " 'lowed them city chaps wuz big enough to pound the daylights outen the Inj'any boys" (*News,* Sept. 10, 1887).

After the 1887 season, the *News* printed a feature explaining the speed of their baseball reporting, which also adds to our knowledge of Dunne's development as a writer. "Two young men" occupy a box on top of the grandstand. "One of them watches the plays as they are made and repeats them to the other, who fashions: 'Anson—home run —Congress Street,' into some such Addisonian language as this: 'Then Capt. Anson, with a mighty lunge, hurled his bat against an out-curve and the ball rose in a sightly parabola and, describing Hogarth's line of beauty, descended beyond the Congress Street wall." The second man, most likely Dunne, "dictates the report just as it must go to the printers, without alteration or substitution." Of him "it can only be said that if he sticks at this sort of business long he will have acquired the rapid use of a vocabulary that would have knocked Lord Macauley silly" (*News,* Sept. 29, 1887). Dunne would always be a fast writer; a flash of inspiration and an hour's work went into most Dooley pieces, and perhaps that habit is rooted here.

In January 1888, Dunne left the *News* for a higher-paying position as a political reporter on the *Chicago Times.* Founded in 1854, the *Times* was one of only three Chicago dailies to have survived the Great Fire of 1871. Through the sixties and seventies it had been edited by one of the most colorful figures in Chicago newspaper history, the fire-breathing Wilbur F. Storey, under whom the *Times* was the most notorious and one of the most popular papers in the city. Storey pursued the news fearlessly and innovatively (his telegraph service had been a model for Chicago journalism) and gloried in opportunities to expose the scandals and hypocrisies of "prominent citizens." He was known for his sensational headlines, the most famous of which, "Jerked to Jesus," announced the hanging of four murderers in 1875.[13]

Since Storey's demise the *Times* had been in decline, and in the late eighties it had come under the control of promoter James J. West, who was building a staff by raiding the other Chicago papers. West approached the already respected Dunne, who saw the chance to move ahead quickly as a political reporter in an election year, and acted on it. His brilliant coverage of the national conventions of 1888 won him the *Times* city editorship. He was twenty-one years old and in charge of the nerve center for gathering and dispensing all Chicago news, undoubtedly one of the most exciting jobs in journalism anywhere. Under West's management, the *Times* had become an outspoken organ of reform in Chicago. In the first six months of Dunne's editorship, the paper proselytized consistently for at least six different causes: a campaign against abortion, a crackdown on gambling in the city (lists of "open resorts" were printed) and on aldermanic graft in the dispensation of utilities franchises, support of the Relief and Aid Society's work with the poor, an exposé of the deplorable conditions at the county madhouse (a *Times* reporter got himself committed in order to study it), and, most vociferously, a campaign for police reform. Attending to these various topics must have provided education with a vengeance.

In addition, Dunne may have conducted his own first experiments with Irish dialect during his tenure on the *Times*. As part of the campaign for police reform in January 1889, the *Times* printed a series of dialect sketches, "Officer Quinn and His Friends," in which a bumbling policeman exemplifies the level of incompetence on the Chicago force. At one point Quinn discovers a suspicious footprint in the snow; shoveling it up, he starts for the station, but is sidetracked into a saloon, from which he emerges several hours later to discover that his clue has melted (Jan. 16, 1889). As the following excerpt indicates, the writer of these sketches is new to the problems of dialect. He gropes uncertainly for the distinctively Irish voice, overwriting to the extent that our understanding is impeded by gratuitous Irishisms and awkward phonetic spellings:

"Begobs!" ejaculated Officer P. Quinn to his friend Officer Weiss-nicht as they stood in Matt Connelly's saloon, next door to the station, looking at the red liquor in their glasses preparatory to engulfing it. "Begobs! 'Tis a gret note, indeed, fin the peppers does be joompin' on the pollis in thish sthyle. Didn't the two av us arresht tin thramps ashlape in a box-car lasht night but wan? . . .

"Be the Powers!" declared P. Quinn, " 'tis in mortial terror I am the whole livelong day, for fear the captain 'll git onto me pluckin' a banandy from the Dago's shtand beyant theer. Fur he's in the divil's own timper now, forbye the peppers does be clemmin' he meks more than his salary, shnoopin' things fin they coom handy. Oh, wirrasthru, 'tis no shnap a poor copper has these days at all, at all." [Jan. 9, 1889]

Also possibly attributable to Dunne in his role of political reporter are the *Times* stories about meetings of the Chicago city council, which are peppered with dialect transcriptions of comical aldermanic rhetoric. In a piece entitled "Spooks Take a Whirl," the ghosts of corrupt city ordinances appear to haunt the final session of the lame-duck council and to applaud speeches in their favor by outgoing aldermen, such as this eloquent plea: "This here orter be passed. . . . There an't no man in that there southwest part of the city but wants that done. I've had thousands of men come to me and ask me to have this here passed" (April 9, 1889).

This technique of dialect reporting followed Dunne to the *Chicago Tribune* when he changed jobs again at the end of July 1889. For example, the *Tribune* front page story of the new council's opening meeting that fall begins with a conversation between Aldermen O'Brien and Burke, of Archer and Parnell avenues, and turns into a report of council proceedings that reproduces the actual language of motions and discussions among the predominantly Irish aldermen.

Around this time, in the summer of 1889, a group of Chicago's bright young journalists, including Peter Dunne, formed a drinking and talking coterie called the Whitechapel Club. Their name and avowed interest in the grotesque and macabre had been inspired by the contemporaneous exploits of "Jack the Ripper" in the Whitechapel section of London. Their clubhouse, located in the newspaper district, was decorated with artifacts of crime and violent death: hanging nooses, authenticated murder weapons of various types, a skeleton or two, and a large, coffin-shaped table draped in black. The club achieved local notice through its "entertainment" of prestigious visitors to Chicago and its many unusual stunts, which included two mayoral campaigns and the midnight cremation of the president of the "Dallas (Texas) Suicide Club" on the shores of Lake Michigan.

The latter diversion particularly exemplifies the Whitechapel spirit. Morris A. Collins, unemployed, depressed, and claiming his dubious presidency, had shot himself to death, leaving a note requesting that the Whitechapel Club take charge of his burial. To finance the cremation, Dunne and Wallace Rice went to their employer at the time, James Scott of the *Herald,* and promised a scoop of the great event in return for the needed funds. Scott advanced $500, and the ceremony took place on Saturday evening, July 16, 1892, at midnight. While the Whitechapelers, in flowing black robes, recited from Shelley, Plato, and their own "works" composed for the occasion, the body of Collins, in a white shroud and crowned with a chaplet of oak leaves, was incinerated atop an eighteen-foot bier of cordwood and driftwood. The Sunday *Herald* gave all of page one to the story, which attracted attention nationally, in the words of Wallace Rice, "as the best example of an American newspaper story prepared in advance and published as a scoop." [14]

The club was much more than a joke, however. It served two valuable functions for Dunne and his fellow journalists. First, the unbridled discussions, especially of radical politics, provided a necessary outlet for ideas that the members' employers would never have printed. As Ellis puts it, "all important Chicago newspapers were conservative, regardless of whether they were Republican or Democratic. Their tone on public questions took its color from the rapidly accumulating wealth of the city, which in the hands of businessmen dominated the expression of political opinion in a brutal manner." [15] In this light, even the Whitechapel Club's apparently frivolous mayoral campaigns become serious and salutary responses to the corrupt state of Chicago politics. In 1891, Frederick U. "Grizzly" Adams ran for mayor under the Whitechapel banner on a platform of "No Gas, No Water, No Police." And two years later the club nominated Hobart C. Chatfield-Taylor, wealthy coeditor of the virulent anti-immigration periodical *America,* describing him as "a bright young Irish-American, who, by close application to literature, has amassed a fortune in this country." Chatfield-Taylor shared the Whitechapel ticket with George M. Pullman, who, a club spokesman declared, had been nominated for city clerk "at the request of a committee of workingmen." [16]

The club's second important function was to provide stern criticism of its members' writing. Ellis describes the Whitechapelers as "tough critics with a malicious delight in destructive criticism. During the organization's life, many a newspaper story was written with as much of an eye for its reception at the Whitechapel Club as at the city desk. Mercilessly pounding bad writing, weak reporting, and unrealistic conceptions of life, it helped immensely to develop a sense of quality." [17]

Moreover, many of the abilities that Dunne was to exercise in the Dooley pieces made earlier appearances at Whitechapel meetings. Dunne was one of the club's five "sharpshooters," along with fellow journalists Charlie Seymour and Charlie Almy, law clerk Charles Perkins, and poet-humorist Ben King. Their favorite pastime was ridiculing the pretensions and hypocrisies of the self-important—Dunne called them "posturers"—and Mr. Dooley's special gift for deflation surely dates from these years. Also, the club entertained itself with grotesque dialogues in imitation of the manners and speech of celebrities and imagined characters.[18] One member's memory of such an occasion suggests that Mr. Dooley's convincing brogue originated in his creator's facility in oral mimicry:

> Peter Dunne entertained his Whitechapel Club associates one night with impersonations of citizens calling at the city room of a morning newspaper which employed two well-known Irishmen. One was James Sullivan, the newspaper's red-cheeked, round-faced political editor, whose every pockmark exuded amiability. The other was John Devoy, expert in revolutionary strategems. Any representative of one class of callers, according to Dunne, opened the door slowly inch by inch, inserted his head cautiously and surveyed with care the occupants of the room. Then tiptoeing in and closing the door noiselessly behind him, he approached the nearest person and, bending over, whispered behind his hand, "Whisht! Is Misther Jawn Devoy in, I dinnaw?" Another type imitated by Dunne entered the city room noisily after flinging the door wide open and roared out, "Where the hell's Jim Sullivan?" [19]

Furthermore, Mr. Dooley could never have been awed by headline figures after Dunne's participation in Whitechapel "roastings" of prominent men who visited the clubhouse; among them humorist Bill Nye, Tammany Hall politicians Bourke Cockran and Richard Croker, and New York railroad magnate Chauncey Depew.[20] All in all, the Whitechapel experience was crucial in Dunne's development as a thinker and a writer.

A stock-watering scandal forced James J. West from management of the *Times* in the summer of 1889, and his city editor was forced to leave with him. Dunne was hired immediately by the *Tribune,* one of the city's most respectable papers and the primary voice of Chicago Republicanism. He stayed for a little over a year, progressing from general reporting to the editorship of the Sunday edition in January 1890.[21] A few examples will suggest the color and quality of the general reporting that Chicago's better journalists were engaged in during these years. Several pieces sound especially like Dunne in their combination of intelligence, cynical wit, and compassion. One feature exposes the condition of the streets in Dunne's home ward, the eighteenth, with cleverness and bite. It opens with praise for "the bouquet of Chicago alleys" on the city's West Side, of which "the heart of the cluster, the large, fragrant jacqueminot rose in the middle is the Eighteenth ward." The reporter goes on to stumble over dead dogs, reeking garbage barrels "not touched in three weeks," a dead cat, "dead for a ducat—yes, for a barrel of them" and "manure piles which don't make proper breakfast reading, but if Mr. Dixon [the chief public works inspector] could take some of the sight . . . down with his coffee and rolls, he might place less reliance on the reports of his inspectors and more on the typhoid fever death reports in the adjoining room." Blame is allocated for the conditions with a cold, clean savagery:

> Where is the blame for this? On the inspectors surely. They are paid by the city to see that the alleys are kept clean, and possibly paid by the scavengers not to see anything. What better can be expected? The low dives and the barrelhouses that produce ward-workers were dragged that these offices might be filled. They are put on the payrolls and given responsible places, not that the city shall be kept clean, but that the machine may work more smoothly. A man can do more powerful politics in a saloon coddling a gin-seller than in fighting shiftless scavengers in a back alley. And it is twice as pleasant to drink barrelhouse whiskey as it is to inhale foul odors. While the alleys are crying for one intelligent, honest, unhypocritical cleaning, the ex-wardworker and plugugly is deaf, and, ten to one, blind, behind a groggery. Such is Democratic politics. [Sept. 27, 1889]

In January 1890, the *Tribune* began a crusade against Chicago's wide-open gambling halls, which culminated in indictments for ten faro-bank proprietors (*Tribune*, Feb. 1, 1890). The clinching testimony before the grand jury was provided by Peter Dunne and a fellow reporter, so we can assume that Dunne wrote some of the colorful descriptions of gambling operations that appeared in the *Tribune* around this time. In one of these a clergyman dresses up "like a young sport up from Amora," in "checkered trousers, a sack coat, brown derby hat and a loud scarf," and accompanies the *Tribune* reporter to George Hankins's gambling house, "the better to preach against it" (Sept. 21, 1889). Another piece details the gambling tragedy of Mrs. Catherine Murphy, who, with an eviction notice at home, drags her son out of Hankins's house after he has lost all but $2.65 of his nine-dollar paycheck. The second piece protests that the gambling houses are already open again, only one month after the grand jury indictments, but the reporter is hardly surprised that "the violent spasm of virtue which recently affected the Democratic city administration has succumbed to treatment" (March 23, 1890).

The *Tribune* management was more responsive to the burgeoning interest in urban local color and dialect features than Dunne's previous employers had been. Their consciousness of a shift in the national taste comes through in a Sunday piece of October 26, 1890, which remarks that the enviable position in American letters of the "realistic branch of Western literature" is "destined soon to be relinquished to the cities of the effete East," for "realism has moved East, or bought a ticket and had its baggage checked," and will soon be found in the columns of the "New York dailies." A band of screaming Apaches may have been exciting some years ago, "but how tame and quiet it is now to an aggregation of Niagara hackmen . . . or a gripman on the Chicago cable cars," and " 'punching steers' now seems a milk and water affair to killing steers in the Chicago Stock-Yards at the rate of a hundred a minute." The *Tribune* contained two regular daily columns of urban local color, "Highway and Byway," and "Gleanings about the City," as well as occasional longer features, including (in a sampling from 1890 alone) visits to Scandinavian and black neighborhoods, a Chinese Sunday school, Italian curio and pawn shops, and the kitchens of Chicago's French chefs. There were often attempts to reproduce local and foreign dialects in these pieces, most of which appeared in the

Sunday *Tribune* during Dunne's association with that edition.[22]

The Chicago Irish community also received its share of attention. Both the "Gleanings" and "Highway" columns contain short sketches that could be prototypes for Mr. Dooley's subsequent explorations of life in Bridgeport: Alderman "Billy" Whelan is interviewed at the opera—"Have to take in all these Dago shows, you know. Pleases the constits. . . . Drink? Certainly, dear boy"; the wife of a striking carpenter tells of not being able to hush the cries of her starving child, because her husband has spent their savings on drink; a Catholic priest details the ingenuity of his parishioners in evading the restrictions of Lent; a young female victim of "poverty and consumption" is buried free to prevent a pauper's funeral by Carroll, the undertaker, who recalls having done the same for her father twenty years earlier.[23] Some of these are probably by Dunne, for his occasional authorship of the "Highway" column is proven by a signed piece in which he indicts melodrama playwrights for their unrealistic depiction of the villain as a "despicable wretch in his appearance and dress" who "dies like a dog without having any fun." On the contrary, says Dunne, "the villain we meet in everyday life . . . goes well dressed and is . . . the fellow whom society takes into its arms—innocently of course.

> Who gets into the church? Who is the ornamental committeeman on great occasions, very frequently? Who sleeps late in the morning and retires late with his stomach laden with the best? Who wheedles the banker into big loans? Who inaugurates schemes for which others put up the money and from which he draws a princely salary? Who marries the pride of some honest old father and mother who made their fortune by grubbing and hoeing and felling the timber out of which the cradles for villains are made? And when he gets her, secures her fortune, beats her, leaves her, and flies to Monte Carlo, or Canada, or some club-house in New York, where he lives like a Prince and struts like a peacock, and wants to know what people are going to do about it? This is the villain of everyday life. It would pay some melodrama playwright to form his acquaintance.
>
> [April 14, 1890]

What we have here is Mr. Dooley without Bridgeport and the brogue: realism leans toward cynicism but is tempered with humor, the questions are phrased with an ear for rhythm and dramatic timing, and the ironic twist that is the point of the piece is developed with unambiguous clarity.

Also worthy of note as possible trial runs for the Dooley pieces are a group of longer Irish dialect sketches that appeared in the Sunday *Tribune* during Dunne's editorship. In one, "They Wanted Violets," an Irish policeman finds two ragged urchins before a flower shop window and tells them that "the blue ones" are "voy-lets, choild." The clerk inside laughs at their five pennies and asks why the children want such expensive flowers. (The asking price is seventy-five cents.) They reply that "They're for maw—she's dead" (April 27, 1890). Equally pathetic is the description of a visit to a run-down West Side Catholic church during Saturday evening confessions. The observer sees a young girl come in sobbing; after she leaves, the priest comes out, and he is crying too, despite the fact that "this scene in a Catholic church was common enough." The bare walls and overall dinginess of the church are captured well and seem to echo the priest's mood of resigned hopelessness (May 11, 1890). Another piece is an interview with "Mrs. Mary Maloney" on the "Cost of Keeping House":

"How much have I spint to kape the hoose an' childer? Faith an' I spind ivery blissed cint I have the day, an' thin the childer don't get all the praties [potatoes] they cud ate.

"There's Mary, and Mickey, and Tom Moore, and Patrick, named after the blissed saint that kilt all the snakes in ould Ireland, till we come to America: thin Dinnis he died and left me a pore widdy woman with four childer, and me the only one big enough to earn a bit. I wash, and scrub, and clane hoose for folks when the sun shines, and a divil a bit they wants me around when it rains. So I earn a dollar and a half a day when I wurruk and lose a dollar and a half when I can't wurruk, and a fine time it is I have with it raining ivery other day. . . .

"They get praties to ate in the morn an' oatmeal an' a sup of milk. At the mission-school they get a bite, an' then for supper praties an' a sup of tay. Arrah, an' it's a fine dinner they have Sundays, what with the lady who gives me a bone for soup. Whin the childer ain't in school they pick up lumps off the railroad track and niver git hurted. The ladies give me clothes an' I cut them off at the bottom, and there we are, as nice an' warm with a penny for the church on Easter, like I gave this blissed day jist past." [April 13, 1890]

Mrs. Maloney's statement appears next to a similar interview with a Michigan Avenue socialite, who outlines a lavish menu for a week's meals and allows $1.50 for a cleaning woman; her weekly expenses rough out to $25.00. There is no forced preaching here; the juxtaposition of the two situations does all the work. (This is a favorite technique of Dunne's, and many of the Dooley poverty pieces depend on just such understatement.)

Another piece stars an Irish bartender, Mr. Patrick Casey, "a great humorist and a most genial gentleman, . . . never given to levity," who helps trick a newly elected state senator, one Isaac Abrams, by showing him the same phony bankroll on six separate occasions, each time declaring it to be money left for Abrams's fellow legislator, Thomas J. McNally. Finally Abrams becomes incensed and explodes into dialect: "Who effer saw de like of dat. Tousands on tousands for MigNally, not a tam cent for me." To get even with McNally, Abrams refuses to vote at all, thus playing into the Irishman's hands (Nov. 30, 1890).

Dialect writing was something of an issue in Chicago in the early nineties. In May 1890, *Tribune* staff reporter Vance Thompson, who did much of the paper's exploring in ethnic neighborhoods and also wrote competent literary criticism, complained that dialect humor had become altogether too popular. While second-rate writers such as humorist Bill Nye were growing rich (Nye appeared regularly in the *Tribune*), "Walt Whitman has been a pauper these ten years—a poor man his life long" (May 18, 1890). Thompson also wrote a clever piece in which he told "The Same Old Story" from four currently popular points of view. He parodies Guy de Maupassant "in his fine cynical way"; Henry James "if he felt, by chance, in a moderately moral mood"; H. Rider Haggard with his "heart-breaking" romanticism; and "any one of the weird throng" of dialect writers. The dialect piece is a chaotic mix of Irish, American cowboy, Scots, and German voices (April 20, 1890).

Thompson's criticism aside, there does seem to have been a general awakening to the vitalizing potential of the various spoken languages of the city. During his 1889 visit, for example, Rudyard Kipling found that in the Chicago newspapers "were faithfully reproduced all the war-cries and 'back-talk' of the Palmer House bar, the slang of the barbers' shops, the mental elevation and integrity of the Pullman-car porter, the dignity of the Dime Museum, and the accuracy of the excited fishwife." [24] In 1891 James Maitland, a Chicago newspaperman, edited an *American Slang Dictionary,* the "first ever to include American and English slang as used today," according to its preface, and dedicated the book to his fellow journalists in Chicago.[25] This flurry of activity could not have been lost on Dunne, who also had the example of several of his fellow Whitechapel Club members. Ben King was a dialect versifier of some wit, and Opie Read of Little Rock had brought his magazine of southern dialect and local color, the *Arkansaw Traveler,* to Chicago in 1887.[26]

More generally, of course, Dunne could have looked for possible models to the tradition of American vernacular philosophizing, which included such names to be conjured with as Major Jack Downing, Sam Slick, Hosea Biglow, and Artemus Ward. Nor was Mr. Dooley the first Irishman to make a place for himself in American literature. An important character in H. H. Brackenridge's early picaresque novel, *Modern Chivalry* (1792–1815), is the mischievous bumbler Teague O'Regan, identified by Arthur R. Williams as "the first live Irish American in the pages of American humor." [27] Then there was Charles Graham Halpine, whose braggart-soldier figure, Private Miles O'Reilly, grew out of his creator's experiences in the Civil War. But O'Reilly is little more than a skeleton, the vehicle for Halpine's now obscure satiric thrusts at wartime politicians and generals.[28] As such, he was no more help to Dunne than Teague O'Regan, who, as a wandering rogue with no communal ties, is much closer to Sancho Panza than to Martin Dooley.

Less literary, but of more potential influence, were the plays of Edward Harrigan, tremendously popular musical farces of the 1870s and 1880s, whose colorful urban settings and Irish slum characters provided some precedent for Dunne's focus on Bridgeport. Behind Harrigan's work were the traditions of American melodrama extending back at least to the 1840s and the figure of the Irish-American Bowery "B'hoy," or tough, the swaggering hero of plays that Richard M. Dorson has called a combination of "urban local color, melodramatic heroics, and the moral fable." [29] In these plays the vitality of city life came through in extravagant crowd and chorus scenes set on the New York streets. Dunne probably did pick up from his predecessors the mechanics of the dialect humorist; for, as Walter Blair points out, they all share a common bag of tricks: cacography; juxtaposition of incongruous predicates, nouns, and proper names; misquotation of classics and the Bible; and many types of word play.[30] And yet, Mr. Dooley owes far less to these prototypes from the wider world than he does to the environment that produced him—big city journalism.

As we have seen, there was plenty of precedent in the Chicago papers for vernacular transcription of urban local color, some of it most likely created by Dunne himself. And the climate at the *Tribune* in 1890 was particularly favorable for a concerted effort in that line of work.

The first Irish dialect pieces attributable positively to Dunne appeared in the *Tribune* during the summer and fall of 1890. Brand Whitlock pointed to them in remembering that "there was a certain Irishman in Chicago responsive to the name of Colonel Thomas Jefferson Dolan, whom, in his capacity of First Ward Democrat, Mr. Dunne frequently interviewed for his paper without the cramping influences of a previous visitation on the Colonel." The real "Colonel" Dolan was a typical small-time political hanger-on who turned out for every function of the County Democracy Marching Club, held a job in the city water office when the Democrats were "in," and ran unsuccessfully for the state legislature several times.[31] Dunne's pieces deal with such Democratic political doings as Boss Mike McDonald's excursion to Niagara Falls with the entire Marching Club, the Democratic party's picnics at Willow Springs, outside the city, and the mechanics of dispensing jobs and favors before the congressional election of 1890. Dunne concentrates on the garish and colorful garb of the Democratic politicians and on their penchant for rollicking good times, describing beef-dressing and dance contests at the picnics and the different footraces for babies, young ladies, married ladies, and men. At one such affair he singles out for special attention a favorite Dooley target, Bridgeport Alderman William J. O'Brien, whose waltzing is "as graceful as the amble of the antelope, as sturdy as the bound of the leopard, yet as easy as the placid movement of the white swan." Clearly a product of "the winter school of dancing in Finucane's Hall," O'Brien wears "an expression of deadly determination; his glassy eye . . . fixed on the roof" (*Tribune,* July 20, 1890).

Dunne has learned a lot already, for the dialect of the Dolan pieces is a great improvement over the attempts that come before it in the Chicago papers. Speech rhythms are more natural and the brogue is altogether smoother and less obtrusive; in fact, if he errs, it is on the side of caution—Irishness is sometimes insufficiently suggested. An example is Colonel Dolan on the proposed trip to Niagara:

"No, Dicky Pindygash can't go. He will have to stay home to look after the Drainage Commission and the fall campaign. There will be 200 go to the Falls, and 1,000 min is today chasin' all over town to find Mike or Capt. Farrell and sign the muster-roll. Nice fellies too, nice fellies—the best in the town, choice min—saloonkeepers and bailiffs, and min that spinds a good dale of their time studyin' law on juries in coorts of record or coorts where the floors is covered with sawdust, or settin' on stiffs. O, the min that will go will be able to handle thimsilves in any emergency.

"Mike is going to get a whole train of Pullman cars. So he is. We are to have the choice of routes, either the Lake Shore, or Wabash, or the Short-Line. All roads going through Canada is barred, because some of the party was in Canada during the Fenian excitement and they don't care to return that way. So they don't. There is no statute of limitations over in Canada. So there isn't, and some of our company would be bagged on the boat betune Detroit and Windsor or at Port Huron." [*Tribune,* July 16, 1890]

Dunne introduces several innovations with the Dolan pieces. They constitute a series, stretching over some three months, whereas the earlier dialect pieces in the *Tribune* had been single, isolated efforts. They describe the Irish-American scene in some detail and, more importantly, from the perspective of a single viewer, who, despite his real-life namesake, is an alter ego for Dunne. And finally, they introduce an Irish dialect voice purer than any that had come before it.

Near the end of 1890, Dunne changed jobs again, this time moving to the Democratic *Herald,* which had the largest morning circulation in Chicago, about 50,000 daily customers. James W. Scott, the *Herald*'s popular publisher, had assembled a group of the brightest young reporters in Chicago, including several of Dunne's Whitechapel associates—Brand Whitlock, Charlie Seymour, "Grizzly" Adams, and Wallace Rice. Whitlock later remembered that "when they induced 'Pete' Dunne to come over from the *Tribune,* the staff seemed to be complete."[32] Being a part of this group must have helped Dunne's writing, as did his association with yet another demanding teacher, *Herald* editor Horatio Seymour, whose rigid standards Whitlock recalls: "The American language not having then been invented, we had to get it out in English, and there was in those days a curious, old-fashioned prejudice in favor of pure English. We were not permitted to invent words, and were hampered by a great many rules that would seem queer today. We were required to find the right words for things." The *Herald* did have style. It was typographically the cleanest, most classically laid out paper in the city, and its reporters thought nothing of beginning their stories with poetic epigraphs; a piece about a shipwreck on Lake Michigan opens with lines from Matthew Prior (Aug. 16, 1891). And its political coverage was often infused with rhetorical ironies of some subtlety. One can picture the Whitechapelers chuckling their approval of a leader such as this for a report of a Republican city committee meeting:

> Benjamin Harrison's face in oil, painted with an armful of dull, brown whiskers, looked east at the Cavalry Armory on Michigan Avenue last night, and an angel of peace, carrying a bough of evergreen, floated across a canvas screen at the other end of the room. The angel of peace was in such a position that when big Colonel Dan Munn leaned back in his chair he left a sample of hair oil on the hem of the angel's garment. It was a hard night that this celestial visitor spent; for not peace, but red-mouthed war stalked through the hall, with a retinue of horrors and amid the screams of a vast contingent of water-office men and tenement inspectors. [Nov. 1, 1891]

Another *Herald* veteran, John Kelley, remembers that "Pete Dunne . . . was writing bang-up stuff for the *Herald* in those days . . . picturesque stories that were a mirror of Chicago life." [33] Most of these cannot be attributed certainly, but Ellis cites as legendary in newspaper circles one Dunne tour de force for the *Herald,* his creation in four hours for the early edition of a 5,000 word feature on a gun battle between police and a Texas racehorse owner at Washington Park track. Dunne had been a chance witness to the shoot-out, in which three persons died, and his story is an exciting, graphic evocation of the event.[34] Ellis identifies one other *Herald* story as Dunne's: the report of a speech by Republican Governor Joseph Foraker of Ohio during the 1892 presidential campaign. Dunne narrates disgustedly Foraker's waving of the bloody shirt: "Harrison volunteered and went to the front, Cleveland volunteered to stay at home. . . . I don't believe any copperhead should be made president of the United States." And his parting shot is worthy of Mr. Dooley: "Then all the people put on their hats and went out to see what news had come from Gettysburg, where a terrible battle is still raging." [35]

I have found no dialect writing in the *Herald* (probably Editor Seymour, linguistic purist that he was, forbade it) but Dunne must have enjoyed these rhetorical exercises, which provided another means of coping with the status quo of corruption and hypocrisy in Chicago. At any rate, when he left the *Herald* for the *Evening Post* in November 1892, his ultimate solution, Mr. Dooley, was less than a year away.

Founded in 1890 by the owners of the *Herald* as their evening affiliate, the *Post* was one of the youngest papers in Chicago but one of the most respected. It was aimed explicitly at an intellectual audience, with a good deal of literary, musical, and artistic coverage and a more sophisticated overall tone than any other paper in the city. Willis Abbot of the *Review of Reviews* judged that "in its news and special features the *Evening Post* may justly be regarded as one of the most admirable afternoon newspapers in the country"; and visiting British journalist W. T. Stead found it "as much in advance of all its evening contemporaries in ability and influence and general quality of make-up and appearance as the *Daily News* is ahead of them in circulation and advertisements." [36]

Dunne took over as editorial chairman, a welcome advancement, for he had become increasingly dissatisfied with the street-pounding life of a reporter. Now he was off the streets and making more direct use of his talents in providing daily commentary from the quieter perspective of an editor's desk. Remembering the lessons of "Butch" White and Horatio Seymour, Dunne made the *Post* editorials pithy and short, usually no longer than three paragraphs. He also enjoyed the added freedom of working for a paper whose political position was officially nonpartisan. Moreover, the *Post*'s managing editor, cigar-eating, shirt-sleeved Cornelius McAuliff, admired Dunne's work and particularly encouraged his satiric bent. As a result, the editorial page fairly sparkled with sophisticated wit. A steady clientele developed swiftly, and by 1893 circulation was a respectable 30,000 daily.[37]

Shortly after moving to the *Post*, Dunne created his first saloon-keeper-commentator, Colonel Malachi McNeery, who bridges the gap between Colonel Dolan and Mr. Dooley. As part of his plan for a Sunday edition, McAuliff asked Dunne to do a weekly humorous piece, for which he would be paid ten dollars extra. His first response was a piece on the death of robber baron Jay Gould, inspired by the remarks of one James McGarry, a noted saloonkeeper-wit whose Dear-

born Street establishment was a favorite gathering place for newspapermen and visiting celebrities. The piece, which appeared in the second
issue of the *Sunday Post,* contains a clear, uncluttered dialect, in line
with that of the Colonel Dolan pieces, and surely developed from their
example.[38] Here it is in full:

"I see our friend Jay Gould is dead," said Colonel McNeery, turning from his regular noonday survey of the procession of fair ones
on Dearborn street. "Jay Gould is dead, Vanderbilt is dead, Mike
Casey is dead. They're all dead and gone, poor men, and none of
them took his money with him. Jay Gould had no fun in life. My
friend there, little Johnny McKenna, would have more fun at a
dance at Brighton Park, ten times over, than Jay Gould had all his
lifetime with $100,000,000. Ten times over, for McKenna could get
up the next morning and eat a side of bacon, cabbage and boiled
potatoes, put on his cambric shirt and come down town as fresh as
e'er a man you know, while Gould, sure, the poor little wisp of a man
if he ate one egg for breakfast, he'd be doubled up with sorrow in his
stomach. Besides, McKenna never had fear of mortal man nailing
him with a bomb. The worst he ever got was some friend of McElli-
gott's soaking him with a brick, and divil a bit they care for that in
Bridgeport. It's a mere diversion, but Gould, the unhappy divil, the
minute he poked his whiskers out of his office some crazy arnychist
was liable to crack away at him with a gas-pipe bomb full of dynamite, or some strong-arm man toss him into a coal hole. Now he's
dead, and what of it? He has a fine box and a mausolyum, but
manny's the boy I've seen as contented and gay in one of Gavin's old
crates as if he was laid out in a rosewood casket, with a satin pillow
under his head; and making no more kick to be dumped into a hole
in Calvary than if he was put on a shelf in a vault like a jar of pickles.
It's little difference it makes to a man when he's dead. He didn't take
anything with him barring a new suit of clothes. He had to leave all
the coin behind. I see he left his son George only $5,000,000 for the
three years' work. It's a burning shame. Faith, I hope the lad will
be able to get through the winter on it, though it's little enough with
hard coal at $8 a ton and Boyle contemplatin' a lift in the price of
steak; and an actress for a wife, at that. Them actresses is spenders.
I wonder if the boy will ever think of his father or will he think of the
money all the time. Aha! it'll be little pleasure he'll take from pon-
dering on the old man if what Shakespeare says is true—that it will
be easier for a camel to go through the eye of one of them little
cambric needles than for a rich man to enter the kingdom of heaven."

[*SP,* Dec. 11, 1892]

This piece marks the real beginning of the Dooley series, with its bartender-patron format, the Dooleyesque comic enumeration— "Gould . . . Vanderbilt . . . Mike Casey"—and the attribution to Shakespeare of a quotation from the Bible. Also, Dunne injects vitality by naming real people—Gavin the undertaker, Billy Boyle, proprietor of a famous Chicago chop-house, and, most important, John McKenna, a genial Irish Republican from the suburban Brighton Park section of the city, who enjoyed being written about and stayed on into the Dooley series as Mr. Dooley's first regular listener. The following week Dunne again presented Colonel McNeery and his patron John McKenna, in a discussion of the relative merits of British and American actors, "thereby," as Ellis puts it, establishing "the form of all his future dialect essays." [39]

This first batch of Colonel McNeery pieces introduces a character less Irish than cosmopolitan, in keeping with Dunne's model, Jim McGarry, whose saloon was something of a cultural center in downtown Chicago. Actors James O'Neill and Edwin Booth frequented the place while touring in the city, as did the boxing champion and hero of the American Irish, John L. Sullivan, a friend of the proprietor, and a large number of Chicago journalists, lawyers, and politicians, great and small.[40] Thus, Colonel McNeery's speech contains very few noticeable Irishisms but a good deal of Chicago slang; for example, "up I was an' out like a chippy-bird an' ready to give a belt in the gob to any man that stud in my way"; or describing a man looking for his glasses, "you'd have died to see the ould amalook crawlin' on his han's an' knees looking for the lamps"; or explaining putting his feet up as "I histed me derricks before th' fire" (*SP,* Dec. 25, 1892, Jan. 15, 1893). Moreover, the humorous analogies that McNeery draws are characteristic of a sophisticated city man: "the divil take me for a toastin' fork," and "Wilson Barrett struttin' across the stage with his front out like a waffle man," and "I've given that boy a silk handkerchief every Christmas for fifteen years. He couldn't use them all if he had a nose like a South American tapir" (*SP,* Dec. 18, 25, 1892). In addition, McNeery quotes from Shakespeare (albeit inaccurately) on several occasions, and his vocabulary is consistently impressive, as when he discusses strange animals, singling out "peecaries" and "cossowaries" for special mention (*SP,* Feb. 5, 1893). In short, McNeery speaks like Jim

McGarry—a long-transplanted Irishman, fully at home among his clever and talented patrons in downtown Chicago.

Nor is the material of these first McNeery pieces Irish-centered. The topics are current events and opinions in Chicago: Jay Gould's death, the debate about actors, the Chicago Charity Ball, which McNeery scorns roundly, and the great educational issue of the day, the introduction of manual training and German language programs in the public schools, both of which the colonel dismisses as frivolous. Only once is the focus on the Chicago Irish community. The piece for New Year's Day 1893 describes the custom of paying holiday calls on friends and relatives. Colonel McNeery and Colonel Cleary, "him that was county commissioner," set out to visit their friends, all real Chicago people, including John McKenna, police detective Jack Shea, and Alderman E. F. Cullerton of Bridgeport. Meeting at Jim Mc-Garry's saloon (an attempt by Dunne to dissociate Colonel McNeery from his prototype), they go first to John McKenna's house in Brighton Park, out beyond Bridgeport. Here, and in passing, Dunne gives us his first description of the place where over the next several years he will ground Mr. Dooley as firmly as any character in American fiction: "Did ye ever go to McKenna's? No? Well, sir, of all th' places! Ye go down Madison street to Halstead an' down Halstead to Archey road an' out Archey road past packin' houses an' rollin' mills an' th' Healy slew an' potato patches till ye get to McKenna's" (*SP*, Jan. 1, 1893). The two callers ring McKenna's bell until one of his neighbors comes out and fires a brick at them; then they march down to "th' place on th' corner" for a drink of "Brighton Park whiskey . . . it feels like a torchlight procession goin' down, as th' fellow says. It would take th' hair off a cow." No one else is home either, and at the end of the evening McNeery and Cleary find their friends all gathered in a downtown saloon, "to give us th' laugh." This piece is entertaining but atypical, and provides the only hint of Dunne's later accomplishment as historian of the Bridgeport Irish. Apparently he became dissatisfied with the series, for he broke it off on February 5, 1893, after only seven pieces had appeared. A hiatus of almost two months followed, and then the stimulus of the Chicago World's Fair brought Colonel McNeery out of retirement and Peter Dunne into his own.

The World's Columbian Exposition of 1893 was the most significant complex of events in the cultural history of the midwestern United

States in the nineteenth century, and the selection of Chicago as its setting was a momentous decision for the midwest's metropolis. First, as I have said, the choice meant acknowledgment by the American people, through an overwhelming congressional vote, of Chicago's coming of age as a great city. Second, there was the resounding impact of the "White City" upon the whole midwest, as the art, music, architecture, technology, ideas, and people of the rest of the world came together at Jackson Park. Finally, the campaign leading up to Chicago's selection and the subsequent planning for the Fair fostered a tremendous amount of self-consciousness among Chicagoans, which the most talented were able to turn to artistic and intellectual advantage.

For many of its visitors, the buildings, exhibitions, and concerts of the Fair constituted a first exposure to high culture, and they were properly impressed, even overwhelmed.[41] In addition, there was the intellectual stimulation of the various "congresses," which provided firsthand exposure to the most advanced thinking on everything under the sun: chronologically, the topics were women, the press, medicine and surgery, temperance reform, moral and social reform, commerce and finance, music, literature, education, engineering, electricity, architecture and art, government, law, political science, labor, religion, public health, and agriculture. There was also the Midway Plaisance, with its introduction to exotic people and places through reproductions of foreign streets and shops, all staffed by natives. And special "Days" scattered through the six-month Fair run provided focuses for particular nationalities and interest groups, uniquely educational for outsiders. These included United States, British Empire, German, Polish, and Irish days, as well as days for several of the individual American states and New York City. On Chicago Day (October 9, the anniversary of the Great Fire) the single-day attendance record was set— at 700,000, which a contemporary Chicago historian claimed was "the largest number ever assembled within one enclosure of the same dimensions in the history of the world."[42] The total attendance of over twenty-seven million for the six months attests to the magnitude of the American response to this extraordinary spectacle.[43]

For Chicago's newspapermen, the World's Fair was a gift from heaven, a once-in-a-lifetime opportunity for imaginative reporting that catalyzed several major talents into action. Brand Whitlock remembers how the *Herald*'s John Eastman "used to get the whole of the World's Fair into a column every night." Wallace Rice, Dunne's friend and fellow Whitechapeler, wrote daily on "Oddities of the Fair" for the *Mail*. Eugene Field mined the Midway regularly for his "Sharps and Flats" in the morning *Record,* which also assigned a young cartoonist-reporter team, John T. McCutcheon and George Ade, to bring back human interest material from Jackson Park. These two created a daily feature, "All Roads Lead to the Fair," a breezy, informative hodge-podge of interviews and sketches that was immediately popular. When the Fair closed, *Record* editor Charles Dennis rewarded Ade and McCutcheon with two columns daily on the editorial page, which they promptly began filling with "Stories of the Streets and of the Towns," flashes of urban local color caught with Ade's words and McCutcheon's pictures. Through attempting to transcribe the speech of the people he met, Ade became interested in the language of the city streets, and his "Stories" evolved into the "Fables in Slang" for which he became famous.[44]

Peter Dunne's response to the great journalistic potential of the Fair was to bring back Colonel McNeery. With this step, he set himself firmly on the road to creating Martin Dooley's saloon on Archer Avenue. Before recalling the Colonel, however, he made an attempt to create a new persona through which to deal with the Fair. On March 19, 1893, the *Sunday Post* printed a conversation in dialect between Irish policeman Steve Rowan, in real life a popular downtown Chicago patrolman, and a statue of Christopher Columbus. The statue gossips about the doings of many prominent Chicagoans, from outgoing Mayor Hempstead Washburne and Police Inspector Johnny Shea to Alderman Billy O'Brien and Colonel McNeery's old friend John McKenna, "a red-faced man . . . from Brighton Park [who] drives down every day and hitches a horse with an oat-bag over his head to my legs." Columbus is particularly critical of the police, who, he declares, specialize in arresting "twelve-year-old prisoners" and detecting "trumps in each other's sleeves." The comments are pointed enough, and the Irish policeman was at least as plausible a model as the Irish bartender for an undertaking such as this, but Dunne rejected the persona immediately, perhaps because of the sensitive, scandal-prone position of Chicago policemen, some of whom were close friends of his.[45]

So it was that on May 21 John McKenna walked into Colonel Mc-

Neery's Dearborn Street saloon and found the colonel dazed, singing Irish airs softly to himself. He had just visited the Midway Plaisance for the first time. "I don't give anything for the fair itself," says the colonel. "What do I ca-are for show cases full of dhried prunes, ould r-rocks an' silk handkerchers! I was f'r goin' over to see Buffalo Willie shootin' Injuns an' rescuin' Annie Oakley from the red divvles, but O'Connor sez: 'No,' he sez, 'come on an' see the Midway,' he sez." Then the fun begins, as McNeery is exposed to a dizzying variety of sights and sounds, ending up in a Midway bar where he finds himself seated between "a lot of black fellows with red towels around their heads an' knives stickin' out of their yellow cloaks," and "half-a-dozen gur-rls with earrings as big as barrelhoops in their ears." McNeery goes on to report that "from that time my mind's a blank. I was like the feller in the story-books. I knew no more. I dunno what happened at all, at all, with dancin' gur-rls an' snake cha-armers an' Boolgarian club swingers an' foreign men goin' around with their legs in mattresses." He concludes by advising McKenna to "go to the fair, ride around in the boats, look at the canned tomatties an' the table-clothes, ride in the electric cars, but beware of that Midway. It'll no do for young men at all, at all. You'd lose your head. You would, you would. Oh, fol-de-rol, de raddle rol" (*SP*, May 21, 1893). The citywise barman quite addled by his exposure to the Midway is a figure for Dunne and his fellow journalists, face to face for the first time in Chicago history with something commensurate to their capacity for wonder.

Throughout the Fair summer that follows, Colonel McNeery pays weekly visits to the White City. He is shocked by the French art exhibition with its preponderance of nudes—"there wasn't a pair of pants or a petticoat in the room. Ne'er a one" (*SP*, June 4, 1893). He rides the giant Ferris wheel with his friend O'Connor, who is frightened into a general confession of his sins while swaying two hundred feet above the Midway (*SP*, July 2, 1893). He criticizes the bowing and scraping of Fair dignitaries before the visiting Princess Eulalia of Spain: "Think o' it—old Mayor Carter Hahr'son bendin' his back till his joints creaked like a cellar dure an' kissin' her hand, with Bath House Jawnny Coughlin standin' prisint arms and Jack McGillen a-crookin' his knee that never was crooked in prayer, I promise ye" (*SP*, June 11, 1893).

Two rival Irish exhibits faced each other across the Midway, replicas of Blarney and Donegal castles, and the colonel explains that the former "is th' real Irish village, for bechune you an' me, Jawnny, I think th' other one from Donegal is a sort of bunk, I do, an' I niver liked Donegal anny how. It was a man from Donegal that hit my fa-ather with a scythe" (*SP*, June 4, 1893).[46] Dunne also wrote two columns describing Irish Day, September 30, which featured speeches by Chicago's Archbishop Feehan, several Irish members of Parliament, and the lord mayor of Dublin. Inclement weather is seen as a blessing because "ye cudden't have got three hundherd thousan' Irishmen to-gether on a fine day without thim breakin' loose. Th' rain kept thim f'um gettin' enthusiastic." [47] Probably Dunne was there, for Ellis reports that his local reputation had grown to the extent that he was appointed to several of the Irish-oriented Fair committees.[48]

Colonel McNeery is also a bemused observer at several of the Fair congresses. He predicts "ructions" at the Parliament of Religions, at which the world's churchmen were gathered for a week of ecumenical discussions, and cites an Irish anecdote about a Protestant-Catholic feud to support his skepticism about toleration (*EP*, Sept. 16, 1893). He also has strong opinions about the Literary Congress, which was the scene of an extension of the heated debate in American letters between practitioners of the new realism and the forces of genteel romance. That issue spilled over into the daily press of Chicago when Eugene Field devoted a series of "Sharps and Flats" columns to a prolonged attack on the realists, aimed primarily at Hamlin Garland and William Dean Howells.[49]

Dunne's response is in keeping with the preference for realism established in his *Tribune* discussion of theatrical melodrama. He takes off from a defense of romanticism delivered at the Literary Congress by critic and novelist Charles Dudley Warner. The concurrently-meeting Folklore Congress has prompted John McKenna to ask "what the divvle is folk-lore?" which allows Colonel McNeery to enter the debate, as follows:

> "Di'lect pothry," replied Colonel McNeery, promptly. "If you was to put ye'er conversations in pothry, Jawn, thim'd be folk-lore an' ye'd be a folk-lorist. Ye have th' hell's own di'lect, Jawn. Ye niver come fr'm Roscommon in all ye'er born days. Ye'er farther down thin that. Folk-lore's di'lect pothry, an' ghost stories an' tales iv th'

pookies that made so much throuble with th' blueberries iv a
hallowe'en, they're folk-lore, too. D'ye mind the ya-arn O'Connor
used to tell about his Uncle Aloysius that had th' rasslin' match with
th' ghost iv Red Hugh O'Neill near Clontarf?"

"I mind it well," said Mr. McKenna.

"Where th' ghost ac-cused O'Connor's uncle iv pickin' up th' mit
he thrun away an' demanded him to give it back because th' poor
ghost couldn't cut his meat with only wan dook," the colonel said.
"Well, that's folk-lore."

"Faith, it may be," said Mr. McKenna. "But it always looked like
a whaling big lie to me."

"McKinna," replied the colonel, sententiously, "ye'er a gom. Ye
know naw more about lithratoor than ye know about th' cathechism
an' ye'er as innocint iv that as the unbaptized haythen. If ye cud've
been down to th' lithry congress with me ye'd 'v larned that truth in
a-art ain't got no more place thin a pool-check in a temp'rance collection. There was a rooster there be th' names iv Char-les Dudley
Warner that gave us that song, an' faith, I'm thinkin' he's right. 'Th'
wan aim,' says Char-les, 'in a-art,' he says, 'is th' beautiful. Naw
slang,' he says, 'or low people,' he says, but beautiful conversations
like thim we larn'd in Hickey's 'Christian Dooty' under th' hedge.
Ah-ha, he's th' boy f'r my money, is Char-les. What th' 'ell do I care
f'r low life an' common people whin I picks up me fambly shtory
paper at night. Th' likes iv you an' th' likes iv me, McKinna, wants
princes an' dooks an' kings an' pottentates an' all th' world full iv
flowers an' sunshine an' music f'r our readin'. Did you niver read
'Thadjus iv Warsaw,' Jawn? Iv coorse not. Faith, I might 've known
betther than t've asked ye. Well, sir, there's my idale iv a good
smashin' book. There's nobody in there lower than th' big casino.
I'm not sure but fr'm what I heerd tell I'm thinkin' me friend Char-les
Dudley wrote that there book."   [*SP,* July 16, 1893] [50]

Of course Dunne is being sarcastic here, for "truth in a-art," as revealed in "slang," "low life," and "common people," is already his
province.

Dunne is much more concerned with things Irish in these columns
than he was in the first batch of McNeery pieces from late 1892 and
early 1893. As we have seen, he tells Irish anecdotes and refers to
Irish folktales. In addition, he lets Colonel McNeery comment on
specifically Irish and Irish-American events, such as the annual August
15 picnic of Chicago's Irish nationalists and the passage in the British
House of Commons of the Home Rule Bill of 1893 (*EP,* Aug. 20,
Sept. 9, 1893). Thus, these later McNeery pieces foreshadow Mr.

Dooley's close connections with Ireland and the Irish in Chicago.

Near the end of the Fair, Colonel McNeery's prototype, Jim Mc-Garry, began to be annoyed at the unsought notoriety that went along with his association with the column. Dunne later recalled the culmination of his friend's annoyance:

> I was going on well and enjoying myself until one afternoon when I happened in at Jim McGarry's. My friend scarcely spoke to me. I tried various topics of conversation. He would have none of them. Suddenly he shook his finger under my nose.
> "You can't put printer's ink on me with impunity," he cried.
> "But, Jim, what have I done?"
> "I'll see ye'er boss, young man. I'll see Jawn R.," he said and turned away.
> Sure enough, the next day I had a visit from John R. Walsh, the banker who owned the Chicago *Herald* and the *Evening Post*. I knew him well and liked him, even if he was a pirate over-punished through President Taft's malignant hatred of him. Walsh said he had a favor to ask of me. I knew at once what it was.
> "Jim McGarry has been to see you," I said.
> "That's it," said my Boss. "You know the old fellow is broken up over those McNeery articles. His friends are laughing at him. Can't you change the name?" [51]

Dunne responded by shipping Colonel McNeery back to Ireland. He appears to have spent about two weeks deciding on a successor, for McNeery's last pronouncement—his reaction to an epidemic of train robberies—comes on September 23, 1893, and the following week finds Officer Steve Rowan and John McKenna discussing his departure and being tested as possible replacements. Steve Rowan has center stage, and his reaction to McNerry's leaving contains a realistic look at Ireland in the nineties and the pretensions of those who returned to it from America:

> "So th' old boy has gone back to th' dart [dirt]. Well, musha, I wish him luck, an', between th' doods on the corners an' th' weight iv this here stick iv timber, manny a time I've been dhriven to wish I was home again where I come from, with a mud wall at me back an' a roof iv rushes over th' head iv me, an' a good potful iv petaties boilin' in the turf-fire, an' maybe, to make the whole thing good, th' tinent nex' dure bein' thrun out f'r not payin' rint. Not that our fam'ly lived much on petaties, Jawn. Don't think that f'r a minyit, me la-ad. I had

an uncle that died iv overatin' reed burruds. I'd give the eye out iv me head to be back with McNeery, cross an old cow as he was. By gar, he'll be th' 'ell's own man, won't he, though. Th' carmen'll take off their hats to him and th' little gossoons [children] 'll chase him down th' sthreet beggin' f'r dough, an' th' parish priest 'll invite him to dinner, an' maybe, by gar, he'll go to parlyment." [*EP,* Sept. 30, 1893]

The voice rings true, but Dunne must have seen immediately that Steve Rowan would not serve. The fact was that to continue the format in which he was most comfortable, that of leisurely dialogue from a position somewhat removed from the urban fray, the saloon setting was perfect. The crucial decision to move that saloon from downtown Chicago out to Bridgeport was partly due to the guidance of the real John McKenna, who remembered later that "Dunne appealed to me, and we went out looking for another character who would stand hitched. We went out to Bridgeport and met the prominent saloon-keepers of that section." Finding that "they too had plenty of brogue and wit," and that there were a good many Dooleys and Hennessys among them, Dunne "decided it would be safe to call his team of characters, destined to fame, by these names, and thus they have remained to this day." [52]

It is important to remember that Dunne had come from a respectable West Side middle-class family, none of whom had known the life of poverty and grinding physical labor common to the Irish of the South Side. Thus, his location of Mr. Dooley in Bridgeport was a freely taken decision to chronicle a way of life different from his own, and not the ambivalent, passionate grappling with his personal origins of, say, James T. Farrell in the 1920s. Actually, while Dunne was reaching down to lower-class life for creative inspiration, he was personally moving up the social ladder, thanks mostly to Mary Ives Abbott, author of two romantic novels and the *Post*'s regular book reviewer. Mrs. Abbott was a proper Bostonian from Salem. The widow of a man who had been engaged in the India trade, she had come to Chicago to be near her brother, a railroad official. Recognizing and encouraging Dunne's ability, she drew him into her social circle, which centered around informal conversational gatherings at her apartment. Dunne had begun to move in Chicago society circles through one of his best friends at the Whitechapel Club, Robert Hamill, a Yale graduate and the son of the president of the Chicago Board of Trade; and the growth of his friendship with Mrs. Abbott cemented his ties with the city's old line wealth, among whom she was a favorite.[53]

Thus begins the curious, persistent split between Dunne's life and his writing, between the successful and social young editor and his persona of an aging, worldly-wise saloonkeeper. Mr. Dooley spends a lot of time laughing at the people his creator spent a lot of time living with and emulating. Indeed, this may be the humorist's curse, for Justin Kaplan also finds it in Mark Twain, remarkable even as Sam Clemens paced the deck of the *San Francisco* on his first trip to New York City in 1867: "He was, at the very least, already a double creature. He wanted to belong, but he also wanted to laugh from the outside. The Hartford literary gentleman lived inside the sage-brush bohemian." [54] Like Clemens, Dunne solidified his doubleness by marriage—in 1902, to Mary Abbott's daughter Margaret. But already in the nineties it was a very real phenomenon, observable in the often widely divergent opinions of Finley Peter Dunne, editor, and Martin Dooley, working-class immigrant sage.

A bar in Bridgeport was a different kind of place from a downtown saloon like Jim McGarry's. The change was from a "social" center and celebrity hang-out to a real social institution with unique and very important community functions. Hull-House researcher Ernest C. Moore acknowledged "The Social Value of the Saloon" in an 1897 study, in which he labeled it "the workingman's club." Clean, warm, and better appointed than the average home, the corner saloon provided the millworkers and draymen of neighborhoods such as Bridgeport with food, drink, and service, with entertainment in the form of cards and billiards, and, most compellingly, with companionship. "It is," found Moore, "the society of his fellows that [the workingman] seeks and must have." [55]

Dunne already had a sense of the peculiar heritage of the working-class saloon when he brought Martin Dooley into existence on Saturday, October 7, 1893. Here are the opening paragraphs of that first piece:

> Business was dull in the liquor-shop of Mr. Martin Dooley in Archey road last Wednesday night and Mr. Dooley was sitting back in the rear of the shop holding a newspaper at arm's length before him and reading the sporting news. In came Mr. John McKenna.

Mr. McKenna has been exceedingly restless since Colonel McNeery went home to Ireland, and on his way out to Brighton Park for consolation he bethought himself of Martin Dooley. The lights were shining in the little tavern and the window decorations—green festoons, a single-sheet poster of a Parnell meeting in McCormick's Hall and a pyramid of bottles filled with Medford rum and flies— evoked such cheery recollections of earlier years that Mr. McKenna hopped off the car and entered briskly.

"Good evening, Martin," he said.

"Hello, Jawnny," replied Mr. Dooley, as if they had parted only the evening before. "How's thricks? I don't mind, Jawnny, if I do. 'Tis duller here than a ray-publican primary in th' fourth wa-ard, th' night. Sure, ye're like a ray iv sunlight, ye are that. There's been no company in these pa-arts since Dominick Riley's big gossoon was took up be th' polis—no, not the Riley that lived down be th' gashouse; he's moved over in th' fifth wa-ard—may th' divil go with him: 'twas him bruk that there mirror with a brick for an' because I said Carey, th' informer, was a Limerick man. This here's Pat Riley, th' big, strappin' kid iv Dominick Riley, that lived beyant the rollin' mills. He was th' 'ell's own hand f'r sport. . . .

"But where've ye been all these days, man alive? I ain't seen ye, Jawn dear, since ye led th' gr-rand ma-arch in Finucane's Hall, this tin years past. D'ye mind th' Grogan girls? A-ha, a musha, I see ye do, ye cute man. An' well ye might. Th' oldest wan—Birdie she called herself in thim days, though she was christened Bridget, an' I knowed it dam well, f'r I was at th' christenin' an' got this here scar on me nut fr'm an unruly Clare man that Jawnny Shea brung over with him—th' oldest wan danced with ye, an' five years aftherward her husband found in her pocketbook a ca-ard sayin' 'Vote f'r Jawn McKinna' an' he was f'r suin' f'r a divorce, by gar, he was. She said ye give her a lot iv thim for to take home to th' old man, an' she on'y kept th' wan. An' ye haven't seen her fr'm that day to this! Oh, dear, oh, dear. How soon forgot we a-are. It's little ye think iv Bridgeport whin ye'er gallopin' aroun' to wakes an' christenin's with Potther Pammer [Potter Palmer] and Hobart What-th'-'ell's-his-name Taylor."   [*EP*, Oct. 7, 1893]

Immediately we are in another world from that of Colonel McNeery. Mr. Dooley's brogue is thicker, with words like "gossoon," "musha," "bruk" and "beyant," and more contractions and expanded "a's," all of which attest to the move down the social scale from Dearborn Street to Archer Avenue. Also, there is an assumption by Mr. Dooley of knowledge common to the Irish-American community, in the reference to "Carey, th' informer," who betrayed the Dublin Phoenix Park murderers in 1883 and was murdered himself in retribution.[56] But most important, we are at once in that community, exposed to the flavor of a particular neighborhood culture, where people are placed by family, geography, and reputation, and where that placement carries real weight. Here are the seeds of Dunne's major accomplishment in the Chicago Dooley pieces—the imaginative evocation of Bridgeport in the 1890s. The following chapters are an attempt to reconstruct that creation.

2

MR. DOOLEY IN BRIDGEPORT

The Creation of a Community

"I know histhry isn't thrue, Hinnissy, because it ain't like what I see ivry day in Halsted Sthreet. If any wan comes along with a histhry iv Greece or Rome that'll show me th' people fightin', gettin' dhrunk, makin' love, gettin' married, owin' th' grocery man an' bein' without hard-coal, I'll believe they was a Greece or Rome, but not befure. Historyans is like doctors. They are always lookin' f'r symptoms. Those iv them that writes about their own times examines th' tongue an' feels th' pulse an' makes a wrong dygnosis. Th' other kind iv histhry is a post-mortem examination. It tells ye what a counthry died iv. But I'd like to know what it lived iv."

Observations by Mr. Dooley [1]

PETER DUNNE's deep and various rendering of Irish-American city life in the 1890s has never been sufficiently acknowledged, mostly because he chose not to republish the bulk of this material in his Dooley collections. An examination of the original newspaper pieces, however, reveals that, by accretion of weekly essay on weekly essay, a whole picture emerges. Bridgeport in the nineties blossoms as a self-contained culture, rich and intensely communal, complete with its private pantheon of heroes and a rigid social hierarchy rooted in place, family, and occupation. A true ghetto, this south side nucleus of the Irish-American working class community had more in common with villages in the old country than with adjacent Chicago neighborhoods; and only Peter Dunne has preserved that village, in fragments to be sure, but in fresh colors that still retain the flush of life. But this is not simply an archeological reconstruction. All that we know of the area we know through Mr. Dooley, so that in a real sense Dunne has created the community for us, has given Bridgeport its only imaginative life.

Dunne observes closely, vividly, but with the economy of a born journalist. From jewellike paragraphs planted everywhere in the Dooley pieces, the individuated colors of Bridgeport flash out. Here is a typical scene—Archer Avenue in winter:

> Up in Archey road the streetcar wheels squeaked along the tracks and the men coming down from the rolling-mills hit themselves on their big chests and wiped their noses on their leather gloves with a peculiar back-handed stroke at which they are most adept. The little girls coming out of the bakeshops with loaves done up in brown paper under their arms had to keep a tight clutch on their thin shawls lest those garments should be caught up by the bitter wind blowing from Brighton Park way and carried down to the gashouse. The frost was so thick on the windows of Mr. Martin Dooley's shop that you could just see the crownless harp on the McCormick's Hall Parnell meeting sheet above it, and you could not see any of the pyramid of Medford rum bottles founded contemporaneously with that celebrated meeting.   [*EP*, Nov. 25, 1893]

So much of quotidian reality is caught here: the roughness of working men defined by a characteristic gesture, the threadbare quality of Bridgeport life as reflected in its children, a hint of nostalgia for Ireland and Parnell, for the brighter days when "the cause" seemed real and victory close at hand.

By his own definition (which heads this chapter), Martin Dooley is the best historian we have of the Irish experience in Chicago, all the way back to its beginnings in the riverside settlement of Hardscrabble, where the first Irish laborers camped, raised shanties, and eventually built solid frame houses. Many of these settlers had moved west after working on the construction of the Erie Canal. In Chicago, they found fifteen years of steady work: first on the Illinois and Michigan Canal, a project to join the Mississippi River and Lake Michigan begun on July 4, 1836, and then on the railroad line that superseded it almost immediately. (The canal opened on April 10, 1848, and the first railroad over the same route began operations in 1851.) Mr. Dooley remembers the building of the canal; in particular, a famous strike "on Dorgan's section." Agitated by an insult (whether real or imagined isn't clear) to their home county, his digging crew of Mayo men demand satisfaction of Dorgan, their boss:

> " 'Why,' says Dorgan, 'ain't every man on me section from th' County May-o?' he says. ' 'Tis true,' says Callaghan, 'but we undherstand ye discriminate,' he says. 'Didn't ye say,' he says, 'that anny man was as good with a pick as a May-o man?' . . . 'What I said,' says Dorgan, 'was that I'd heer tell of good pick-min,' he says, 'out iv May-o,' he says, gettin' his back up. 'An' be hivins I stand by it,' he says. 'Thin,' says Callaghan, 'we strike,' he says. 'We like ye, Cornelius,' he says, 'as a man,' he says; 'but on principle we'll break your back,' he says. An' they thrun him into th' canal."
>
> [*EP,* June 30, 1894]

When the canal opened in 1848, the little Irish community, rechristened Bridgeport, became for a few years a booming, brawling river town, overrun with muleskinners, teamsters and bargemen, and Mr. Dooley resurrects several tall tales from this fertile but forgotten time. An epic prize fight between "Con Murphy, th' champine hivvyweight iv th' ya-ards," and "th' German blacksmith" lasts from four in the morning until after sunset, "whin Murphy's backer put a horseshoe on th' big man's fist," and the canal-side battle finally ends (*EP,* Nov. 2, 1895). Another piece describes a legendary race the length of the canal between the scows of O'Brien and Dorsey: "O'Brien had th' fastest mule. He was out iv th' most famous mule on th' canal—

Lady Annabel, ownded be a man be th' name iv Clancy." Each scow
fouls the other, so the race itself is inconclusive, but the participants
settle their grudge by "rollin' each other into th' canal" (*EP*, Sept. 14,
1895). Those were lively days, and Mr. Dooley is properly nostalgic
about their passing.

The Irish Famine of the late 1840s had been the great shared experience of the immigrant generation of which Mr. Dooley was hypo-
thetically a member, and he tells chilling stories of suffering and
violence from that terrible time, during which the population of Ireland
dropped, through death and emigration, by two million souls in ten
years. In one of his harshest pieces, Dunne used the connotative power
of the Famine to indict George Pullman's callousness during the citywide strike of his workers in the summer of 1894. To make his point,
Mr. Dooley compares strike-bound Chicago with Ireland in the forties:

> " 'Tis not th' min, ye mind; 'tis th' women an' childhren. Glory be
> to Gawd, I can scarce go out f'r a wa-alk f'r pity at seein' th' little
> wans settin' on th' stoops an' th' women with thim lines in th' fa-ace
> that I seen but wanst befure, an' that in our parish over beyant, whin
> th' potatoes was all kilt be th' frost an' th' oats rotted with th' dhrivin'
> rain. Go into wan iv th' side sthreets about supper time an' see thim,
> Jawn—thim women sittin' at th' windies with th' babies at their
> breasts an' waitin' f'r th' ol' man to come home. . . . Musha, but 'tis
> a sound to dhrive ye'er heart cold whin a woman sobs an' th' young
> wans cries, an' both because there's no bread in th' house."
> [*EP*, Aug. 25, 1894]

Closely related to the Famine, for a man of Martin Dooley's age,
was the experience of emigration itself, which Dunne has described in
an early piece, "The Wanderers." He serves notice immediately that
the mood of sentimental melancholy associated with departure from
Ireland in so much Irish-American writing will not be here indulged—
not even to the end of one sentence: "We watched th' little ol' island
fadin' away behind us, with th' sun sthrikin' th' white house-tops iv
Queenstown an' lightin' up th' chimbleys iv Martin Hogan's liquor
store" (*EP*, Feb. 16, 1895). What we get instead is a realistic depiction of the hardships of crossing in the overcrowded, unsanitary emi-
grant ships of the late 1840s, with Dooley's focus on a widower and
his child, only one of whom survives. The piece ends with the abate-
ment of a six-day storm at sea:

"[The widower] had been settin' on a stool, but he come over to me. 'Th' storm' says I, 'is over.' 'Yis,' says he, ' 'tis over.' ' 'Twas wild while it lasted,' says I. 'Ye may say so,' says he. 'Well, please Gawd,' says I, 'that it left none worse off thin us.' 'It blew ill f'r some an' aise f'r others,' says he. 'Th' babby is gone.'

"An' so it was, Jawn, f'r all his rockin' an' singin'. An' in th' avnin' they burried it over th' side into th' sea. An' th' little man see thim do it."

Memories such as this die hard, and they must have been plentiful in Bridgeport.[2]

Mr. Dooley also gives us glimpses of the early years in Chicago of the Famine generation, available nowhere else and likely based on reminiscences by those who made the trip, such as Dunne's parents. From the perspective of age and experience Dooley looks back wryly at his youthful illusions about America as the place "where all ye had to do was to hold ye'er hat an' th' goold guineas'd dhrop into it." Those illusions turned quickly to the reality of actual employment opportunities for the Irish in America in the 1840s and 1850s:

"But, faith, whin I'd been here a week, I seen that there was nawthin' but mud undher th' pavement—I larned that be means iv a pick-axe at tin shillin's th' day—an' that, though there was plenty iv goold, thim that had it were froze to it: an' I came west, still lookin' f'r mines. Th' on'y mine I sthruck at Pittsburgh was a hole f'r sewer pipe. I made it. Siven shillin's th' day. Smaller thin New York, but th' livin' was cheaper, with Mon'gahela rye at five a throw, put ye'er hand around th' glass.

"I was still dreamin' goold, an' I wint down to Saint Looey. Th' nearest I come to a fortune there was findin' a quarter on th' sthreet as I leaned over th' dashboard iv a car to whack th' off mule. Whin I got to Chicago, I looked around f'r th' goold mine. They was Injuns here thin. But they wasn't anny mines I cud see. They was mud to be shovelled an' dhrays to be dhruv an' beats to be walked. I chose th' dhray; f'r I was niver cut out f'r a copper, an' I'd had me fill iv excavatin'. An' I dhruv th' dhray till I wint into business."

[*EP,* July 17, 1897]

In the 1850s jobs appeared in Bridgeport lumberyards and stockyards to take up the slack of declining canal trade, and in 1865 the first steel rolling mill opened at Archer and Ashland avenues. Rolling mills subsequently operated on that spot until 1896, providing work for thousands of Bridgeporters. These factories and yards kept Bridgeport a working-class community, a place to be left behind on the road to respectability in St. Patrick's parish.[3]

When Dunne created Mr. Dooley in 1893, the line between the West Side middle-class and the South Side working-class Irish was still clear, although both neighborhoods were showing signs of erosion. Dunne described the changing character of Bridgeport in the preface to his first collection, *Mr. Dooley in Peace and in War* (1898):

> There was a time when Archey Road was purely Irish. But the Huns, turned back from the Adriatic and the stock-yards and over-running Archey Road, have nearly exhausted the original popula-tion,—not driven them out as they drove out less vigorous races, with thick clubs and spears, but edged them out with the more biting weapons of modern civilization,—overworked and undereaten them into more languid surroundings remote from the tanks of the gas-house and the blast furnaces of the rolling mill.[4]

The "new immigration" from southern and eastern Europe was chang-ing Bridgeport before Dunne's eyes, and he was faced with the difficult task of bringing a community into existence during the very years of its transformation into something else. He solved this problem by translating his own sense of urgency into Mr. Dooley's various reac-tions to the dissolution of his way of life, which range from resignation to confusion and near-panic. Moreover, the sense of flux running through them gives a dramatic quality to the Dooley pieces: first a culture is created for us; then we watch it die. The rest of this chapter explores the creation; the next chapter will deal with the death.

A full round of community events comes spinning from Dunne's pen: a world of fairs and raffles; holidays, graduations, and games; mar-riages and births and funerals. There are reports of church plays, staged by the parish young people for an eager audience of parents whose inability to distinguish art from life provides most of the humor. For example, in the "St. Patrick's Stock Company" production of "The Doomed Markey," the plight of a disinherited French aristocrat, née Denny Hogan, prompts the following brisk exchange:

> "Well, sir, Dinny was all broke up. 'What,' he says, 'shall I do?' he says. 'What shall I do?' . . . 'Go to wurruk,' says wan iv th' Dorgan twins in th' back iv th' hall. 'I want ye to undherstand he has a good job promised to him on th' ca-ars,' said Mrs. Hogan, tur-rnin' 'round

on th' Dorgan twin. ' 'Tis ye'er own fam'ly 'll be scratchin' a beggar's
back whin I'm ridin' up an' down to Mrs. Potther Pammers without
payin' no more thin how-d'ye-do to me own son,' she says. So they
thrun out th' Dorgan twin an' th' play wint on." [*EP,* Nov. 16, 1895]

Sporting events also brought Bridgeporters together. At Thanksgiving time, Dunne described riotous football games between parochial
schools (the Christian Brothers School played the St. Aloysius Tigers
in 1897) or between rival youth clubs with Irish-nationalist orientation
(the "young Parnells" vs. the "young Sarsfields" in 1895). The appeal
of football seems to lie in its violence, which Mr. Dooley sees as a
natural outgrowth of life on Archer Avenue: "Downtown it's football;
out here it's the Irish killin' each other. Downtown the spectators sees
it f'r a dollar apiece; out here it costs th' spectators ne'er a cent, but
th' players has to pay tin dollars an' costs" (*EP,* Nov. 28, 1896). In
a piece which mocks the golfing fad among Chicago's upper classes—
Dunne had recently taken it up—Mr. Dooley produces a list of Bridgeport's sporting heroes, none of whom can understand the strange game.
These include "Dorsey, th' polisman," who "was th' best hurler in th'
county whin he was young," "Flannagan, th' fireman, that is th' rough-
est tosser in a handball coort," and "Carmody, th' captain iv th'
Motorman's baseball nine" (*EP,* Sept. 18, 1897). This appeal to men
of obvious stature, occupational as well as athletic, is decisive, and
Dooley concludes that there is no justification "f'r a game that a man
can't begin to undherstand without he knows Gaelic as it's talked in
Scotland." Golf will never replace hurling, handball, or baseball in
Bridgeport, because it is too complicated and too tame: "It lacks th'
wan issintial for a good time, iv homicide."

Dunne also turned out occasional pieces describing the habitual ob-
servance of various holidays in Bridgeport, from the custom of going
calling on New Year's Eve (*EP,* Jan. 1, 1893), to the Memorial Day
parade and its pathetic adjunct, "th' women marchin' to Calv'ry
[Calvary Cemetery, where most of Chicago's Irish were buried] with
their veils over their heads an' thim little pots iv gyraniums in their
hands" (*EP,* June 2, 1894). He pays particular attention to the specifically Irish celebrations, notably St. Patrick's Day, and these will be
discussed later together with Irish nationalism. The Lenten season, of
major significance in Catholic Bridgeport, causes Mr. Dooley perennial
trouble. When John McKenna finds him mixing a hot toddy during

Lent, Dooley responds to censure by recalling his father's difficulties with giving up smoking back in Roscommon. As that attempt was unsuccessful, Dooley has decided that he is his father's son, "a'most to th' hour an' day," and that to resist his destiny as a sinner is impossible. Besides, as the parish priest has explained to him, "starvation don't always mean salvation. . . . They'se a little priest down be th' Ninth Ward that niver was known to keep a fast day; but Lent or Christmas tide, day in an' day out, he goes to th' hospital where they put th' people that has th' small-pox" (*EP*, March 7, 1896).

One other Lent the narration of his annual downfall contains a crackling exchange between Mr. Dooley and a witty adversary from the County Clare. Having made up his mind to "stop off swearin', drinkin', smokin' and playin' ca-ards till afther Easter," he holds out until the second day, when, after cracking his shin, "I swore till half the women along th' road begun to call in their childher. Iv coorse I had to scratch off swearin' an' thry to play th' shtring out with th' other three.

> I done all right through th' afthernoon, but at night that big Clare man, O'Toole, he come in. I don't like a hair iv his head an' he knows it, so I says, 'Terence,' I says, 'I'm glad to see ye.'
> " 'How ar-re ye?' says he. 'I was goin' by,' he says, 'an' I thought I'd come in an' play ye a little game iv forty-fives.' ' 'Tis Lint,' says I. ' 'Tis a good excuse,' says he. 'What's that?' says I. 'Oh,' he says, with a laugh, 'I don't blame ye,' he says, with that mane smile iv his. 'I don't blame ye,' he says. 'There's very few min fr'm ye'er part iv Connack that can play games,' he says. 'That ray-quires intillegence,' he says. 'Ye'er betther a long way at pitchin' quates,' he says. I was hoppin' mad in a minyet. Says I: 'There niver was a man born in th' County Clare,' says I, 'that could bate me playin' forty-fives,' I says. 'Come on,' says I. 'What for?' says he. 'Th' dhrinks,' says I. 'An' th' see-gars,' says he. 'It's a go,' says I, an' there I was, all me good intintions down at wanst. 'Twas a judgment on him f'r challengin' me that he lost tin straight games an' had to walk clear to Brighton f'r lack iv car fare."   [*EP*, March 24, 1894]

Let us look now at one of Mr. Dooley's more extended descriptions of the social scene, typical in its sharply observed detail. The occasion is the parish fair at "St. Honoria's" at Christmastime, 1894:

> " 'Twas a gr-rand fair. They had Roddy's Hibernyun band playin' on th' cor-rner an' th' basemint iv th' church was packed. In th'

ba-ack they had a shootin' gall'ry where ye got five shots f'r tin cints. Hogan, th' milkman, was shootin' whin I wint in an' iverybody was out iv th' gall'ry. He missed eight shots an' thin he thrun two lumps iv coal at th' ta-arget an' made two bull's-eyes. He is a Tipp'rary man an' th' raison he's over here is he hit a polisman with a rock at twinty ya-ards—without sights.

"I'd no more thin inthered th' fair thin who should come up but Malachi Dorsey's little girl, Dalia. 'Good avnin,' she says. 'Won't ye take a chanst?' she says. 'On what?' says I. 'On a foldin' bed,' says she. 'Faith, I will not,' I says. 'I'll take no chances on no foldin' bed,' I says. 'I was locked up in wan wanst,' I says, 'an' it took a habees corpis to get me out,' I says. She lift me alone afther that, but she must've tipped me off to th' others f'r whin I come away I stood to win a doll, a rockin' chair, a picture iv th' pope done by Mary Ann O'Donoghue, a deck iv ca-ards an' a tidy. I'm all right if th' combination comes out ayether way fr'm th' rockin' chair to th' doll 'r th' tidy. But I wuddent know what th' divvle to do if I sh'd catch th' pope iv R-rome an' th' ca-ards.

"Th' booths was something iligant. Mrs. Dorsey had th' first wan where she sold mottoes an' babies' clothes. Next to hers was the ice crame layout, with the Widow Lonergan in cha-arge. Some wan touted big Hinnisy again it. He got wan mouthful iv it an' began to holler: 'F'r th' love iv hivin, won't some wan give me a cup iv tay,' he says. 'Me insides is like a skatin' rink.' He wint over an' shtud be th' fire with his coattails apart till th' sexton put him out.

"Acrost th' hall was th' table f'r church articles, where ye cud get 'Keys iv Hevin' an' 'St. Thomas a Kempises' an' ros'ries. It done a poor business, they tell me, an' Miss Dolan was that sore at th' eyesther shtew thrade done be Mrs. Cassidy next dure that she come near soakin' her with th' 'Life iv St. Rose iv Lima.' 'Twas tur-r-rible."

[*EP*, Dec. 29, 1894]

Notice that in the midst of describing the color and chaos of the fair Mr. Dooley takes the time to identify the sharpshooter Hogan as a milkman, a native of County Tipperary, and a fugitive from justice in Ireland. Such exact placement is not merely pedantic gossip. Rather, through Mr. Dooley, Dunne is charting the social structure of Bridgeport from the inside. The result is a delineation, unique in American writing of the 1890s, of the social dynamics of an urban Irish community. By piecing together Mr. Dooley's various exercises in placement, we too can plot the hierarchy of status that operated there.

In the first place, one had to reckon the Irish background: where were you from in Ireland, and what had your family done there?

Having hit a policeman with a rock was a point probably in Hogan's favor, but having come from Tipperary decidedly was not; not, that is, if, like Mr. Dooley, you were from Roscommon. "Tips," as he refers to them, were known only for rock throwing and for their ability to incite riots. Many Bridgeporters were from the agrarian west of Ireland, but Martin himself is quick to deny any connection with "farmer Dooleys" when John McKenna gets his family confused with another:

> "No wan iv our fam'ly iver lived in th' counthry. We live in th' city, where they burn gas an' have a polis foorce to get on to. We're no farmers, divvle th' bit. We belong to th' industhreel classes. Thim must be th' Fermanagh Dooleys, a poor lot, Jawn, an' always on good terms with th' landlord, bad ciss to thim, says I. We're from Roscommon."   [*EP,* Aug. 24, 1895]

Dunne was having none of the literary sentimentalism about the western peasantry fostered in the nineties by Yeats, Hyde, and the Gaelic Leaguers; thus, Mr. Dooley, always the hard-headed realist, finds nothing romantic about rural life in Ireland. On the contrary, he tells one chilling story of the famine time on a rackrented farm in which a landlord is murdered by his starving tenant, "a black man be th' name iv Shaughnessy, that had thramped acrost th' hills fr'm Galway just in time to rent f'r th' potato rot" (*EP,* Feb. 6, 1897). Dooley also provokes John McKenna, by reminding him of his peasant origins:

> "There was places in th' pa-art iv Ireland ye'er people come fr'm, Jawn, with ye'er di'mons an' ye'er gol'-headed umbrella, where a piece iv bacon an' an exthra allowance iv pitaties was a feast f'r th' kids. 'Twas in ye'er town, Jawn, that th' little girl, whin she wanted to remimber something, says to th' ol' man: 'Why,' she says, 'ye remimber 'twas th' day they had mate,' says she. She remimbered it because 'twas th' day they had mate, Jawn. 'Twas like Christmas an' th' Foorth iv July an' Pathrick's day, whin they had mate in ye'er part iv Ireland, Jawn. On other oc-casions they had pitaties an' butthermilk, or, if their neighbors wuz kind, oatmale stirabout. Poor things!"
>   [*EP,* Dec. 23, 1893]

Moreover, while Irish intellectuals were romanticizing the supposed purity and classicism of the peasant culture, Mr. Dooley reports that Bridgeport children had stoned the house of a Gaelic-speaking Galway woman, thinking her a witch because of her foreign mutterings (*EP,* Dec. 5, 1896). And another Galway native lives in Bridgeport as a total outcast for espousing a heathenism that Yeats would have found charming and proper to his origins (*EP*, Jan. 30, 1897).

Dooley often describes natives of the western counties as "black," an adjective that seems to connote antisocial remoteness, obstinacy, and a tendency to sudden, violent anger. "Ye know how they ar-re whin they're black," he says of the Galway woman, "an' she was worse an' blacker." His favorite enemy is Dorsey, "th' cross-eyed May-o man that come to this counthry about wan day in advance iv a warrant f'r sheep-stealin'," and he counts it "a luxury that I can't go without in me ol' days" to have "a rale sthrong inimy, specially a May-o inimy—wan that hates ye ha-ard, an' that ye'd take th' coat off yer back to do a bad tur-rn to" (*EP*, Jan. 2, 1897). Similarly, it is a "black Mayo man" named O'Malley who disrupts a benefit crap game by rolling the highest possible number, then swallowing the dice to insure victory (*EP*, Jan. 12, 1895).

Certainly, Irish county rivalries carried over to America; if anything, they were more intense here. Mr. Dooley's employment history in Chicago is one long series of fights because all of the jobs he tries are monopolized by men from counties other than his own Roscommon. Kilkenny men drive him from the "Northwistrun freighthouse"; he leaves the rival Chicago Railroad Company when Limerick "butthermilks" attempt "to make a couplin' iv me bechune two freightcars"; "Shannyvogles an' Perkladdies" from Waterford and Dublin "jackeens" make him feel unwelcome on two other railroad jobs, and he finally goes into business for himself out of sheer exasperation (*EP,* Dec. 22, 1894). Moreover, Bridgeporters always answered challenges to county pride. We have seen Mr. Dooley break his Lenten resolves to answer a Clare man, and section boss Dorgan ends up in the canal for insulting his Mayo pick men. Love of county also inspires Fireman Clancy from Mayo to a dangerous rescue, which he justifies to his wife in this way: "Did ye see th' captain? He wanted to go. Did ye think I'd follow a Kerry man with all th' ward lukkin' on?" (*EP*, Nov. 23, 1895). Finally, hardly a month goes by without Mr. Dooley describing the disruption of some public gathering by clashing county factions. The Irish background remained a vital, emotional issue in the Bridgeport community.

To further complicate the fixing of social position, family history was at least as important as county of origin. To be sure, Mr. Dooley claims that "Ye don't often hear nowadays iv wan iv us sayin' he's descended fr'm wan iv th' kings iv Ireland. Who the divvle'd care? . . . Th' kings an' queens are played out." But he contradicts himself immediately, by sliding in a reference to his own family credentials: "F'r mesilf I'd as lave have a plastherer f'r a grandfather—me own was married to th' niece iv th' parish priest—as th' Imp'ror iv Roosha or th' Sultan iv Boolgaria. I would that." The occasion here is a lecture in the school hall on the origins of the Irish people, which leads to a heated genealogical debate between Clancy and Grogan:

> " 'Th' main guy iv our fam'ly was Murtagh, th' first king iv Connock,' says Clancy. 'An' he had a gr-reat deal iv goold in his three-asury.' 'Me folks is fr'm Owen, the first,' says Robert Immitt Grogan. 'I've heerd till iv him,' says Clancy. 'Me father mintioned his name often,' he says. 'He was a grand jook, Grogan,' he says. 'He wur-rked f'r King Murtagh,' he says, 'an' was a sober, industhrious man,' he says. ' 'Tis a lie,' says Grogan. 'Owen, the first,' he says, 'niver'd take any such job as jook,' he says. 'An', furthermore,' he says, 'no Grogan,' he says, 'iver wur-rked f'r a Clancy,' he says, 'ayether in Persia,' he says, 'in Connock,' he says, 'or in th' rowlin' mills,' he says. An' if I hadn't got in bechune thim [says Dooley] they'd been rile [royal] blood spilt on that there floor." [*EP*, March 2, 1895]

There is trouble of a similar nature at the Dooley family reunion, a ritual regathering of relatives scattered by the Famine. Mr. Dooley charts the emotional progression of the evening from nostalgia to name-calling:

> "On a Saturdah night we come together in a rinted hall an' held th' reunion. 'Twas great sport f'r a while. Some iv us hadn't spoke frindly to each other f'r twinty years, an' we set around an' tol' stories iv Roscommon an' its green fields, an' th' stirabout pot that was niver filled, an' th' blue sky overhead an' th' boggy ground undherfoot. 'Which Dooley was it that hamsthrung th' cows?' 'Mike Dooley's Pat.' 'Naw such thing: 'twas Pat Dooley's Mike. I mane Pat Dooley's Mike's Pat.' . . . They was lashins iv dhrink an' story-tellin', an' Felix's boy Aloysius histed a banner he had made with 'Dooley aboo' painted on it. But afther th' night got along, some iv us begun to raymimber that most iv us hadn't been frinds f'r long. Mrs. Morgan Dooley, she that was Molly Dooley befure she married Morgan, she turns to me, an' says she, ' 'Tis sthrange they let in that Hogan

woman,' she says,—that Hogan woman, Jawn, bein' th' wife iv her husband's brother. She heerd her say it, an' she says, 'I'd have ye undherstand that no wan iver come out iv Roscommon that cud hold up their heads with th' Hogans,' she says. ' 'Tis not f'r th' likes iv ye to slandher a fam'ly that's iv th' landed gintry iv Ireland, an' f'r two pins I'd hit ye a poke in th' eye,' she says. . . . Well, they wasn't two Dooleys in th' hall'd speak whin th' meetin' broke up; an' th' Lord knows, but I don't to this day, who's th' head iv th' Dooley fam'ly."   [*EP*, Aug. 24, 1895]

Martin's Uncle Mike, "as rough a man as iver laid hands on a polisman," puts an end to the status scrambling by hurling the ultimate insult: "Th' back iv me hand an' th' sowl iv me fut to all iv ye, . . . I quit ye. . . . Ye're all livin' here undher assumed names."

Reversals of family fortune between the old country and the new rankled the most. Mr. Dooley accentuates the plight of a blacklisted former railroad worker, Hagan, by placing him as "a Kilkenny man, whose father was a schoolmaster near where Dan'l O'Connell come fr'm" (*EP,* Nov. 30, 1895). Hagan keeps up appearances by sheer force of will. A friend of Mr. Dooley's meets him "comin' home in th' dark, staggerin' like a dhrunken man an' with his gray face down in his chist." Even though he has spent the day "walkin' fr'm house to house, carryin' coal an' poundin' with a hose at carpets, thin thrampin' home to save th' nickel or, more like, without enough money in his pocket to pay ca-ar fare," Hagan musters "a smile an' a proud bow f'r th' bist iv thim." " 'I like th' walk,' he says. ' 'Tis gran' to be out loosenin' me ol' bones such a night as th' like.' " His wife slams the door on the Ladies Aid Committee, led by a "pompious little fat ol' washerwoman," whose occupation seems to be as insulting as her errand, but the piece ends happily when Hagan returns to work, his father's good name intact. Another family in a similar situation is not so fortunate. Although her husband has been out of work for six months, Mrs. Callaghan refuses to accept charity, in part because the father of the relief committee chairman was one of her father's farmhands back in Roscommon. Callaghan himself visits the committee and instructs them to "take ye'er charity . . . an' shove it down ye'er throats" (*EP,* Nov. 24, 1894). No more attempts are made to help the family, and Mrs. Callaghan dies within the year, her resistance to pneumonia having been destroyed by near-starvation. Ironically, just before the fatal attack she has reasserted her community "position" by renting a pew at church, a luxury purchased at the expense of steady diet.

Failing proper county and family placement, a Bridgeporter could always marry well, although Mr. Dooley easily undercuts spurious social climbing by this means: "She marrid young Coogan. Ye mind him? He was in th' rale-estate business Mrs. Dorgan the bride's mother tould me, an' bydad she was r-right, f'r I see him wur-rukin' on a dredge in th' river" (*EP*, May 5, 1894). Still, courtship and marriage in Bridgeport are favorite Dooley topics, as long as the discussion stays in the third person. A keen observer of his society, Mr. Dooley knows all the signs of incipient matrimony, "as sure as I know 'tis goin' to r-rain whin me leg pains me." For example he offers the Casey boy, lately engaged:

> "He use to talk iv her whin he had his r-rollers on. Thin he begun to wear a white necktie an' wash his hands an' face befure supper. That's wan thing, Jawn, love does f'r a man. It makes him clane, an' marridge, conthrarywise, makes him dirty. Thin he let th' polisman on th' bate pass him by without peggin' a brick—which was onusu'l. Afther awhile he wint to dances, an' wan day I see him pass th' plate at early mass. Thin I knowed 'twas all off." [*EP*, May 5, 1894]

Most of the humor in the courtship pieces comes from the reluctance of the prospective groom, an established comic convention but particularly applicable in Bridgeport; for, as Dooley generalizes, "f'r an impetchoos an' darin' people th' Irish is th' mos' cowardly when it comes to mathrimony that iver I heerd tell iv." Stories of "th' bashfulness iv th' Archey road lads" are plentiful: "There was Dolan's daughter, who was coorted be Hannigan th' fireman f'r fifteen years, an' would be coorted now if she hadn't shamed him be sindin' him a wig f'r his bald head las' Christmas. Thin there was Dacey, the plumber, who'd niver'v marrid if he hadn't got into th' wrong buildin' whin he wint to take out a license f'r his dog, an' got a marridge license instid." In the most extreme anecdote Father Kelly actually proposes for the tongue-tied Danny Duggan, who comes out of the ordeal "lookin' as if he was goin' to kill a Chineyman, an' th' dear little colleen thrimblin' an' cryin', but holdin' on to him like a pair iv ice tongs" (*EP*, Dec. 8, 1894).

At their wittiest these sketches anticipate Frank O'Connor's studies of Irish mating habits; yet Dunne's satire is gentled by his sympathy for these rough, bumbling boys, and by his realistic perspective on the limits imposed on them by their environment:

"People that can't afford it always have marrid an' always will. 'Tis on'y th' rich that don't. They niver did. That's wan reason why they're rich, too. But whin a young man is so poor that he can't afford to keep a dog an' has no more prospects thin a sound-money dimmycratic newspaper [this was written during William Jennings Bryan's domination of the Democratic party], he finds a girl who's got less an' proposes to her an' they're marrid at th' expinse iv th' grocers iv th' neighborhood an' they live unhappy iver after, bringin' up a large fam'ly to go an' do likewise. There've been more people marrid since hard times set in thin iver befure in th' histhry iv th' wurruld. This here wave iv prosperity that's comin', if it's on th' square, will rejooce th' income of the marredge license department fifty per cint. Still, there'll be plenty. All th' wurruld can't get rich in a minyit, and so long as there's broken people on earth there'll be marredges. I tell ye that f'r th' truth. They may fall off in Mitchigan avenoo. They always do whin stocks go up. But over on this side iv th' thracks there niver has been enough prosperity to keep anny man's front stoop clear iv poor an' hopeless bridegrooms. Th' fewer th' jobs in Archey road th' bigger th' vote iv th' sixth wa-ard."

[*EP*, July 31, 1897]

One of the most moving Dooley pieces, "Shaughnessy," depicts the sorrow that a marriage brings to the father of the bride. "A quite [quiet] man that come into th' road befure th' fire," Shaughnessy "wurruked f'r Larkin, th' conthractor, f'r near twenty years without skip or break, an' seen th' fam'ly grow up be candle-light." The story of this family reads like an O'Neill tragedy in miniature, for Shaughnessy's children fail socially, and in ways that seem peculiarly Irish.

"Th' oldest boy was intinded f'r a priest. 'Tis a poor fam'ly that hasn't some wan that's bein' iddycated f'r the priesthood while all th' rest wear themsilves to skeletons f'r him, an' call him Father Jawn 'r Father Mike whin he comes home wanst a year, light-hearted an' free, to eat with thim."

The situation described here, evidently a familiar one in Bridgeport, is close to that of "The Sisters" in Joyce's short story. Worn out by caring for their brother, Father Flynn, they are left with nothing when he dies.[5] Shaughnessy's boy dies too, and like Father Flynn, he dies embittered by having been driven toward a vocation that he never felt:

> "Shaughnessy's lad wint wrong in his lungs, an' they fought death f'r him f'r five years, sindin' him out to th' Wist an' havin' masses said f'r him; an', poor divvle, he kept comin' back cross an' crool, with th' fire in his cheeks, till wan day he laid down, an' says he: 'Pah,' he says, 'I'm goin' to give up,' he says. 'An' I on'y ask that ye'll have th' mass sung over me be some man besides Father Kelly,' he says. An' he wint, an' Shaughnessy come clumpin' down th' aisle like a man in a thrance."

The next child, a daughter, goes bad—"She didn't die; but, th' less said, th' sooner mended"—and the next is Terrence, a charming ne'er-do-well like Jamie Tyrone or Synge's Christy Mahon, "a big, bould, curly-headed lad that cocked his hat at anny man,—or woman." Terrence burns himself out and dies young. He is followed soon after by his mother and then by the Shaughnessy twins, "th' prettiest pair that wint to first communion." This leaves Theresa, "a big, clean-lookin' child" who "thought on'y iv th' ol' man, an' he leaned on her as if she was a crutch." Their love comes alive in one sharp detail: "She was out to meet him in th' avnin'; an' in th' mornin' he, th' simple ol' man, 'd stop to blow a kiss at her an' wave his dinner-pail, lookin' up an' down th' r-road to see that no wan was watchin' him."

In time, Theresa makes a good marriage—to the "prisident iv th' sodality"—but in relieving the weight of the family's accumulated social failure she leaves her father with a worse burden. After the wedding reception, Mr. Dooley waits up for a time with the old man and leaves with us a simple and powerful image of his loneliness.

> "Him an' me sat a long time smokin' across th' stove. Fin'lly, says I, 'Well,' I says, 'I must be movin'.' 'What's th' hurry?' says he. 'I've got to go,' says I. 'Wait a moment,' says he. 'Theresa 'll'—He stopped right there f'r a minyit, holdin' to th' back iv th' chair. 'Well,' says he, 'if ye've got to go, ye must,' he says. 'I'll show ye out,' he says. An' he come with me to th' dure, holdin' th' lamp over his head. I looked back at him as I wint by; an' he was settin' be th' stove, with his elbows on his knees an' th' empty pipe between his teeth."

[*EP*, March 28, 1896]

Dunne had opened this piece with a reflection on the nature of heroism: " 'Jawn,' said Mr. Dooley in the course of the conversation, 'whin ye come to think iv it, th' heroes iv th' wurruld,—an' be thim I mean th' lads that've buckled on th' gloves, an' gone out to do th' best they cud,—they ain't in it with th' quite people nayether you nor me hears tell iv fr'm wan end iv th' year to another.' " The story of Shaughnessy is one of many Dooley sketches intended to illustrate this point. Another features Pat Doherty, a legitimate hero of the Civil War who returns quietly to his job pushing a wheelbarrow at the mills, while blowhard politicians who never left Chicago wave the bloody shirt. Infuriated by the Memorial Day mouthings of a political hack named O'Toole in Mr. Dooley's saloon, Doherty delivers a withering blast, aimed as directly at war itself as at O'Toole's hypocrisy:

> "Doherty was movin' up to him. 'What rig'ment?' says he. 'What's that?' says O'Toole. 'Did ye inlist in th' army, brave man?' says Pat. 'I swore him over age,' says I [Mr. Dooley]. 'Was ye dhrafted in?' says th' little man. 'No,' says O'Toole. 'Him an' me was in th' same cellar,' says I. 'Did ye iver hear iv Ree-saca, 'r Vicksburg, 'r Lookout Mountain?' th' little man wint on. 'Did anny man iver shoot at ye with annything but a siltzer bottle? Did ye iver have to lay on ye'er stummick with ye'er nose burrid in th' Lord knows what while things was whistlin' over ye that, if they iver stopped whistlin', 'd make ye'er backbone look like a broom? Did ye iver see a man that ye'd slept with th' night befure cough, an' go out with his hands ahead iv his face? Did ye iver have to wipe ye'er most intimate frinds off ye'er clothes, whin ye wint home at night? Where was he durin' th' war?' he says. 'He was dhrivin' a grocery wagon f'r Philip Reidy,' says I. 'An' what's he makin' th' roar about?' says th' little man. 'He don't want anny wan to get onto him,' says I."   [*EP,* June 1, 1895]

Many Bridgeporters worked in the South Chicago steel mills at hot, dangerous, poorly paid jobs. (On March 31, 1895, the *Times-Herald* featured an interview with a mill watchman who declared that "I've seen them sweat until their shoes were full. . . . I've seen lots of big husky fellows dry up and die since I came here. They seem to sort o' shrivel away in the heat. I guess that's one kind of work that a man can't get accustomed to so he can stand it.") Another of these quiet heroes is little Tim Clancy, who "wurruks out in th' mills, tin hours a day, runnin' a wheelbarrow loaded with cindhers." Somehow he remains the optimist, displaying "th' patience iv Job" in coping cheerfully with the hardships of life in the culture of poverty:

> "He lives down beyant. Wan side iv his house is up again a brewery, an' th' other touches elbows with Twinty-Percint Murphy's flats. A few years back they found out that he didn't own on'y th' front half iv th' lot, an' he can set on his back stoop an' put his feet over th' fince now. He can, faith. Whin he's indures, he breathes up th' chimbly; an' he has a wife an' eight kids. He dhraws wan twinty-five a day—whin he wurruks." [*EP,* June 8, 1895]

But nothing daunts Clancy: a murderous heat wave, "promotion" to "th' big cinder pile" after the previous tender has collapsed with sunstroke, the sickness of his wife and one child—all are faced with such equanimity that Mr. Dooley confesses "whin I think iv th' thoughts that's been in my head f'r a week, I don't dare to look Tim Clancy in th' eye."

Mr. Dooley's favorite listener after 1896, the stolid, infinitely patient Hennessy, is also a mill worker with a large family to support. Not very bright, he misses most of his friend's witticisms and is often, in fact, the butt of Dooley's jokes. Yet he is good-hearted, dependable, and always there, managing, as John Kelleher has said, "a vivid existence on little more than silent bewilderment." Significantly, Dunne dedicated his third collection "To the Hennessys of the world who suffer and are silent." [6]

By these characterizations, Dunne was attempting to redress an inequality that Mr. Dooley first remarks upon in his column for Memorial Day, 1894: "Th' sojers has thim that'll fire salutes over their graves an' la-ads to talk about thim, but there's none but th' widdy f'r to break her hear-rt above th' poor soul that died afther his hands had tur-rned to leather fr'm handlin' a pick" (*EP,* June 2, 1894). Certainly this effort constitutes a revision of the accepted hierarchy of status and respect that the settlers of Bridgeport had brought with them from Ireland. In Catholic Ireland the social scale had run from beggar to priest, passing through the stages of unskilled day laborer (the cottier class), tenant farmer, the small farmer who owned his land (ranked by the size of the holding), and the townsmen (shopkeepers and semiprofessional people). The Anglo-Irish gentry, mostly Protestants, monopolized the professions and the large estates, and their lofty positions were not on the scale of possibility open to the Catholic lower classes. Nor did they end up in Bridgeport. Mr. Dooley's refusal to admit a farming background and Shaughnessy's ill-fated attempt to make his son a priest illustrate that the poles of status remained pretty much the same in America. The major difference was that in Chicago the unskilled factory and railroad workers (like Pat Doherty, Shaughnessy, and little Tim Clancy) replaced the Irish cottiers and small tenants on the lower end of the scale. For the mill worker of Bridgeport, "success" lay in promotion to foremanship or the big break into a civil service job—at city hall, "on the force," or as a fireman—and community admiration was mostly focused on figures from this world. Thus, Mr. Dooley's case for the unskilled urban laborer as hero is a departure from Bridgeport custom that marks him as much more of a thinker than his customers. It is also a measure of Dunne's compassion and central to his contribution to American realism, a movement dedicated in part to discovering the common life for literature.

As for the men of acknowledged status in Bridgeport, Mr. Dooley strings them out, in significant order, in his report on a benefit raffle for an ailing fellow bartender:

> "Near ivry wan along th' r-road was at Donovan's, f'r Harrity was a pop'lar man who give good measure. Th' aldherman was there, an' th' sinitor, an' th' loot fr'm th' station, an' th' captain iv th' fire depa-artment—a coorajoos man, that. He niver wint to a fire yet that he didn't sthrip to his red flannel shirt. He wears his hat an' coat indoors, but no wan iver see him with ayether, though th' big wind sh'd blow again, whin on his way to a fire." [EP, Jan. 12, 1895]

This list is hierarchical. Bridgeporters were ambivalent toward their political leaders; they could respect a politician's power but not his character, for, as a later chapter will show, Chicago's spoils system in the 1890s was as rotten as any in the country. On the other hand, her firemen were Bridgeport's undisputed heroes; in a wooden city famous for its fires, they risked their lives daily for the safety of the community. As for the police, their position was more ambiguous; public opinion about them was, at best, mixed.

Police work had always been popular among the urban Irish; they dominated the Chicago force from its inception in 1835, when one

James Sweeny banded "twelve men of Connaught" into a "law and order league." [7] By 1890 the anti-immigration periodical *America* was still alarmed because "one tenth of the voters of Chicago are Irish, but they have one third of the police force." [8] *America* is a prejudiced source, but there were many valid reasons for the unpopularity of the Chicago Police Department in these years. In June 1887, William J. McGarigle, until 1882 the city's police chief, was convicted of complicity in a huge Cook County graft ring. He fled to Canada and returned to Chicago two years later, exonerated of all twenty-three pending indictments after having paid a token fine of $1,000 (*Tribune,* Jan. 31, 1889). In 1889 the sensational Cronin murder case broke with the arrest of Chicago police Sergeant Daniel Coughlin, who had been the first detective assigned to solve it. As the case dragged on into the early nineties, a jury-tampering exposé reinforced the growing public conviction that green-tinted corruption lay behind the whole of the city's law enforcement and judiciary systems. In March 1890, the *Tribune* called for general reform so that "Irishness will not be a necessary qualification for police" (March 16), and similar newspaper campaigns followed similar revelations of police corruption and brutality on a yearly basis all through the nineties. [9]

Two points are important here: first, that the Chicago police force was demonstrably corrupt; and second, that a tradition of outspoken criticism of that corruption existed in the city. And yet, despite his voluble concern in so many causes, Mr. Dooley never really goes after the police. He delivers an occasional light jab: to "th' polisman that dhrinks this beat," to back room card games involving on-duty policemen, to the "doctrine" of Officer Jerry Hoolihan ("Niver stop to fight whin ye'er goin' to supper"), which Dooley advocates as a substitute for the Monroe Doctrine. [10] But this is as far as it goes. Dunne simply refused to unleash his powerful satire on this most vulnerable target. He is similarly reticent about the evil of drink, which Mr. Dooley hits hard only once in the nearly three hundred pieces that Dunne wrote before leaving Chicago in 1900. [11] The reason for restraint in both cases lies, I think, in Dunne's sympathy and identification with the Bridgeport community, for which Mr. Dooley was the one articulate spokesman during the 1890s. Alcoholism was simply too sensitive a problem, affecting too many people in Bridgeport. To attack it would have been cruel and pointless, especially for a saloonkeeper. And the same held true for police work, which Dunne could see was one of the few legitimate ways for a Bridgeporter to get out of the mills. Whatever his shortcomings, the policeman was both necessary and official, a uniformed figure of authority who enjoyed the security of civil service employment. Thus, Mr. Dooley numbers the "loot fr'm th' station" in his litany of important community figures. As a symbol of ascent from the slough of unskilled labor, he continued to command respect.[12]

In this matter of the police, we can observe for the first time a remarkable divergence of attitude between Dunne as *Post* editor and Mr. Dooley. Compare a Dooley pronouncement and a Dunne editorial on the same subject, the unpopularity of the police:

> "How is it?" asked Mr. Dooley, "that whin a fireman dies th' whole city mourns an' whin a polisman dies all annywan says is: 'Who's th' first illigible on th' list?' How is it?"
>
> "I dinnaw," said Mr. Hennessy, "but 'tis so."
>
> "No doubt iv it," continued Mr. Dooley. "I think th' reason is we're bumpin' too much into th' polis foorce. If we was to see thim on'y goin' by in th' get-ap wagon, with th' horses chargin' along an' the gong ringin' we'd play thim f'r pop'lar heroes. A polisman always looks good whin he's goin' by in a hurry. But whin he gets out iv th' chariot an' goes to bat he's no man's frind, an' anny citizen is entitled to move things fr'm th' roof on his head. He mixes in with th' populace an' familyarity breeds contempt, as Shakespeare says."

Notice how much farther the editorial goes:

> A misfortune to the Chicago fire department is a misfortune to the whole community. The death of a fireman afflicts everybody with a sense of personal loss, and such a catastrophe as that of Thursday [five firemen had died in a grain elevator explosion] awakens a profound sympathy that would be unknown if the victims were civilians —or policemen. A majority of the community feel about the police force as the gambler felt when he was asked for $5 "to bury a policeman." "Here," he said, "take $10 and bury two policemen."
>
> Of course the superficial cause of this difference in the feeling toward the two departments is one of sentiment. The firemen are always seen "on parade." They appear in the role of protectors of property and saviors of life, while the drudgery of police work brings the unfortunate "copper" into harsh opposition to individual liberty. But beyond this is the knowledge that the fire department is a clean,

well-disciplined body, in which there is no such thing as politics. Under Chief Swenie promotion has been by merit alone. Removals have been few. Scandals have never touched the fire brigade. The police department, on the other hand, is full of unrest, intrigue and self-seeking. Merit has never counted in promotions. No reward is offered for courage or fidelity. The principal officers have never been beyond suspicion.[13]

The split is virtually schizophrenic. Mr. Dooley's case rests on a common-sense appeal to human nature: no one wants to be interfered with, so the police are bound to be unpopular. On the other hand, Dunne brands the Dooley explanation "superficial," and goes "beyond" it to blame corruption and politics on the force for its unpopularity. The rising young editor seems committed to the reformist outlook of the budding progressive movement; while the older, more pragmatic saloonkeeper remains loyal to his fellow Bridgeporters on the force. Thus, to label Dunne a standard-issue progressive, whose aim in creating Mr. Dooley was simply to further the cause of social reform, is to misunderstand Dooley's role as it emerges in the Chicago years. In a very real sense, he became the spokesman for Bridgeport, for the point of view of an urban ethnic community whose values and attitudes were often in conflict with those held more generally in Chicago and America. Embodying that point of view in a believable character, at the expense, possibly, of his own more objective attitudes, constitutes Dunne's real creative accomplishment.

The situation, as Mr. Dooley puts it in the piece just discussed, was "altogether diffrent with th' fireman." He was truly a man apart:

"No wan is on really intimate terms with him. We may call him by his first name an' play dominoes with him or pitch horseshoes behind th' barn, but we have a secret feelin' that he's a shuperior person that it's not safe to take liberties with. Ye may be settin' in th' injine-house with a fireman as calm an' frindly as ye plaze, an' it's 'Ye'er move, Tom,' an' 'There goes ye'er king row, Felix;' but lave th' ticker buzz wanst an' the gong ring an' ye've suddenly lost equality. Over goes th' boord, out come th' horses an' it's 'Get out iv th' way, there, blast ye,' an' 'All right, Misther Casey.' I niver see th' day whin I felt just right in th' prisince iv a man in a helmet. Did ye iver know a fireman to be slugged? Or robbed? Niver. Th' toughest thief that iver roamed th' shtreets 'll lave alone a lad with a brown sthraw hat an' silver buttons."

Indeed, Chicago was intensely proud of her fire department. Even the cantankerous W. T. Stead praised it as "the ideal" toward which the police force should strive, "the best equipped and most efficient fire department in the world." [14]

Like the police, and for the same reasons, America's urban fire-fighting ranks were dominated by the Irish. The foremost example in Chicago was the career of Denis Swenie, Irish immigrant, fireman since 1850, and chief since 1879; a living legend and one of the city's most admired men. The *Post* editorial on the occasion of his forty-fifth anniversary as a fireman called the Chief "the boss fire-fighter of the United States. . . . as resolute, as fearless, as skillful as ever, still pre-pared to back water against fire or any other divvlish agency . . . be-cause he has kept his heart green and his faith in the fluid constant." [15] Dunne also acknowledged the impact of Swenie's career in a Dooley piece. The Chief has made it to the respectable West Side, as we learn from Dooley's vivid picture of the figure he cuts at St. Patrick's Church. His timing seems perfect, for "ivry Sunday about th' gospel" he is called out to a fire:

> "Thin ivry wan'd lave his devotions an' give an' eye an' an ear. Ye cud ha-ardly hould th' althar byes, an' avin th' soggarth the priest himsilf'd take a squint over his shoulder—no more thin a squint, d'ye mind. . . . 'What box?' ye'd hear th' chafe say. 'Twinty-sicond an' Loomis,' an' they was off."

Returning to Bridgeport to fight a fire personally after ten years away, Chief Swenie receives a hero's welcome:

> "Well, sir, I niver see such a greetin' as th' chafe got las' night. 'Twas 'Good avnin' to ye, Misther Swenie,' an' 'Misther Swenie, will ye have a glass iv beer befure ye go in, f'r th' fire's hot?' an' 'Have ye forgot all ye'er ol' frins that know'd ye whin ye r-run with Avalanche tin?' Well, sir, th' chafe looked that plazed. 'Good avnin', Mrs. Doolan,' he'd say. 'Pla-ay away there sivinteen. How's Mike? I hope ye've brought him up well. Why th' 'ell don't ye come along with that pipe. Pla-ay away there tin, d'ye think ye'er here to make a bonfire? Oh, they're all well, thanks be to Gawd, Mrs. Casey. An' how's ye'er own? That's good. Campeen, get ye'er min to stop playin' croquet an' put a laddher up that there tannery. No, I thank ye kindly, Mrs. Dinnihy, I niver indulge. Dorgan, ye big bosthoon, if ye shtand here a minyit longer I'll hitch me horse to ye. D'ye think

that laddher was put up to shave that there house?' An' so he'd go on convarsin' iv social doings an' ordherin' th' min till th' fire was out. Faith, he's a gr-reat ma-an. What county is he from?"

[*EP*, Aug. 11, 1894]

Swenie's triumph prompts Mr. Dooley to exclaim, "If I had a child iv me own . . . I'd give him th' finest schoolin' th' land'd affoord an' thin I'd put him on th' fire depa-artment."

Civil-service-administered fire departments like Chicago's were the direct descendants of the volunteer fire companies of pre-Civil War America. These had been Irish-dominated, rough and boozy fraternal clubs, by turns heroic and ludicrous, and an important part of the folklore of American city life. In the 1850s (Cincinnati was first in 1853) the institution of paid, full-time professional fire departments forced the elimination of slapstick elements, such as rival companies racing to fires, sabotaging one another's equipment, and suddenly dropping their hoses to engage in free-for-all brawls. Before its demise, though, the rough-and-tumble romanticism of fire-fighting carried over into the American theater, notably in the character of "Mose the Bowery B'hoy," first dramatized in 1848 and described by Richard M. Dorson as a "unique compound of East Side swell, gutter bum, and volunteer fire laddie evolved by some curious alchemy from the swirling currents of the melting pot, and in a moment of theatrical genius snatched from the water-front alleys and thrust on to the boards in living likeness." In the many plays that grew up around him, Mose was at once comic buffoon, fist- and fire-fighting champion, and heroic guardian angel of the Bowery. As "the first fully developed folk-hero of an urban culture" (Dorson's distinction), he begins a tradition of fireman-heroes to which Dunne contributed.[16]

Because she was a notorious firetrap, Chicago supplied epic challenges for fire-fighting, many of which caught the imagination of the entire city. For example, when seventeen firemen died before 130,000 horrified spectators in a warehouse fire at the World's Fair, the *Post* editorialized that the heroism of firemen on that terrible day was "proof that the godlike is not yet dead in man" (July 11, 1893). Indeed, Dunne's own best pieces on firemen were immediate responses to actual fire tragedies. In his piece following the grain elevator explosion that killed five, an image of the fireman-hero emerges sharply. Pipeman Shay is a dark, brooding man, whose aloofness, fierce pride, and heroic defense of his calling inspire something akin to awe in the usually irreverent Mr. Dooley. Here is his story in full:

"There used to be a man up here be th' name iv Duggan, an', havin' a large fam'ly, he lived on th' fifth flure iv th' Flaherty Buildin' near the roof. He was a jealous man whin he was dhrunk, an' that was sometimes, an' he used to roar about th' aisy life iv th' firemen. 'Here,' he says, 'am I, a man with a good hot intilleck condimned to wurruk in th' broilin' sun shovellin' coal f'r wan sivinty-five a day,' he says, 'while th' likes iv ye set in ye'er aisy cheers,' he says, 'smokin' ye'er pipes, with nawthin' to do,' he says, 'but decide who's th' champeen dominoes player,' he says. 'Fr'm morn to night ye don't do a tap iv wurruk, an' I an' th' likes iv me pay ye f'r it,' he says. He talked this way in th' injine house day an' night an' th' lads laughed at him an' wint on playin'. On'y wan man didn't like th' talk. He was a dark man be th' name of Shay with a big horseshoe mustache, an' he used to eat half iv it off iviry time Duggan made his speech. I seen he was achin' f'r Duggan's throat, but it's a rule iv th' departmint that mimbers 'r not allowed f'r to lick civilyans. They can lick polisman, if they're able to, but not citizens.

"Th' Flaherty flats took fire wan night an' bein' consthructed f'r poor people out iv nice varnished pine an' cotton waste they burned up without anny loss iv time. Duggan counted his childher an' found wan missing. He had a good manny—twelve or thirteen, I think— but he needed thim all in his business. He counted again an' again, but there was still wan short, an' afther awhile he figured it was th' baby, be th' name iv Honoria. She's a great big girl now—with red hair. Whin Duggan found he was shy a chip he proceeded to throw fits on th' sthreet an' wanted to go into th' buildin', which wud've been th' end iv him, f'r he was full iv rum and wud've burned like a celluloid collar. Cap Kenny iv thruck twinty-nine heerd his ravin' and wanted to know what ailed him. 'He's short a kid,' said th' polisman that was holdin' him be th' hair. Kenny begun cursin' like a tug captain, an' in less thin a minyit he was shinnin' up a ladder with three or four others, among thim bein' our frind Shay. Th' cap wint in first an' stayed in five minyits an' had to be carrid out. Thin two others staggered to th' window an' was dhragged out be th' legs. But Shay stuck. We waited an' waited, with all th' pipes playing on th' wan window, an' fin'lly th' Connemara man come out carryin' something in his ar-rums. Glory be, but he was a sight. He was as black as a lump iv coal an' he had no more hair on him thin a lookin'-glass. He slid out to th' ladder an' climbed down, scornin' assistance. Th' women gathered around him, weepin' an' callin' on all th' saints in th' catalogue to bless him, an' th' men swore an' ran to get dhrinks. But Shay paid no attintion to thim. He pegged th' baby at a sthrange

woman an' walked over to Duggan. 'What ye said to me las' Choos-
dah night,' he roared, 'was a lie, an' I'm goin' to club ye'er head off.'
An' he fell on th' weepin' father an' wud've kilt him. Cap Kenny
pulled him away, an' Shay, lookin' ashamed to death undher th' soot,
saluted. 'Pipeman Shay,' says th' cap, 'I will recomind ye f'r th'
Three medal,' he says, 'but I fine ye five days' pay f'r lickin' a
civilyan.' he says. 'Lord help us, I hope Swenie won't hear iv this,'
he says.

"That man Shay used to come into my place an' play forty-fives
with me. But d'ye suppose I cud challenge his count as I do other
people's, or ask to cut his ca-ards?"

"Ye'd be afraid he'd lick ye," suggested Mr. Hennessy.

"That was wan reason," said Mr. Dooley.   [*EP,* Aug. 7, 1897] [17]

Shay has affinities with the line of silent, enigmatic heroes of Irish
history and legend. Cuchulain comes to mind, or the mystique of
Charles Stewart Parnell. Moreover, his exploit borders on the fool-
hardy, suggesting the classic tragic element of hubris, of which there
were plentiful examples in the annals of Chicago fire-fighting. Fire
Marshall Edward Murphy, after Chief Swenie the city's most prominent fireman, was indicted by a grand jury after the World's Fair
warehouse fire on a charge of responsibility for the deaths of his seventeen firemen. He had ordered them, some said rashly and stupidly,
to the top of the building's tower, from which they fell to their deaths.
The charges were dropped when Murphy's long career of exemplary
heroism was cited. Ten days later, still bandaged and suffering from
injuries received in the warehouse fire, Murphy climbed 200 feet on
girders to the roof of the Fair's Manufactures Building to extinguish
a blaze in the decorative bunting.[18]

Dunne's greatest piece on the Irish fireman brings together the elements discussed severally above: vaudeville, heroism and hubris, community respect and tragedy. The Saturday response to a Friday fire in
which four Irish firemen lost their lives, it is a remarkable occasional
performance. Again, an editorial on the same day illustrates the split
between Dunne and Mr. Dooley. In the editorial, Dunne rues the loss
of life but criticizes the tendency toward hubris among firemen in a
detached and reasonable tone:

   The fireman lives in an atmosphere of peril. Perhaps the realization of the constant menace makes him the more reckless and causes
   him to take chances which are not always justified. It is difficult to

say where true bravery ends and unnecessary hardihood begins; it is enough to know that when a fireman gives his life to his calling he is always in his line of duty, which is perilous at the best. For this reason he is a hero in death and inspires the gratitude of the city for what he tried to do, and grief for the fate he so bravely meets.

[*EP,* Nov. 23, 1895]

Mr. Dooley, on the other hand, begins concretely and with emotion, by naming the four dead firemen and praising their example as a counterweight to the anti-Irish prejudice engendered in Chicago by unsavory politicians:

"O'Donnell, Sherrick, Downs, Prendergast," Mr. Dooley repeated slowly. "Poor la-ads. Poor la-ads. Plaze Gawd, they wint to th' long home like thrue min. 'Tis good to read th' names, Jawn. Thanks be, we're not all in th' council. . . . They'se an Irishman 'r two on th' fire departmint an' in th' army, too, Jawn, though ye'd think be hearin' some talk they was all runnin' prim-ries an' thryin' to be cinthral comitymen. So ye wud. Ye niver hear iv thim on'y whin they die; an' thin, murther, what funerals they have!"

Dunne then moves into fiction to relate the story of fireman Mike Clancy, whose deeds of great and irrational courage are reminiscent of Edward Murphy's Chicago career. "Whin th' big organ facthry burnt, he carrid th' hose up to th' fourth story an' was squirtin' whin th' walls fell. They dug him out with pick an' shovel, an' he come up fr'm th' brick an' boards an' saluted th' chief." Clancy's heroics include impossible rescues embellished with stunts worthy of Mose, the Bowery B'hoy, and perhaps recalling Mose specifically. (At one point Clancy carries a girl down a ladder face first, explaining afterwards that "I seen a man do it at th' Lyceem whin I was a kid.") He also drives the hose cart around corners on one wheel, refuses to wear cap or coat to a fire, and has an incomparable reputation for readiness, "jumpin' whin he heerd a man so much as hit a glass to make it ring." Clancy is the most admired man on Archer Avenue:

"All th' r-road was proud iv him, an' faith he was proud iv himself. He r-rode free on th' sthreet ca-ars, an' was th' champeen hand-ball player f'r miles around. Ye shud see him goin' down th' sthreet, with his blue shirt an' his blue coat with th' buttons on it, an' his cap on his ear. . . . All th' people looked up to him, an' th' kids followed him down th' sthreet; an' 'twas th' gr-reatest priv'lige f'r anny wan f'r to play dominos with him near th' joker."

Clancy is flawed, though, and in the heroic tradition, as John Kelleher has pointed out: "But like Achilles or Cuchulain, Clancy cannot die in bed. The hero must break his taboos. Clancy's are worn-out luck and onsetting age. He knows that the time has come to quit. He will quit—after the last battle." [19] That battle comes, and the conclusion to his story is muted, even lyrical; a lasting image of the common man as tragic hero, and one of the few such images allowed and indigenous to the Irish-American community in the nineteenth century.

"About a year ago he came in to see me, an' says he, 'Well, I'm goin' to quit.' 'Why,' says I, 'Ye'er a young man yet,' I says. 'Faith,' he says, 'look at me hair,' he says,—'young heart, ol' head. I've been at it these twenty year, an' th' good woman's wantin' to see more iv me thin blowin' into a saucer iv coffee,' he says. 'I'm goin' to quit,' he says, 'on'y I want to see wan more good fire,' he says. 'A rale good ol' hot wan,' he says, 'with th' win' blowin' f'r it an' a good dhraft in th' ilivator-shaft, an' about two stories, with pitcher-frames an' gasoline an' excelsior, an' to hear th' chief yellin': ' "Play 'way, sivinteen. What th' hell an' damnation are ye standin' aroun' with that pipe f'r? Is this a fire 'r a dam livin' pitcher? I'll break ivry man iv eighteen, four, six, an' chem'cal five to-morrah mornin' befure breakfast." ' 'Oh,' he says, bringin' his fist down, 'wan more, an' I'll quit.'

"An' he did, Jawn. Th' day th' Carpenter Brothers' box factory burnt. 'Twas wan iv thim big, fine-lookin' buildings that pious men built out iv celluloid an' plasther iv Paris. An' Clancy was wan iv th' men undher whin th' wall fell. I seen thim bringin' him home; an' th' little woman met him at th' dure, rumplin' her apron in her hands."   [*EP*, Nov. 23, 1895]

3

MR. DOOLEY IN BRIDGEPORT

The Dissolution of a Community

A nation scattered in the boundless reaches of America resembles rays diverging from a focus. All the rays remain, but the heat is gone. Their power consisted in their concentration: when they are dispersed, they have no effect.

SAMUEL JOHNSON [1]

BECAUSE Mr. Dooley and his creator were, respectively, immigrant and first-generation Americans, the sum of those weekly columns between 1892 and 1900 is a unique firsthand account of the process of assimilation into American city life of a large ethnic group. As an immigrant community, Bridgeport was culturally unstable, and the Dooley pieces help us to chart the forces for change within such a community, as well as the often painful effects of the breakdown of the tenuous balance between old and new that its members attempted to strike. Dunne's vantage point in the 1890s is particularly revealing, for those years marked the coming to power and prestige of the American Irish. Themselves born in this country, the sons and daughters of the Famine immigrants were just then beginning to reap the fruits of their parents' struggles to establish a new life. At the same time, their numbers and know-how had so increased that the Irish were emerging as the most significant new political power on the American urban scene. These blessings were not unalloyed, of course, and many disturbed Irish-Americans found that the price of assimilation was loss of their very identity, and thus far too dear. Through Martin Dooley and his friends, Peter Dunne recreates the peculiar combination of fulfillment and frustration, satisfaction and bewilderment, that went along with being Irish in America in the nineties. In this chapter Mr. Dooley's scattered observations on the problems of the immigrant experience are organized thematically: first, his general commentary about the city as a place to live; and second, his delineation of three important indicators of dissolving community in Bridgeport—the scramble for material success and respectability in the older generation, the questioning and overturning of the old ways by the young, and the twin specters of poverty and crime among the least fortunate.

The tradition of intellectual opposition to the urban environment in America runs back at least to Thomas Jefferson and includes most of our formidable nineteenth-century thinkers, among them Emerson, Thoreau, Hawthorne, Melville, Poe, Henry James, and Henry Adams. In the 1890s and early 1900s further indictments of the American city were registered by architects Louis Sullivan and Frank Lloyd Wright, whose Chicago roots give them added relevance here; by John Dewey, the founder of the Chicago School of philosophy; and by municipal re-

formers such as Lincoln Steffens and W. T. Stead.[2] This prevalent view
of the city as a pernicious influence on its inhabitants was applied
specifically to the Irish by a number of writers.

In an 1896 *Atlantic* piece on "The Irish in American Life," Henry
Childs Merwin faults the American government for allowing the almost four million Irish immigrants to congregate in cities, rather than
providing transportation to the west, land, and enough money so that
they could have become farmers again. Instead, says Merwin, ignored
by the authorities, "they remained largely in the great cities where
they landed," with disastrous results. "The herding of the Irish in our
large cities, and their sudden contact with new social and political
conditions, have made the average of pauperism, crime, and mortality
very high among them." Moreover, the naturally contaminating city
is worse for the Irish than for other groups because of their overly
developed sense of loyalty to their own kind: "for want of anything
better, [they are] compelled to fall back upon Irish politicians, orators,
and saloon-keepers." In fact, Merwin generalizes, "the Irish in America, of the second generation, degenerate. The children of Irish birth,
born and brought up in this country, are morally inferior to their parents." On the other hand, "in country places, descendants of Irishmen
are an improvement upon the old stock almost in all cases." [3]

A significant negative response to city life by the Irish themselves
was the colonization movement. Even before the diaspora, isolated
groups of Irish immigrants, choosing to remain farmers, bought land
collectively in the Midwest and established rural communities. But the
great immigrant tide of the 1840s and 1850s flowed to the cities for
reasons both economic and social. Many Irish lacked the funds to
travel further than their port of entry, and they also felt comfortable
in close-knit city neighborhoods among their own. In Ireland they had
tilled plots tiny by American standards, where subsistence depended
partly on cooperation, and the isolation of the American prairies was
an unfamiliar, terrifying prospect. In addition, for most, their last
farming experience in Ireland had been the harrowing potato blight.
Still, the poor living conditions in the urban ghettoes disturbed prominent Irish-American journalists and clergymen, and various "back to
the land" colonization schemes were tried from the fifties through the
eighties. The movement reached its high point in 1879 with the formation, at a Chicago convention, of the Irish Catholic Colonization Asso-

ciation of the United States, but no large scale exodus from the cities resulted, and the idea soon died out.[4] The colonizers were convinced that "the great blot upon our people is their wretchedness in large cities and in manufacturing centers. . . . Until it is remedied, all of our efforts in their behalf, all partial means of redress, are small indeed." [5] This simplistic indictment of urbanism was shared by many intellectuals in Ireland as well in the 1890s. Douglas Hyde's Gaelic League and the literary program of Yeats and Lady Gregory contained a good deal of sentimentalism about the superiority of the pastoral peasant society in the Irish west.

Dunne's judgment of the city was more complex. He had the native's love for Chicago crossed with the newspaperman's experience of her many shortcomings, and he combined these contradictory reactions in a style of dry wit and wryly stated paradox to express a realistic ambivalence toward the urban environment. "All the various accents of Ireland" can be heard on Archey Road, he observes in the preface to his first Dooley collection, but "with the difference that would naturally arise from substituting cinders and sulphuretted hydrogen for soft misty air and peat smoke." He goes on to play off city and country against each other by explaining that Bridgeport is the right place for philosophy; he doesn't know where it's likely to go better.

> From the cool heights of life in the Archey Road, uninterrupted by the jarring noises of crickets and cows, Mr. Dooley observes the passing show, and meditates thereon. . . .
> "There's no better place to see what's goin' on thin the Ar-rchey Road," says Mr. Dooley. "Whin th' ilicthric cars is hummin' down th' sthreet an' th' blast goin' sthrong at th' mills, th' noise is that gr-reat ye can't think." [6]

Similarly equivocal is Mr. Dooley's nostalgic description of the Chicago River in the old days; his enthusiasm almost makes us forget that the source of its color was industrial waste:

> " 'Twas th' prettiest river f'r to look at that ye'll iver see. Ye niver was annything iv a pote, Hinnissy, but if ye cud get down on th' Miller dock some night whin ye an' th' likes iv ye was makin' fireworks in th' blast, an' see th' flames blazin' on th' wather an' th' lights dancin', green at th' sausage facthry, blue at th' soap facthry, yellow at th' tannery, ye'd not thrade it f'r annything but th' Liffey, that's thinner but more powerfuller."

Dooley denies that the river is unhealthy—"Did ye iver see a healthier lot iv childher, or more iv thim, than lives along th' river?"—and claims that those who criticize it have simply mistaken its purpose:

> "Th' Chicago river niver was intinded as a dhrink. It didn't go ar-round advertisin' itself as a saisonable beverage! It ain't moxie, an' it ain't sasparilly, an' it ain't ice crame soda wather. It had other business more suited to it, an' 'twas consistent in ivery way."
>
> [*Journal,* Jan. 13, 1900] [7]

Pollution was a large issue in Chicago in the nineties, and all of the papers for which Dunne worked ran editorials on the problem, along with luridly detailed feature stories exposing abuses of the sanitation laws, like the piece on filth in the streets discussed in chapter 1. But Mr. Dooley is never so single-minded or serious about it. Instead, his love for Chicago—noise, dirt, smell, and all—undercuts the reforming impulse at every turn.

His classic statement of the Irish city-dweller's ambivalence toward his home is a piece that Dunne wrote in September 1897 about the unwholesome effects of a city man's trip to the country. Though never collected, "The Vacation Habit" is one of his best efforts—a tour de force of linguistic inventiveness applied to a central Irish-American theme. Here it is in full. [8]

> "Ye shud take a vacation," said Mr. Hennessy when the philosopher complained of a slight headache. "Ye ought to go away an' have a few weeks' fishin' or r-run down to Westbaden an' be biled out, or indulge in some other form iv spoort."
>
> "I shud not," retorted Mr. Dooley firmly. "I'm well enough off where I am. They'se no disease that afflicts th' American people akel to th' vacation habit. Ye take a big, sthrong man that's lived in Chicago all his life, an' if he stays on here he'll niver know a day iv ill health. He goes out in th' mornin' and dhrinks in th' impure an' healthy air, filled with mickrobes an' soot an' iron filin's, an' his chest expands. He ates onwholesome, rich an' appetizin' food. His muscles is kept firm be dodgin' cable cars an' express wagons. His mind is rooned an' made ca-am be readin' th' newspapers. His happy home is infested with sewer gas, an' if he survives he's th' sthrongest thing that iver was made. But ye take that man out iv his parnicious an' agreeable atmosphere an' sind him to th' country. He ates wholesome food that his stomach, bein' used to th' best

Luetgert society, rayfuses to intertain. His lungs cave in fr'm con-
sumin' pure air that, like ivrything pure, is too thin. He misses his
daily sewer gas an' he finds cow's milk a poor substitute for
docthered whisky an' beer with aloes in it. Th' man suffers. He
does so. He rayturns to Chicago a shattered invalid an' it takes
months iv livin' in onsanitary tinimints an' a steady dite iv cigaroots
an' bakin' powdher biscuits to restore him to his proper condition iv
robust bad health.

"Now, look at ol' Duggan. There was th' healthiest man in th'
wa-ard f'r his age. He was bor-rn an' raised on th' banks iv th' slip
where ye can hear th' water poppin' fr'm wan year's ind to another
like a shelf iv catsup bottles on a hot night. Th' air was so thick with
poisonous gases that a wagon loaded with scrap iron wud float at
an ilivation iv tin feet. He lived below th' grade an' th' rain backed
into his bedroom. He wurrked in a white lead facthry at night an'
had to cross twinty-five railroad thracks an' an ilictric switch on his
way to wurruk. He lived mos'ly on canned goods an' fried pork an'
drank his beer at an Irish saloon an' his whisky at a German's. Not
bein' a corpse befure he was twinty-five, it was a sure thing he'd
be a joynt [giant] at fifty. An' so he was. A sthronger man niver
breathed. But some wan put it in his head he ought to go off to th'
counthry f'r his vacation, an' he wint dhrivin' a canal boat mule or
cuttin' hay. Whin he come back he was that weak a child cud go to
th' flure with him. 'Where have ye been?' says I. 'On me vacation,'
says he. 'Well,' I says, 'ye'er pretty near vacated,' I says. 'Yis,' he
says, 'I'm glad to get back,' he says. 'I need tinder care,' he says.
They nursed him back to life, but 'twas not till his house'd been
declared unfit f'r habitation be th' health departmint an' he'd been
ejicted afther a free fight be his landlord an' r-run in wanst be th'
polis an' over twict be a mail wagon an' was back to wurruk
breathin' lead dust be th' quart that he raycovered his ol' sperrits.

"I niver leave town mesilf. I take a vacation be sittin' here at me
front dure lookin' up at Gawd's an' th' Illinye Steel Company's
black-an'-blue sky. Th' ilictric ca-ars go singin' by an' th' air is
filled with th' melody iv goats an' cur dogs. Ivry breeze that blows
fr'm th' south brings th' welcome tidings that me frind Phil Armour
is still stickin' to th' glue business. I cannot see th' river, but I know
that it's rollin' grandly backward tord its sewerce laden with lumber
hookers an' ol' vigitables. Occasin'lly I hear a tugboat cooin' to its
mate an' now an' thin a pathrol wagon flits by on its errand iv love.
At night th' tired but unhappy lab'rers rayturns fr'm their tile an' th'
air is laden with th' sound iv fryin' liver an' th' cheery perfume iv
bilin' cabbage. Whin I want more active amusemint I go in an' start
a bung or angle with a fork f'r a sardine. So whin me vacation is

over I rayturn rayfrished an' eager f'r th' battle iv life. I don't have
to get th' taste iv good butter out iv me mouth.

"They'se no use f'r a Chicago man thryin' to take his vacation out
iv town till they put up a summer hotel in th' crather iv Mount
Vasuvyous. Ayether he ought niver to go away, or—"

"He ought niver to come back," suggested Mr. Hennessy.

"Ye'er r-right," said Mr. Dooley.   [*EP*, Sept. 4, 1897]

Dooley is at his oxymoronic best in describing the "impure an' healthy
air" and the Chicagoan's "proper condition iv robust bad health."
Double-edged words help too, like the vacation that "vacated" old
Duggan and the river that flows back toward its "sewerce." And he
mocks both pastoral rhetoric and the urban environment by praising
the "black-an'-blue sky," "th' melody iv goats an' cur dogs" and the
southerly breeze from Armour's glue works. Add to these Joycean
language games the exuberant tall-tale exaggeration of Duggan's up-
bringing—in an atmosphere that could float wagonloads of scrap iron
—and the result is a lyrical recreation of daily life in the polluted city,
along with a buoyant celebration of the toughness of those who survive: "Not bein' a corpse befure he was twenty-five, it was a sure thing
he'd be a joynt at fifty." Mr. Dooley's ambiguous attitude comes
through clearly, as he alternately gives with one phrase and takes away
with the next throughout the piece, resting negatively only in the characteristic ending twist: "Ayether he ought niver to go away, or—. . .
He ought niver to come back."

While to some extent these problems of city life were common to
all Chicagoans, of special, compelling concern to Bridgeporters was
the crumbling of community that provides Mr. Dooley with his saddest
subjects. That crumbling was, first of all, superficially evident in the
changing ethnic makeup of the Bridgeport population. Already well in
evidence in the nineties was the familiar rhythm of neighborhood take-
over by newer and less privileged groups, as the older, more established groups move out into more attractive areas. As has been
discussed, the Chicago Irish exodus was from the South Side to the
West Side of the city. Mr. Dooley measures this change in two pieces
for May of 1897. First, a conversation with "Hogan's lad" on the
decadence of Greece (the war against Turkey had been going badly)
leads him to remark on similar erosion in the tenth precinct of the
sixth ward (part of Bridgeport):

"D'ye raymimber th' fightin' tenth precint? Ye must've heerd ye'er father tell about it. It was famous f'r th' quality an' quantity iv th' warfare put up in it. Ivry man in th' tenth precint cud fight his weight in scrap-iron. Most iv thim come fr'm th' ancient Hellenic province iv May-o; but they was a fair sprinklin' iv Greek heroes fr'm Roscommon an' Tipperary, an' a few from th' historic spot where th' Head iv Kinsale looks out on th' sea, an' th' sea looks up at th' Head iv Kinsale. Th' little boys cud box befure they was out iv skirts. Far an' wide, th' tenth precint was th' turror iv its inimies. . . .

"F'r manny years th' tenth precint was th' banner precint iv th' Sixth Wa-ard, an' its gallant heroes repelled all attacks by land or Healey's slough. But, as time wint by, changes come over it. Th' Hannigans an' Leonidases an' Caseys moved out, havin' made their pile. Some iv th' grandest iv th' heroes died, an' their fam'lies were broke up. Polish Jews an' Swedes an' Germans an' Hollanders swarmed in, settlin' down on th' sacred sites. . . ."

The effect on the precinct is dramatic. A band of toughs from ward eight comes over one night, and the neophyte sixth warders turn and run, disgracing the heritage of the "fightin' tenth." The moral is clear:

" 'On account iv th' fluctuations in rint an' throuble with th' land-lord it's not safe to presoom that th' same fam'ly always lives in th' wan house. Th' very thing happened to Greece that has happened to th' tenth precint iv th' Sixth Ward. The Greeks have moved out, an' th' Swedes come in. Ye yet may live to see th' day,' says I, 'whin what is thrue iv Athens an' th' tenth precint will be thrue iv th' whole Sixth Wa-ard.' "

"Ye don't mean that," said Mr. Hennessy, gasping.

"I do," said Mr. Dooley, with solemnity. " 'Tis histhry."

[*EP,* May 8, 1897]

His prediction had been fulfilled by 1936 (and probably well before), when a WPA neighborhood study found that the original Bridgeport area was 90 percent Polish.[9]

The following week Mr. Dooley cites more evidence of "change an' decay in all around I see": namely, that "they have put a Polacker on th' r-red bridge" (*EP,* May 15, 1897). The notoriously unstrenuous job of bridgetender was a traditional political sinecure in Chicago, a city of many bridges and much water traffic, and Hennessy is properly shocked by this development: " 'Tis but a step fr'm that to a Swede loot at Deerin' sthreet an' a Bohemian aldherman. I niver thought I'd live to see th' day." Dunne explains that "the command of the 'red bridge' is a matter of infinite concern" among Bridgeporters, for the bridgetender is a major source of news, and "every citizen" visits with him practically "day by day." The bridge at issue here must have been the one that spanned the South Branch of the Chicago River at Halsted Street. Before the days of expressways, it would have been the main entrance to Bridgeport and the entire south side of the city. In this piece Dooley recalls the time when Clancy, the tender, turned the bridge to keep the Illinois National Guard from capturing a group of striking mill workers who had run for refuge back into Bridgeport. Thus, the appointment of a "Polacker" to the bridge takes an important gate-keeping control out of Irish hands.[10] Mr. Dooley sees the appointment as "all part iv what I tol' ye th' other day iv th' decay iv this ward," but he sees no immediate danger to Irish-American political dominance, "f'r if ye put wan Irishman among twenty thousand Polackers, Bohemians, Rooshians, Germans an' Boolgaharians he'll be th' leader iv thim all." Still, Dooley concludes, the appointment is a sign that "th' foreign ilimints have to get some recognition nowadays. They're too sthrong to be left out."

The Dooley pieces are full of references to a general cooling of the emotional climate in Bridgeport, a decline in truculent ethnocentrism, as the old country receded into memory and the climb began toward acceptance and respectability in the new. The rabid Irish nationalism that crested with Parnell had ebbed considerably after his tragic fall in 1890, and politics was also much calmer than before, as we shall see in later chapters. Mr. Dooley constantly bemoans the passing of techniques such as armed attack against polling places and the feeding of excess Republican ballots to Dorsey's goat.

All over Bridgeport the colorful rough and tumble of the "old days" has disappeared, replaced by the new craving for respectability, which Dooley considers an insidious disease. He points to the change in a piece about Bridgeport's new attitude toward the newspapers:

"Whin I was young, if a rayporther wint rubberin' around a dance we might give him a dhrink an' we might throw him in th' canal. It depinded on how we felt tord him. It wasn't rispictable in thim days to have ye'er name in th' paper. It niver got in except whin ye was undher arrest. Now I see har-rd wurkin' men thrampin' down to th' newspaper offices with little items about a christenin' or a wake an' havin' it read to thim in th' mornin' at breakfuss before they start to th' mills.' "

He even catches Hennessy in the act of advertising a "progressive euchre party" to be held at his house, and the piece ends with "Mr. Dooley, the untainted one," standing alone, "the solitary green spot in a desert of 'society' " (*EP,* June 26, 1897).

Mr. Dooley further examines the new respectability in a sharp satiric piece (which Dunne never reprinted) on the naming of his friend Hogan's tenth child. Each previous addition to the Hogan family has occasioned a battle royal, and poor Hogan has "growed gray haired an' bald thryin' f'r to inthrodjooce th' name iv Michael or Bridget [his own father and mother] in th' family." Mrs. Hogan, who wins every time, has other, higher-toned ideas:

"Th' first wan was a boy an' afther Mrs. Hogan had th' polis in 'twas called Sarsfield. Th' second was a girl an' 'twas called Lucy, d'ye mind? Lucy! Yes, by dad, Lucy Hogan. Thin they was Honoria an' Veronica an' Arthur an' Charles Stewart Parnell, bor-rn durin' the land lague, an' Paul an' Madge an' William Joyce Hogan, an' th' ol' ma-an all this time tryin' f'r to edge in Michael or Bridget.

"Well, Hogan does be gettin' on in years now an' whin the last come an' th' good woman was sthrong enough f'r to walk around, says he: 'Whin ar-re ye goin' to christen little Mike,' he says. 'Little who?' says she. 'Little Mike,' he says. 'Little Mike Hogan,' he says. 'Th' kid.' 'Ther'll be no little Mikes around this house,' says she, 'unless they walk over me dead body,' she says. Jawn, she's County May-o to th' backbone. 'D'ye think I'm goin' to sind th' child out into th' wurruld,' she says, 'with a name,' she says, 'that'll keep him from anny employmint,' she says, 'but goin' on th' polis for-rce,' she says. 'Mike is a good name,' says Hogan. ' 'Twas me fa-ather's,' he says, 'an' he was as good an anny.' 'Don't tell me about ye'er father,' says she. 'Didn't I know him,' she says, 'carryin' around a piece iv ol' chalk,' she says, 'atin' wan ind iv it f'r heartburn an' usin' th' other ind iv it to chalk up for-rty-fives scores on th' table,' she says. 'I had a cousin a priest,' says Hogan. 'Match that if ye dahr.' 'Ye had wan a lamplighter,' says she. 'Me mother's brother kep' a cow,' he says. 'Not afther th' polis found it out,' says Mrs. Hogan. ' 'Twas me aunt Ayleonara's.' That thrun Hogan, but he come back sthrong. 'Ye'll be namin' no more children iv mine out iv dime novels,' he says. 'An' ye'll name no more iv mine out iv th' payroll iv th' bridge

depar-rtmint,' says she. Thin Hogan wakened. 'What ar-re ye goin'
to call it?' he says. 'Augustus,' says she. An' be hivins 'twas Augustus
th' priest give it. Th' poor, poor child!"   [*EP*, Nov. 17, 1894] [11]

These pieces on Irish social climbing once again reveal Dunne's doubleness, for he was at the same time delineator and victim of assimilation. As he wrote the Dooley pieces, his reputation in journalism and
as a brilliant conversationalist was gaining him access to the higher
reaches of Chicago society.

Several of Mr. Dooley's vignettes are really capsule biographies,
illustrating the assimilation process on the individual level. In one, he
describes the effects of getting rich, using his listener, Hennessy, as the
hypothetical new millionaire:

> "I tell ye what ye'd do, . . . Ye'd come back here an' sthrut up
> an' down th' sthreet with ye'er thumbs in ye'er armpits; an' ye'd
> dhrink too much, an' ride in sthreet ca-ars. Thin ye'd buy foldin'
> beds an' piannies, an' start a reel estate office. Ye'd be fooled a good
> deal an' lose a lot iv ye'er money, an' thin ye'd tighten up. Ye'd be
> in a cold fear night an' day that ye'd lose ye'er fortune. Ye'd wake
> up in th' middle iv th' night, dhreamin' that ye was back at th'
> gas-house with ye'er money gone. Ye'd be prisidint iv a charitable
> society. Ye'd have to wear ye'er shoes in th' house, an' ye'er wife'd
> have ye around to rayciptions an' dances. Ye'd move to Mitchigan
> Avnoo, an' ye'd hire a coachman that'd laugh at ye. Ye'er boys'd
> be joods an' ashamed iv ye, an' ye'd support ye'er daughters' hus-
> bands. Ye'd rackrint ye'er tinants an' lie about ye'er taxes. Ye'd go
> back to Ireland on a visit, an' put on airs with ye'er cousin Mike.
> Ye'd be a mane, close-fisted, onscrupulous ol' curmudgeon; an',
> whin ye'd die, it'd take half ye'er fortune f'r rayqueems to put ye
> r-right."   [*EP*, July 17, 1897]

In Dooley's experience, Irish-Americans who have "made it" often
turn into arrogant dispensers of charity or heartless misers; for example, Old O'Brien from

> down be th' dumps. . . . [who] put in his time from morn till night
> handin' out contimpt an' hathred to all mankind. No wan was harder
> to rent fr'm. He had some houses near Halsted Sthreet, an' I've see
> him servin' five days' notices on his tenants whin th' weather was
> that cold ye cudden't see th' inside iv th' furnace-rooms at th' mill f'r
> th' frost on th' window.

Such performances lead Dooley to generalize: "Of all th' landlords on earth, th' Lord deliver me fr'm an Irish wan. Whether 'tis that fr'm niver holdin' anny land in th' ol' counthry they put too high a fondness on their places whin they get a lot or two over here, I don't know; but they're quicker with th' constable thin anny others" (*EP*, May 30, 1896). Eugene O'Neill's unforgettable portrayal of his father's parsimony and land hunger in *Long Day's Journey into Night* comes to mind, especially Act Four, where James Tyrone describes to his son the terrible poverty of his childhood in Ireland.

The biographical vignettes about Chicago Irish politicians in Mr. Dooley's columns all follow a pattern of slow, painful advancement from poverty to power and wealth via brute strength, corruption, and the boss system. But Dunne almost always implies that these men could not have risen by other means to embrace the success ethic of their adopted country. The pressure to assimilate is the villain of these pieces. Throughout these explorations of the Irish movement toward middle-class respectability, Mr. Dooley's dominant tone is sad and nostalgic: somehow, despite the hardships, life in the wide-open, brawling, early days was both simpler and more straightforward. To an old-schooler like Martin Dooley, the competitive scramble for "lace-curtain" status can only be petty and demeaning.[12]

Signs of dissolving cultural unity naturally appeared early among the younger generation, the sons and daughters of the immigrants, and Dunne created a group of characters to illustrate the generation gap that is always so pronounced within an immigrant community. Molly Donahue, a lively, fad-conscious Bridgeport teenager, and her Irish father square off some half dozen times in a battle of generations that is aggravated by the assimilation process. In an 1894 Dooley piece Molly first appears—on a bicycle, in bloomers, riding down Archer Avenue at rush hour on a Friday evening. The neighborhood is scandalized, and her father reacts by repossessing the bicycle and sending her off to church, where she receives "a pinance . . . th' like iv which ain't been knowed in Bridgeport since Cassidy said Charles Stewart Parnell was a bigger man thin th' pope" (*EP*, Sept. 22, Oct. 20, 1894). Dooley blames her outré conduct on education, for Molly has attended a convent school, where "she larned to pass th' butther in Frinch an' to paint all th' chiny dishes in th' cubb'rd, so that, whin Donahue come home wan night an' et his supper, he ate a green paint ha-arp along with his cabbage, an' they had to sind f'r Docthor Hinnissy f'r to pump th' a-art work out iv him." [13]

Next, Molly attempts to vote. In the fall of 1894, Illinois took its first step toward woman suffrage when the legislature passed a law allowing women to vote for statewide school officers. A hot debate ensued when the state's attorney general (his name was Maloney) still refused to register women or to print ballots for them. But the law was upheld, and 25,000 women registered on October 16. On October 20, Mr. Dooley reports that Molly's attempt to register has been thwarted by her father, an election judge, who sends her home, declaring that "Mattchew Xavier Donahue'll do all th' votin' f'r th' Donahue family in this here precinct." Donahue reinforces his ruling by chaining his daughter to the bed and "makin' preparations f'r to have a noveeney said f'r her recov'ry."

Molly also embraces the women's liberation movement of the 1890s, the aim of which was the emergence of the "New Woman." Suffrage was only one point in this controversial program, which demanded equal rights for women all across the board. Thus, Dunne deals with a fiery contemporary issue when Molly confronts her father as follows:

> " ' 'Tis th' era iv th' new woman,' says Molly. 'Ye're right,' says th' mother. 'What d'ye mean be the new woman?' says Donahue, holdin' his boot in his hand. 'Th' new woman,' says Molly, ' 'll be free fr'm th' opprision iv man,' she says. 'She'll wurruk out her own way, without help or hinderance,' she says. 'She'll wear what clothes she wants,' she says, 'an' she'll be no man's slave,' she says. 'They'll be no such thing as givin' a girl in marredge to a clown an' makin' her dipindant on his whims,' she says. 'Th' women'll earn their own livin',' she says; 'an' mebbe,' she says, 'th' men'll stay at home an' dredge in th' house wurruk,' she says." [EP, May 4, 1895]

Mr. Donahue defeats the movement by becoming the "new man": he stays in bed the next morning, tells Molly to bring in the coal, and orders his wife off to the mills. Molly gets the coal, but Mrs. Donahue backs down—"Ye wudden't have th' ol' woman wurrukin' in th' mills. . . . 'Twas all a joke"—and the subject is dropped, temporarily. However, when Elizabeth Cady Stanton and the Sisterhood of Advanced Women draft a plan for a Woman's Bible, in which passages implying the inferiority of women would be deleted or "improved," Molly throws her support to this project as well. Mr. Dooley reports that "they'll attimpt to show that they was a combination again Eve iv th' snake an' her husband, an' fr'm that come all th' throuble," and gives his blessing (*EP,* May 18, 1895).

Dunne satirizes the pretensions of the Irish-American middle class when the Donahues get a piano, the ultimate symbol of the new respectability.[14] On the subject of music, Molly and her mother oppose "ol' man Donahue" and his cronies in a classic confrontation between old customs and new pretensions. Old Donahue breaks a precedent himself by inviting Slavin and Cassidy into the parlor (they are usually relegated to the dining room) in order to impress them with his daughter's piano playing, and there the battle is joined.

> "At anny other time Mrs. Donahue'd give him th' marble heart. But they wasn't a man in th' party that had a pianny to his name, an' she knew they'd be throuble whin they wint home an' tould about it. ''Tis a mel-odjious insthrument,' says she. 'I cud sit here be the hour an' listen to Bootoven and Choochooski,' she says.
>
> "'What did thim write?' says Cassidy. 'Chunes,' says Donahue, 'chunes. Molly,' he says, 'fetch 'er th' wallop to make th' gintlemen feel good,' he says. 'What'll it be, la-ads?' 'D'ye know 'The Rambler fr'm Clare'?' says Slavin. 'No,' says Molly. 'It goes like this,' says Slavin. 'A-ah, din yadden, yooden a-yadden, arrah yadden ay-a.' 'I dinnaw it,' says th' girl. ' 'Tis a low chune, annyhow,' says Mrs. Donahue. 'Misther Slavin ividintly thinks he's at a polis picnic,' she says. 'I'll have no come-all-ye's in this house,' she says. 'Molly, give us a few ba-ars fr'm Wagner.' 'What Wagner's that?' says Flanagan. 'No wan ye know,' says Donahue; 'he's a German musician.' 'Thim Germans is hot people f'r music,' says Cassidy. 'I knowed wan that cud play th' 'Wacht am Rhine' on a pair iv cymbals,' he says. 'Whisht!' says Donahue. 'Give th' girl a chanst.' "

Molly's rendition of Wagner drives her father out of his chair and into an admission of his real feelings and a quarrel with his wife:

> " 'Hol' on!' he says. 'That's not a rented pianny, ye daft girl,' he says. 'Why, pap-pah,' says Molly, 'what d'ye mean?' she says. 'That's Wagner,' she says. ' 'Tis th' music iv th' future,' she says. 'Yes,' says Donahue, 'but I don't want me hell on earth. I can wait f'r it,' he says, 'with th' kind permission iv Mrs. Donahue,' he says. 'Play us th' 'Wicklow Mountaineer,' he says, 'an' threat th' masheen kindly,' he says. 'She'll play no 'Wicklow Mountaineer,' says Mrs. Donahue.

'If ye want to hear that kind iv chune, ye can go down to Finucane's Hall,' she says, 'an' call in Crowley, th' blind piper,' she says. 'Molly,' she says, 'give us wan iv thim Choochooski things,' she says. 'They're so ginteel.' "

The piece ends with Donahue's friends laughing last. Slavin, "with th' politeness iv a man who's gettin' even," recalls that his brother used to play Choochooski's "chunes"—"me brother Mike, that run th' grip ca-ar"—and adds, on his way out the door, that the "wan thing missin' fr'm Molly's playin' " is "an ax" (*EP,* Aug. 20, 1895).[15]

In a final attempt at gentility, Molly stages a home vaudeville show in retaliation for the Hogans' "progressive spoil-five party." (Dunne connects a "low" Irish card game and the contemporary social fad of progressive parties.) This time her father agrees that the Hogans must be "thrown," because "they wurked f'r me father on th' ol' sod an' I'd be th' poor stick iv a man f'r to let thim put th' comether over Molly." But all does not go well, and the star of the show, an exotic dancer, is thrown out by old Donahue in a memorable scene, which ends with a pointed reassertion of perspective:

" 'Woman, lave me house,' he says. 'Go,' he says, 'an' sin no more,' he says. 'As f'r th' rist iv ye,' he says, 'if ye think th' house iv Dona-hue is th' Lyceem or th' dime museem ye've made th' mistake iv ye'er life,' he says. 'If ye're not all out on th' sthreet within th' minyit Monseer Terence Donahue'll give ye an imitation iv a poor, tired assistant night foreman at th' mills inthrojoocin' a novelty in society be clanin' out his guests with th' leg iv a stove.' "

[*EP,* Feb. 22, 1896][16]

Molly's attempts at revolution always fail, but they remind us that change was very much in the air of Bridgeport in the nineties, espe-cially within the younger generation. Education was a key issue here, for Mr. Dooley blames Molly's convent schooling for her intransigence, and he frequently deplores the relaxation of discipline that differen-tiates American from Irish schools. His report of the graduation from eighth grade of "Hennessy's youngest" is revealing, for the boy's valedictory speech suggests a cockiness that was no part of the edu-cation in respect for authority of the old hedge schools: "He said that he was lookin' th' future square in th' eye, an' though th' past was bad he'd thry to do the bist he cud f'r th' wurruld. . . . He'd been very busy at school for some years, but now that he'd gradjooated he thought he'd have time to put things in ordher." In his closing, Dooley's brusque wit leavens Hennessy's mixture of pride, melancholy, and remorse:

"His father come over with me afther th' intertainment an' he looked blue. 'What's th' matther with ye?' says I 'Does it remind ye iv ye'er own boyhood days,' I says, 'whin ye was gradjooated be th' toe iv th' hidge schoolmasther's boot?' I says. 'No,' says he. ' 'Tis not that,' he says. 'I was on'y thinkin' afther hearin' Joe's o-ration,' he says, 'that I've lived a misspent life,' he says. 'I niver give care nor thought to th' higher jooties iv citizenship,' he says. 'Mebbe,' he says, 'I had to wurruk too hard,' he says. 'Go home,' says I. 'I'm goin' to close up,' I says."   [*EP*, July 6, 1895]

Hennessy cannot quite understand or articulate how his disturbance is rooted in the changing times, but he does make a valid point—he *has* had to work too hard—and Dooley brushes him aside simply because he is powerless to answer or alleviate the situation.

College begins to be possible for Irish-American youth in these years, and Dooley's reports on Thanksgiving football contain proud references to the contributions of the Irish at Wisconsin and Notre Dame. Another rumble of change registers when the Dennehy boy comes home from Notre Dame to overturn the pattern of parental authority that had been a rigid constant in the old country. On an Irish farm, a boy was a "boy" for as long as he remained at home and his father was still alive; he had few privileges, fewer prospects, and no say in how the farm was run. When Mr. Dooley presents the situation in the Dennehy household, the distance between Ireland and Chicago comes clear:

"He come back fr'm Nother Da-ame Collidge las' summer with his head so full iv quare notions that his poor ol' man, as simple a soul, Jawn, d'ye mind, as iver put a pick on his shoulder, was afraid to open his mouth f'r fear he'd say something that'd affind th' dam jood. He got Dennehy that there scared, d'ye mind, that he wore his shoes afther supper an' had to r-roll th' growler f'r a pint in a handbag. He'd larned to ride a bicycle—th' la-ad had—an' all winter he's been tellin' me he was gawn to get a wheel. 'Ye'd betther be gettin' a wheelbarrow,' I says. ' 'Tis more in th' line iv yer fam'ly,' I says. They're not much, Jawn. Not a priest belongin' to thim."

[*EP*, May 19, 1894]

A final and summarizing piece linking assimilation and the younger generation finds Hennessy beginning to worry about his own son's potential waywardness.

> "I'm havin' a time iv it with Terence," said Mr. Hennessy, despondently.
> "What's th' la-ad been doin'?" asked Mr. Dooley.
> "It ain't so much what he's doin'," Mr. Hennessy explained, "as what he ain't doin'. He ain't stayin' home iv nights, an' he ain't wurrukin'; but he does be out on th' corner with th' Cromleys an' th' rest, dancin' jig steps an' whistlin' th' 'Rogue's March' whin a polisman goes by. Sure, I can do nawthin' with him, f'r he's that kind an' good at home that he'd melt th' heart iv a man iv stone. But it's gray me life is, thinkin' iv what's to become iv him whin he gets to be a man grown. Ye're lucky, Martin, thet ye're childless."

Mr. Dooley reacts with disturbed bewilderment: "Is there somethin' in th' air or is it in oursilves that makes th' childher nowadays turn out to curse th' lives iv thim that give thim life?" The answer, he continues, may be

> "in th' thrainin'. Whin I was a kid, they were brought up to love, honor, an' respect th' ol' folks, that their days might be long in th' land. Amen. If they didn't, th' best they cud do was to say nawthin' about it. 'Twas th' back iv th' hand an' th' sowl iv th' fut to th' la-ad that put his spoon first into th' stirabout."

With a vignette, Dooley then illustrates that " 'tis th' other way about now." An Irish cobbler named Ahearn emigrates to Chicago, realizes the potential of land, and is infected with avarice:

> "He picked up money be livin' off iv leather findings an' wooden pegs, an' bought pieces iv th' prairie, an' starved an' bought more, an' starved an' starved till his heart was shrivelled up like a washerwoman's hand. But he made money. An' th' more he made, th' more he wanted, an', wantin' nawthin' more, it come to him fr'm th' divvle, who kept th' curse f'r his own time."

Ahearn becomes a miserly, rackrenting landlord, with "tinants be th' scoor that prayed at nights f'r him that he might live long an' taste sorrow." He marries late, and his wife dies giving birth to a son, on whom he then lavishes every attention: "Nawthin' was too good f'r th'

kid. He had nurses an' servants to wait on him. He had clothes that'd
stock this ba-ar f'r a year." But the boy grows up weak, without backbone—a crushing failure in his father's eyes: "He did nawthin' that
was bad; an' yet he was no good at all, at all,—just a slow, tired,
aisy-goin', shamblin' la-ad,—th' sort that'd wrench th' heart iv a father
like Ahearn." Finally exasperated by what he has created, Ahearn
takes the most extreme of actions in this family-oriented society: he
disowns the boy and throws him out of the house (*EP,* Nov. 13, 1897).

Ahearn has ruined his son by spoiling him rotten, so that Dooley
has made his ostensible point with the vignette, but the trouble here
lies deeper than the matter of discipline in child-rearing. Ahearn's has
been an American success story: by hard work and thrift he has gained
a real estate empire, only to lose his own soul and his son. The devil
who kept his curse for Ahearn was born of the process of assimilation.
By embracing the individualistic business ethic of Gilded Age America,
Ahearn has committed the sin of putting himself before the community: "th' love iv money was knitted into his heart; an' . . . th' way he
ground th' people that lived in his houses was death an' destruction."
Thus, his punishment is deserved by Irish standards, implied in Mr.
Dooley's merciless characterization of him, although he is only following the natural way of American business, with its rationale in Social
Darwinism. Dunne expresses here the moral dilemma of a culture
caught between two worlds, with the balance ever tending toward the
new, and with constant questioning of the old values. The resulting
hopeless tangle seems unavoidable.

Perhaps the greatest force for the dissolution of the Bridgeport community in the nineties was poverty, which hung over the neighborhood
like a fixed black cloud all through the decade. The national economic
depression of 1893–1898 aggravated the local problems of exploding
immigrant population, labor unrest, and bitter-cold winters to produce
a crisis of major proportions. At the same time, the settlement movement, ushered into Chicago by the opening of Hull-House in 1889,
brought the first organized and published investigations of the living
and working conditions of the city's poor. An associate of Jane
Addams, Florence Kelley, directed a revealing study of one square
mile of the nineteenth ward in 1893. The following year brought W. T.
Stead's *If Christ Came to Chicago,* which dealt extensively with the

poverty problem. Chicago in the nineties also became the main source for settlement worker and sociologist Robert Hunter's watershed study of *Poverty,* which appeared in 1904.[17]

Mr. Dooley's first winter on the *Evening Post* was the "Black Winter" of 1893–1894, when the panic that the rest of the country had begun to feel the previous summer caught up to Chicago in the wake of the temporary prosperity brought by the World's Fair. Intensified by the numbers of unemployed left stranded after the Fair closed, the depression, when it finally hit, precipitated a staggering relief crisis. W. T. Stead describes a city swarming with tramps, "like the frogs in the Egyptian plague." For thousands of destitute people there were only three available lodging places: the run-down Harrison Street police station, where they could sleep stacked head to foot along the corridors of cell blocks, "like herrings in a barrel"; the Pacific Garden Mission, which accommodated five hundred men but made them sleep sitting up on chairs; and the corridors of City Hall, where 2,000 sleepers huddled nightly through the winter. In *Twenty Years at Hull-House,* Jane Addams also recalls the chaos of 1893: the lack of municipal regulation, the inadequacy of existing charitable organizations, the waste of energy as social workers discussed general principles and the poor themselves blindly blamed an abstraction called "poverty" for their plight.[18]

Stead and Miss Addams make the same two observations: that the poor reach out remarkably to help those who have less; and, on the other side, that official charities are often guilty of self-defeating coldness and "scientific" detachment.[19] Indeed, all through the nineties reformers puzzled over the question of how to combine the humanitarian sympathy of personal charity with the greater efficiency and inclusiveness of organized efforts; and Chicago responded to the "Black Winter" crisis with new initiatives on both fronts. At least half the city's seven thousand saloons dispensed free lunches daily, prompting Stead to declare that "without pretending to be of much account from a charitable point of view," the saloons had "nevertheless fed more hungry people this winter in Chicago than all the other agencies, religious, charitable and municipal, put together." And at the same time, in February 1894, a group of concerned citizens was forming the Civic Federation, which moved immediately to organize the city's scattered philanthropic groups into the Chicago Bureau of Charities.[20]

Mr. Dooley faces Bridgeport's poverty not with the detachment of a social scientist or political reformer, but with the mingled anger and frustration, compassion and bewilderment of a member of the afflicted community. He agrees in substance with the criticisms of Addams and Stead by depicting several humiliating confrontations between destitute Bridgeporters and the unfeeling purveyors of organized charity. In Mr. Dooley's view, however, these confrontations are dramatically linked to internal pressures unique to the immigrant Irish culture. This view prevents him from seeing poverty as just another social problem, solvable by the application of principles through politics. In the real world of Bridgeport, unreasoning pride and the relentless battle for improved social position combine in situations where humiliation is the certain price exacted from the Irish poor by Irish alms-givers, and going on relief is the most crushing of personal defeats and social stigmas. Moreover, the poor of Bridgeport are not idlers and loafers. Most want desperately to make their way with self-respect, but forces beyond their control or understanding keep them from honest labor or a living wage, and the disgrace of enforced idleness or want is almost more than they can bear. As both a sign that their culture is crumbling around them and an agency of the dissolution, the fact of poverty terrifies the Irish of Bridgeport, and brings their spokesman, Martin Dooley, to the brink of despair. The mélange of conflicting emotions that Bridgeport feels through Mr. Dooley adds a dimension to the poverty issue that outsiders like Addams, Hunter, and Stead miss entirely. Thus, the importance of these pieces as living, corroborative social history can hardly be exaggerated.

The important distinction in the Irish-American community between official and personal charity is a major theme of the Dooley poverty pieces. The case against organized charity is clearly made in the story of the St. Vincent de Paul Society, the leading relief agency in Bridgeport, and the impoverished Callaghan family.

"They'd had th' divvle's own winter an' spring iv it—Callaghan out iv wurruk an' th' good woman down with pnoomony iv th' lungs an' ne'er a dollar in th' house but what he picked up wanst in a while doin' odd jobs around. An' him as proud as a pr-rince an' patient as a nun! I mind whin th' Saint Vincent de Pauls wint out f'r to investigate his case. Well, Jawn, ye know what th' Irish is whin they have money. Head and tail up. Give me thim that haven't

enough to ate iv their own to help their neighbors. I've seen th'
stirabout divided whin th' eyes iv th' childher was poppin' out iv
their heads. Well, the chairman iv th' comity that wint to investigate
Callaghan's case was old Peter Coogan—an' ye know him—big
hear-rt enough but desp-rate r-rough. Mrs. Callaghan was up whin
they called an' 'twas 'me good woman this' an' 'me good woman
that' an' 'th' mimbers is always r-ready f'r to help th' desarvin' poor.'
Con Hogan who was in th' comity tol' me Mrs. Callaghan answered
niver a wur-rud, but th' tears come to her big, gray eyes an' she
held on to th' table. Coogan's father was wan iv her fa-ather's farmhands in Roscommon, d'ye mind." [*EP*, Nov. 24, 1894]

In the tragic dénouement of this tale of pride and humiliation (already
discussed in chapter 2), Callaghan insults the relief committee, all
organized efforts to help the family cease, and Mrs. Callaghan dies of
pneumonia.

Mr. Dooley much prefers the unofficial dispensation of aid from
family to family, a practice for which the Famine years in Ireland provided familiar precedent; those of the peasantry who survived did so
only by helping one another. He illustrates in one of the earliest
pieces, an incisive sketch of a child caught in the web of poverty, which
turns into an exemplum of personal charity.

A rattle at the door and a short cry caused Mr. Dooley to pause
and listen and finally to toddle out grumbling complaints about the
Donohue goat, whose only diversion was to batter down the tenements of dacint people. As he opened the door his grumbling ceased,
and presently he came in carrying something that looked like a rather
large parcel of rags, but on close inspection turned out to be a very
small girl carrying a very big can.

"Glory be to Gawd," said Mr. Dooley, setting the little girl down
in the chair. "Glory be to Gawd, an' did ye iver see th' likes iv
that? Luk at her, Jawn, th' unfortunate chick, lyin' out there froze
in this murdhrin' night with a can in her hand. Who are ye, poor
thing? Let me take a luk at ye. By gar, I thought so. 'Tis Grady's
kid—Grady, th' villain, th' black-hearted thafe, to send th' poor
choild out to her death. Don't stand there, ye big numbskull, like a
cigar store injun starin'. Go over an' fetch that can iv milk. Musha,
musha, ye poor dear. . . ."

Mr. Dooley stood with hands on his hips and saw the little Grady
girl laving her purple nose in the warm milk. Meantime he narrated
the history of her father in forcible language, touching upon his

failure to work and provide, his bibulous habits and his tendency toward riotous misconduct. Finally, he walked behind the bar and set out the glasses, as his custom was for closing time. He placed the cash drawer in the small iron safe in the corner and tucked a $5 bill in his vest pocket. Then he turned out the lights in the window and put on his overcoat.

"Where are you going?" asked Mr. McKenna.

"I'm goin' over to lick Grady," said Mr. Dooley.

"Then," said Mr. McKenna, "by heavens," he said, "I'll go with you."

And they marched out together, with the little Grady girl between them.   [*EP*, Nov. 25, 1893]

This is the first of many Dooley vignettes in which charity is administered more "from the heart" than "from the ledger," in the words of a *Post* editorial around the same time.[21]

Dunne's poverty studies continued throughout the Chicago years, appearing most often in the wintertime, and especially during the Christmas season. The holidays always brought out Mr. Dooley's dark side, for Dunne felt keenly the collision of heightened expectations and maximum deprivation that was the order of the day for many Bridgeporters. "The approach of Christmas," says Dunne in the introduction to one Dooley piece, "is heralded in Archey Road by many of the signs that are known to the less civilized and more prosperous parts of the city. The people look poorer, colder, and more hopeful than at other times" (*EP*, Dec. 18, 1897).[22]

During the winter of 1896–1897, the fourth of hard times in a row, and the worst, Dunne wrote the harshest and most tragic of the Dooley pieces, harrowing tales in which his indictment of the structure of American urban society is so specific and damning that he never chose to republish them, despite their obvious power. That winter in Chicago the relief crisis was extreme. As early as November 30, the Bureau of Associated Charities estimated that 8,000 families were destitute (*T–H*, Nov. 30, 1896). A wave of bitter cold struck and held on all through December and into January. The *Times-Herald* editorial page, for which Dunne was then writing, called daily for more and faster action by the various charitable organizations. The first responses attributable with any certainty to Dunne came on Saturday, December 5, when an editorial and a Dooley piece appeared on the same subject—the necessity of helping all of the poor, regardless of their "qualifications." Once again, Editor Dunne and Mr. Dooley are in striking disagreement.

The editorial praises the Relief and Aid Society for its work among "the worthy and deserving poor," but goes on to caution that "all these things are good, but they do not exhaust the charitable field":

> The deserving poor and the investigatable poor are not the only sufferers entitled to relief at our hands. There is a considerable army of people who are not in themselves worthy persons who must be helped, and often with the eyes shut. Organized charity is apt to frown upon these, not in any very Pharasaic way either, but simply because they cannot give an account of themselves. They are sometimes drunkards, sometimes worse, and always liars, and yet they are not outcasts, nor subjects for the bridewell [city jail] or the poorhouse. Everybody knows some of these persons, existing as they do on the fringe of society, frequently with an air of respectability or the memory of better days about them. They could no more stand a cross-examination by the agent of organized charity as to the whys and wherefores of their present condition and what they would do with a little money if it were given them than they could tell what had become of the lost tribes of Israel, and yet they have got to be assisted. This is one field for the occupation of unorganized charity, and where the ready hand must fly to the open pocket without much thought.

Once again, as we saw in chapter 2, the corresponding Dooley piece exemplifies a shift in perspective—from outside to inside, from detached observer to committed participant. Instead of praising the Relief and Aid Society, Mr. Dooley attacks its self-defeating regulations by reducing them to absurdity:

> "If they'se annything will make a person ongrateful an' depindent it's to give thim something to eat whin they're hungry without knowin' whether they are desarvin' iv th' delicate attintion. A man, or a woman ayether, has to have what ye may call peculiar qualifications f'r to gain th' lump iv coal or th' pound iv steak that an organized charity gives out. He must be honest an' sober an' industhrious. He must have a frind in th' organization. He must have arned th' right to beg his bread be th' sweat iv his brow. He must be able to comport himself like a gintleman in fair society an' play a good hand at whist. He must have a marridge license over th' pianny an' a goold-edged Bible on th' marble-topped table. A pauper

that wud disbelieve there was a God afther thrampin' th' sthreets
in search iv food an' calmin' an onreasonable stomach with th' east
wind is no object iv charity. What he needs is th' attintion iv a
polisman. I've aften wondered why a man that was fit to dhraw a
ton iv slate coal an' a gob iv liver fr'm th' relief an' aid society
didn't apply f'r a cabinet position or a place in a bank. He'd be
sthrong f'r ayether."

Instead of condescending to ask aid for "drunkards" and "liars,"
Dooley goes on to tell a haunting story, important not only for its
treatment of the poverty problem, but also for its picture of a stoical
peasant from the west of Ireland, transplanted to alien soil, the kind
of person for whom Yeats wanted to write "one/Poem maybe as cold/
And passionate as the dawn." [23]

"I mind wanst there was a woman lived down near Main sthreet
be th' name iv Clancy, Mother Clancy th' kids called her. She come
fr'm away off to th' wist, a Galway woman fr'm bechune mountain
an' sea. Ye know what they ar-re whin they're black, an' she was
worse an' blacker. She was tall an' thin, with a face white th' way a
corpse is white, an' she had wan child, a lame la-ad that used to
play be himsilf in th' sthreet, th' lawn bein' limited. I niver heerd tell
iv her havin' a husband, poor thing, an' what she'd need wan f'r,
but to dhrag out her misery f'r her in th' gray year sivinty-foor,
I cudden't say. She talked to hersilf in Gaelic whin she walked an'
'twas Gaelic she an' th' kid used whin they wint out together. Th'
kids thought she was a witch an' broke th' windows iv her house an'
ivry wan was afraid iv her but th' little priest. He shook his head
whin she was mintioned an' wint to see her wanst in awhile an' come
away with a throubled face.

"Sivinty-foor was a hard winter f'r th' r-road. Th' mills was shut
down an' ye cud've stood half th' population iv some iv th' precints
on their heads an' got nothin' but five days' notices out iv thim.
Th' nights came cold, an' bechune relievin' th' sick an' givin'
extremunction to th' dyin' an' comfortin' th' widows an' orphans
th' little priest was sore pressed fr'm week's end to week's end.
They was smallpox in wan part iv th' wa-ard an' diphtheria in
another an' bechune th' two there was starvation an' cold an' not
enough blankets on th' bed.

"Th' Galway woman was th' las' to complain. How she iver stud
it as long as she did I lave f'r others to say. Annyhow, whin she
come down to Halsted sthreet to make application f'r help to th'
Society f'r th' Relief iv th' Desarvin' Poor she looked tin feet tall
an' all white cheek bones an' burnin' black eyes. It took her a long

time to make up her mind to go in, but she done it an' stepped up to where th' reel-estate man Dougherty, cheerman iv th' comity, was standin' with his back to th' stove an' his hands undher his coat tails. They was those that said Dougherty was a big-hear-rted man an' give freely to th' poor, but I'd rather take rough-on-rats fr'm you, Hinnissy, thin sponge cake fr'm him or th' likes iv him. He looked at her, finished a discoorse on th' folly iv givin' to persons with a bad moral charackter an' thin turned suddenly an' said: 'What can we do fr ye?' She told him in her own way. 'Well, me good woman,' says he, 'ye'll undherstand that th' comity is much besieged be th' imporchunities iv th' poor,' he says. 'We can't do anything fr ye on ye're own say so, but we'll sind a man to invistigate ye're case, an',' he says, 'we'll attind to ye.'

"I dinnaw what it was, but th' matther popped out iv Dougherty's head an' nayether that day nor th' nex' nor th' nex' afther that was annything done fr th' Galway woman. I'll say this fr Dougherty, that whin th' thing come back to his mind again he put on his coat an' hurried over to Main sthreet. They was a wagon in th' sthreet, but Dougherty took no notice iv it. He walked up an' rapped on th' dure, an' th' little priest stepped out, th' breast iv his overcoat bulgin'. 'Why, father,' he says, 'ar-re ye here? I jus' come fr to see—' 'Peace,' said th' little priest, closin' th' dure behind him an' takin' Dougherty be th' ar-rm. 'We were both late.' But 'twas not till they got to th' foot iv th' stairs that Dougherty noticed that th' wagon come fr'm th' county undertaker, an' that 'twas th' chalice made th' little priest's coat to bulge."   [*EP,* Dec. 5, 1896]

There is a miracle of transformation here, as editorial condescension toward those "on the fringe of society" yields to a stark tragedy of unassimilable peasant pride.

The crisis grew even worse in January 1897. At the *Times-Herald,* the editorial staff was concentrating on the theme of "hunger amid plenty" and beginning to criticize openly the red-tape delays of the city's relief bureaucracy. On January 23 came another Dunne-Dooley pairing. A *Times-Herald* editorial that Saturday morning called for acceleration of the process of relief, for

the present crisis, when ill-clad, half-famished shapes confront us on the streets; when the cold pinches the denizens of hovels and tenements, when the children in a thousand squalid homes cry for sustenance, when women fight for bread at the county agent's door, and able-bodied men swarm on the railway tracks, eagerly bagging fragments of coal—this crisis is not to be met with perfunctory measures.[24]

That evening in the *Post,* Mr. Dooley told the story of one of those destitute coal-pickers, a Polish immigrant named Sobieski. Again the difference is striking between the generality of the editorial writer's statement of the problem and the specifics of Sobieski's tragedy, which Dunne presents as a clear case of failed assimilation. Understanding that the problems of the Irish poor were magnified tremendously for the unfortunates of the newer immigration, up against both a language barrier and a more virulent prejudice, Dunne brought to his subject a savage and concentrated indignation in the tradition of Swift.

"Ye didn't know a man named Sobieski, that lived down be Grove sthreet, did ye? Ah-ha! Well, he was not so bad, afther all. He's dead, ye know. Last week. Ye see, this here Sobieski had no more sinse thin a grasshopper. He arned enormous wages f'r a man with eight childher—wan twinty-five a day, half a week in good times, sidintary imploymint carryin' pigs iv steel at th' mills. Bimeby th' saviors iv their counthry, believin' th' market was overstocked, shut down an' left time and grocers' bills heavy on Sobieski's hands. The col' weather come on, an' Sobieski grew tired iv inaction. Also th' childher were freezin' to death. So he put a bag on his shoulder an' wint over to th' railway thracks to pick up some coal. Wan man can't pick up much coal on th' railway thracks, Hinnissy, but it is an unpardonable crime, just th' same. 'Tis far worse thin breakin' th' intherstate commerce act. Anny offense again' a railway company is high threason, but pickin' up coal is so villainous that they'se no forgiveness f'r th' hidyous wretch that commits it.

"Sobieski walked along th' thracks, gettin' a chunk here an' there, till a watchman seen him, an' pintin' a revolver at him, called 'Halt!' Sobieski didn't know th' English language very well. 'Dam Pole' was about his limit, an' he had that thrained into him be th' foreman at th' mills. But he knew what a revolver meant, an' th' ignorant fool tur-ned an' run with his three cints' worth iv coal rattlin' at his back. Th' watchman was a good shot, an' a Pole with heavy boots is no tin-second man in a fut race. Sobieski pitched over on his face, thried to further injure th' comp'ny be pullin' up th' rails with his hands, an' thin passed to where—him bein' a Pole, an' dyin' in such a horrible sin—they'se no need iv coal iv anny kind.

"That shows wan iv th' evils iv a lack iv idyacation," Mr. Dooley continued. "If Sobieski had known th' language—"

"He'd a halted," said Mr. Hennessy.

"He wud not," said the Philosopher. "He'd niver been there at all. While th' watchman was walkin' knee-deep in snow, Sobieski'd been comfortably joltin' th' watchman's boss in a dark alley downtown. Idyacation is a gr-reat thing."   [*EP,* Jan. 23, 1897]

Mr. Dooley's cruel cynicism about the education necessary for survival in Chicago indicates the gravity of the poverty crisis and Dunne's frustration concerning its alleviation.

Meanwhile, the cold wave continued. It was thirteen below zero at noon on Sunday, January 24. On Monday, Mayor Swift issued a proclamation stating that instant relief would be provided to all the needy, regardless of their qualifications. The police, who were to act as relief agents, were instructed to "feed and warm them first. Inquire about it afterwards." There were to be "no investigations, lectures or homilies" dispensed with food and fuel. By Tuesday, when the police relief program began, $12,000 had been subscribed to a central fund.[25]

The next weekend, as a rejoinder to the mayor's proclamation, Dunne provided another moral exemplum of personal charity. Mr. Dooley registers his dissatisfaction with the entire relief system, which he sees as little more than conscience balm for the rich: "To think that a man can square himsilf with his conscience be givin' wan thousan' dollars to a polisman an' tellin' him to disthribute it! Why don't they get the poor up in a cage in Lincoln Park an' hand thim food on th' ind iv a window-pole, if they're afraid they'll bite?" Dooley feels that cooperation within the Bridgeport community is the only charity worthy of the name, and he illustrates with a vignette:

"Afther all 'tis th' poor that keeps th' poor. They ain't wan sthrugglin' fam'ly in this war-rd that ain't carryin' three others on its back. A pound iv tay in ye'er house means a hot cup f'r thim poor Schwartzs' and ye'er encouragin' petty larceny be lavin' ye'er soft coal out—I seen ye do it, ye miserable man—so that th' Dugan boys cud steal it because ye don't speak to their father. Th' man Clancy down th' sthreet that nobody likes, him bein' a notoryous infidel, 'd be dead if it wasn't f'r th' poor iv a poor parish."

Having been put on the police relief roll, the starving Clancy receives "a sprinklin' pot, a pair iv corsets, a bar iv soap, an ax an' a hammick." He weeps "tears iv joy," and asks the dispensing policemen for salt

and pepper to "make a salad out iv this hammick." Then Father Kelly
hears of the case:

> "He's wan iv th' poor iv th' parish; th' saint got an appetite f'r
> thruffles at colledge, an' has been satisfyin' it on oatmeal iver since.
> He'd saved up tin dollars f'r to buy th' 'Life iv Saint Jerome,' but
> whin he heerd iv Clancy he give a sigh an' says he, 'Martin,' he says,
> 'Jerome'll have to wait,' he says, an' we wint down th' sthreet an'
> rough-an'-tumbled ivery coal dealer, butcher, grocer an' baker—
> most iv thim broke thimselves—till we had a wagonload iv stuff.
> We dumped it at Clancy's, an' th' pagan came out an' wanted
> Father Kelly to set on th' coal while he proved that th' Bible was
> nawthin' more nor less thin a book of anecdotes an' that if historical
> tistimony was believed Queen Victoria'd be pope in Rome to-day.
> I was f'r feedin' him a piece iv coal, but th' good man says, 'What
> talk have ye? Go an' starve no more,' an' come away with a grin
> on his face."   [*EP,* Jan. 30, 1897]

Examples like Hennessy's and Father Kelly's seem to suggest that
in the crisis situations of these bitter Chicago winters, the Bridgeport
community was holding together. And yet Mr. Dooley has many more
negative than positive examples of the effects of poverty in Bridgeport:
for every Clancy there are Sobieskis, Mother Clancys, and Mrs. Cal-
laghans; for every Father Kelly there are gloating Coogans and
Doughertys, bolstering their egos at the expense of their neighbors'
self-respect. An indication of the extent of the crisis in January and
February 1897 was the cancellation of the St. Patrick's Day parade
for the first time in recent memory, because the treasuries of the various
Irish societies were so depleted by the work of relief. The archdiocesan
newspaper, the *New World,* agreed with the vote of the societies by
declaring that it would be "little short of a crime to lavish money on
bands and horses and uniforms for a parade in times such as these." [26]
Such a breakdown on the ceremonial level is significant evidence that
personal charity was no more than a stopgap measure to shore up a
community whose dissolution was only a matter of time.

Moreover, Dunne's perspective on the seriousness of the poverty
issue is sure and steady, for in the piece about Clancy, the infidel, he
goes deeper than the debate about forms of charity, to reveal not only
sympathy for the victims of poverty, but also a profound understanding
of its roots in the Protestant ethic:

"Yis, I know th' wur-ruk iv relief is goin' on, but what th' la-ads need is th' relief iv wur-ruk. I'm not much iv a believer in wur-ruk personally, but that's because I was raised a pet. Annyhow, it's ruinin' th' temper iv th' human race. But manny a man doesn't know anny betther thin to think he's servin' Gawd best be poundin' slag fr'm daybreak to sunset an' thin goin' home too tired to stand or set or lay down. We've hammered it into their heads that they'se some connection between a pickax an' a dish iv ham an' eggs, an' bedad they can't be made to believe that wan ain't th' fruit iv th' other."

Here is a flash of Dunne as a true radical, questioning not simply the existence of poverty, but the entire complex of beliefs and social structures that makes life so hard for so many.

The following week Dunne further expressed his deepening sense of crisis by making a chilling comparison between Chicago in 1897 and Ireland during the Great Famine. The occasion was a controversy that had been underscoring the galling disparities between rich and poor in depression-ridden America. The Bradley-Martins of New York had announced a masked ball for February 10—estimated cost: $300,000. The country's newspapers were full of the affair, especially after Dr. William Rainsford of St. George's Episcopal Church in New York publicly denounced the Bradley-Martins for callously flaunting their wealth in a time of widespread destitution. Acceptances poured in, however, and Mr. Bradley-Martin argued back that actually he was performing a service—in sending so much money into circulation among the designers, artisans, and shopkeepers of New York. The Chicago papers tended to agree. Dunne's *Times-Herald* editorialized against the "popular wealth-hating fad in this country" and its loudest spokesman, Mary Ellen Lease, who had blasted the Bradley-Martins. Because "the foundations of the Bradley-Martin fortune were laid in patient industry and frugality," they should be allowed to "send it into the channels of usefulness" in any way they pleased (*T–H,* Jan. 24, 30, 31, 1897).

While Dunne may have been convinced by the arguments of his editorial page, Mr. Dooley most certainly was not. On February 6 he presents his opinion, stacking the cards from the start by having the hapless Hennessy take the side of the Bradley-Martins:

"If these people didn't let go iv their coin here, they'd take it away with thim to Paris or West Baden, Indiana, an' spind it instid iv puttin' it in circulation amongst th' florists an' dhressmakers an' hackmen they'll have to hire. I believe in encouragin' th' rich to walk away fr'm their change. 'Tis gr-reat f'r business."

Mr. Dooley then refutes Hennessy with a story from the Famine years in Ireland. A wealthy landlord, one "Willum Fitzgerald Dorsey, justice iv th' peace, mimber iv Parlymint," continues the round of gay entertaining for which he is famous even though his tenants are starving. Further, he demands that they continue to pay rent, or else he will evict them and seize all their cattle and goods. His self-justification is very like that of the Bradley-Martins; he has supported the shopkeepers of the area by the demands of his lavish scale of entertainment. The rub, of course, is that neither Dorsey nor the Bradley-Martins have considered the plight of the really poor. One night a starving peasant, "that had thramped acrost th' hills fr'm Galway just in time to rent f'r th' potato rot," murders Dorsey in sheer blind hatred, and Mr. Dooley diagnoses the case as follows:

> "An' Dorsey was a fool. He might've evicted twinty thousan' tinants, an' lived to joke about it over his bottle. 'Twas th' music iv th' band an' th' dancin' on th' hill an' th' lights th' Galway man seen whin he wint up th' muddy road with his babby in his arrums that done th' business f'r Dorsey." [*EP*, Feb. 6, 1897]

The application of this tale to the Bradley-Martins is plain and ominous, softened only by the distance Dunne creates by setting it in Ireland in the 1840s. Moreover, as a moving, imaginative recreation of the terrors and frustrations of the Famine time, the piece demonstrates the depth of Dunne's emotional connection with his Irish heritage.[27] All in all, these Dooley pieces from the winter of 1896–1897 constitute a testament of concern for the urban poor, as well as a significant historical record of a crisis potentially as destructive to the Chicago Irish community as the Famine had been to the peasants of Ireland.

Dunne also sees the spread of crime in Bridgeport as a part of the irreversible, tragic process of assimilation. The continual erosion of their old culture has left the Irish without a steady moral base. And because young people feel most strongly the disjunction between their parents' precepts for conduct and the reality of life on the streets, they are the first to lose their bearings. Dunne has the good sense and art to withhold his own fuller perspective on the problem, so that Mr. Dooley's sad stories of Bridgeport's young criminals embody convincingly the reactions of the middle-aged immigrant to the failure of the younger generation: bewildered apprehension that something—God knows what—has gone wrong with his world, and utter frustration at his powerlessness to set it right. These pieces further differentiate Mr. Dooley's outlook from that of the municipal reformers, who could look at urban crime as one more "city problem" with a set of simple solutions: clean up the city; find jobs for its people; put honest men in power. For Mr. Dooley the problem goes deeper, and the reformist-progressive formula is no help in solving it.

Again, we can compare Dunne as editorial writer and Dooley as Bridgeport villager, and the same startling difference of perspective emerges. On October 11, 1895, Henry "Butch" Lyons, twenty-seven years old and a convicted murderer, was hanged in Chicago. The next day Dunne responded. The *Post* carried a Dooley piece that was subsequently republished as "The Idle Apprentice," and the *Times-Herald* ran an editorial, "The Case of Henry Lyons, Deceased," which is here reprinted in full:

> Henry Lyons was born in 1868. His father was a drunkard, his mother a poverty-stricken working woman.
> At the age of 9 he was sent to the bridewell. He served terms repeatedly for minor offenses between 1877 and 1885, when he was committed to the house of correction for the serious crime of robbery. In 1888 he was arrested for rape. In 1889 he was sent to the bridewell for burglary. In 1894 he was arrested for burglary. Within six months he was again arrested for a criminal assault. When he mauled a companion to death he had served one term in the penitentiary and twenty-one in the bridewell. He had been arrested over 200 times!
> The judge who sentenced him could find nothing in his career that appealed for mercy. The state's attorney who prosecuted him declared he was a criminal from birth. The question is whether Henry Lyons, alcoholic by birth, encouraged to crime by environment, a wolf-child among men, could have closed his career elsewhere than on the gallows. Did he have a fair chance?

The editorial contains a dispassionate enumeration of events and statistics that lead inexorably to the gallows. The writer knows and fingers clearly the villains in this tragedy—heredity and environment, equal parts of congenital alcoholism and the streets of the city. The ending question is rhetorical: Butch Lyons did not have a fair chance, and we all know why he went wrong.

Mr. Dooley's story about young Jack Carey, "the idle apprentice," is factually the same, but with an entirely different focus and conclusion. Because Carey was a native Bridgeporter, Mr. Dooley begins by placing him solidly in a particular family and neighborhood, with the result that his downfall becomes part of the larger tragedy, inexplicable to Dooley, of the decline of the whole community.

"D'ye raymimber th' Carey kid? Ye do. Well, I knowed his grandfather; an' a dacinter ol' man niver wint to his jooty [his Catholic duty to receive the sacraments] wanst a month. Whin he come over to live down be th' slip, 'twas as good a place as iver ye see. Th' honest men an' women wint an' come as they pleased, an' laid hands on no wan. His boy Jim was as straight as th' r-roads in Kildare, but he took to dhrink; an' whin Jack Carey was born, he was a thramp on th' sthreets an' th' good woman was wurrukin' down-town, scrubbin' away at th' flures in th' city hall, where Dennehy got her.

"Be that time around th' slip was rough-an'-tumble. It was dhrink an' fight ivry night an' all day Sundah. Th' little la-ads come together under sidewalks, an' rushed th' can over to Burke's on th' corner an' listened to what th' big lads tol' thim. Th' first instruction that Jack Carey had was how to take a man's pocket handkerchief without his feelin' it, an' th' nex' he had was larnin' how to get over th' fence iv th' Reform School at Halsted Sthreet in his stockin' feet.

"He was a thief at tin year, an' th' polis'd run f'r him if he'd showed his head. At twelve they sint him to th' bridewell f'r breakin' into a freight car. He come out, up to anny game. I see him whin he was a lad hardly to me waist stand on th' roof iv Finucane's Hall an' throw bricks at th' polisman."

Branded a chronic criminal, Carey is hounded by the police, and a bitter feud develops between him and a fellow Bridgeport native, Officer Clancy. Clancy wins the first round. He surprises Carey one night, beats him to a pulp, and sends him "over th' road" to the state penitentiary. When the boy returns, revenge is his only thought. At the first opportunity, he murders Clancy in cold blood in broad daylight on Archer Avenue, thereby sealing his own fate.

"They got him within twinty yards iv me store. He was down in th' shadow iv th' house, an' they was shootin' at him fr'm roofs an' behind barns. Whin he see it was all up, he come out with his eyes closed, firin' straight ahead; an' they filled him so full iv lead he broke th' hub iv th' pathrol wagon takin' him to th' morgue."

"It served him right," said Mr. McKenna.

"Who?" said Mr. Dooley. "Carey or Clancy?" [*EP,* Oct. 12, 1895]

There is nothing rhetorical about Mr. Dooley's question. He is genuinely bewildered, unable to sort out causes and assign blame. The social-science certainties of Editor Dunne yield before a group of complex and disturbing reactions—a shared sense of the play of ambiguous external forces and the loss of community. All of Bridgeport is threatened when two of her sons turn against and destroy each other.

The summer following the Lyons hanging, a similar tragedy elicited a similar dual response from Dunne. Daniel Carroll, an Irish-American orphan, was accused of brutally murdering another youth. A *Times-Herald* editorial, "Another Victim of the Slums," recounted the dismal events of his short life:

It is said that he never knew his father or mother, but, like Topsy, "he just growed." From his earliest childhood he has lived a hunted life, like the dogs and cats of the alleys. When he committed some petty offense he was sent to the bridewell, and when released was watched as a suspect. The wonder is that he ever tried to earn an honest living, but it appears that he has been a waiter, a cook, and a peddler. Every circumstance of his recent crime shows that he has no moral sense and no realization of the dreadful nature of his offense.

He is called a "degenerate"—a euphemistic term now generally applied to people that never had a chance. And he most assuredly is that. What responsibility society owes on his account, or for his like, is something that society has been wrangling about for several centuries or more without much agreement. As a rule, when it comes to an individual case like this, society puts a rope around the degenerate's neck and that ends the particular discussion. And there are scores of children growing up in this city to become as this man is!

If we owe nothing to Carroll do we owe anything to these?

[*T–H,* June 17, 1896]

Again the tone is positive, the question rhetorical. "Society" is to blame for the Daniel Carrolls, and taking "responsibility" is, by implication, the cure.

Mr. Dooley deals obliquely with the Carroll case in his piece "On Criminals," which tells the story of young Petey Scanlan, child of exemplary parents, who grows up to become, inexplicably, "th' scoorge iv th' polis." As in the case of Jack Carey, Dooley begins by placing the boy in the social structure of Bridgeport:

> "I minded th' first time I iver see him,—a bit iv a curly-haired boy that played tag around me place, an' 'd sing "Blest Saint Joseph" with a smile on his face like an angel's. Who'll tell what makes wan man a thief an' another man a saint? I dinnaw. This here boy's father wurrked fr'm morn till night in th' mills, was at early mass Sundah mornin' befure th' alkalis lit th' candles, an' niver knowed a month whin he failed his jooty. An' his mother was a sweet-faced little woman, though fr'm th' County Kerry, that nursed th' sick an' waked th' dead, an' niver had a hard thought in her simple mind f'r anny iv Gawd's creatures. Poor sowl, she's dead now. May she rest in peace!"

Dunne has changed the facts of the Carroll case, has given Petey Scanlan an eminently respectable background, in order to convey once again the fear and frustration of an immigrant faced with the mystery of dissolving community:

> "He didn't git th' shtreak fr'm his father or fr'm his mother. His brothers an' sisters was as fine a lot as iver lived. But this la-ad Petey Scanlan growed up fr'm bein' a curly-haired angel f'r to be th' toughest villyun in th' r-road. What was it at all, at all? Sometimes I think they'se poison in th' life iv a big city. Th' flowers won't grow here no more thin they wud in a tannery, an' th' bur-rds have no song; an' th' childher iv dacint men an' women come up hard in th' mouth an' with their hands raised again their kind."

Like Carey and Clancy, Petey has turned against his own people. Dooley tries blaming the city itself, but he cannot specify the "poison," for the problem goes deeper than environment. His entire culture, the self-contained immigrant community with its tenuous balance between two worlds, is breaking down. The story's climax comes after Petey has robbed a store, terrorized half the city, and fled for asylum to his parents' home:

> "In three minyits th' r-road was full iv polismin . . . an' they'd r-run Scanlan through th' alleys to his father's house. That was as far as they'd go. They was enough iv thim to've kicked down th' little cot-

tage with their heavy boots, but they knew he was standin' behind th' dure with th' big gun in his hand; an', though they was manny a good lad there, they was none that cared f'r that short odds.

"They talked an' palavered outside, an' telephoned th' chief iv polis, an' more pathrol wagons come up. Some was f'r settin' fire to th' buildin', but no wan moved ahead. Thin th' fr-ront dure opened, an' who shud come out but th' little mother. She was thin an' pale, an' she had her apron in her hands, pluckin' at it. 'Gintlemin,' she says, 'what is it ye want iv me?' she says. 'Liftinant Cassidy,' she says, '' 'tis sthrange f'r ye that I've knowed so long to make scandal iv me befure me neighbors,' she says. 'Mrs. Scanlan,' says he, 'we want th' boy. I'm sorry, ma'am, but he's mixed up in a bad scrape, an' we must have him,' he says. She made a curtsy to thim, an' wint indures. 'Twas less than a minyit befure she come out, clingin' to th' la-ad's ar-rm. 'He'll go,' she says. 'Thanks be, though he's wild, they'se no crime on his head. Is there, dear?' 'No,' says he, like th' game kid he is. Wan iv th' polismin stharted to take hold iv him, but th' la-ad pushed him back; an' he wint to th' wagon on his mother's ar-rm."

"And was he really innocent?" Mr. McKenna asked.

"No," said Mr. Dooley. "But she niver knowed it. Th' ol' man come home an' found her: she was settin' in a big chair with her apron in her hands an th' picture iv th' la-ad th' day he made his first c'munion in her lap."   [*EP,* June 13, 1896] [28]

This piece echoed resonantly in Chicago for years after its appearance. It was read annually as a sermon in one of the city's Catholic churches, and the *Times-Herald* reviewer of *Mr. Dooley in Peace and in War* thought it the best piece in the book.[29] Also, the piece provides one of the few indications we have of Dunne's impact on the people he was writing about, Chicago's working-class Irish. In his front-porch revery at the opening of James T. Farrell's great trilogy, Studs Lonigan's father recalls Peter Dunne in recalling Petey Scanlan:

And Mike had run off and married a woman older than himself, and he was now in the east, and not doing so well, and his wife was an old crow, slobbering in a wheel chair. And Joe was a motorman. And Catherine, well, he hadn't even better think of her. Letting a traveling salesman get her like that, and expecting to come home with her fatherless baby; and then going out and becoming . . . a scarlet woman. His own sister, too! God! Nope, his family had not turned out so well. They hadn't had, none of them, the persistence that he had. He had stuck to his job and nearly killed himself working. But now he was reaping his rewards. It had been no soft job when he had started as a painter's apprentice, and there weren't strong unions then like there were now, and there was no eight-hour day, neither, and the pay was nothing. In them days, many's the good man that fell off a scaffold to die or become permanently injured. Well, Pat Lonigan had gone through the mill, and he had pulled himself up by his own bootstraps, and while he was not exactly sitting in the plush on Easy Street, he was a boss painter, and had his own business, and pretty soon maybe he'd even be worth a cool hundred thousand berries. But life was a funny thing, all right. It was like Mr. Dooley said, and he had never forgotten that remark, because Dooley, that is Finley Peter Dunne, was a real philosopher. Who'll tell what makes wan man a thief, and another man a saint? [30]

These Dooley pieces constitute the most complete creative account we have of the late nineteenth-century urban Irish community, and they are of an extraordinary richness, considering their genesis as weekly performances for the insatiable city newspaper. Taken together, they are sufficient to place Dunne among the pioneers of American literary realism—as a writer who accepted the commonplace on its own terms, with faith in its value as material for art. Indeed, had the Spanish-American War not propelled Dunne to national fame, the slouching Hennessy boy might well have been the Studs Lonigan of his generation; and knowing Martin Dooley, we can imagine that his story would have been told with subtlety and compassion.

4

THE IRISH IN AMERICAN POLITICS

The View from Archer Avenue

I slept six deep in a bunk short as a coffin
Between a poisoned pup of a seasick boy
And a slaughtered pig of a snorer from Kildare,
Who wrestled elephants the wild nights through,
And sweated sour milk. I wolfed my meals,
Green water, and salt beef, and wooden biscuits,
On my hunkers like an ape, in a four-foot aisle
As choked as the one door of a burning school.
I crossed in mid-December: seven weeks
Of driving rain that kept the hatches battened
In a hold so low of beam a man my height
Could never lift his head. And I couldn't wash.
Water was low; the place was like an icehouse;
And girls were thick as field mice in a haystack
In the bunk across. I would have died of shame,
When I stood in the landing shed of this "promised land,"
As naked as the day I first saw light,
Defiled with my own waste like a dying cat,
And a lousy red beard on me like a tinker's,
While a bitch of a doctor, with his nails too long,
Dared tell me: "In Amurrica, we bathe!"
I'd have died with shame, had I sailed here to die.
I swallowed pride and rage, and made a vow
The time would come when I could spit both out
In the face of the likes of him. I made a vow
I'd fight my way to power if it killed me,
Not only for myself, but for our kind,
For the men behind me, laughing out of fear,
At their own shame as well as mine, for the women,
Behind the board partition, frightened dumb
With worry they'd be sent back home to starve
Because they'd dirty feet. I was born again.
It came to me as brutal as the cold
That made us flinch the day the midwife takes
Our wet heels in her fist, and punches breath
Into our dangling carcasses: Get power!
Without it, there can be no decency,
No virtue and no grace.

WILLIAM ALFRED [1]

POLITICAL life provided the most visible and controversial career opportunities for the Irish in American cities in the late nineteenth century. Between the Famine time of the 1840s and the turn of the century, over three million Irishmen came to America, and the 1890 census showed an all-time high of 1,872,000 Americans of Irish birth. The combination of numbers, linguistic and organizational talents, previous experience as political underdogs under British rule, and a ghetto community cohesive both ethnically and religiously made for success in city politics.[2] The most obvious product was the urban machine, a tightly woven network of single-minded men, from the boss at the top to the precinct captain at the bottom, through which few votes were allowed to slip. The aim, of course, was to get power. To that end, however, various good works were incidentally performed. The poor received food and fuel and sometimes jobs; the financial burden of burials and christenings and weddings was made lighter; Christmas turkeys and Easter hams found their way to tables that otherwise would have been bare; and, most important, if you had a complaint, someone was there to listen. Judgment on the boss system oscillates between the extremes of indictment as wholly corrupt, self-serving spoilsmanship, and praise as a social welfare system in embryo, responding to the needs of city dwellers before the provision of governmental apparatus.[3] The middle view holds that while the machine did provide social services, it did so only in a limited, stop-gap way, and as a means to power. Lacking an overall social vision, machine bosses were unable to see politics as an instrument of social change.[4]

In the 1890s there was much criticism nationally of what one writer called "The Irish Conquest of Our Cities."[5] In his 1896 *Atlantic* series on the Irish in America, H. C. Merwin points to the "almost entire absence of [the] reform element" in Irish-American politics, which "have been distinguished more by corruption and intrigue than by any better qualities."[6] Another writer at this time sees the influence of the Irish in American politics as "great out of all proportion to their actual number" and complains of their "viciously mistaken idea of the nature of public office as a business opening for private gain."[7] The classic example of Irish boss rule, cited in all of these pieces, was New York's Tammany Hall, which was in the news a great deal in the nineties because of a series of scandals that finally forced Boss Richard Croker to flee the country. Another significant response was an increase in anti-Irish activity by the American Protective Association, a Know-Nothing group that survived on fear that Ireland and Catholicism were taking over America.[8]

In Chicago in the 1890s the boss system was flourishing. The mayor and the city council, made up of two aldermen from each of thirty-odd wards, presided over the dispensation of a seemingly endless supply of franchises and ordinances necessary to the continued expansion of the fastest growing city in America. Every new road or building, every railroad, streetcar, and telegraph line, every installation of gas, electricity, and water provided a potential source of graft. In 1894, W. T. Stead estimated that the right of way on Chicago streets was "a property the net value of which cannot be valued at less than five million dollars a year." The people of Chicago almost never benefited from this money, however, for the council of "gray wolves," as they were widely known, sold most of the franchises under the table through a process known as "boodling," which Stead defines as "a euphemism signifying the corrupt disposal of public property by the representatives of the people in return for a price paid not to the public but to their dishonest representatives." Stead declared that "fewer than eighteen" of the sixty-eight aldermen in the 1894–1895 council were honest, and that "boodling remains the chief motive power of the city council of Chicago."[9] Moreover, gambling and prostitution, both illegal, flourished in the first ward, the city's tenderloin area, with the tacit blessing of amply rewarded aldermen and police officials.[10]

In all of this, the contribution of the Irish was considerable. The Democratic machine was strong, Irish-dominated, and firmly entrenched, thanks especially to its alliance with Carter H. Harrison, who, despite his Anglo-Saxon background, had thrown in with the Irish and had subsequently been elected mayor an unprecedented five times in the 1880s and 1890s. (He was assassinated in October 1893 while serving his fifth term.) A colorful figure, fond of leading parades on a white stallion, Harrison was known for his underworld connections and his laxity toward professional gambling and prostitution, none of which hurt him at election time. Gambler-politician Mike McDonald, the nearest to being a citywide boss in Chicago, was close to Harrison. In semiretirement after 1890, he was succeeded by a small group of aldermen and bosses with such names as O'Brien, Brennan, Whelan, and Powers, all of whom were unmistakably "out for the stuff." Despite yearly antiboodle campaigns in the newspapers, the machine rolled on through the nineties, helping itself over the rough spots by means of questionable election procedures. In short, the Irish controlled Chicago, they were guilty of large-scale abuses of that control, and everyone, including Peter Dunne, knew it.

As an experienced political reporter who had been close to the action in Chicago since the 1880s, Dunne was well qualified to describe his city's governmental processes. He had been good enough to cover the national conventions for each of the papers that he worked on in election years: the *Times* in 1888, the *Herald* in 1892, the *Times-Herald* in 1896, and the *Journal* in 1900. In 1890 he investigated ties between politics and professional gambling for the *Tribune* and testified before a grand jury. As we saw earlier, his first dialect experiments may have involved city council meetings. Finally, he was obviously playing to a strength when his first dialect series featured ridicule of the plots and picnics of the city Democratic Club and "Colonel" Thomas Jefferson Dolan.

Thus, by the time Mr. Dooley appeared in 1893, his creator was already an expert political observer, hardened to the realities of the boss system, Chicago style. And the Dooley political pieces do not disappoint. They constitute an important inside narrative of the Irish preoccupation with power, a vivid microcosm of the urban political machine in America at the turn of the century. From his knowledgeable position as former precinct captain in ward six, Bridgeport, Mr. Dooley gives us much otherwise unavailable information—from descriptions of the yearly tribal rite, the aldermanic election, to capsule biographies of real Chicago politicians, to glimpses of the inner workings of the mayor's office and the city council.

In a 1936 introduction to his work, Dunne recalled that the Dooley persona and the mask of humor had allowed him to attack by name some of the worst boodlers in the city council, such as Johnny Powers of the nineteenth ward and William J. O'Brien of the sixth: "If I had written the same thing in English I would inevitably have been pistolled or slugged, as other critics were. But my victims did not dare to complain. They felt bound to smile and treat these highly libellous articles as mere humorous skits." [11] There is some truth in this memory, but I think that Dunne is confusing his position as a reform-oriented editorial writer with Mr. Dooley's often quite different slant on politics. Examination of the Dooley political pieces in the context of the various municipal elections that prompted them, and in comparison to the corresponding Dunne editorials, will illuminate that difference, which is another element of the split between Dunne and Mr. Dooley that is being traced here.

To begin with, a common theme of Mr. Dooley's responses to the yearly aldermanic election in April is nostalgia for the "old days" when, like so much of Bridgeport life, politics was rougher and more "lively" than in the more respectable nineties. On the other hand, corresponding *Post, Times-Herald,* and *Journal* editorials always deplore whatever bluster and bullying remain in the electoral process, and in most years of the nineties that was considerable. Certainly the old days had been lively: I have checked back as far as 1880, and no city election passed by quietly through that entire decade. Rioting and fist fights were common at the polling places, which were often in saloons, and charges of ballot-box stuffing and stealing and fraudulent vote counting were yearly occurrences. Contrary to Mr. Dooley's reports, however, the turn of the decade brought few reforms in the process. In 1890, for example, the April election caused pistol and hand-to-hand assaults in several wards, and the *Tribune* claimed "the worst interference by police and officials ever." In ward nineteen, "all the patrolmen, bridgetenders, city hall clerks and official cormorants" came out to "help" boodle prince Johnny Powers, and in Bridgeport (ward six) police lieutenants drove from poll to poll in "support" of Eddie Burke (April 3, 1890). At the end of the month, an election fraud scandal broke, involving several score of prominent Democratic politicians, election judges, and police officers. The charge was that a troop of Bridgeport Democrats had been enlisted by the party machine to travel around from ward to ward and to vote several times under a series of assumed names. Casting 400 fraudulent votes, they had affected the outcome of the election in six different wards (*Tribune,* April 30, May 1, 7, 18, 1890). Moreover, in September 1890, the County Democratic Convention turned into a donnybrook of fists, brass knuckles, knives, and revolvers. In one of its strongest indictments of the "ruling race," the *Tribune* described the convention as "two packs fighting with each other in Tipperary fashion to get at the plunder" (Oct. 1, 1890).

Mr. Dunne and Mr. Dooley, a poster by William Nicholson advertising *Mr. Dooley's Philosophy,* a collection of Dunne's columns published in 1900. Chicago Historical Society.

"It seems to me, Hinnissy, that this here thing called bi-ography is a kind iv an offset f'r histhry. Histhry lies on wan side, an' bi-ography comes along an' makes it rowl over an' lie on th' other side. Th' historyan says, go up; th' bi-ographer says, come down among us. I don't believe ayether iv thim."

Left: Dearborn Street, Chicago, in 1892, the locale and date of Colonel McNeery, Dunne's first fictional Irish saloonkeeper. Chicago Historical Society.

Below: A view of the "White City," the World's Columbian Exposition of 1893, which marked Chicago's coming of age. Chicago Historical Society.

"But, faith, whin I'd been here a week, I seen that there was nawthin' but mud undher th' pavement—I larned that be means iv a pick-axe at tin shillin's th' day—an' that, though there was plenty iv goold, thim that had it were froze to it."

Fire Marshall Denis J. Swenie, apotheosized at the height of his long career. Painted in 1899 by F. L. Van Ness. One of the city's most admired men, Swenie, an Irish immigrant, was a Chicago fireman from 1850 to 1901. Chicago Historical Society.

"They'se an Irishman 'r two on th' fire departmint an' in th' army, too, Jawn, though ye'd think be hearin' some talk they was all runnin' prim'ries an' thryin' to be cinthral comitymen. So ye wud. Ye niver hear iv thim on'y whin they die; an' thin, murther, what funerals they have!"

St. Patrick's Church in Chicago's Irish West Side in a
nineteenth-century picture. Dunne was born across the street
and baptized in St. Patrick's in 1867. Hull-House Collection.

The Holy Family football team in 1895. Hull-House Collection.
"Downtown it's football," says Mr. Dooley. "Out here it's
the Irish killin' each other."

A parish parade and parochial school graduation in a Chicago Irish neighborhood. Hull-House Collection.

Scene from a Chicago parish theatrical production of the 1890s. Hull-House Collection.

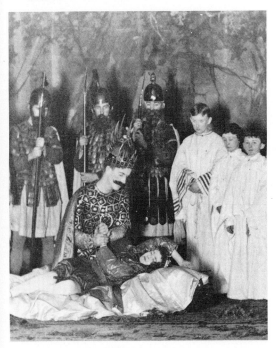

" 'Twas a gr-rand fair. They had Roddy's Hibernyun band playin' on th' cor-rner an' th' basemint iv th' church was packed. In th' ba-ack they had a shootin' gall'ry where ye got five shots f'r tin cints. . . . Thin they was a thrajeedy an' all th' lads took th' parts iv play-acthors."

Archer Avenue, Bridgeport, in 1885. Dunne placed Mr. Dooley's saloon here in the heart of Chicago's Irish working-class community. Chicago Historical Society.

Regan's Tavern on South Halsted St., Bridgeport, in the 1880s. A shop such as this may have served as the model for Mr. Dooley's saloon. Chicago Historical Society.

Michael "Hinky Dink" Kenna and Johnny Powers, Chicago
aldermen and two of the most visible Irish political
"boodlers" of the 1890s. Hull-House Collection.

A Chicago firehouse, proudly displaying its two engines and teams,
some time in the 1890s. Hull-House Collection.

A Chicago street scene in a working-class neighborhood such as Bridgeport, probably in the 1890s. Hull-House Collection.

"Th' elictric ca-ars go singin' by an' th' air is filled with th' melody iv goats an' cur dogs. . . . Occasin'lly I hear a tugboat cooin' to its mate an' now an' thin a pathrol wagon flits by on its errand iv love. At night th' tired but unhappy lab'rers rayturns fr'm their tile an' th' air is laden with th' cheery perfume iv bilin' cabbage."

In the spring of 1892, the *Herald* reported the continuation of hostilities—at least in Bridgeport—this time between Irish and German political armies engaged in a battle for sixth ward alderman. All over Bridgeport there were skirmishes between torch-carrying supporters of incumbent Eddie Burke and challenger Henry Stuckart, and "the enlisted men in both parties were hopeful of beating each other with the lard oil torches before midnight" (April 5, 1892). In that hotly contested race, "every man, woman, and child in the sixth ward [was] for Burke or Stuckart, and wildly for him," according to the *Herald,* and groups of children, saloonkeepers and their patrons, even a streetcar conductor and driver, had come to blows before the election was over.[12]

And yet Mr. Dooley draws his fond memories of tough Chicago politics, complete with torchlight parades, from his own experience as a Bridgeport precinct captain, dated by Dunne as 1873–1875.[13] Especially detailed is the piece that appeared just before the municipal election of April 1895, in which the unsuccessful Republican mayoral candidate was Frank Wenter, a Bohemian-American:

> "Ilictions ain't what they was, Jawn. Runnin' a Bohemian f'r office! Why, whin I was takin' a hand in politics an' captain iv me precinct, with conthrol iv two shut-off min an' half th' r-rid bridge, 'twas th' proud boast iv th' pa-arty that th' Bohemian vote cud be got to a man be promisin' wan Bohemian to let him go downtown an' look at th' lake. 'Twas so. . . . 'Tis no time iv year to be talkin' politics, an' annyhow politics ain't what they was, Jawn. I've sold nothin' all day but a bottle iv pop, an' I've had so manny pictures iv candydates in th' window that I've had to light th' gas at noon.
>
> "D'ye suppose in th' old days I cud've hung thim posters without a rite [riot]? I sh'd say not."

As his example, Mr. Dooley uses another Irish-German contest. (Not surprisingly, the opposition of Chicago's two largest and best established immigrant groups had been a feature of local politics for years.)

> "I mind whin Eddie O'Reilly an' Schultze was runnin'. Torchlight procission iv'ry night. O'Reilly'd 've won if they hadn't let th' Dutchman's lads vote fr'm th' 'ospital. But annyhow, I had up a picture iv O'Reilly in th' window, whin in come little Slatthery. D'ye mind him? He was a nervous little la-ad fr'm th' County Kerry. . . . 'What have ye th' face iv that man frightenin' away custom f'r?' he says. 'Who?'

says I. 'O'Reilly,' says he. 'What's th' matther with O'Reilly?' says I. 'He's no good,' says he. 'He throws down all his frinds,' says he. 'But th' other man's Dutch,' says I. 'Naw he ain't,' says he. 'He's marrid wan iv Doherty's daughters,' he says. 'An' if Prince Bismark was to marry an Irish girl,' says he, 'he'd be th' head cinter iv th' fanians [Fenians] within wan month.' 'I guess ye'er right,' says I. So I took down O'Reilly an' put up Schultze. I'd no more thin turned me back whin bang! come a brick through th' window. I wint out, an' there was th' prisident, secrity, an' thre-asurer iv th' Eddie O'Reilly Lith'ry Club thryin' to pry up th' sthreet f'r ammunition.

"Now look at it. I aven put up a picture iv th' prohibition candydate an' no one set fire to th' house. Little Cassidy come in here yesterday, an', says he, 'Who's all thim ye have in th' window?' he says. 'Thim befure-an-afther-takin' pictures?' says he. 'Thim 'r th' candydates f'r mayor,' I says. 'Are they?' says he. 'They's always some wan runnin' f'r something,' he says. 'Ain't they?' he says. 'Give me a glass iv beer—a high wan,' he says. An' I've seen that man r-run fr'm th' bridge to th' mills with a ballot-box under his ar-rm fr'm th' pure love iv th' thing.

"Why on'y this afthernoon I met Willum Joyce walkin' down th' sthreet, doin' what? R-readin' a book, no less. D'ye think he'd 've done that tin years ago three days befure iliction? I've seen him goin' downtown settin' on th' flure iv th' car."

Mr. Dooley brushed away a tear and counted up.

[*EP,* March 30, 1895]

Actually, the election of April 1895 was far from quiet. There were stabbings, shootings, and full saloons, and the *Evening Post* deplored editorially both the conditions and the results, pointing to the lavish use of whiskey and money to buy votes, and tallying the final score at "for boodle—45, against boodle—23" in the new council (*EP,* April 2, 1895). These grave editorial judgments clearly belie Mr. Dooley's teary nostalgia on the same occasion.

In the same way, his response to the previous year's equally chaotic municipal election diverges from the tone and concerns of the *Post* editorial page. In February 1894, a citizens' organization for clean government, the Civic Federation, was founded, and the *Post* gave it strong support, with daily editorials condemning boodle candidates and dishonest election practices. Just before the April election, the *Post* singled out the sixth ward as having the worst lineup of election judges in the city, including men previously convicted of arson, assault, robbery, stuffing ballot boxes, picking pockets, and horse-stealing

(March 27, 1894). The election itself was distinguished by two shootings, more than forty cases of assault, indictments for election fraud in four wards, and the return to the council of such notorious boodlers as "Bathhouse John" Coughlin in the first ward.[14] To all of this, Mr. Dooley was strangely oblivious, for he declared on the Saturday after the election that "politics don't intherest me no more. They ain't no liveliness in thim." He proceeds to illustrate this point with a proud recollection of his own complicity in election tampering:

> "Whin Andy Duggan r-run f'r aldherman against Schwartzmeister, th' big Dutchman,—I was precinct captain then, Jawn,—there was an iliction f'r ye. 'Twas on our precinct they relied to ilict Duggan; f'r th' Dutch was sthrong down be th' thrack, an' Schwartzmeister had a band out playin' 'Th' Watch on th' Rhine.' Well, sir, we opened th' polls at six o'clock, an' there was tin Schwartzmeister men there to protect his intherests. At sivin o'clock there was only three, an' wan iv thim was goin' up th' sthreet with Hinnissy kickin' at him. At eight o'clock, be dad, there was on'y wan; an' he was sittin' on th' roof iv Gavin's blacksmith shop, an' th' la-ads was thryin' to borrow a laddher fr'm th' injine-house f'r to get at him. . . .
>
> "We cast twenty-wan hundhred votes f'r Duggan, an' they was on'y five hundhred votes in th' precinct. We'd cast more, but th' tickets give out. They was tin votes in th' box f'r Schwartzmeister whin we counted up; an' I felt that mortified I near died, me bein' precinct captain, an' responsible. 'What'll we do with thim?' says Dorsey th' plumber. 'Throw thim out th' window,' says I. Just thin Dorsey's nanny-goat that died next year put her head through th' dure. 'Monica,' says Dorsey (he had pretty names for all his goats), 'Monica, are ye hungry,' he says, 'ye poor dear.' Th' goat give him a pleadin' look out iv her big brown eyes. 'Can't I make ye up a nice supper?' says Dorsey. 'Do ye like paper?' he says. 'Would ye like to help desthroy a Dutchman,' he says, 'an' perform a sarvice f'r ye'er counthry?' he says. Thin he wint out in th' next room, an' come back with a bottle iv catsup; an' he poured it on th' Schwartzmeister ballots, an' Monica et thim without winkin'."　　[*EP*, April 7, 1894][15]

It seems to me that in these pieces Dunne's desire to capture the unique flavor of election day in an Irish ward far outweighed his concern for the crises and challenges of the actual political situation in Chicago. Rather than making Mr. Dooley a voice for reform, Dunne used the persona to describe a phenomenon still very much in evidence but one whose life would not be long. As the contemporary newspaper reports demonstrate, the old days were not yet gone; but in setting Mr. Dooley's renderings of rough-and-tumble electioneering in the past, Dunne was able to sanction more easily his fascination with the customs of people who were willfully, if vibrantly, corrupt.

In 1896 and 1897, however, Mr. Dooley did deal directly with the aldermanic elections, though very differently each year. In 1896, he throws his weight behind the Municipal Voters' League, another citizens' group that had been established in January in response to the passage in council of a particularly blatant boodle ordinance. A week before the April election, the League issued a detailed scorecard on all candidates for alderman, rating them overall as "good, indifferent, or very, very bad." Mr. Dooley predicts defeat for the worst candidates, "fourteen as good lads as iver swung a lead pipe in a yarn stockin' or shelled an overcoat pocket," and he isolates three of the "very, very bad" for special attention:

> "Will Colvin go back, d'ye think, an' little Mike Ryan an' Jawnny Powers? Oh, there'd be th' crowd iv honest an' upright min to r-run th' city. . . . What'd th' iv-ryday, hard-wurrukin' aldherman that's busy fr'm morn to night stealin' annything fr'm a milk can to a mile iv paved sthreet, what'd he do with thim three buckos runnin' th' machine? I tell ye, it'll be a ha-ard winter f'r th' poor but dishonest gazabo if they break in. . . . I view with alarm th' threatened impoverishment iv th' fink aldhermin if th' Big Three take hold."
>
> [*EP*, April 4, 1896]

The *Times-Herald* (Dunne was on its editorial staff now) kept up a barrage of daily editorials aimed at the boodlers throughout the month of March, and the results, for once, seemed encouraging. Twenty-one of the thirty-three M.V.L.-endorsed candidates were elected, and the *Times-Herald* estimated that the new council would probably line up 37–31 against boodle ordinances (*T-H*, April 5-8, 1896). As for the "Big Three," Colvin and Ryan lost to League candidates, and although Powers was returned, his majority was 1,000 votes less than it had been two years earlier.

A year later, these ostensible gains were dramatically reversed in an exciting election to which Dunne responded with one of his longest sustained performances—a series of four Dooley pieces focused emphatically on exposure of municipal corruption. Curiously, though, these same pieces reveal sharply two major weaknesses of the Dooley persona as a vehicle of reform: Dunne's congenital pessimism about social change through political means, and his insider's sympathy for the Irish-American politician as the product of a harsh environment with few viable options for escape.

The great issue before the public in April 1897 was the vast and frightening influence on Chicago and Illinois politics of streetcar magnate Charles Tyson Yerkes. Immortalized as the protagonist of Theodore Dreiser's Cowperwood trilogy, Yerkes was a giant among the robber barons, a ruthless promoter who, since his arrival in Chicago in 1881, had wrestled his way to control of the city's entire streetrailway system.[16] Now a bill lay on the floor of the state legislature that if passed would turn the streets of Chicago over to the existing streetcar companies (that is, to Yerkes) for the next forty years. Even getting such a bill to the floor was an awesome accomplishment, and passage was a real possibility, despite the clamoring of every major Chicago newspaper that this was the worst and most audacious boodle ordinance ever conceived in the city.

Concurrently, Carter Harrison, Jr., was nominated as Democratic candidate for mayor, apparently on the basis of his father's name and the promise, as the *Times-Herald* put it, of a return to "public gambling, all-night saloons, a political police force, the spoils system, no compensation for franchises, and extravagance in city affairs" (March 13, 1897). It was widely believed also that young Harrison was intimately associated with Charles T. Yerkes. Worse still, the opposition vote was almost hopelessly divided between Judge Nathaniel Sears, the regular Republican nominee, and John M. Harlan, a reform alderman, son of a U. S. Supreme Court justice, and the Municipal Voters' League choice, running on the "Citizens' Party" ticket. In addition, five other men had insisted on entering the race, the best known of whom was Washington Hesing, owner-editor of the influential German-language newspaper, the *Illinois Staats-Zeitung*, and former postmaster of Chicago.

This was the situation on March 27 when Mr. Dooley declared his candidacy for mayor. Refusing "to stay at home hidin' me lights undher this bar whin a majority iv me fellow citizens is proposin' to emolyate thimsilves on th' althar iv our beloved city," Dooley articu-

lates a tongue-in-cheek platform of direct appeal to the business interests of the community—"I don't mean th' business intherests in
Janooary, whin th' rayform banquets ar-re held, but th' business intherests in March, just befure th' iliction.

> In th' first place I'm f'r that gran' old man Yerkuss. I am aware bad
> things are said about him be people that ride on his sthreet-cars, but
> ye must admit that he's done manny things f'r th' divilopmint iv this
> gr-reat an' growin' city. I believe in encouragin' him, f'r he carries
> th' prosperity iv Chicago on his shoulders, an' 'tis betther to give him
> more sthreets than to make him take thim away fr'm us with an ax. If
> I am mayor I pledge mesilf to give Yerkuss anything he wants—at
> rejooced rates."   [*EP,* March 27, 1897]

Dooley's pro-business platform includes other planks too: fair tax
assessments, "provided th' rale esthate boord an' th' capitalists don't
have to pay thim"; civil service reform, "afther I've put me own people
in office"; clean streets, "provided no taxes is paid f'r to clean them.
. . . Instead iv hirin' men an' puttin' sweepers to wurruk I'll organize
prayer meetins to pray f'r rain"; and gambling reform—"I wud rigidly
rigulate it to th' downtown sthreets, where it wud help th' business
intherests iv this gr-reat an' growin' city iv ours." Now it may be
argued that Dunne designed this sarcastic platform to direct attention
and votes to a sincerely reformist candidate such as Harlan, who had
no ties to the "business intherests"; but he has chosen a curiously
negative approach, for the message here is really Mr. Dooley's mockery of the hypocrisy of campaign promises in general, and his cynical
tone is killing to reform.

The following week Dooley reiterates his platform and his support
of Yerkes, promising, if elected, "to deliver over a blanket morgedge
on th' town to that saint on earth th' Sthreet Ca-ar Magnum," and
praising Yerkes's practical approach to political life: "They's no frills
on this great an' good philanthropist. He searches out th' hear-rts iv
men an' whin he finds thim r-rings thim up. Ye can't deceive a lad
that meets Virtue whin it comes f'r a dividend an' that knows where
th' rayform ilimint does its bankin'." However, Mr. Dooley then
proceeds to praise Harlan's candidacy in earnest:

> "A man comes along with a fair front concealin' th' divilish purpose
> iv givin' th' people iv this city a chanst f'r their lives—wan chanst in

tin thousand f'r to lift their heads an' thank th' Lord f'r livin'. He
wants to make it so a man can go to th' city hall to pay his taxes
without havin' his pocket picked. He wants to write acrost th' page,
dark with bloodshed an' plunder, wan line iv goold that our childher
—ye'ers, not mine, f'r I have none, thank th' Lord—can r-read
without shame. An' people believe in him, an' crowd to hear him,
an' cheer him, an' bid him good luck. But not th' Sthreet Ca-ar
Magnum. Thank th' saints f'r wan man clear-sighted enough to
pinithrate human motives. Thank th' Lord f'r th' crooked yardstick.
Th' Sthreet Ca-ar Magnum says: 'He's a fraud an' an ass.' A fraud
an' an ass!" [17]

Dooley's sarcasm here is heavy and strained almost to the breaking
point, and it crumbles into a disturbing sincerity when he continues
this line of thought:

"An' mebbe he is, too. An ass, anyhow, to think that annything can be done that th' Sthreet Ca-ar Magnum doesn't write
"eempreematoor" in, like an archbishop in a caddychism. Th'
on'y candydate that has a r-right to live is th' wan that turns in
his platform like a thrip-sheet iv a conductor f'r th' Sthreet Ca-ar
Magnum to approve. An' th' Sthreet Ca-ar Magnum knows his business. He has what th' pa-apers calls 'th' key iv th' situation.' I butt
up again a man on th' sthreet an' he falls again another man an'
that man reels again you, Hinnissy, walkin' along th' curb, ca'm an'
peaceful, an' out ye go into th' mud. I don't like Schwartzmeister—
an' I don't—an' I heave a rock through his window, an' lo! an' be-
hold, I hit me cousin Mike standin' at th' ba-ar takin' his quiet dhrink.
I go out to make th' Sthreet Ca-ar Magnum give back part iv what
he took, an' th' first thing I know me banker that has his bonds
piled up like cordwood in his safe tells me to take th' little account
that I'm savin' against license day around th' corner an' lave it in
th' ash bar'l. Th' crow is up in th' three, no doubt, black an' ugly,
stealin' me potatoes an' makin' me life miserable with his noise, but
whin I throw a club at him he's out iv th' way an' it smashes into
a nest full iv eggs that some frind of mine has been hatchin' out.
    "An' that's why I'm th' sthreetcar candydate. I believe in th'
Magnum. I am in favor iv corruption an' bribery, f'r 'tis on'y be
means iv thim we can live comfortably, die happy an' dhraw inthrest.
Virtue is shovellin' coal at a dollar-an'-a-half a day."

[*EP*, April 3, 1897]

The notes of cynicism and despair are overwhelming here. There
seems to be no clean, equitable way to cut through the mess and

tangle of self-serving and selfless interests in big city politics, and we are left with only a bitter taste and nowhere to turn for redress of wrongs. It is just this hopelessness about the political process, grounded, to be sure, in Dunne's own experience of Chicago, that unfits Mr. Dooley for the role of reformer.

Unfortunately for Chicago, the election on Tuesday corroborated Dunne's Saturday pessimism. Carter Harrison won a landslide victory, and a safe majority of known boodlers was returned to the council. And because the vote was the heaviest ever in a city election—a 90 percent turnout—the newspapers saw it as a mandate for corruption.[18] At the end of the week, Mr. Dooley explained the election as a product of the combined stupidity of the electorate and the reformers. He discovers that one of his patrons, Dugan, a pick-and-shovel laborer, had thought he was voting for Carter Harrison's father:

> " 'I voted f'r Charter Haitch,' says he. 'I've been with him in six ilictions, an' he's a good man,' he says. 'D'ye think ye're votin' f'r th' best?' says I. 'Why, man alive,' I says, 'Charter Haitch was assassinated three years ago,' I says. 'Was he?' says Dugan. 'Ah, well, he's lived that down be this time. He was a good man,' he says.
>
> "Ye see, [Dooley continues] that's what thim rayform lads wint up again."

Dooley then goes on to indict the reformers for their blindness to the very existence of the working-class electorate, citing in contrast the perspicacity of Bridgeport's Billy O'Brien, who had just been reelected to the council after a stint as state senator.

> "If I liked rayformers, Hinnissy, an' wanted f'r to see thim win out wanst in their lifetime, I'd buy thim each a suit iv chilled steel, ar-rm thim with raypeatin' rifles, an' take thim east iv State Sthreet an' south iv Jackson Bullyvard. At prisint th' opinion that pre-vails in th' ranks iv th' gloryous ar-rmy iv ray-form is that there ain't anny-thing worth seein' in this lar-rge an' commodyous desert but th' pest-house an' the bridewell. Me frind Willum J. O'Brien is no ray-former. But Willum J. undherstands that there's a few hundherds iv thousands iv people livin' in a part iv th' town that looks like nawthin' but smoke fr'm th' roof iv th' Onion League Club [the Union League, an exclusive Chicago men's club] that have on'y two pleasures in life, to wur-ruk an' to vote, both iv which they do at th' uniform rate iv wan dollar an' a half a day. That's why Willum

J. O'Brien is now a sinitor an' will be an aldherman afther next Thursday, an' it's why other people are sinding him flowers."

Finally, Dooley presents a parable of the election just past. "Th' boys down town" decide that "th' time has come f'r good citizens f'r to brace up an' do somethin'." They agree to nominate "Willie Boye" as a reform candidate for alderman, and to "set th' alar-rm clock f'r half-past three on th' afthernoon iv iliction day, so's to be up in time to vote f'r th' riprisintitive iv pure gover'mint." Then they sit back in the "Onion League Club" and wait for election day.

> " 'Tis some time befure they comprehind that there ar-re other candydates in th' field. But th' other candydates know it. Th' sthrongest iv thim—his name is Flannigan, an' he's a re-tail dealer in wines an' liquors, an' he lives over his establishment. Flannigan was nomynated enthusyastically at a prim'ry held in his bar-rn; an' befure Willie Boye had picked out pants that wud match th' color iv th' Austhreelyan ballot this here Flannigan had put a man on th' day watch, tol' him to speak gently to anny raygistered voter that wint to sleep behind th' sthove, an' was out that night visitin' his frinds. Who was it judged th' cake walk? Flannigan. Who was it carrid th' pall? Flannigan. Who was it sthud up at th' christening? Flannigan. Whose ca-ards did th' grievin' widow, th' blushin' bride-groom, or th' happy father find in th' hack? Flannigan's. Ye bet ye'er life. Ye see Flannigan wasn't out f'r the good iv th' community. Flannigan was out f'r Flannigan an' th' stuff." [*EP*, April 10, 1897]

Naturally, however self-motivated, Flannigan's solicitude for his pro-spective constituents wins him the election—easily—as it did, by im-plication, for Carter Harrison, Jr., William J. O'Brien, and the rest of the boodlers. And again, Dunne has described the workings of ward politics so compellingly and with such a sense of logical inevi-tability that any impetus he might have felt to change the system is drained from the piece.

The last piece in this four-part series brings out Dunne's second major weakness as a reformer: his sympathy for the Irish-American politician. The piece is a biographical sketch of Bridgeport alderman Thomas Reed,[19] and it opens with a compassionate picture of his father, "a man fr'm th' wist iv Ireland, a har-rd wur-rkin', quite, stoop-shouldhered man, that slept tin hours a night an' wurrked twelve a day and put in th' other two eatin' food that didn't always agree with him. He wint to his jooty reg'lar an' whin he died had a large an' continted fun'ral." The young Reed

> "played in th' sthreets night an' day an' was dhragged to school be th' ear iv'ry month or so. He seemed to be a dacint enough little thing as kids go till he begun to dhrift down to'rd Halsted sthreet an' r-run with th' gang iv big boys. Thin th' polis got to layin' hands on him an' 'twas a crool thing to see a big copper comin' up th' sthreet with little Tom be th' coat collar, him cryin' an' screamin' an' bringin' all th' women to th' dure to cur-rse th' polis foorce."

Eventually, the boy is sent to reform school for petty theft, "where he added pickin' pockets to his other accomplishments," and graduates to a career that encompasses "annything fr'm dhrunk an' disorderly to poundin' in a man's head with a brick." It is this reputation that gets him into politics, for "long befure he was a voter . . . he was considered handy at th' primaries." After performing various services for the ward leaders, Reed makes his strongest political move: "He had a change iv hear-rt and he see a gr-reat light an' he opened a saloon an' gamblin'-house." Soon he has his own built-in following and, in due time, the aldermanic nomination:

> "Ye know his record since. He's got rich an' powerful. He on'y comes in th' ward th' week befure iliction. He gives liberal to th' poor, he keeps his horses, he wears a diamond as big as an inkstand an' almost anny day ye'er lible to see him an' th' prisidint iv th' sthreet ca-ar comp'ny ar-rm-in-ar-rm."   [*EP*, April 17, 1897]

Until he enters politics, Reed's career is identical with that of Petey Scanlan, the young criminal in the tragic Dooley piece discussed earlier. Dunne's feel for the grim realities of the culture of poverty, for the context that explains, though it can never justify, a career such as Reed's, runs counter to the simplistic moralizing mind of the professional reformer.

The treatments by Editor Dunne and Mr. Dooley of the aldermanic election of 1898 provide one of the clearest examples of their nearly schizophrenic split on certain issues, and a kind of crystallization of their thinking about politics. In January 1898, Jane Addams began a serious effort to unseat the Hull-House representative in the city council, who was none other than the notorious Johnny Powers. The saloon-keeping partner of William J. O'Brien, "Johnny de Pow" served a total of thirty-eight years (1888–1927) as nineteenth ward alderman and acknowledged "prince of boodle" in Chicago. Because by 1898 he was well established as the city's most visible symbol of municipal corruption, the Municipal Voter's League and the press of Chicago ranged themselves solidly behind the Hull-House campaign to replace him with a reform alderman.[20]

Around this time, Peter Dunne made his final job change in Chicago—to the *Journal* as managing editor with charge of the editorial page.[21] There the policy on the Powers issue consisted of repeated, emphatic denunciations of the man and everything he stood for. The *Journal* editorial of January 17, early in the campaign, is typical. In it, the writer sees "the roots of political corruption in city, state, and national government" in "the rank soil of ward politics," and especially in the nineteenth Chicago ward, "one of the strongholds of corruption in this city." He goes on to outline the machinery of the boss system as manipulated by Powers. Until very recently, ward nineteen has been "well under control of the bosses, who were well under control of the corrupting, illegal, privilege-buying corporations." The machine ran on patronage ("that is, the handing out of public jobs in return for ward work, with no regard to the efficiency or honesty of the appointee"), and on fear ("a great many poor people . . . could easily be made to feel dependence on the boss, and terror of him as a vague and hence greatly to be feared power"). "But," the editorial continues, "a different attitude is beginning to manifest itself in the Nineteenth. The shams and pretenses of the crocodile martyr boss are beginning to show through." (Powers often bemoaned adverse criticism.) "The people have had their attention called to the shameless disposal of franchises and to other abuses by the council gang, and they have been compelled to notice Ald. Powers."

Encouraged by the growing strength of Powers's opposition in the ward, the *Journal* writer sees the possibility of defeating him in April, toward which end he issues an earnest plea, couched in a rhetoric of uplift for which Mr. Dooley could have had only scorn:

> If one of the worst members that ever sat in the Chicago common council can be overthrown in his own stronghold, it will show most encouraging gains for decency, intelligence, and good government.

It will show that the cause of decency, intelligence, and good government is gaining ground at an astonishing rate in a most unpromising locality.

If only for this reason it should be supremely a matter of pride for the people of the Nineteenth to dig a deep, deep political grave for Weeping Johnny, tumble his political corpse into it, and roll stones on the top.

But there is the additional reason that the political funeral of Johnny Powers will be one of the most encouraging events to the friends of reform that ever occurred in the history of this city. . . . It would give Chicago new hope, new courage, new pride. It would be a victory worth achieving, worth praising, worth the gratitude of the entire respectable city toward the free voters of the Nineteenth Ward.[22]

Two days earlier, Mr. Dooley had spoken out on the Powers issue from a radically different position:

"I'm not settin' up nights wishin' f'r th' desthruction iv Jawnny Powers an' th' likes iv him. I've knowed Jawnny f'r manny years, iver since he come here fr'm Waterford, with a face on him f'r all th' wurruld like th' flap iv a envelope, an' wint to wurruk in th' grocery store down be Jefferson an' Harrison sthreet. He was a smooth little lad an' bimeby he marrid th' lady what ownded th' store an' wint into politics.

"I don't believe they was anny reason in Jawnny Powers' eddication f'r to think that he'd throw away money because iv his conscience throublin' him. Th' place he lived in was th' toughest on earth. They was hardly a house around that didn't shelter a man that was able to go out anny night with half a brick or th' end iv a bullyard cue an' arn his daily bread. Acrost fr'm where he sold groceries was Law avnoo, a sthreet that no polisman iver enthered an' come out with a whole skin. Back iv him was Sebor sthreet, where th' Cashin twins used f'r to burn th' path-rol boxes, an' a few blocks west 'twas a sthrange night whin ye cudden't hear Chick McMillan's big revolever roarin' like a batthry iv artillry."

The facts of Powers's immigration and environment are accurate. Just as he did with Tom Reed, Mr. Dooley has placed John Powers sympathetically, in a context that goes a long way toward explaining his subsequent conduct as an alderman. Moreover, Dooley goes on to suggest that large-scale municipal corruption flows from the council to the ward, not in the other direction:

"They raise no saints in that part iv th' nineteenth ward, an' they was nawthin' Jawnny Powers seen afther he got into th' council that'd make him think th' worse iv Alick Swan iv Law Avnoo. He didn't meet so manny men that'd steal a ham an' thin shoot a polisman over it. But he met a lot that'd steal the whole West Side iv Chicago an' thin fix a gr-rand jury to get away with it. It must've been a shock to Jawnny Powers, thim first two years in th' council. Think iv this quite, innocent little grocery-man that knew no thieves but thim that lurked along alleys with their hats pulled over their eyes, bein' inthrojooced to bigger thieves that stole in th' light iv day, that paraded their stovepipe hats an' goold watches an' chains in Mitchigan avnoo."

Dooley then details Powers's "education" into the council, which involves his having to unlearn the naive notions that "whin a man dhresses dacint he's respectible an' whin he has money he won't steal," and that "th' la-ads that presided over th' municipyal purity meetin's was on th' square." At this point, Hennessy injects an uncommonly bright remark: "Somethin' ought to be done to rayform th' rayformers." Dooley agrees, and suggests a two part organization to do just that. One part, with branches "in ivry church an' charitable society in Chicago an' in ivry club," would watch out to expose the hypocrisy of "anny man that abuses Jawnny Powers an' Yerkuss while buyin' th' wan an' guaranteein' th' bonds iv th' other." The second part would be a kind of Hull-House in reverse, a "social colony" to be placed "down town near th' banks an' th' boord iv thrade an' th' stock exchange," where leading citizens could come and be instructed in the mores of the culture of poverty. Dooley explains his solicitude for the rich with pointed irony:

"I think th' Hull House idee is right, but I'd apply it diff'rent. A man wurrukin' in a bank all day thryin' to get money anny way he can, how's he goin' to know anny diff'rent? What he needs is to be cheered up, have th' pianny played to him be nice-lookin' girls, an' find out somethin' iv th' beauties iv honest poverty be convarsin' with poor an' honest people." [*EP,* Jan. 15, 1898]

Mr. Dooley thus takes the side of Powers against the hypocritical mugwump reformers from "down town," many of whom, he suspects, profit from the corruption that they publicly deplore. (The Civic Federation was led by Lyman J. Gage, a prominent Chicago banker and later secretary of the treasury under McKinley.) In this response Dooley is a Bridgeport Irishman through and through, for protecting one's own is the natural reaction of a community member to criticism from outside. That Dunne could so totally contradict his new employer's editorial position demonstrates how deeply he has imagined the Dooley persona and controlled it artistically.

Another accomplishment of the Dooley political pieces is the creation as rounded characters of politicians such as John Powers and William J. O'Brien. We already knew quite a bit about Powers; his long tenure in the council, his running feud with Hull-House, and his natural flamboyance made him a favorite with the newspapermen. (He once incensed the entire city by declaring himself unbeatable because "I have 750 saloons at my back. It is true you have the church and the press. But the people of the nineteenth ward are a people that are governed by saloons—not by the church—not by the press. I am as good as elected now" [*Tribune,* April 1, 1890]. He was, of course, right.) But Billy O'Brien exists for us only because of Dunne's efforts to establish him as the essential Bridgeport politician. I can find nothing about O'Brien in the various Chicago biographical dictionaries, despite the fact that some of them are specifically slanted toward politics, Democrats, and Irish-Americans. Yet he was a real person who served three terms in the city council as Bridgeport's alderman (1889–1893 and 1897–1899).[23]

Judging from the accuracy of Dunne's portrait of Powers, we can assume that he has also given us an honest look at O'Brien. "Willum J." is mentioned often in the Dooley pieces, but his personal success story is narrated in greatest detail during the exciting 1896 Democratic national convention in Chicago. In this piece, Hennessy confuses William J. with William Jennings Bryan, the Democratic presidential nominee, and begins to write a campaign biography for O'Brien. He reads some of it to Mr. Dooley:

"Willum J. O'Brien was born in th' County iv Mayo forty years ago. He received a limited education, his parents even thin designin' him f'r th' Prisidency. Bein' unable to complete a coorse at th' rayform school, he wint to wurruk; but soon, tired iv this, he started a saloon. Fr'm thince he dhrifted into politics, an' become noted as th' boy welter-weight iv th' South Branch. He was ilicted aldherman at a time whin comparatively nawthin' was doin' in th' council. Subsequent he become a sinitor, an' later enthered into partnership with th' Hon. Jawn Powers in th' retail liquor traffic. Mr. O'Brien is a fine built man, an' can lick anny wan iv his age west iv th' river, give 'r take tin pounds, color no bar. His heart beats up close to th' ribs iv th' common people, an' he would make opprissors iv th' poor wish they'd died early if ye give him a chance with a beer bottle." [*EP*, July 11, 1896]

O'Brien's life follows a familiar pattern of advancement from youthful hardship and humiliation to political power, a pattern which, whenever Dunne employs it, carries the implied question of alternatives. How many roads were open to a poor Irish boy in the 1860s and 1870s? There being no seats available on the stock exchange, wasn't politics preferable to being ground down in the mills and ditches and railroad beds? Johnny Powers's big break was marrying the boss's daughter; O'Brien's was discovering that his considerable physical toughness was an attribute in politics. And generally it is brute force, not intelligence or cunning, that provides Dunne's politicians with their first foothold on the ladder.

"Th' people up here likes spirit. How did Billy O'Brien hol' his own all these years but because he done dumb-bell exercise with a beer kag in wan hand an' a German polisman in th' other? How come Eddie Burke—may he rest in peace—to have th' ward f'r so long but because, bit iv a man that he was, with on'y th' leg iv a cuk stove in his hand, he wint through a roomful iv his innimies, back an' forward twict? Sure, politics ain't bean-bag. 'Tis a man's game, an' women, childer, cripples an' prohybitionists 'd do well to keep out iv it." [*EP*, Oct. 5, 1895]

Actually, O'Brien emerges as a kind of folk hero, holding his position against continual attack from pretenders to the throne by means of his legendary strength:

" 'Tis thrue, O'Broyn have bate near ivery wan wist iv Halsted street, but sure he's got to do that anyhow ivery month whether there do be an iliction on or not. He's a sthrong bit iv a la-ad, that there O'Broyn. He's a athlete, d'ye mind, Jawn. Whin he comes home at night th' first thing he does is to carry th' kitchen shtove up an' down th' house twinty-wan times. Thin he have a thrained goat that he got fr'm Doheny's shtud out be th' mills an' he spinds wan hour havin' th' goat butt him. Whin th' goat can't butt him har-rd enough to hurt it gets no supper. Thin he punches a cast-iron man, ates a light male an' goes out an' licks two polismin befure bedtime. He's thrained so much an' got so sthrong that if he loses th' money he's got an' laves pollytics he need niver look f'r a job. He can take th' place iv anny bridge hor-rse Yerkuss have." [*EP,* June 16, 1894]

O'Brien understands the system thoroughly, though, and he always runs a model campaign. First he gets the superintendent of the rolling mills on his side; then he puts "three or four good fam'lies" to work in the gashouse. He makes regular calls on "th' bar-rn boss iv th' sthreet-ca-ars." He goes to picnics, hires the orchestra for dances, gets himself voted the most popular man at the church fair "at an expinse iv at laste five hundherd dollars"; and finally he establishes headquarters "in ivry saloon fr'm wan end iv th' ward to th' other." After defeating a long-winded but insolvent reformer, O'Brien articulates the guiding principle of his political success: "th' roly-boly [bribe money] is th' gr-reatest or-rator on earth. . . . Th' American nation in th' Sixth Ward is a fine people. . . . They love th' eagle, on th' back iv a dollar" (*EP,* July 18, 1896). In the end, though, O'Brien always relies on his characteristic forthrightness. When a ward committee led by "Big Casey, th' house-mover" asks his opinion on "th' tariff, th' currency question, pensions, an' th' interstate commerce act," William J. answers with this classic distinction between platform issues and the realities of machine politics:

" 'Well, . . . th' issue on which I'm appealin' to th' free an' intilligent suffrages of Ar-rchey Road an' th' assistance iv Deerin' Sthreet Station,' he says, 'is whether little Mike Kelly will have th' bridge or not,' he says. 'On that I stand,' he says. 'As f'r th' minor issues,' he says, 'I may have me opinions on thim an' I may not. Anny information I possess I'll keep tucked away in this large an' commodjous mind cage, an' not be dealin' it out to th' likes iv ye, as though I was a comity iv th' Civic Featheration,' he says. 'Moreover,' he says, 'I'd like to know what in 'ell you, Casey, have got to do comin' roun' to my house and pryin' into my domestic affairs,' he says. ' 'Tis th' interstate commerce act now, but th' nex' thing'll be where I got th' pianny,' he says; an', f'r fear ye may not stop where ye are, here goes to mount ye.' An' he climbed th' big man, an' rolled him. Well sir will ye believe me, ivry man on th' comity but wan voted f'r him. Casey was still in bed iliction day.

"I met Tom Dorsey afther th' comity called [continues Dooley]. 'Well,' says I, 'I heerd ye was up to O'Brien's questionin' him on th' issues iv th' day,' I says. 'We was,' says he. 'Was his answers satisfacthry?' says I. 'Perfectly so,' he says. 'Whin th' comity left, we were all convinced that he was th' strongest man that cud be nommynated,' he says." [*EP*, May 16, 1896]

While O'Brien and Powers are presented humorously and even sympathetically, Mr. Dooley can also see the dark side of politics, and several of his political biographies are tragic. He remains consistent, however, in refusing to tell the sad stories at election time, when they could be construed as sell-outs to mugwump reformism. Blood is always thicker than the tie to Civic Federation liberalism. Moreover, when he does discuss the pernicious effects of political life, it is never the city as a whole that suffers: the tragedies are community affairs, affecting only Dooley's fellow Bridgeporters. Two examples will suffice, one involving a successful boss, the other, a losing candidate.

Tammany boss Richard Croker's flight to avoid prosecution prompted one of Dunne's most tragic political stories, in which a Bridgeport ward leader commits the unpardonable sin (as has Croker in Dooley's view) of turning against the community. Mr. Dooley recalls first seeing Boss Flannagan when "he'd th' smell iv Castle Garden on him, . . . an' he was goin' out with pick an' shovel f'r to dig in th' canal,—a big, sthrappin', black-haired lad, with a neck like a bull's an' covered with a hide as thick as wan's, fr'm thryin' to get a crop iv oats out iv a Clare farm that growed divvle th' thing but nice, big bolders." In a month Flannagan has licked every man in his section gang, including the boss; in a year "he was knowed fr'm wan end iv th' canal to th' other as th' man that no wan cud stand befure. He got so pop'lar fr'm lickin' all his frinds that he opened up a liquor store beyant th' bridge, an' wan night he shot some la-ads fr'm th' ya-ards that come over f'r to r-run him. That made him sthronger still." From this point Flannagan's rise is inexorable. He loads the ballot box and is voted most popular man in the parish, and goes on to become boss of the ward, with the aldermen serving as his minions. "He niver wint to th' council, d'ye mind; but, whin he was gin'rous, he give th' aldhermen tin per cint iv what they made." Growing rich, Flannagan builds a brick house, moves in a piano for his daughter, and wears "a dimon as big as ye'er fist." Next, he sells the liquor business and goes into real estate: "D'ye mind, Jawn," says Dooley, "that th' r-rale estate business includes near ivrything fr'm vagrancy to manslaughter." Then, "wan day without th' wink iv th' eye he moved up in th' avnoo [Michigan Avenue], an' no wan seen him in Bridgeport afther that." Rejecting the old neighborhood is, of course, the beginning of the end, which follows swiftly:

> " 'Twas a month or two later whin a lot iv th' la-ads was thrun into jail f'r a little diviltry they'd done f'r him. A comity iv th' fathers iv th' la-ads wint to see him. He raceived thim in a room as big as wan iv their whole houses, with pitchers on th' walls an' a carpet as deep an' soft as a bog. Th' comity asked him to get th' la-ads out on bail.
>
> " 'Gintlemen,' he says, 'ye must excuse me,' he says, 'in such matthers.' 'D'ye mane to say,' says Cassidy, th' plumber, 'that ye won't do annything f'r my son?' 'Do annything,' says Flannigan. (I'll say this f'r him: a more darin' man niver drew breath; an', whin his time come to go sthandin' off th' mob an' defindin' his sthone quarry in th' rites iv sivinty-siven, he faced death without a wink.) 'Do?' he says. 'Why,' he says, 'yes,' he says; 'I've subscribed wan thousand dollars,' he says, 'to th' citizen's comity,' he says, 'f'r to prosecute him; an',' he says, 'gintlemen,' he says, 'there's th' dure.'
>
> "I seen Cassidy that night, an' he was as white as a ghost. 'What ails ye?' says I. 'Have ye seen th' divvle?' 'Yes,' he says, bendin' his head over th' bar, an' lookin' sivinty years instead iv forty-five."
>
> [*EP*, May 12, 1894]

Flannagan's total corruption by politics has been established in the harshest terms known to the Irish. Forgetting the bog for the carpet, he has denied his own people and become a force for the dissolution of community.

The second piece tells the tragic story of "little Flannagan," a decent man ruined by misplaced political aspiration. Deceived by the idle predictions of his friends that he can win a seat in the state legislature, Flannagan quits his job, draws all his money from the bank, and even puts a mortgage on the house—all to further his campaign; while his friends insist that "ye'll get it all back th' first day in th' legis-lachure." The whole family begins to put on airs, as "night afther night ye'd see th' touchers comin' up to Flannagan's an' goin' away with th' little man an' him sthruttin' with his mass coat on his back an' his shtove-pipe on the side iv his head an' all th' fam'ly peekin' out iv th'

window at him. He'd come home singin' later." Election night finds
him a beaten and a ruined man, however, and we are left with another
of Mr. Dooley's striking images of the Irish-American as solitary
victim:

> "He wint to th' station iliction night f'r to hear th' returns. He
> come away early. 'Twas a raw night with a smother iv fog in th'
> sthreet but I see him comin' home, crouched down like with his
> coat wide open an' his hands be his side. They was lights in th'
> house but he wint around be th' back dure."

Flannagan's has been a family tragedy, so that once more we have
seen politics as destructive of community. In addition, this story is the
setting for a powerful, general condemnation of politics and politicians,
focused, as so often in the Dooley pieces, on the perennial sufferers
from deprivation, Bridgeport's women and children. Mr. Dooley is
recalling his own misspent youth as precinct captain:

> "But 'tis all th' game in politics, Jawn, tubby sure. Whin I was a
> young man there was no handier in th' precint with anny manes iv
> reform, fr'm a piece iv gaspipe in a stockin' to a speech to th' Ger-
> man voters. I was well liked be th' Germans in thim days, though
> they're again me now. I was always out peddlin' tickets an' bur-rnin'
> ballots f'r th' good iv th' cause. But the likin' lift me long ago, an'
> small loss. 'Tis all white stockin' an' no leg inside like th' Kilkenny
> girls. Bluff an' cheat. 'Good mornin', Casey, an' how's th' good
> woman' th' da-ay before iliction an' 'Th' 'ell with Casey' th' da-ay
> afther. Bad ciss to thim. They're howlin' about th' ol' flag an' th'
> rights iv workinmin at Finucane's an' down be th' slough th' women
> goes about with their feet thrippin' wan another an' th' childher's
> eyes gets bigger an' their faces smaller day be day. Dimmycrat or
> raypublican—what th' 'ell."   [*EP*, Oct. 27, 1894]

Dunne's refusal to write these sentiments at the behest of reformers
from outside the Irish community in no way mitigates the force of his
disillusionment and cynicism here.[24]

In addition to his descriptions of electioneering and political biography,
Mr. Dooley provides valuable first-hand insight into the functioning
and failures of big city government in the nineties. First of all, he
examines in detail the qualifications, duties, and privileges of a Chicago

alderman. The occasion is Hogan's attempt to decide whether his son should be a lawyer or a priest—the two most respectable paths to status in the community. Mr. Dooley emphatically sets him straight:

" 'Don't ye do it,' says I. 'There's priests an' lawyers enough,' I says, 'to sind two worlds to hell,' I says, 'an' get thim out again,' I says. 'Make him an aldherman,' I says. An' thin what d'ye think th' big fool asks me? 'Where can I find a school,' he says, 'to sind him to.' School, mind ye, Jawn. 'School,' says I. 'Faith, Hogan, if ye don't sind him to school at all, at all, he's sure,' I says, 'to be wan.'

"But 'tis thrue I've told ye there's no job like it. No work or worry. Nawthin' but to sit down with ye'er hat cocked over ye'er eye an' ye'er feet on a mahogany table, an' watch th' roly boly dhrop into ye'er mit. Th' most wurruk an aldherman has to do is to presint himself with a gold shtar wanst a year so he won't forget he's an aldherman. Whin he has th' shtar upon him he can go anny-where an' divvle th' cint to pay. 'Tis good f'r annything fr'm a ball to a christenin', an' by gar Billy O'Broyn wurrked it on th' church. He wint to mass over at Father Kelly's wan Sundah mornin' to square himsilf, an' whin Dinnis Nugent passed th' plate to him he showed th' shtar. 'Ar-re ye an aldherman?' says Nugent. 'I am that,' says O'Broyn. 'Thin,' says Nugent, stickin' th' plate undher his nose, 'thin,' he says, 'lave half f'r th' parish,' he says. Well, sir, O'Broyn was that mad he waited till afther mass an' he made Nugent ate th' 'Key iv Hiven' and four chapters in 'The Lives iv the Saints' in the vesthry."

Dooley then enumerates the fringe benefits of a seat in the council, which include free theater seats in the best location, meal tickets to all the banquets, hack rides in parades, and license to be as drunk and disorderly as you damn well please without fear of arrest, because "th' polisman that'd arrist an aldherman wouldn't get off short iv tin years." He summarizes neatly that

"Tis an iligant job. . . . Ye have nawthin' to worry ye. Whin ye'er hungry ye go to a bankit. Whin ye'er broke all ye have to do is to give something away that don't belong to ye. 'Tis th' only thrade left f'r a young man, an' I'm goin' to have Hogan begin tachin' his boy rough-an'-tumble fightin' to-morrow an' give him th' proper shtart."   [*EP,* Feb. 10, 1894]

As a retired politician, Mr. Dooley is privy to the complex dispen-sation of jobs and favors by which the spoils system perpetuates itself, and several pieces comment effectively on the procedure. For example,

even the Pope's elevation of Bishop Satolli to cardinal disturbs a misguided local job-seeker: " 'Th' 'ell he has,' says Hogan, sthrikin' th'
ba-ar. 'Thin, by dad, I'll niver vote f'r Casey again,' he says. 'He
promised that to me' " (*EP,* Jan. 12, 1895). Judging from the number
of references to it, the water office was the catch-all political employment vehicle, and bridgetenders and water inspectors were likely to be
friends and relatives of men currently in power. (As I mentioned earlier, the placement of a "Polack" on the red bridge signaled the decline
of Irish influence in Chicago.) Occasionally, these political appoint-
ments must have come back to haunt the dispensing angel, and Mr.
Dooley recalls some comical cases, such as the bridgetender who
complained to the mayor that whistling tugboats were keeping him
awake: " 'An' what do they be whistlin' f'r,' says th' Whole Thing.
'F'r me to open th' bridge an' let thim through,' says me brave Tom"
(*EP,* March 3, 1894). Or, better still, the water inspector who was
allergic to the element:

> "Jawn, I knowed a man named Hannigan, Francis Xavier Hannigan,
> a Wexford man, an' a bum be th' same token. Hahrson give him
> a job in th' wather office an' he was to be a wather inspector. Well,
> sir, d'ye suppose that Hannigan iver inspicted wather? Not be a
> dam sight. He avoided it. He used beer as th' chaser. I seen him
> hangin' round th' corner playin' forty-fives on th' top iv a bar'l an'
> dancin' jig stips an' says I: 'Hannigan' I says, 'why ain't ye down
> be th' city hall,' I says, 'inspictin' wather,' I says. 'I hear,' says I,
> 'there's microbes an' th' divvle knows what all in it,' says I. 'It
> needs to be sieved,' I says. 'Goowan now,' says he, 'an' mix me a
> proosic acid cocktail,' he says. 'I'm no ga-arden hose.' Well, sir,
> no wan in th' city hall iver see hide nor hair iv Hannigan excipt
> whin he'd dhrop in to get his letthers on Choosdahs, Thursdahs an'
> Saturdahs, an' he become that ins'lint he rayfused to sal-oot Willum
> Joyce whin he see him. Bedad, Willum didn't like that an' whin
> Hannigan fin'ly sint wurrud down to th' mayor to have his letthers
> fetched out to him they picked him up an' thrun him down, they
> did so, they did. Th' last I see iv him he was ma-archin' at th' hid
> iv a pro-cession carryin' a banner f'r 'We wants bread or wurruk.'
> Faith, Hannigan wanted nayther. What he wanted was jelly cake
> an' a foldin' bid."   [*EP,* Jan. 6, 1894]

To illustrate how the mayor's office and the city council work together to pass legislation, Mr. Dooley recalls an exchange between
Billy O'Brien and Mayor Carter Harrison, who, during his last ad-

ministration, wanted to install a garbage dump in Bridgeport. When O'Brien successfully blocks passage of Harrison's ordinance, all hell breaks loose. First, the mayor fires young Malachi Googin from his position as tender of the red bridge, and when old man Googin comes in to complain, Harrison blames Alderman O'Brien. Googin returns to Bridgeport "with tears in his eyes, swearin' vengeance," which turns out to be no idle threat, given the political leverage of the Googin family.

> "He was a strong man, that Googin. He had eight lads, all iv thim vote getters. Four iv thim worked in th' rollin' mills an' wan was conductor iv a street ca-ar. Th' oldest lad was marrid to Mary Haley, an' her father was foreman up in a packin' house an' voted two hundred Dutch. Thin Mrs. Googin, she that was O'Donnell, was related to th' Dorneys an' th' Coughlins, an' Tim Coughlin's youngest son was prisident iv th' young men's sodality. Ye knew th' Dorneys. They were th' best men that iver captained th' gashouse precinct, an' they had a pull like a bridge horse. Wan iv th' Dorney girls was marrid to th' liftnant at Deering sthreet an' another was sparkin' th' paymaster at th' ca-ar barns.
>
> "They was all fr'm th' war part iv May-o, an' whin Googin come home an' rayported what th' Main Guy told him 'twas like whin they used to spread th' light over beyant. First they formed th' Dennis Googin Anti-O'Brien Club an' then they formed th' County Mayo Phalanx, which was christened be Coughlin's kid, and they had eight hundred mimbers before Sundah. They put up a Dutchman named Schwartzmeister that kep' a beer cellar down be Halsted sthreet f'r alderman an' wint up in a body to burn O'Brien's bar-rn."
>
> [*EP*, Oct. 21, 1893]

Needless to say, the alderman gets the message and promises to change his vote on the garbage dump if only Mayor Harrison will "haul th' Googins off." The piece is a lesson on the way in which the density and cohesiveness of the Irish community operated as a formidable political force.

Citywide, and sometimes national, attention centered on the journeys through the council of large boodle ordinances. Every year or so a bill such as Yerkes's forty-year streetcar franchise request would come up, most often to be passed amid a loud and wholly ineffectual chorus of journalistic indignation.[25] In the midst of the controversy in December 1898 over a Yerkes-sponsored ordinance that would have extended the current street-railway franchises another fifty years, Mr. Dooley explained the distribution of boodle in the council:

> " 'Tis not, Hinnissy, that this man Yerkuss goes up to an aldherman an' says out sthraight, 'Here, Bill, take this bundle, an' be an infamyous scoundhrel.' That's th' way th' man in Mitchigan Avnoo sees it, but 'tis not sthraight. D'ye mind Dochney that was wanst aldherman here? Ye don't. Well, I do. He ran a little conthractin' business down be Halsted Sthreet. 'Twas him built th' big shed f'r th' ice comp'ny. He was a fine man an' a sthrong wan. He begun his political career be lickin' a plasthrer be th' name iv Egan, a man that had th' County Clare thrip an' was thought to be th' akel [equal] iv anny man in town."

Dochney beats up the first man who approaches him with a five thousand dollar bribe, but he listens to the second, who explains that support for the big companies is really support for "th' widdies an' orphans . . . that has their har-rd-earned coin invisted." He begins to ponder the problem:

> " 'Twas a shame to give th' comp'nies what they wanted, but th' five thousan' was a lot iv money. 'Twud lift th' morgedge. 'Twud clane up th' notes on th' new conthract. 'Twud buy a new dhress f'r Mrs. Dochney. He begun to feel sorrowful f'r th' widdies an' orphans. 'Poor things!' says he to himsilf, says he. 'Poor things, how they must suffer!' he says; 'an' I need th' money.' "

In the end, Dochney takes the bribe, and Mr. Dooley records his progressive moral decline and financial rise:

> "He begun missin' his [Catholic sacramental] jooty at wanst. Aldhermen always do that after th' first few weeks. 'Ye got ye'er money,' says Father Kelly; 'an' much good may it do ye,' he says. 'Well,' says Dochney, 'I'd be a long time prayin' mesilf into five thousan',' he says. An' he become leader in th' council. Th' las' ordhnance he inthrojooced was wan establishin' a license f'r churches, an' compellin' thim to keep their fr-ront dure closed an' th' blinds drawn on Sundah. He was expelled fr'm th' St. Vincent de Pauls, an' ilicted a director iv a bank th' same day."

Dooley has no reformist solution for this situation. Instead, he turns bitterly sarcastic:

"Now, Hinnissy, that there man niver knowed he was bribed—th' first time. Th' second time he knew. He ast f'r it. An' I wudden't hang Dochney. I wudden't if I was sthrong enough. But some day I'm goin' to let me temper r-run away with me, an' get a comity together, an' go out an' hang ivry dam widdy an' orphan between th' rollin' mills an' th' foundlin's' home. If it wasn't f'r thim ray-pechious crathers, they'd be no boodle annywhere."

[*Journal,* Dec. 17, 1898]

Mr. Dooley almost makes a run for alderman himself in 1896, backing off only after attending a city council meeting, which provides an example of aldermanic sophistry in the passage of boodle ordinances. Alderman Buck McCarthy introduces "an ord'nance givin' th' Internaytional Microbe Company a right to lay pipes an' pump microbes throughout the city." The seconding speech by a friend of McCarthy's parodies what must have been a familiar defense of boodle against legitimate payment to the city for franchises:

"'I want to say,' says another aldherman, 'that th' ord'nance is all right. While I feel that th' cramped condition iv th' city three-asury is such that some income might be exthracted fr'm th' company, still,' he says, 'I feel that it'd be a mistake,' he says, 'to put new burdens on an industhry that's conthri-buted so much to th' prosperity iv this gr-reat an' imperyal city,' he says. 'Look,' he says, 'at our audjiotorums an' our a-art institoots an' our Columbus mony-mints an' our other pinal institutions,' he says. 'Look at our bridewell an' our insane asylum,' he says. 'Who built thim an' who supply thim but our gr-reat corporations?' he says. 'I say th' prosperity iv th' gr-reat an' imperyal an' rootytoot City iv Chicago dipinds upon th' way ye threat these corporations,' he says. 'Refuse,' he says, 'an ord'nance in this here matther,' he says, 'an' th' whole microbe industhry 'll be desthroyed in this city,' he says. 'These people 'll go to New York an' get capitalists to back thim an' set up microbe foundhries an' roon th' thrade iv Chicago,' he says."

[*EP,* Feb. 15, 1896]

An alderman who questions the need for microbes in Chicago is hooted down as a reformer but allowed to expound at length because "he doesn't count . . . an' th' more he talks th' betther f'r us." At this point, Mr. Dooley drops out of the race, fearing that "if I was in th' council I might turn out as a rayformer, an' I don't want to take anny chances on that."

Thus, we have seen that Mr. Dooley is no protoprogressive political reformer. For one thing, this role would be inconsistent with his character as a Bridgeport Irishman; for another, it would be foreign to Dunne's own pervasive skepticism. As the piece on Hull-House vs. Johnny Powers demonstrates, he is more suspicious of self-styled reformers than of those they intend to reform. And so the reformers that Mr. Dooley meets are all ineffectual rhetoricians or hypocritical profiteers or both. Even in Bridgeport, a reform committee is organized by the principle that "ivry man that took a dollar iv a bribe is sent down th' r-road. Thim that takes two goes on th' comity iv th' wave iv rayform." Furthermore, as exposed by a friend of Dooley's, the Bridgeport committee is seen to be made up of the community's least sympathetic members:

> "I see befure me in a chair a gintleman who wud steal a red-hot stove an' freeze th' lid befure he got home. On me right is th' gintleman who advanced th' wave iv rayform tin years ago be puttin' Mrs. Geohegan out on th' sthreet in a snowstorm whin she was roarin' with a cough. Mrs. Geohegan have rayformed, peace be with her, undher th' dhrifts iv Calv'ry! . . . An' you, Misther Brannigan, who knows about vacant lots, an' you Misther Clancy, th' frind iv th' dhrunk an' disordherly, we're proud to have ye here. 'Tis be such as ye that th' polisman who dhrinks on th' sly, an' th' saloon-keeper that keeps open f'r th' la-ads an' th' newsboys that shoots craps, 'll be brought to justice. Down with crime! says I."
>
> [*EP*, Jan. 5, 1895]

Mr. Dooley's moral in this piece is undiluted cynicism: "Niver steal a dure-mat, . . . If ye do, ye'll be invistigated, hanged, an' maybe rayformed. Steal a bank, me boy, steal a bank."

Dunne's contempt for hypocritical reformers carried over from his knowledge of the persecution of the poor by unfeeling corporate interests, whose leaders were likely to be Civic Federation members. This kind of injustice prompted some of his most powerful writing: hard-nosed, direct accusations which, like so many of the poverty pieces, he chose not to republish.[26] One example is the merciless portrait of George Pullman's callousness, which follows Mr. Dooley's comparison of the effects of the Pullman strike to the Famine years in Ireland:

> "But what's it all to Pullman? Whin Gawd quarried his heart a happy man was made. He cares no more f'r thim little matthers iv

life an' death thin I do f'r O'Connor's tab. 'Th' women an' childher is dyin' iv hunger,' they says. 'Will ye not put out ye'er hand to help thim?' they says. 'Ah, what th' 'ell,' says George. 'What th' 'ell,' he says. 'What th' 'ell,' he says. 'James,' he says, 'a bottle iv champagne an' a piece iv crambree pie. What th' 'ell, what th' 'ell, what th' 'ell."

"I heard two died yesterday," said Mr. McKenna. "Two women."

"Poor things, poor things. But," said Mr. Dooley, once more swabbing the bar, "what th' 'ell."   [*EP,* Aug. 25, 1894] [27]

Similarly, when President Stuyvesant Fish of the Illinois Central refused to install pedestrian crossings over the railroad's lakeside tracks, Dunne again shaped his rage into a parable of the sufferings of the weak at the hands of the strong. Hennessy suggests that a new catechism be written, in which the Illinois Central takes the place of God: " 'Who made ye?' 'Th' Illinye Cinthral made me,' 'An' why did it make ye?' 'That I might know it, love it, an' serve it all me days.' " Mr. Dooley agrees, because "they's naw use teachin' th' childher what ain't thrue. What's th' good iv tellin' thim that th' Lord made th' wurruld whin they'll grow up an' find it in th' possission iv th' Illinye Cinthral?" To illustrate, he tells this story:

"Ye mind th' Mulligans—thim that lives over beyant Casey's— th' little quite man with th' r-red whiskers. He wurruks hard, but all he's been able to lay up is throuble an' childher. He has tin iv thim old an' young, an' th' last come is sick an' feverish. I seen th' good woman rockin' it wan day on th' stoop, an' says I: 'How's th' kid?' 'Poorly, thank ye,' says she. 'He seems throubled be th' heat. 'Tis mortial hot,' she says. 'Why don't ye take him where 'tis cool?' I says. 'I'm goin' to to-morrah, praise Gawd,' she says. 'I'm goin' to take him down an' give him a r-ride around on th' steamboat. Th' doctor tells me th' lake air'll make him right,' she says. ' 'Tis ixpinsive,' she says. 'Five cints on th' ca-ars wan way an' five cints th' other, an' tin cints on th' boat, but 'tis betther than to have th' poor chick sufferin' an' I'm goin' to do it.'

"Ye see, she'd been brought up on th' ol' caddychism an' thought Gawd ownded th' wurruld, an' she'd niver heerd tell iv th' man-Fish. So I see her goin' off downtown with th' baby in her arms, shieldin' its face fr'm th' blazin' sun, bright an' early. How she found her way acrost th' city I dinnaw. F'r mesilf, I'd as lave attimpt to cross hell as State sthreet. I was r-run over be a gripca-ar th' last time I was there. But annyhow she got acrost to where she cud see th' blue wather iv th' la-ake an' th' crib that Tom Gahan built. 'Twas there she found who ownded th' wurruld. She wint along th' irne fince lookin' f'r a gate an' they was no gate. Thin she wint into th' little deepo an' says she: 'I want to go over to thim boats,' she says. 'Ye'll have to buy a ticket beyant,' says th' man. 'An' how much is it?' says she. 'Tin cints,' says th' man. 'But,' says she, 'I've on'y th' fifteen left,' she says, 'an' th' boat costs tin cints,' she says. 'Lave me in,' she says. 'I can't help it,' says th' man. ' 'Tis me ordhers,' he says. Ye see, th' man-Fish had tol' thim not to let annywan go to his lake, th' wan he made, d'ye mind, on th' sicond day. An' there she stood, peerin' through th' irne fince an' lookin' out at th' lake— at th' Illinye Cinthral's lake—an' glory be, I suppose she didn't undherstand it, but no more does she undherstand why it is f'r some to live off th' fat iv th' land an' f'r her on'y to bear childher an' see thim die or go to th' bad.

"She come home afther awhile whin th' baby got cross again. I seen her that night. 'Did ye like th' lake?' I says. 'I didn't go,' she says. 'F'r why?' says I. 'Th' Illinye Cinthral wudden' let me,' she says. 'I think it'd done th' baby good,' she says. 'He's onaisy to-night. Maria,' says she, 'will ye take Tiddy while I cuk ye'er father's supper?'

"So I think with Hinnissy they'll have to make a new caddychism, Jawn. I hope th' Illinye Cinthral'll be kinder to Mulligan's baby in th' nix' wurruld than it's been in this, f'r unless me eyes have gone back on me, they'll be another sthring iv crape on Mulligan's dure tomo-rah mornin'." [*EP,* Aug. 10, 1895]

Maybe there is poison in the life of a big city, but Dunne-as-Dooley locates the most virulent source of contamination not in Bridgeport but on Michigan Avenue. And invariably those who are least able to defend themselves suffer the most. This bleak angle of vision, which he simply cannot deflect or ignore, makes Mr. Dooley, at best, a compassionate observer of social evils that he has no hope of alleviating.

5

CATHLEEN NI HOULIHAN IN CHICAGO

Dunne & Irish-American Nationalism

What need you, being come to sense,
But fumble in a greasy till
And add the halfpence to the pence
And prayer to shivering prayer, until
You have dried the marrow from the bone?
For men were born to pray and save:
Romantic Ireland's dead and gone,
It's with O'Leary in the grave.

W. B. YEATS [1]

THE QUESTION of the political connection between Ireland and Great Britain is a desperately thorny problem, snarled into the Irish identity since Henry II landed near Waterford in 1171, and unfortunately as compelling today as it was in the 1890s. The American contribution to the movement to free Ireland has always been a confused and confusing, a tragicomic business: taken far too grimly by fanatic adherents, too easily mocked from outside, and impossible to assess to the satisfaction of all. There was, first of all, the pain of the struggle itself: seven hundred years of bungled conspiracies, abortive or disastrous risings, and repressive reactions from Britain, all of which had been sharpened in the too-recent memory of Irish-Americans in Mr. Dooley's day by the experience of the Famine. Secondly, those involved in the movement in America were immigrants as well as ostensible Irish patriots. In a country with strong nativist and Anglophile strains, they were exposed to malicious mockery and accusations of subversion and "divided loyalties." Widely misunderstood, suspected, and ridiculed, their position was vulnerable; their sensitivity to criticism was razor sharp.

On the other hand, there was much that deserved laughter and badly needed changing in the Irish-American nationalist organizations. The trick was to separate unjust from just and well-meaning criticism. Unfortunately, pain and sensitivity kept most nationalists from so discriminating, especially in Chicago, where a string of calamities in 1889 and 1890 plunged morale to an all-time low. Despite these considerable difficulties, Finley Peter Dunne did not shirk the emotion-laden issue of Irish freedom. Through Mr. Dooley he became an outspoken, incisive critic of the nationalist movement in America. Not surprisingly, for his trouble he was rewarded, not with an official vote of thanks, but with several enemies—of the "rale sthrong" Mayo variety, the kind "that hates ye ha-ard." A further reason for this animosity was that the people Mr. Dooley judiciously chose to criticize most often were those in control of the politics and media of the movement in Chicago.

Throughout the 1880s and 1890s, Chicago's most visible Irish nationalist was John F. Finerty, the editor of *The Citizen,* a weekly newspaper concerned almost exclusively with the American Irish and the fight for Irish freedom. Born in Galway City in 1846, Finerty was deported from Ireland because of nationalist activities at the age

of eighteen. He came straight to Chicago, where he threw himself into
the American movement, then known as the Fenian Brotherhood (so
called after the Fianna, warrior-heroes of Irish legend).[2] To support
himself, he became a crack correspondent for Wilbur Storey's *Chicago
Times,* making a reputation with his exciting coverage of the Indian
wars of 1876–1881, which he later turned into a popular book,
Warpath and Bivouac, or the Conquest of the Sioux.[3] He next became
an active Republican politician, winning a seat in Congress in 1882,
the same year that he founded *The Citizen.* Finerty was only a one-
term congressman, partly because of his notorious interest in Irish
rather than Chicago affairs. Mr. Dooley recalls the time "me frind
Jawn Finerty come out iv th' House iv Riprisintatives; an', whin some
wan ast him what was goin' on, he says, 'Oh, nawthin' at all but some
damned American business' " (*Journal,* March 11, 1899). He was
more successful with *The Citizen,* which quickly became the leading
Irish-American organ of the Midwest.[4] By 1893, however, Finerty
had been at it for too long. The fiery young patriot had become a
middle-aged rhetorician, out of touch with Ireland, obsessed with "the
Cause," and a sitting duck for Mr. Dooley. Inevitably they clashed,
in an intermittent war of words that reveals a good deal about Irish-
American nationalism in their time.

In the first place, Mr. Dooley provides humorous perspective on
the past history of the nationalist movement in America—a history
that Finerty took with utmost seriousness, in part because he had
helped to make it. Mr. Dooley's memory goes back to the earliest
and most incredible of nationalist events: the Fenian invasion of
Canada. The Brotherhood had been bolstered by the Civil War, for
many of the "Irish Brigades" formed in both the North and the South
had stayed together after Appomattox and simply changed their command to Fenian leadership. Moreover, Fenian "circles" (as their
smallest units were called) had been organized within the regular
army and navy, where they also profited from sanctioned military
training. Immediately after the war, at a convention in Philadelphia
in October 1865, the American Fenians founded a provisional government for the Irish republic in exile, modeled on the United States
Constitution. Among the elected officials were a secretary of war and
a full complement of generals, most of whom had seen service during
the Civil War. At once, the organization's strategists quarrelled over

the question of how to strike the hardest blow for Ireland. One faction favored planning toward a new rising in Ireland itself; the other conceived the fantastic scheme of invading Canada, in hopes of provoking an international incident between England and the United States, thereby aiding the Irish cause indirectly. Amazingly, the invasion took place. In June 1866, some eight hundred Fenians under the command of "General" John O'Neil crossed the Niagara River and engaged Canadian troops in several small skirmishes before retreating to Buffalo, New York. The invasion produced some eighty casualties but no international crisis.[5]

John Finerty participated in the Canadian raid, so he could not have appreciated Mr. Dooley's version, which takes full advantage of its comic potential. Significantly, the family representative to the invasion was Dooley's Uncle Mike, whom Dunne often brought in to illustrate the roughness of Bridgeport life in the old days. Here the implication is clear that for many Fenians patriotism was overshadowed by mean egotism and temperamental belligerency.

"I'll niver forget th' night me uncle Mike come back fr'm Canada. Ye know he was wan iv th' most des'prit Fenians that iver lived; an', whin th' movement begun, he had to thread on no wan's shadow befure he was off f'r th' battle. Ivry wan in town knew he was goin'; an' he wint away with a thrunk full iv bottles an' all th' good wishes iv th' neighborhood, more be reason iv th' fact that he was a boistherous man whin he was th' worse f'r wear, with a bad habit iv throwin' bricks through his neighbors' windows. We cud see him as th' thrain moved out, walkin' up an' down th' aisle, askin' if there was anny Englishman in th' car that'd like to go out on th' platform an' rowl off with him.

"Well, he got up in New York an' met a lot iv other des'prit men like himself, an' they wint across th' bordher singin' songs an' carryin' on, an' all th' militia iv New York was undher ar-rms; f'r it 'd been just like thim to turn round an' do their fightin' in New York. 'Twas little me uncle Mike cared where he fought.

"But, be hook or crook, they got to where th' other Fenians was, an' jined th' army. They come fr'm far an' near; an' they were young an' old, poor lads, some iv thim bent on sthrikin' th' blow that'd break th' back iv British tyranny an' some jus' crazed f'r fightin'. They had big guns an' little guns an' soord canes an' pitchforks an' scythes, an' wan or two men had come over armed with baseball bats. They had more gin'rals thin ye cud find in a Raypublican West Town convintion, an' ivry private was at laste a colonel.

They made me uncle Mike a brigadier gin'ral. 'That'll do f'r a time,' says he; 'but, whin th' fun begins, I'll pull Dorney off his horse, an' be a major gin'ral,' he says. An' he'd 've done it, too, on'y they was no fightin'.' "

Instead of redcoats, the battalion finds only a rainstorm, in which they sit "shiverin' an' swearin' " until Uncle Mike leads a delegation to see Major General Dorney:

> " 'Dorney,' says me uncle Mike, f'r he was chairman iv th' comity, 'Dorney,' he says, 'me an' me associated warriors wants to know what th' 'ell,' he says. 'What d'ye mane?' says Dorney. 'Ye brought us up here,' says me uncle Mike, 'to fight th' British,' he says. 'If ye think,' he says, 'that we come over,' he says, 'to engage in a six days' go-as-you-please walkin' match,' he says, 'ye'd betther go an' have ye'er head looked into be a vethrinary surgeon,' he says. 'Have ye anny British around here? Have ye e'er a Sassenach concealed about ye'er clothes?' he says. 'We can't do annything if they won't stand f'r us,' says Dorney. 'Thin,' says me uncle Mike, 'I wash me hands iv th' whole invasion,' he says. 'I'll trouble ye f'r me voucher,' he says. 'I'm goin' back to a counthry where they grow men that'll stand up an' fight back,' he says; an' he an' his la-ads wint over to Buffalo, an' was locked up f'r rivolution.
>
> "Me uncle Mike come home on th' bumpers iv a freight car, which is th' way most rivolutioners come home, excipt thim that comes home in th' baggage car in crates. 'Uncle Mike,' says I to him, 'what's war like, annyhow?' 'Well,' says he, 'in some rayspicts it is like missin' th' last car,' he says; 'an' in other rayspicts 'tis like gettin' gay in front iv a polis station,' he says.   [*EP*, June 15, 1895] [6]

The second faction of Fenian military thinking also failed, with the collapse of a nearly planless rising in Ireland on March 5 and 6, 1867. This fiasco prepared the way for the revival of parliamentary methods of agitation for Irish freedom, which reached their climax in the brilliant but doomed career of Charles Stewart Parnell. In America, however, the more extreme nationalists came to the fore and were able to turn the energies of the movement into a new secret organization aimed at violent revolution. The Clan na Gael (or Brotherhood of the Gaels) was founded by Irish-American "physical force" men in 1867 and had about ten thousand members by the time of its formal affiliation with its counterpart in Ireland, the Irish Republican Brotherhood, by means of a joint revolutionary directory ten years later. Replete with codes, secret handshakes, and an elaborate hierarchy of officers and "camps," the Clan was easy game for Mr. Dooley, although it had been serious business indeed in the seventies and eighties.[7]

Throughout the 1870s, while Parnell was building his powerful political machine in Ireland, debate raged in America between those who favored parliamentary agitation, or "moral force," and the advocates of violent revolution, including most of the leadership of the Clan na Gael. That debate resolved itself as far as the Clan was concerned in March 1883, with the opening of the Dynamite Campaign, a systematic plan to blow up the major symbols of British nationality, which planted the Irish cause firmly on the front pages of America's newspapers. Three factors influenced the Clan na Gael to begin this campaign of terrorism by dynamite. The first was the repressive situation in Ireland after May 1882, when a band of fanatical physical force men murdered the two highest ranking British officials in Ireland in Dublin's Phoenix Park. England reacted by passing a special Crimes Act which tightened security and suspended most Irish civil liberties. Second, a new famine was threatening, particularly in Donegal and other counties of the north and west, and no one had forgotten the black years of the late forties. Third, Parnell and his party were laying back, even, some said, capitulating to the British, and Parliament seemed particularly deaf to Ireland's problems. In this atmosphere of repression, fear, and frustration, America's physical force men swung into action. From a "Skirmishing Fund" in New York, the Clan na Gael hierarchy dispensed money for dynamite and passage to England for those who were to use it.[8]

The bombings began on St. Patrick's Eve in 1883, with explosions at Britain's Local Government Board in Whitehall and at the offices of the London *Times,* which immediately blamed "Irish crime and the assassin press in America." Over the next two years several more explosions occurred—at London's Victoria Station, in Scotland Yard itself, underneath London Bridge, and the *coup de grâce,* the simultaneous bombing of Parliament and the Tower of London in January 1885. Although there were no serious injuries, anti-Irish sentiment in England rose to a fever pitch. Vigilance committees were organized, M.P.'s demanded more repressive legislation in Ireland, and British employers began dismissing their Irish workers in droves. But the campaign was already over; there were several more threats but no more bombings. For one thing, the Clan and the IRB feared the continuance of economic retaliation against Irish employees in England. For another, Parnell's parliamentary group began to make significant headway, culminating in Prime Minister Gladstone's introduction of a bill for Irish home rule in April 1886. Finally, internal dissension was eating away at the Clan, and the days of consensus around a policy of physical force were over.[9]

Many London-bound dynamiters had departed from Chicago camps of the Clan na Gael, which were solidly in favor of violent means. In fact, the entire campaign may have been masterminded by Alexander Sullivan, a brilliant and sinister Chicago lawyer and the apex of the "Triangle," the ruling triumvirate of the Clan in the early and middle eighties.[10] Moreover, *The Citizen* had been vociferously behind the dynamiting—so much so that its editor became known in the British press as "Finerty the Dynamitard." Throughout the campaign the paper praised what one headline called "God's Mercy Manifested in Atlas Powder," and the Victoria Station bombing prompted the editorial opinion that "deeds, not words, should be weighed. . . . It is only dynamite or some other blessed agency created by God, utilized by science and wielded with heroic purpose that makes them thump their craws and talk about measures of redress." [11] Such sentiments mark Finerty as already a fanatic (which Mr. Dooley defined as "a man that does what he thinks th' Lord wud do if He knew th' facts iv th' case." [12]).

The *Citizen* editor is obviously the target when Mr. Dooley pointedly distinguishes rhetoric from performance in a piece comparing the jingoist press just before the Spanish-American War with the Irish nationalist press of Chicago during the Dynamite Campaign. Counseling Hennessy that, despite their war-mongering, the Chicago papers cannot be counted on for concrete assistance should war be declared, Mr. Dooley recalls the lightning conversion to pacifism of Editor Grady:

> "When th' movement to free Ireland be freein' quantities iv dinnymite was goin' on, a man be th' name iv Grady had a pa-aper he called 'Th' Explosive' down on Halstead sthreet. It was a pathrite [patriot] pa-aper an' it advised me an' others f'r to go acrost

th' sea an' spoil th' ancient architecsure iv Great Britain. I didn't go. But wan day I got me a small piece iv gas pipe plugged at both inds with a fuse in wan, an' took Dorsey down with me to see Grady. 'Misther Grady,' says I, 'I'm goin' over,' I says. 'Good,' says he. 'That's right,' he says. ' 'Tis on'y through th' courage an' fidelity iv her sons that Ireland can be freed. Ar-re ye fixed with th' stuff?' he says. 'I am,' says I, an' I pulled th' gas pipe. He tur-rned white as his shirt. 'Take that out,' he says. 'Take it away fr'm here or I'll—Oh, merciful powers, that I should have let this loonatic into me office. Take it away, I tell ye.' 'Ye needn't be afraid,' I says. 'I'm very careful. I'll give it to Dorsey. Here, Tim,' an' I tossed th' gas pipe to him. Grady give a scream iv turror an' in two leaps was at th' window. Another wan took him to th' sthreet an' it was a whole day before he cud be injooced to come back. He changed th' pa-aper into an organ iv th' undhertakers' association."

[*EP*, Oct. 2, 1897]

Mr. Dooley has no more reverence for those "pathrites" who actually followed the advice of *The Explosive*, for he has it on good authority that "th' reason Ireland wasn't free long ago was because th' good la-ads we give th' materyel to to blow up th' Prince iv Wales was so glad to get ashore they forgot what they was sint for. Some iv thim wint on th' polis foorce" (*EP*, May 11, 1895).

Dunne presents Mr. Dooley as a lapsed Clansman, a one-time believer in physical force who has been converted to a saner view of "the Cause." In addition, Mr. Dooley's patrons, notably John Mc-Kenna and Hennessy, are equally conversant with the organization and interests of the Clan na Gael. Such involvement on the part of a saloonkeeper and his working-class clientele tallies with the conclusion of Thomas N. Brown that Irish-American nationalism was "largely the cause of the poor . . . who felt no scruples over the institutionaliz-ing of the fact of alienation that was so manifest in their lives." The wealthier Irish kept themselves aloof from a movement that was rooted in "the realities of loneliness and alienation, and of poverty and prejudice," Brown states. "For its formal content this peculiar nationalism owed much to the thought and traditions of Tone, O'Connell, and Young Ireland, but it was from life in America that it derived its most distinctive attitudes: a pervasive sense of in-feriority, intense longing for acceptance and respectability, and an acute sensitivity to criticism.[13] As well as justifying Mr. Dooley's nationalist background, this analysis illuminates John Finerty's limitations.

At the time of the British-American dispute about the boundary of Venezuela, Mr. Dooley rejected the possibility of war, citing an experience in his camp of the Clan na Gael during the Dynamite Campaign, about which he had few illusions:

> "Jawn," he said; "ye may take off ye'r ep'lets an' lay down ye'er double-bar'd shot gun an' hang up ye'er fife an' dhrum. They'll be no war.
>
> "F'r why?—They was a man be th' name iv McGuire wanst that lived in th' twinty sicond ward, but belonged to th' same camp with me. He was th' mos' rarin', tarin' dinnymiter that iver lived. Whiniver I wint to th' lodgeroom f'r to smoke a see-gar an' have a talk with th' la-ads I knew an' hear Tim Darsy sing 'Let Ireland ray-ha-mimber th' da-ays iv old' me ears'd be split with this man McGuire's orathry. 'Ah,' says he, 'Ar-re ye min or ar-re ye slaves?' he says. 'Will ye sit idly here with ye'er hands in ye'er pockets while th' craven flag iv th' Sassenach floats o'er th' green land,' he says, 'an' a brave people is gr-round down beneath th' feet iv ty-ranny?' he says. 'Or will ye ray-mimber O'Donnell an' O'Neill iv th' r-red hand, an' Sarsfield an' Immit an' Meagher an' Wolf Tone an' John Mitchel an' sthrike wan blow f'r freedom?' he says. 'Oh,' he says, 'if 'twas lift to me not wan shtone'd stand on another in that ac-cursed land,' he says. 'I'd give th' las' cint iv me money an' th' las' dhrop iv me blood f'r th' cause,' he says, 'if I cud die,' he says, 'cryin' Ireland free,' says McGuire, th' cooper iv th' twinty sicond ward."

Dooley places McGuire in the Bridgeport community hierarchy in order to undercut his rhetoric, which is overblown in typical nationalist fashion, complete with the required litany of Irish heroes. He goes on to give a vivid thumbnail sketch of a Clan meeting, at the same time admitting his own former acquiescence in the dynamite philosophy:

> "Well wan night th' camp was more quite whin I wint in, an' afther awhile th' dure was bolted an' th' sanyor garjeen [senior guardian] got up. He was white in th' face an' low-spoken, f'r he believed th' way to conquer England was f'r to hoist a church or two an' kill a polisman. An' be th' same token I believed th' same mesilf in thim days. I know diff'rent now. He said they had lads planted in London an' Liverpool, an' at a certain signal 'twas th' intintion f'r to blow up Windsor Castle an' maybe take a leg off th'

Prince iv Wales. Th' cinthral exicutive had ordhered an assismint iv five dollars apiece, an' he'd put th' matther to a vote. Thin me bould McGuire he ups an' says 'Wait a minyit,' he says. 'Wait a minyit,' he says. 'Sure, now, ye don't mane we have to give up five?' he says. 'F'r th' cause iv freedom,' says the s. g. 'Well, now,' says McGuire, 'I think 'tis too much,' he says. 'I'm as sthrong f'r th' cause as annywan,' he says, 'but,' says he, 'it looks as though ye was thryin' to crowd this here thing. Five dollars is a lot iv money to spind,' he says. 'I vote no,' says McGuire, the cooper. Th' rist iv us paid down, but th' nix' time I see McGuire he'd jined th' peace movement." [*EP*, Dec. 28, 1895]

The point here in the context of December 1895 is that war with England would be opposed by American moneyed interests and thus will not come. But the piece also further exposes the gap between talk and action among many so-called patriots of the 1880s.

Several details here demonstrate Dunne's familiarity with the Clan na Gael. The term "senior guardian," for instance, is correct for a camp leader of the Clan, and the Fenians bequeathed to their successors a fondness for initials that Dooley mocks in referring to "the s. g." Similar references crop up in other pieces. Mr. Dooley remembers a vote for "head center," an office in the Fenian Brotherhood (*EP*, Nov. 10, 1894). He recalls the spy Henri LeCaron and the new secret sign devised by the Clan after his exposure (*EP*, March 13, 1897). He boosts a friend's political ambitions by vouching that he was "in the Fenian raid" (*Journal*, Aug. 13, 1898). Never does Dunne feel it necessary to explain these things, so the Irish freedom movement must have been very familiar to the Chicago reading public in the nineties.

A bizarre, anachronistic series of events in September 1896 prompted Mr. Dooley's best satiric look at the phenomenon of the Irish-American dynamiter. On September 13 in Boulogne, France, one P. J. P. Tynan was arrested by British detectives and accused of fomenting "a Fenian-Russian Nihilist" plot to assassinate both Queen Victoria and the czar on the occasion of the czar's impending visit to England. According to Scotland Yard, the conspirators, four more of whom were arrested within twenty-four hours, had intended to tunnel under the Queen's London residence from a neighboring building and to set a charge big enough to blow up the entire palace. The tip-off had come, it was reported, from a Chicago informer.

Tynan was a well-known eccentric in England and America, having written and published at his own expense a seven-hundred-page book "proving" that he had masterminded the Phoenix Park murders and the Dynamite Campaign. Scotland Yard quickly dropped the charges after learning that he had been outlining the details of his plot for years in New York saloons. Coincident with the Tynan affair were the release and return to America of three Irish-Americans who had been convicted of dynamite conspiracy in England in the 1880s: Alfred Whitehead, Dr. Thomas Gallagher, and Dr. John Daly.[14]

Dunne responded to this flurry of publicity with a tour de force piece in his vein of exaggeration to absurdity, in which Tynan is cast—legitimately, it seems—as the archetypal boastful and blundering Irish-American revolutionary. The force of history is behind Mr. Dooley's opening contention that "they'se nawthin' in the wide wurruld as aisy to undherstand as a rivoluchonary plot be our own people." He illustrates by narrating the events that led up to Tynan's arrest:

> "Well, th' first thing th' la-ads done was to go to Madison Square Garden an' hold a secret meetin', in which thim that was to hand th' package to th' queen and thim that was to toss a piece iv gas pipe to his cza-ars was told off. Thin a comity was sint around to th' newspaper offices to tell thim th' expedition was about to start. Th' conspirators, heavily disgeesed, was attinded to th' boat be a long procission. First come Tynan ridin' on a wagon-load iv nithroglycerin; thin th' other conspirators, with gas-pipe bombs an' picks an' chuvvels f'r tunnellin' undher Winzer Castle; thin th' Ah-o-haitches; thin th' raypoorthers; thin a brigade iv Scotland Ya-ard spies in th' ga-arb iv polismin. An' so off they wint on their secret mission, with th' band playin' 'Th' Wearin' iv th' Green,' an' Tynan standin' on th' quarther deck, smilin' an' bowin' an' wavin' a bag iv jint powdher over his head.
> "No sooner had th' conspirators landed thin th' British gover-mint begun to grow suspicious iv thim. Tynan was shadowed be detictives in citizens' clothes; an', whin he was seen out in his backyard practisin' blowin' up a bar'l that he'd dhressed in a shawl an' a little lace cap, th' suspicions growed." [15]

After several more steps in this vein, Tynan makes his fatal mistake: "He wint to France. It's always been obsarved that, whin a dinnymiter had to blow up annything in London, he laves the counthry. Th' polis, now thoroughly aroused, acted with commindable promptness.

They arristed Tynan in Booloon f'r th' murdher iv Cavendish [Lord Frederick Cavendish, killed in Phoenix Park in 1882]." [16] Mr. Dooley finishes with a flourish: a few bars of mock-heroic nationalist rhetoric, and a nod toward the greatest failing of the old-time patriots— stupidity.

> "Thus," said Mr. Dooley, sadly, "thus is th' vengeance f'r which our beloved counthry has awaited so long delayed be th' hand iv onscrupulious tyranny. Sthrive as our heroes may, no secrecy is secure against th' corruption iv British goold. Oh, Ireland, is this to be thy fate forever? Ar-re ye niver to escape th' vigilance iv th' polis, thim cold-eyed sleuths that seem to read th' very thoughts iv ye'er pathriot sons?"
>
> "There must have been a spy in th' ranks," said Mr. Hennessy.
>
> "Sure thing," said Mr. Dooley, winking at Mr. McKenna. "Sure thing, Hinnissy. Ayether that or th' accomplished detictives at Scotland Yards keep a close watch iv the newspapers. Or it may be— who knows?—that Tynan was indiscreet. He may have dhropped a hint of his intintions."   [*EP*, Sept. 19, 1896]

Again we see Dunne's ability to seize a particular event and generalize from it. How well this piece must have captured the mood of the city on the day it appeared; but besides being topical, and without any of the background provided here, it remains effective as satire at the expense of the dynamite philosophy of Irish revolution and the limited men who espoused it. John Finerty's only response to the Tynan case was an editorial conjecture that the "plot" had been invented by Scotland Yard to blacken the Irish character.

A final comment on Tynan followed his release from jail. A *Times-Herald* editorial that day focused on his sins against the language with such liveliness and wit that it must have been Dunne's. It is worth quoting in full:

> The release of P. J. P. Tynan from prison in Boulogne-Sur-Mer is like opening the cave of the winds. The air is filled with the splinters of rhetoric, the mangled limbs of policemen, joists from Windsor Castle, fragments of crowns and scepters. You cannot see the sun for the flying debris. Tynan the All Destroying is abroad again.
>
> He did not intend to blow up the czar. Oh, no! He would not harm the poor old queen or the Prince of Wales. In fact, if you come to analyze the intentions of this awful man you may find that

he seeks only to destroy silence. He hates the speechless gloom which hangs over the world. He would blast and rend it, scatter it in multitudinous echoes, fill its place with the billowy roar of his own voice. No despot's heel shall be laid upon his vocal organs. No mailed hand shall stifle his sounding-board jaws. When all the world sleeps listen to Tynan making a conch of the dome of heaven, Tynan the most illustrious Megaphone of all time, Tynan who has the caged thunder sing to him as a bullfinch and tunes his notes to the hurricane's blast.

Ireland will gain her heritage some day, we have no doubt. Haste the happy hour when the unhappy land will be free—from Tynan.   [Oct. 17, 1896]

In 1896 Mr. Dooley could joke easily about a residual dynamiter and crackpot like Tynan, but the real Dynamite Campaign twelve years before had done serious damage to the none too stable reputation of the immigrant Irish in America. Because of it, the new middle class had continued to stay away from the nationalist movement. With the emergence of Parnell's Irish parliamentary party as a political force, however, Irish-American nationalism was moving toward respectability in the late eighties. Even after the failure of Gladstone's Home Rule Bill of 1886, there continued to be widespread faith, even in Chicago, in the parliamentary agitation. Thus, the Irish party and its American subsidiary, the National League of America, began to attract the support of moderates from the Irish-American bourgeoisie. The old association of fanaticism and Irish nationalism seemed finally to be dissolving. Then disaster struck. Irish nationalism in Chicago was dealt two staggering blows in as many years: in 1889 came the murder of Dr. Patrick Henry Cronin, in 1890, the scandal of Parnell's affair with Mrs. Katharine O'Shea. It is important that we see Mr. Dooley's treatment of Irish-American nationalism and John Finerty's reactions in this context, especially as Dunne had himself been involved in the grotesque Cronin case.

Dr. Cronin was a well known Chicago physician, social singer, and Irish nationalist. As a stalwart and fairly well-placed member of the Clan na Gael, he had participated in the machinations of Aleck Sullivan and his cohorts during the Dynamite Campaign. Cronin was convinced—probably rightly—that Sullivan had embezzled Clan funds collected for dynamite and Land League agitation and gambled them away on the Chicago Board of Trade. Cronin's accusations, first in Clan councils and then more and more publicly, made Sullivan his bitter enemy and led directly to his murder on the evening of May 4, 1889, the anniversary of Chicago's Haymarket massacre of 1886 and of the Dublin Phoenix Park murders of 1882.[17]

Dunne found himself in the middle of all this: first, because he was, at twenty-two, the city editor of the *Chicago Times,* and the Cronin case was the biggest news in the city for six months running; and second, because he was a friend of John Devoy, a powerful Clan na Gael leader with whom he had worked on the *Daily News.* Devoy had been working lately in New York, but upon hearing of Cronin's disappearance, he quit his job and rushed back to Chicago to help in the investigation.[18] There was no love lost between Devoy and Aleck Sullivan. Cronin's evidence of Sullivan's dishonesty had convinced Devoy, and he began insisting on a link between Sullivan and the Cronin case upon his return to Chicago.

The case broke shockingly with the indictment of Sergeant Daniel Coughlin, the Chicago detective who had been in charge of the investigation. In his memoir "On the Irish," Dunne gives himself a central role in the implication of Coughlin and the *Times* scoop of his arrest, tracing both to a conversation he had with an ex-detective in Billy Boyle's chophouse, during which Coughlin's animosity toward Cronin was revealed. Dunne remembered that "I could think of nothing but the Cronin case. I slept with it. I ate with it. I drew on the cashier of our struggling newspaper for what he considered enormous sums to pay the expenses of reporters lodging in the same houses with a score of persons under suspicion." Evidently the *Times* coverage of the case grew out of such sources, as well as Dunne's connections with John Devoy and detective William Pinkerton. And the arrest of Coughlin, as Dunne remembers it, followed a conference at the *Times* editorial offices involving Dunne, his publisher James J. West, the mayor of Chicago, and the chief of police, at which the evidence against Coughlin was presented.[19]

Cronin's brutal murder—he had been bludgeoned and his body stuffed in a catch basin—gripped the imagination of the city. His funeral was the largest in Chicago since that of Stephen A. Douglas, twenty-five years earlier. Twelve thousand people passed the bier at the First Cavalry Armory; the funeral procession of the city's Irish societies (including the Clan na Gael Guards) was 8,000 strong; and some 25,000 were on hand at the depot as the body was entrained for burial in Calvary Cemetery, north of the city proper. Mass meetings were held denouncing Cronin's murderers at which money was raised to help the prosecution.[20] Dime museums sprang up featuring reenactments of the murder, including one of the actual murder scene, the Carlson Cottage on the North Side. Street vendors sold replicas of the horse-and-buggy murder vehicle.

Several men were arrested and cleared, including Aleck Sullivan, and there were confessions by a few notoriety seekers. When all the dust had settled, five indictments for murder were handed down by the grand jury: to John Kunze, a German-American laborer, to Coughlin, and to three other members of Clan na Gael Camp 20 (Patrick O'Sullivan, Martin Burke, and John F. Beggs). The trial itself aggravated the already tense and tangled situation. Over eleven hundred men had to be examined before a jury was selected, a jury-tampering scandal broke in midtrial, and the whole messy proceeding dragged on for 108 days, making it the longest trial on record in the United States. Finally, on December 16, 1889, Coughlin, O'Sullivan, and Burke were found guilty of murder in the first degree and were sentenced to life imprisonment.[21]

The second blow struck almost immediately. Eight days after the Cronin verdict, on December 24, 1889, Captain William O'Shea filed a petition in London for divorce from his wife, Katharine, naming as co-respondent Charles Stewart Parnell. The Cronin case had split Chicago's nationalists into two warring factions, named by the press "Trianglers" and "anti-Trianglers," for their support of Sullivan's or Cronin's position regarding the administration of the Clan. Now the Parnell controversy made the situation worse by causing these two factions to splinter further. Following the announcement of Captain O'Shea's uncontested divorce on November 17, 1890, both the Trianglers and the anti-Trianglers divided into pro- and anti-Parnell factions. All of Chicago's major daily newspapers came out against Parnell, and hardly a day went by in December without front-page stories and elaborate editorial interpretations, all of which were embarrassing to the Irish community. As it became evident that Parnell would not step down from his position as leader of the parliamentary party, the *Tribune* expressed its shocked disbelief at his "callousness," concluding that "he will have to go or the Irish cause is lost for this

generation"; while the *Herald* saw his decision as "insolent defiance
of a public opinion based on moral laws that must hold good unless
civilization is to lapse into something worse than barbarism. . . . A man
who cannot rule himself ought not to be considered necessary to a
political party that seeks to rule a nation." [22]

The fierce debate about Parnell's fate came home to Chicago with
the arrival on November 28, 1890, of a fund-raising delegation from
the Irish party, led by John Dillon, William O'Brien, and Timothy
Harrington—all names to be conjured with in nationalist circles. Eight
thousand people packed the Battery D Armory to receive the delegates,
to pledge money to the party, and (presumably) to hear something
about Parnell. Here they were disappointed, for none of the Irish
speakers mentioned the name or the issue that was on everyone's mind.
It was left to a Chicago Irishman to bring it up, in an outburst from
the audience calling for Parnell's continuance as party leader, which
was cheered resoundingly. Finley Peter Dunne was listed among "those
on the platform" at the meeting, attesting to his proximity to this controversy as well (*Tribune,* Nov. 22, 29, 30, 1890).[23] Two days after
the meeting, five of the six Irish delegates (Harrington abstaining)
issued from their Chicago hotel a manifesto calling for Parnell's resignation as leader of their party. With this encouragement, denunciation
of Parnell in the daily press intensified, and there followed general
editorial approval of both the Irish Catholic hierarchy's rejection of
Parnell as leader of the people on December 3 and the secession from
Committee Room 15 of Justin McCarthy and a majority of the Irish
party on December 6 (*Tribune* and *Herald,* Dec. 1–10, 1890).

Parnell's tragic, unreasoning pride and its consequences continued
to be front-page news in Chicago all through the long agony of the
three unsuccessful by-elections (Kilkenny on December 22, North
Sligo in April 1891, and Carlow in July) in which the fallen leader
wore himself out trying to win popular support for his increasingly
untenable position. When he died at Brighton on October 6, 1891,
the cause of Irish nationality was once again in shambles. In America,
the Irish National League expired simultaneously. At its last convention, held in Chicago on October 1 and 2, 1891, with less than two
hundred attending, President Michael V. Gannon spoke this bitter valediction: "The enemies of our race are great and powerful. . . . Even
here in this broad and free land we are the objects of their malice. . . .

We are today the least organized nationality in America, while we have the most to contend with." [24] Certainly this was true in Chicago, where the increasingly prevalent view of the Irish nationalist as an immoral, faction-loving murderer had two faces—Alexander Sullivan's and Parnell's.

The year 1890 was thus a watershed for the Chicago Irish community. These tragic events had wrecked the nationalist movement for a generation and wreaked havoc with the public image of the Irishman in America. The horrible Cronin murder with its overtones of sinister secret-society plottings, the long and tainted trial, the strong hint of police corruption through Dan Coughlin, the ignominious divorce proceeding and Parnell's subsequent drive to self-destruction—all combined to shatter the veneer of respectability that had barely begun to attach itself to the nationalist movement and the whole Irish community in Chicago. By laying bare the violence and (by genteel standards) the immorality that lay beneath the surface of the movement, the Cronin and Parnell publicity drove the emerging Irish-American middle class back into the defensive position of an unwelcome immigrant group.

There was still more for Chicago's Irish to face in 1890. Locally, a rash of political and gambling scandals broke, all of them involving Irishmen. There was a huge exposure of election tampering in late April. In September, the County Democratic Convention erupted into a slugfest. And in January and October, well known Irish-American politicians of dubious reputation were shot to death in saloons (*Tribune,* Jan. 28–31, Feb. 1, 2, Oct. 27, 1890). Moreover, these home-town debacles were echoed nationally when Boss Richard Croker's Tammany Hall machine crumbled in New York in April. So demoralized was the Chicago Irish community that the Irish-American council voted to cancel the St. Patrick's Day parade for 1890. One delegate explained bitterly that "professional leaders and agitators in this town will have to take a back seat. The honest Irish have sense enough to know and say that this is no time to make a display of our nationality" (*Tribune,* Feb. 17, 1890).

Surely, in Dunne's close connections with Irish-American affairs during these harrowing months lie the roots of Mr. Dooley's unillusioned perspective on the nationalists. John Finerty, in contrast, reacted by turning his back on the trouble. While daily headlines blazed of Dan Coughlin and Mrs. O'Shea, he relegated both issues to small articles on inside pages, mention so disproportionate to their importance to *The Citizen*'s audience as to reveal how disturbed he really was. And certainly the effect of it all on him must have been devastating. Irish freedom was his fixed idea, and his hopes had been high while Parnell was in the ascendant. Now the entire program had turned to ashes in a series of humiliating defeats in both Ireland and Chicago. As a result, any remaining perspective that he might have had was destroyed forever, and thwarted obsession became permanent, shrill paranoia.

In his St. Patrick's Day editorial for 1890, Finerty saw "a tidal wave of bigotry" sweeping the United States, directed particularly at the Irish. And when the British-American Association of Chicago condemned the Cronin murderers as foreign anarchists, he declared that "Chicago is now looked upon, and quite justly, as the champion Know-nothing city of the United States. There is a bitter and growing dislike of Irishmen in Chicago, which is not at all to its credit." Moreover, he went on to accuse the Chicago daily press of labeling all Irish candidates for public office "trianglers, murderers, etc." [25] All through the nineties, and until his death in 1908, Finerty continued to turn out speeches and editorials of a grinding sameness: formulaic idealized encomiums of Ireland and bitter denunciations of her enemies, both studded with litanies of the canonical battles and heroes, like the beads of a well-worn rosary. Sarsfield and Robert Emmet, the pikemen of '98, Aughrim and Drogheda and the Boyne—it is as if he were seeking a charm, some magic configuration of the old names that would infuse the dying movement with life. Always he took the paranoid stance of beleaguered defender of the Irish against attack from all sides. And his energies for composing invective were prodigious: most weeks *The Citizen* contained two full pages, sixteen columns, of editorials—a sad, bleak, humorless pile of words.

Certainly Finerty had no patience left for Mr. Dooley. He had long since come to resent any attempt to write in brogue, however salutary the message.[26] He had complained in *The Citizen* about the use of "the devil of dialectism" to degrade the Irish race. In addition, his animosity extended to most other literary attempts to picture the

Irish: he had criticized the plays of Harrigan and Hart as "drama from the slums," and condemned the innocuous Dion Boucicault for having "held the mirror up to . . . the rags and tatters of our enemy's worn-out stage-Irishman" in plays that "owe their being to Anglo-Saxon hatred."

In like manner, Finerty returned Dunne's explicit references to him in kind. During Mr. Dooley's first year, 1893, Finerty called the *Evening Post* Chicago's most "ill-natured" newspaper, singling out the *Post*'s owner and "the numerous cranks who compose its editorial staff." He continued as follows:

> Every Saturday this Democratic organ, which, no doubt, Irish-Americans subscribe for in large numbers, contains a vile screed on their alleged peculiarities—supposed to be written in what fools call the 'Irish brogue' vernacular—which is an insult to common-sense and a disgrace to respectable journalism. The chief proprietor of the *Post* is, by birth, an Irishman, and ought to have, at least, enough race pride to prevent the libeling of his kindred people in a journal controlled by himself. [*Citizen,* Dec. 9, 1893].[27]

The exaggerated sense of personal insult and the appeal to "race pride" are typical of the special blindness of the fanatic nationalist. Similarly, in 1895 Finerty chose to read Mr. Dooley with simplistic narrowness:

> Some young men of Irish blood, born in this country, imagine that they elevate themselves in public estimation by caricaturing the accent and manners of their Irish-born kindred. On the contrary, they render themselves objects of well-merited contempt on the part of non-Irish-Americans, who always respect the country and the race from which they sprang. [*Citizen,* July 13, 1895, in an editorial entitled "Lampooning the Irish"]

Finally, in 1898, the *Citizen* editor called his opponent to task by name for gross misuse of his considerable abilities:

> The *Journal* is, we understand, mainly edited by "Pete" Dunne, better known as "Dooley," a talented gentleman whose patriotism has chiefly developed itself in the form of an atrocious brogue, such as only the very lowest of the Irish peasantry indulge in. Mr. Dunne has "infinite wit" and is worthy of better things than murdering two languages, by a bad combination of both, in order to make fools and bigots laugh. By using his talents properly, this brilliant, red-

headed son of an Irishman, and Irish woman too, could do much
to advance Celtic race pride and crush "Anglo-Saxon" assumption
and ignorance in this city. We hope he will see the better way before
it is too late. [*Citizen,* July 2, 1898]

Here Finerty reveals himself to be confused by his own conflicting
motives. The desire for acceptance into the American middle class
comes across in his disparagement of "the very lowest of the Irish
peasantry." But that same disparagement contradicts his advocacy of
"Celtic race pride." Thus, he embodies the classic immigrant dilemma
of attempting to straddle two worlds. At the same time he fails to
perceive that his Celticism is of one racist cloth with the supposed
" 'Anglo-Saxon' assumption and ignorance" of his adversaries.

Finerty's inability to acknowledge Dunne's accomplishment illustrates what Thomas N. Brown has seen as the increasingly narrow
philistinism of Irish-American nationalism, evidenced later on by the
New York *Playboy* riots of 1911, when Dunne's old friend John
Devoy led an eggs-and-cabbage assault on the Abbey Theatre production of Synge's play, considered by the nationalists to be a libel against
the Irish character.[28] Because the fanatic heart denies itself perspective and the accompanying release of laughter, Finerty remained blind
to the only spokesman of genius that his community was ever to have.

About the moribund nationalist movement as it had survived into
the nineties Dunne had mixed emotions. Mr. Dooley sympathizes with
the rank and file nationalists, whose sincere concern for Ireland he
never questions, but he has only contempt for the leaders, whose
ulterior motives are all too obvious:

"Did ye iver see a man that wanted to free Ireland th' day afther
to-morrah that didn't run f'r aldherman soon or late? Most iv th'
great pathriotic orators iv th' da-ay is railroad lawyers. That's a
fact, I'm tellin' ye. Most iv th' rale pathriots wurruks f'r th' railroads too—tampin' th' thracks."   [*EP,* Aug. 17, 1895] [29]

Dunne further underscores his separation of the sincere from the self-
serving nationalists in a piece describing a meeting of the "Cuban
Sympathy League" at Finucane's Hall in February 1897. Speeches in
support of Cuba's struggle against Spain are delivered by Dorsey, the
director of the building and loan association, Clancy, the lawyer, and
Schwartz, the cashier of the bank, all of whom leave when Joe

Gallagher suggests that war may threaten the stability of the economy. In the crowd that remains, Dooley counts "twinty Fenians," none of whom has more than two dollars or credit at Schwartz's bank. Moreover, they all support Casey's resolution "that we declare war at wanst an' for-rm a rigimint, an' here goes me last dollar f'r to buy dinnymite." Dooley reports that "I niver see such a r-rush iv money. Ivrybody dug, an' in less than no time they was thirty dollars an' eighty cints in th' pot. Ol' man Duggan was mortified that he had on'y a nickel, but as he wint flyin' out th' dure he called back: 'Wait f'r me, boys, till I can get at th' childher's bank!' " (*EP,* Feb. 27, 1897).

The connection between hypocritical nationalism and political spoilsmanship comes clear when Mr. Dooley visits a nationalist meeting in 1893:

> "I was down at a meetin' iv th' Hugh O'Neills, an' a most intherestin' meetin' it was, Jawn. I'd been niglictful iv me jooty to th' cause iv late, an' I was surprised an' shocked to hear how poor ol' Ireland was sufferin'. Th' rayport fr'm th' Twenty-third Wa-ard, which is in th' County Mayo, showed that th' sthreet clanin' conthract had been give to a Swede be th' name iv Oleson; an' over in th' Nineteenth Wa-ard th' County Watherford is all stirred up because Johnny Powers is filled th' pipe-ya-ard with his own rilitives. I felt dam lonely, an' with raison, too; f'r I was th' on'y man in th' camp that didn't have a job. An' says I, 'Gintlemen,' says I, 'can't I do something f'r Ireland, too?' I says. 'I'd make th' 'ell's own conthroller,' says I, 'if ye've th' job handy,' I says; and at that they give me th' laugh, and we tuk up a subscription for Finerty, an' adjourned." [*EP,* Nov. 18, 1893] [30]

Certainly the business of dispensing jobs here is a far cry from Dooley's recollection of dynamite plotting by the earnest, if misguided, clansmen of the eighties. He makes the same ironic point in reporting that John Finerty has joined the Japanese navy, which had just fired on the British flag, thereby accomplishing "what th' Sarsfields an' th' Wolf Tone Lithry Club have been sacrificin' thimsilves in th' wather office an' on th' bridges f'r years to accomplish" (*EP,* Aug. 4, 1894). Thomas N. Brown has remarked that as far back as 1864 "Fenians were too frequently aspirants for public office," and Mr. Dooley's observations of the movement in the nineties corroborate Brown's judgment that "in fact Irish-American nationalism was directed chiefly toward American, not Irish, ends." [31]

As a talented journalist and lover of good prose, Dunne objected strongly to the excesses and simplifications of the nationalist rhetoric. We have already seen his definitive dissections of P. J. P. Tynan. The Finerty style was, of course, also a frequent target for Mr. Dooley, as were two other prominent nationalist orators, William Joyce and Matthew P. Brady. Not much information exists about Joyce, who seems to have been a king-maker, never holding public office himself. High in nationalist circles, he served as president of the United Irish Societies in 1891 and delivered the major address at their August 15 picnic, which he chaired several years running (*Tribune,* Aug. 16, 1891). Brady was a famous, perhaps notorious, speaker, who practiced law and served as a city prosecutor; he could be counted on to orate at the drop of a hat at both Democratic party and Irish nationalist functions.[32] At one point Mr. Dooley proclaims Finerty to be the champion paper revolutionary, at the expense of "Macchew P."

> "I'll say this f'r [Finerty], he's hit some thunderin' blows at th' Sassenach. 'Dad, there's th' lad to throw th' ink acrost th' pa-aper, an' make thrones an' dy-nasties thremble. Gawd bless him for th' good he's done. I use t' think Brady was his akel, but th' captain has wiped up th' earth with him. D'ye know that Macchew P. has give it up f'r good an' all an' has took to writin' come-all-yes? He have so. Molly Donahue had one iv his songs—'Walkin' with Looloo in th' Pa-ark'—with ne'er a wurrud about dinnymite in it. They've give him a vote iv censure in th' Wolf Tones. They have so."
>
> [*EP*, June 29, 1895]

Dunne often reproduced the nationalist oratory of Finerty, Brady, and Joyce, as in the speech by "McGuire, the cooper iv th' twenty-sicond ward," discussed earlier, or in this report from the United Irish Societies picnic of 1894, which ends with a characteristic Dooley undercutting:

> "Th' first man I see was Dorgan, the sanyor guarjeen in the Wolfe Tone Lithry Society. He's th' la-ad that have made th' Prince iv Wales thrimble in his moccasins. I heerd him wanst makin' a speech that near injooced me to take a bomb in me hand an' blow up Westminsther Cathedral. 'Ar-re ye,' he says, 'men, or ar-re ye slaves?' he says. 'Will ye,' he says, 'set idly by,' he says, 'while th' Sassenach,' he says, 'has th' counthry iv Immitt an' O'Connell,' he says, 'an' Jawn Im Smyth' [a Chicago Irish-American furniture dealer], he says, 'undher his heel?' he says. 'Arouse,' he says, 'slaves an' despots!'

he says. 'Clear th' way!' he says. 'Cowards an' thraitors!' he says. 'Faugh-a-ballagh!' he says. He had th' beer privilege at th' picnic, Jawn." [*EP*, Aug. 18, 1894]

Dunne recognized that these blowhard, blood-and-thunder speeches were wholly out of touch with the realities of life in Ireland. William Joyce's analysis of the British cabinet crisis of June 1895, when Lord Rosebery was forced to resign as Prime Minister, is typically callous and wrongheaded:

"Willum Joyce come in here las' night an' he said it was a big thing f'r Ireland. 'How is that?' says I. 'Well,' says he, 'they'll be a crool man put in to rule th' counthry,' he says, 'an' he'll burn th' houses an' seize th' cattle an' mebbe kill a lot iv people,' he says, 'an' thin there'll be throuble,' he says. 'Ireland is niver well off,' he says, 'but whin she's unfortunate,' he says. I hear th' mimbers iv th' Wolf Tones is goin' about with so manny dinnymite bombs in' tails iv their coats they don't dare to set down." [*EP*, June 29, 1895]

Nor is Joyce's position that much of an exaggeration on Dunne's part. The treasurer of the Irish National League of America, William Lyman of Harlem, New York City, actually delivered a speech with a similar message the year before this Dooley piece appeared. In his speech, Lyman called for an end to Irish-American contributions toward famine relief in Ireland, because it is "better to be famine stricken, to fight and be shot down by the hundreds until all nations cry 'Hands Off' to England, than to become craven beggars before the world." An *Evening Post* editorial writer (possibly Dunne) proceeded to put Lyman in his place as follows: "Little does William care for the redcoat file or the potato rot. Little fears he the wrath of the Queen of England. Bold and undaunted, like Mr. Brennan of the song, he stands fearing naught while the liberty of dear old Ireland is in the balance. Hooroo! Hooroo! Harlem is only 3,000 miles from the city of London" (*EP*, Jan. 22, 1894).

Even earlier, Dunne had made this point in a lyrical Dooley piece about the seeming paradox of Irish accomplishment abroad and failure at home:

"There's Mac's an' O's in ivry capital iv Europe atin' off silver plates whin their relations is staggerin' under th' creels iv turf in th' Connaught bogs.

"Wirra, 'tis hard. Ye'd sa-ay off hand, 'Why don't they do as much for their own counthry?' Light-spoken are thim that suggests th' like iv that. 'Tis aisier said than done. Ye can't grow flowers in a granite block, Jawn dear, much less whin th' first shoot 'd be thrampled under foot without pity. 'Tis aisy f'r us over here, with our bellies full, to talk iv th' cowardice iv th' Irish; but what would ye have wan man iv thim do again a rig'mint? 'Tis little fightin' th' lad will want that will have to be up before sunrise to keep th' smoke curlin' fr'm th' chimbley or to patch th' rush roof to keep out th' March rain. No, faith, Jawn, there's no soil in Ireland f'r th' greatness iv th' race; an' there has been none since th' wild geese wint across th' say to France, hangin' like flies to th' side iv th' Fr-rinch ship. 'Tis on'y f'r women an' childher now, an' thim that can't get away. Will th' good days ever come again? says ye. Who knows! Who knows!"

[*EP*, Nov. 4, 1893]

The rhythms here are haunting, and expressive of a sadness that leaves no doubt about Dunne's feeling for Ireland.

The cluster of nationalist-oriented commemorative occasions in the Irish community provided a yearly seismograph of the decline and corruption of the nationalist movement in Chicago in the nineties. Mr. Dooley often attended these functions, but he always came away clear-eyed and judging, untouched by beery sentimentality. Yearly meetings were held on the anniversaries of the birth of the Irish poet Tom Moore (May 28) and of the execution of three Fenian heroes, the Manchester Martyrs (November 23).[33] The Moore celebration was an assertion of pride in Irish culture, marked by orations on Moore's works and Irish literature generally; while the Manchester memorial meeting had a more narrowly nationalist cast, the speeches consisting largely of exhortations to the defense of Ireland. *The Citizen* advertized these meetings loudly and long, and crowd estimates ran between two and five thousand every year. After the Moore celebration of 1894, Finerty lamented the small turnout, blaming "the factious spirit exhibited in Ireland, the purposeless policy pursued by the Irish parliamentary leaders, the general apathy following the hanging up of home rule by the Whigs, after the ignominious close of Gladstone's public career, and the repeated calls on the more patriotic section of the Irish people in this city" (*Citizen*, June 2, 1894). Feeling that the movement in America was "relapsing into the coldness of death," he called with characteristic blind bravado for a return to physical force, "the platform of Tone, Emmet, Mitchel, and the Fenians."

Certainly Ireland had not cornered the market on "factious spirit."
Every August 15 during the nineties the spectacle of two separate and
opposed Irish Societies' picnics symbolized the persisting Cronin split
in Chicago's nationalist ranks. Mr. Dooley's predecessor, Colonel Mc-
Neery, in his report on the picnics of 1893, concludes that faction is
a natural manifestation of Irishness:

> "There do be always two Irishmen or two sits iv Irishmen, on'y at
> a prize fight wan or th' other is licked an' done for, an' there'll be
> two Irish picnics so long's there do be two Irishmen f'r to hould thim.
>   " 'Tis the nathure iv the race an' 'tis what keeps thim haughty but
> poor to this day, an' will lave thim unsubdued be th' Sassenach, or
> be thimsilves f'r th' matther iv that, 'till th' last Turk is undher th'
> sod." [EP, Aug. 20, 1893]

The following year, Mr. Dooley attends one of the picnics, bringing to
it his memories of the Cause in the days of dynamite, when nationalism
was more exciting but equally ineffective.

> "Jawn, th' la-ads have got th' thrick iv freein' Ireland down to a
> sinsible basis. In th' ol' days they wint over with dinnymite bombs
> in their pockets, an' ayether got their rowlers on thim in Cork an'
> blew thimsilves up or was arristed in Queenstown f'r disordherly
> conduct. 'Twas a divvle iv a risky job to be a pathrite in thim days,
> an' none but those that had no wan dipindint on thim cud affoord it.
> But what was th' use? Ireland wint on bein' th' same opprissed green
> oil it had always been, an' th' on'y difference th' rivolutions made
> was ye sa-aw new faces on th' bridges an' th' Wolfe Tones passed
> another set iv resolutions. [Here Dunne again connects nationalism
> and political spoilsmanship, revealed in the dispensation of bridge-
> tenders' jobs.]
>   " 'Tis different now. Whin we wants to smash th' Sassenach an'
> restore th' land iv th' birth iv some iv us to her thrue place among
> th' nations, we gives a picnic. 'Tis a dam sight aisier thin goin' over
> with a slug iv joynt powder an' blowin' up a polis station with no
> wan in it. It costs less; an', whin 'tis done, a man can lep aboord a
> Clyburn Avnoo ca-ar, an' come to his family an' sleep it off."

The inevitable nationalist speeches at the picnic are undercut by
Dooley's description of the carnival atmosphere, complete with shoot-
ing galleries, beer concessions, and a "knock-th'-babby-down-an'-get-
a-nice-seegar jint." The day ends with a brawl between natives of
Limerick and Tipperary, which is broken up only because the chief of

police has had the foresight to send German policemen to keep the peace. Dooley's observations act as a corrective to the solemnity with which the picnics were always treated by Finerty, who usually presided and spoke at one of them. And John McKenna's closing question is well taken:

> "What's that all got to do with freeing Ireland?" asked Mr. McKenna.
> "Well, 'tis no worse off thin it was befure, annyhow," said Mr. Dooley.   [*EP,* Aug. 18, 1894]

The Cronin case, with its legacy of faction, refused to disappear from the public eye. Like Banquo's ghost, it hovered over Chicago all through the nineties, making frequent and embarrassing appearances. Between the end of the trial in 1889 and December 1892, twenty-one people connected with the case died, including (in prison) two of the convicted murderers (*EP,* Dec. 10, 1892). Many of the deaths occurred under strange circumstances, and each added to a growing mystery. Moreover, the defendants kept themselves in the news by filing motions for new trials at regular intervals. When Dan Coughlin was granted one in June 1893, the whole mess came to the surface once again. The retrial ran from November 1893 through early March 1894—even longer than the original—and it was marred, nightmarishly, by yet another jury tampering scandal. This time Coughlin was acquitted, on March 9, 1894, and a new round of fierce debate ensued. As had been his policy during the original troubles, John Finerty all but ignored the second Cronin trial; he acknowledged the verdict grudgingly with a small editorial praising the defense lawyers.[34] Mr. Dooley was now also on the scene, and he jumped at the chance to contribute. The day after the verdict was announced, he explained his difficulties in attempting to please the various factions among his customers.

> "Well sir, whin this here verdict was brought in ivry wan in th' r-road asked me me opinion iv it. Schneider, the low Dutchman what keeps down below, he comes in an' he says, says he, in his German brogue, he says: 'Well, Mr. Dooley, what ye t'ink iv dis here Coughlin peezness,' he says. 'Well,' says I, 'Bisma-ark,' I says (I allways calls him Bisma-ark), 'Bisma-ark,' I says, 'I'm ashamed iv me race,' I says. ' 'Tis a low outrage,' I says. ' 'Tis time some wan stopped this here business,' says I. 'F'r,' I says, 'if 'twas wan iv ye'er

people he'd be hung,' I says. He bought a dhrink or two an' wint away.

"Pretty soon I hears a r-roar an' in bounds Maloney, th' new sanyer guardjean iv the Wolf Tone Timp'rance an' Beniv'lent Sodality. 'Huroo!' he says. 'Huroo!' says I. 'Who's ilicted?' 'He's acquitted,' says he. 'Huroo! huroo!' says I. 'Huroo!' I says. ' 'Tis a vindication iv us again th' dips,' says I. ' 'Tis that,' says he. An' he bought an' wint away. Well, sir, he'd got no further than th' bridge whin in comes Hogan that's wan iv th' other side. 'Give us a dhrink,' he says. 'What d'ye think iv it?' ' 'Tis a nice clear day,' I says, duckin'. 'I mean th' verdict,' he says, lukin' at me ha-ard. 'What verdict?' says I. 'Haven't ye hear-rd?' he says, brightenin' up. 'They've acquitted him.' 'Acquitted him!' says I. 'Glory be to Gawd,' I says. 'How cud they do it?' says I. ' 'Tis a disgrace,' I says, an' he bought another wan an' wint away."   [*EP*, March 10, 1894]

Dooley's strategy backfires when the Croninite and anti-Croninite representatives, Maloney and Hogan, return at the same time to trade insults and begin a shop-clearing brawl that is only broken up when Dooley calls for a German policeman. The scene is humorous, but its implications for the nationalist cause are not. As at the picnic, the Irish have demonstrated that they cannot control themselves or argue peaceably about their differences.

In the nineties, St. Patrick's Day was already well established as the most important emotional focus for attitudes about Irishness. Dunne's pieces on the annual parade succeed, first of all, in evoking the pomp and circumstances of the celebration. The typical line of march included police and firemen, Irish-American militia companies (the Hibernian Rifles and Clan na Gael Guards), the Father Mathew Temperance Band and cadets, several parochial school bands and marching groups, and delegations from the city's Ancient Order of Hibernians divisions, one from every parish. As many as ten thousand would march, with over a hundred thousand spectators yearly. The day began, as it does to this day, with high mass at St. Patrick's Church, which prompted the *Chicago Times* to remark in 1889 that a "religious consciousness" had replaced the "old traditions" of "a day's enthusiasm, poteen, and a general high old time, concluding with the dilapidation of the celebrant, his regalia, and his high silk hat" (March 17, 1889). Mr. Dooley's descriptions, however, suggest that there was some carry-over of "enthusiasm" into the nineties. For example, here he mimics the grand marshall of the 1896 parade:

"Attintion! Carry ar-rms. Where's th' band? Officer Mulcahy, go
over to Dochney's an' chop that band away fr'm th' bar. Hol' on
there! Casey, don't back that big sawhorse again me. Ma, look at da-
da in Gavin's hack. Ar-re ye ready? Play up th' wearin' iv the green,
ye baloon-headed Dutchmin. Hannigan, go an' get th' polis to inther-
fere—th' Sons iv Saint Patrick an' th' Ancient Order's come together.
Glory be, me saddle's slippin'. Ar-re ye ready? For-wa-ard, march!"

[*EP,* March 21, 1896]

Dooley also details the yearly difficulty with horses, stemming from
the fact that riding is no more the forte of Chicago's Irish leaders than
of their ancestors in the old country, where only the gentry rode.

"There don't seem to be anny way iv makin' th' man's movements
agree with th' hor-rse's. Whin wan is comin' down th' other is goin'
up, an' whin wan is goin' up th' other is comin' down, an' ridin's
like holdin' a resarved seat on th' piston rod iv an ingine.

"But they stick. That's wan thing f'r thim. They stick. Ye niver
knowed a marshal to be thrown be th' mos' savage horse that iver
dhrew a dump-cart. They stick, an' r-ride it out, though r-ridin' is
th' same as sittin' on a roarin' volcano, an' they're sheddin' teeth an'
pocketpieces, an' suspinder buttons in plain view iv his grace an' th'
faculty iv th' collidge."   [*Journal,* March 19, 1898]

More important, though, are Mr. Dooley's criticisms of the parade,
through which Dunne registers his abhorrence of "professional Irishmen" and his objection to the transformation of St. Patrick's Day from
a cultural to a political event. In 1894 he complains that " 'Tis not like
it was, Jawn. In them days the pollyticians had dam'd little to do with
th' purcession an' sare a foot we put on th' South Side. 'Twas only
Pathrick's Day on th' West Side an' we liked it all th' betther" (*EP,*
March 17, 1894). Two years later, he returns to this objection and
clarifies it:

"What business have we in Mitchigan Avenoo? There ain't a vote
or a subscriber to th' Citizen there an' they'se twenty-sivin blocks iv
unfrindly houses without enough dhrink to start a fight on. Sure,
we'd a-done betther if we'd stuck where we belonged. Displaines
street, right flank ristin' again Alderman Brinnan's; south to Harr'son,
wist to Bloo I'land avnoo, south-wist to Twilfth, where th' procission
'll counthermarch befure th' Jesuit Church an' be reviewed be his
grace th' archbishop, be th' clargy an' th' mayor an' th' board iv
aldhermin. . . . The ol' days has gone, an' here are th' joods [dudes]

marchin' up an' down Mitchigan Avenoo in new clothes like masons
or thrade unions. Sure I'd 've give an eye to be back at th' ol' times
befure they put on style an' thried to impriss th' wur-ruld with how
many votes we cud tur-rn out, rain 'r shine. 'Twas Pathrick's day
thin. But now it might as well be th' annivarsary iv th' openin' iv
th' first clothin' store in Chicago."   [*EP*, March 21, 1896]

The parade route charted here falls strictly within the old eighteenth
and nineteenth wards, the Irish-American middle-class neighborhood
on Chicago's West Side in which Dunne was raised. The movement
downtown to the central business district and its major artery, Michigan Avenue, symbolizes the corruption of Irishness, and in particular
of Irish nationalism, into a saleable commodity in the marketplace of
American city politics.

In 1893 that corruption had been illustrated vividly. Alderman M. J.
O'Brien of ward nineteen introduced an ordinance to the effect that
city hall be closed on St. Patrick's Day. Few council members cared
to risk the wrath of their Irish constituents, so the motion passed
easily. A heated controversy ensued, during which most of the city's
prominent Irishmen repudiated the closing order. William J. Onahan,
moderate spokesman for Irishmen of wealth in the city, who was
serving as Chicago comptroller, refused to close his own office and
issued a statement condemning the closing as "a scheme of small fry
politicians to gain a little popularity in some quarters." [35] John Finerty
declared that the closing was "well meant, but an error," and that
"Irish-Americans want equality, not ascendancy" (*Citizen*, March 25,
1893). And Dunne's *Evening Post* editorial page blasted Alderman
O'Brien as representing "nothing in Chicago but himself and the other
groggery keepers, in council and out of it, who will reap the only profit
from turning their heelers in the city hall loose for a holiday. It is an
insult to religion and a disgrace to the much abused Irish cause that
such miscreants should appear in public to speak for either" (March
16, 1893). A follow-up editorial calls for the discontinuance of the
parade, which the writer feels to be "out of harmony with Irish sentiment of to-day, which finds more appropriate, more intelligent and
practical ways of honoring Ireland's patron saint and serving the national cause" (March 19, 1893).[36] At least some shift of perspective
had occurred by 1896, when a second city hall closing proposal was
introduced by Alderman Johnny Powers and was soundly defeated in

council. This time around, the highlight of the debate was Alderman Larsen's remark that "St. Patrick been dead and gone years ago" (*T-H*, March 16, 1896).

Mr. Dooley's interest in St. Patrick reaches its low point in his last March 17 piece in Chicago. Hennessy has to remind him of the planned celebration, which he claims to have forgotten: "Patrick's Day? It seems to me I've heard th' name befure. Oh, ye mane th' day th' low Irish that hasn't anny votes cillybrates th' birth iv their naytional saint, who was a Fr-rinchman" (*Journal*, March 11, 1899). The point of Dooley's memory lapse is that most of America's leaders, including President McKinley, have proven to be fair weather (that is, election year) friends of the Irish:

"A few years ago ye'd see the President iv th' United States marchin' down Pinnsylvanya Avnoo, with the green scarf iv th' Ancient Ordher on his shoulders an' a shamrock in his hat. Now what is Mack doin'? He's settin' in his parlor, writin' letthers to th' queen, be hivins, askin' afther her health." [*Journal,* March 11, 1899]

So weak and divided against themselves are the Irish, in both Ireland and America, that McKinley considers them politically expendable. At any rate, this is Dooley's somewhat cynical conclusion: "There are different kinds iv hands from acrost th' sea. There are pothry [poetry] hands an' rollin'-mill hands; but on'y wan kind has votes."

Another sign that the nationalist spirit was on the wane in Chicago was the Orange parade of 1895. On July 12 the Protestant Irish of the city marched in celebration of the 1690 Battle of the Boyne, a kind of counter-St. Patrick's Day that marked British ascendancy over the Irish. Dooley reports somewhat wistfully that the 1895 parade went off without incident, unlike the situation in previous years, "whin an Orangey'd as lave go through hell in a celluloid suit as march in this here town on the twelfth iv July" (*EP*, July 13, 1895). He goes on to regale John McKenna with hair-raising tales of Catholic-Protestant battles of the past and, unregenerate, ends up asking McKenna to find him some bricks to "hand" at a passing Armagh man who "digs with his left foot" (meaning that he's a Protestant). A *Journal* editorial on July 12, 1898, almost certainly by Dunne, makes the same point—the days of nationalist-unionist disruption are gone—but makes it very differently. Here again we find the split between Dunne the editorial writer and his Dooley persona, for the editorial ridicules the Boyne issue, concluding that "perhaps Irishmen are beginning to appreciate the absurdity of celebrating a battle that transferred the rule of their country from a wooden-headed Scotchman to a bigoted Dutchman and solidified religious hatreds that have kept Ireland poor and troubled for two hundred years." [37]

Nor does an important upcoming nationalist celebration generate much enthusiasm in Chicago. Mr. Dooley is contemptuous of the Irish who plan to commemorate the centennial of the 1798 rising.

> "An' 'twill be th' gran' thing to see all th' good la-ads marchin' down Sackville sthreet singin' 'Who fears to speak iv ninety-eight, who blushes at th' name?' No wan, an' that's th' throuble. If they were afeerd to speak iv it, 'twud be dangerous, an' I'm thinkin' th' more public it is th' less it amounts to."   [*EP*, Dec. 31, 1897]

He was right, of course. Very little of a politically constructive nature was being accomplished in Ireland in the nineties. After the Parnell split, the Irish parliamentary party was hopelessly splintered for years; even the much stronger anti-Parnellite forces were divided, as Tim Healy and John Dillon struggled for control throughout the decade. Moreover, as F. S. L. Lyons has pointed out, Dillon's reestablishing of an essentially Parnellite unity and discipline within the party in 1910 was itself illusory. It remained for the "terrible beauty" of Easter 1916 to bring the country together again.[38] Thus, Mr. Dooley mirrors what must have been a pervasive Irish-American attitude in looking back longingly to the days when "Charles Stewart Parnell was a bigger man thin th' pope" in Bridgeport (*EP*, Oct. 20, 1894).

When Gladstone's third home rule bill passes the House of Commons in September 1893, Colonel McNeery and his patrons hardly blink, for they know the House of Lords will kill it, and besides, the "prisint gin'ration" of Irish party members are "a poor, spiritless, washed out lot," judging from those who have come to Chicago soliciting funds. "Those iv thim I've seen over here wears white pa-ants an' smokes cigareets an' thries to talk with an English accint which is as r-raspin' on th' nerves as to hear a Dutchman singin' 'Fa-ather O'Flynn'" (*EP*, Sept. 9, 1893). Mr. Dooley takes the occasion of Gladstone's retirement in March 1894 to further lament the new breed of Irish and English politicians, all of whom look to him like "play-actors," especially the new prime minister, Lord "Raspberry," his inevitable rendering of the dandyish Rosebery. Dooley goes on here to recall the glorious days of the Gladstone-Parnell alliance of 1886, when home rule seemed a certainty:

> "Well, I was sayin'," said Mr. Dooley, "that Gladstun was a great man. But there was wan gr-reater. 'Twas Charles Stewart Parnell. Mind ye, Jawn, Gladstun wasn't always a frind of Ireland, mind ye that. By dad, he put more dinnymiters in th' booby-hatch thin anny man iv his day. An' he an' Parnell, they had it out an' out at th' prim'ries an' th' convintions. They was just like Billy O'Broyn an' Willum Joyce, d'ye mind. An' though most iv th' time Gladstun'd win out he always knew he had an argymint, f'r Parnell had th' la-ads back iv him, an' whiniver the comity'd give him a judge, by dad, 'twas all day moosh with Gladstun. Well, sir, wan day th' ol' la-ad he goes to Parnell an' says he: 'Parnell, we've had many a scrap,' he says. 'We have that,' says Parnell. 'But there's no ha-ard feelin',' says Gladstun. 'Divvle th' bit,' says Parnell. ' 'Twas all in the line iv di-varsion f'r me.' 'Well,' says Gladstun, 'we're all good fellows,' he says. 'Let's be good fellows together,' he says. 'An' we can skin Salsbry,' he says, 'Salsbry's a dip'ty.' 'He is,' says Parnell. 'I know it,' says Gladstun. 'I know the ca-amp he belongs to,' says he. 'Thin,' says Parnell, 'I'm right along with ye.' An' they had a frish wan together an' they niver parted till poor Parnell passed away, may his sowl—"
>
> "But—Ireland isn't free yet!" said Mr. McKenna.
>
> "No," said Mr. Dooley. "Th' Prince iv Wales thrun thim down."
>
> [*EP*, March 3, 1894] [39]

Mr. Dooley is similarly unimpressed by the Venezuela boundary dispute between the United States and Great Britain in the fall of 1895. He treats with proper scorn the flurry of "England's misfortune is Ireland's opportunity" talk that circulates in his saloon during that crisis; and when the Wolf Tones resolve "to invade Canada the first time they get a day off at the rolling-mills," he can only shake his head. Those days seem to be gone forever (*EP*, Dec. 21, 28, 1895).

When Dunne moved on to a New York-based commentary on the wider world, Irish-American nationalism in Chicago lost a valuable critic. To those who were listening, Mr. Dooley provided many things: perspective on the Clan na Gael and Fenian past, warnings to the nationalists of the threat of internal dissension and venal political aspiration, determined deflation of the excesses and hypocrisies of nationalistic rhetoric, and a realistic assessment of the unpromising status of the movement in Ireland and America. Still, his pieces were misconstrued by the nationalist leaders. In addition to John Finerty's opposition, Dunne was periodically accused of affiliation with the American Protective Association, an Anglo-Saxon supremacist, anti-immigration group; and Patrick Ford of *The Irish World* (New York's answer to *The Citizen*) even refused in 1899 to carry advertisements for Dunne's second book, *Mr. Dooley in the Hearts of His Country-men*.[40] That these men ignored Mr. Dooley's valid and illuminating examinations of their cause is one more illustration of W. B. Yeats's sad maxim: "Too long a sacrifice/ Can make a stone of the heart." [41]

6

FROM BRIDGEPORT
TO MANILA

Mr. Dooley Becomes a National Sage

Then fare you well, McNarry!
An' farewell Pether Dunne!
I'm swallowed up in "Dooley"
An' vanished is my fun!
Oh for th' owld time evenings
When I heard th' bull-frogs mew,
And watched th' purple sunset
On th' banks of Healy's Slough!

"DOOLEY'S LAMENTATION" [1]

MR. DOOLEY did not wake from uneasy dreams to find himself suddenly changed into a national sage. His timely satiric illuminations of American folly in the Spanish-American War marked the final step in what was a gradual transformation from spokesman and chronicler of the Chicago Irish community to commentator on the affairs of America and the world. In fact, a three-stage progression to his ultimate role is observable in a chronological reading of all the Chicago pieces.

Mr. Dooley's interests had never been narrowly parochial. From the beginning he was a habitual reader of "th' pa-apers," commenting on national and international affairs with the same bemused fascination that he brought to his descriptions of life in Bridgeport. In the earliest pieces, however, his attention is always focused on Archer Avenue. National events invariably inspire Bridgeport anecdotes, which take up more space and are clearly more important to Dooley than the events themselves. Grover Cleveland's difficulty with an intractable Congress in the fall of 1893 prompts Dooley to advise the president to adopt the tactical spoilsmanship of Chicago's Mayor Carter Harrison, whose plan for a garbage dump in Bridgeport is opposed by Alderman Billy O'Brien (*EP,* Oct. 21, 1893). The Corbett-Mitchell heavyweight title fight of January 1894 reminds him of the longer and bloodier match between Mr. and Mrs. Malachi Duggan (*EP*, Jan. 27, 1894). And the scandalous conviction in a breach of promise suit against a Kentucky legislator leads into the story of the theft of Hogan's goat by Sarsfield Dugan, "th' most rispictable man that ever come over th' hills" (*EP, April 14, 1894*). This technique is operating well when Mr. Dooley turns the march on Washington by Coxey's Army into a vignette about the parish collection in Bridgeport:

"So be Coxey. Th' omadhon [Irish for clumsy oaf], he gets a lot of gazaboys together an' he says to thim: 'Let's go down to Washin'ton,' says he, 'an' in-vade it,' he says, 'an' we'll tache thim what's what,' he says. He calls it the commonwheel, he does; an' why, I dinnaw, f'r all iv thim has to walk. By gar, I sh'd think he'd ca-al it th' common fut. 'Tis more thrue to nathure. So they're off, an' whin those iv thim that ain't thrun into th' booby hatch gets down to Washin'ton 'twill be time f'r Cleveland to put on his hat an' coat. F'r if I ain't much mistaken 'twill go ha-ard with him. As I said, this here Coxey is a determined man, Jawn, an' whin he

makes up his mind he's as ris'lute as th' parish priest takin' subscrip-
tions f'r a new church. Gawd, be good to me that shouldn't be sayin'
th' like iv that. Did I niver tell ye how th' little soggarth [priest] up
wist iv th' bridge put th' comether on me wan time. He wanted to
have a spire on th' church an' I was th' soft ma-ark iv th' parish. He
wint out afther me, an' by gar, I made up me mind to escape. I
hired Dorney's lad to watch f'r him, an' whin he see th' good man
comin' he passed th' wurrud an' I pulled down th' blinds an' sneaked
out th' ba-ack way. Well, sir, we had it to an' fro f'r near a month
an' I wint to mass all that time in th' little Frinch church beyant
where ye'd expect to see th' pastor doin' a jig step ivry time he
r-read th' gospel fr'm Saint Jawn. Hivin help me, me tongue's r-run
away. Well, sir, th' little soggarth thried be letters an' be missingers
to land me, but I stud him off till wan day I was standin' down at
th' dure an' see him comin' up th' r-road. I r-run inside an' bolted
th' dure. Thin I waited. I heerd him talkin' with th' la-ad an' thin
there come a knock. 'Misther Dooley,' says th' kid, 'he's gone.'
'He's not,' says I. 'He is,' says th' little rogue. 'He's gone an' he lef'
a goold watch an' chain f'r ye,' he says, says th' la-ad, 'that they
voted ye as th' mos' pop'lar man in th' parish.' Well, Jawn, ye know
I was dam sthrong in thim days an' I thought it was on th' square
an' I opened th' dure. Th' minyit I did in come a good-sized broad-
cloth leg an' th' smilin' face iv th' little soggarth. Me strenth left me
an' I let him all in. 'Well,' I says, 'ye've bate me,' I says. 'But savin'
ye'r prisince,' I says, ' 'tis a strange example ye give.' 'Be what?'
says he. 'Be lyin',' says I. 'Sure,' says he, 'I didn't lie,' he says. ' 'Twas
th' la-ad, an' I'll give him a pinance that'll br-reak his back. An' now,'
he says, 'about that spire ye wa-ant so bad.' Well, sir, he got me
f'r wan hundhred bucks, an' afther all I didn't begredge it, Jawn.
He was a good man, the little soggarth that died along in sixty-sivin
iv nursin' th' chollery patients. Pax vobiscum."   [*EP*, April 21, 1894]

The second stage emerges in 1895, when there begins to be more
balance between the Bridgeport vignettes and the national events that
spark them. For example, the threat of war with Spain over Cuba in
March 1895 prompts an Archer Avenue parable on the subject of
barroom brawling, the moral of which is never pick on a little man
when you're spoiling for a fight. But here Mr. Dooley follows through
by carefully applying the anecdote to the Spanish dispute, indicating
that Dunne was concerned about both parts of the essay.

"Now, 'tis much th' same with counthries, Jawn. Clancy'd had a
bad wurrud flung in his face an' he hadn't took it up an' he'd

brooded on it, an' whin he'd dhrunk himself blind he come up lookin' f'r fight. An' he picked out th' wrong man. So be th' United States. 'Tis not f'r me to sa-ay who does be right an' who does be wrong in this here thing. I'm r-runnin' me little liquor shop an' Gresham [Cleveland's secretary of state] does be r-runnin' his own job. But it looks to me like as if we was so dam cocky just f'r an' because Spain is a lightweight counthry an' not much out f'r throuble. Look out that we don't get our hands full. A big dhrunk man is th' littlest man there is, an' there are dhrunk min an' dhrunk counthries, Jawn." [*EP,* March 23, 1895]

Similarly, Mr. Dooley gives equal time to the Monroe and Hoolihan doctrines in discussing the British-American quarrel over the boundary of Venezuela in October 1895. He spends half the piece describing British "incroachmints" on this continent and "Doc Mon-roe's" prescription: "if . . . anny iv th' Eur-opyean powers attimpted to throw th' boots into anny counthry on this continent, we'd throw th' boots into thim." Then comes Hoolihan's opposite principle:

"Jerry Hoolihan was a polisman an' he held his job f'r thirty year. He was thravelin' beat wan night an' a woman put her head out iv a window an' says she, 'Officer!'—like that. 'What can I do f'r ye, lady?' says Hoolihan. 'Me husband's dhrunk,' says she, 'I thried to subdue him with a flat iron an' he's gone f'r an ax,' she says. 'I can do nawthin' f'r ye,' says Hoolihan. ' 'Tis on ye'er beat,' says th' lady. 'I know it,' says Hoolihan. 'But there's pig's feet on me beat, too. I'm goin' f'r some at this minyit,' he says.
    " 'I don't see what that's got to do with Vin-ezwala,' says Hinnissy. 'Well,' says I, ' 'tis th' Hoolihan doctorin'. Niver stop to fight whin ye'er goin' to supper,' says I." [*EP,* Oct. 19, 1895]

The tendency toward balance in these pieces of 1895 and 1896 slips steadily toward the third and last stage of Dunne's treatment of national and international materials, in which all that remains of Bridgeport is Mr. Dooley's voice, engaged exclusively in discussions of the wider world.

The subject of Mr. Dooley's first extended foray into national affairs was not the Spanish-American War, which made him famous and sealed his fate, but the Bryan-McKinley presidential campaign of 1896. Dunne had covered both national conventions that year for the *Chicago Times-Herald,* a newspaper that had recently been converted

from a Democratic to a Republican organ. The context of that conversion is important to the Dooley pieces on the campaign, which appeared in the *Post,* the *Times-Herald*'s evening affiliate. The product
of a March 1895 merger of the two most popular Democratic newspapers in Chicago, the *Times-Herald* had been the brainchild of *Herald*
publisher James W. Scott. His untimely death six weeks after the merger caused the new paper and the *Evening Post* to be thrown onto the
open market for sale. They were bought by Herman H. Kohlsaat, a
wealthy Chicago bakery and restaurant owner, a staunch Republican,
and an early McKinley supporter. Declaring that "this paper is going
to be strictly independent, except that it will be for protection, for
William McKinley, and for anything he wants," Kohlsaat dictated and
supervised the *Times-Herald*'s editorial shift from Democratic to Republican and also brought the *Evening Post* along, thereby destroying
its longstanding reputation for nonpartisan, scholarly treatment of issues. The Kohlsaat regime also brought significant changes in Dunne's
journalistic life. He was transferred from his position as *Post* editorial
chairman to the staff of the *Times-Herald,* where his colleagues included Alexander Sullivan's wife, Margaret, and Slason Thompson,
former editor of *America.* (Strange bedfellows—a committed Irish
nationalist and an anti-immigration, Anglo-Saxon supremacist!) More
important, as Ellis points out, the earnest Republican tone of the new
Times-Herald editorial page left Mr. Dooley as "the only real outlet
for Dunne's gift of witty and satirical writing." [2] No doubt Mr. Dooley's increased consciousness of national politics at this time is directly
related to the strictures placed on Dunne as an editorial writer.

At any rate, Mr. Dooley begins to be interested in the question of
coinage in April and May 1895, simultaneously with a *Times-Herald*
campaign of daily editorial refutation of William H. "Coin" Harvey's
free silver arguments.[3] Keeping himself impartial, Mr. Dooley ridicules
the extreme positions of both sides, and concludes by warning that

> "th' nex' man that opins his head to mintion it, I'll bounce into th'
> middle iv th' sthreet at a ratio iv sixteen to wan—sixteen wallops
> with th' bungstarter to wan head. . . . An' I give notice that hince-
> forth all bimettalic conf'rinces 'll pay cash in advance. I'll restore th'
> paratty bechune a shell iv beer an' th' nickel iv commerce if I have to
> break some wan's back." [EP, April 27, 1895] [4]

The following summer, ten days before the Republican National Convention, Dunne began a series of Dooley pieces on the campaign. The scope of the series has not been noticed because so few of the eighteen pieces have been republished. Dunne also kept these pieces free of the militant McKinleyism of the *Post* and *Times-Herald* editorial pages by establishing Mr. Dooley's neutrality—primarily by introducing Hennessy, a mill-worker and typical Irish Democrat whose free-silver position balances the goldbug-McKinleyism of Dooley's original listener, John McKenna.[5] Each takes an extreme and dogmatic stand, which allows Mr. Dooley to stand comfortably in the middle, exploiting the comic potential of both camps. Hennessy's name had come up in a few Dooley-McKenna conversations as an undifferentiated member of the Bridgeport community, but Dunne had never before included him as a contributing, center-stage personality. After the campaign, however, Hennessy replaced McKenna entirely, for Dunne realized the advantages of his new character as a foil for Mr. Dooley. Stolid and a little slow, Hennessy could be expected to listen quietly and sometimes uncomprehendingly to Mr. Dooley's flights of fancy. Also, as a working man with a large family, he was a more typical Bridgeporter than McKenna. Finally, as a wholly fictional creation, he allowed freer play to Dunne's imagination.

Coinage and the heated campaign were ideal targets for Mr. Dooley's skeptical scrutiny. Few presidential contests have been fought on so definite and controversial an issue as that of 1896, and few key issues have been so fraught with mathematical and economic complications as that of coinage. Dunne simply picked up the thread of his earlier coinage pieces, and Mr. Dooley had a high old time from June to November. A major theme is his cutting through the lofty talk of principles to see the silver question as a debate between lobbying interest groups of rich and poor, with the forgotten middle class left voiceless and unrepresented.

"On wan side I see a lad that's niver had eight dollars together at wan time an' that borrahs money fr'm th' hired girl to get downtown on, ready an' willin' to issue wan hundherd millions iv greenbacks on his own hook, an' on th' other hand I see a man that a year ago looked as though he was thryin' to do a back somerset whin a poor divvil come by with a dinner pail in his hand, an' that was f'r

standin' ivrybody that cudden't show a passbook up in a line f'r to
have a lot iv Swedes fr'm Fort Sheridan shoot at thim, now gatherin'
a happy fam'ly 'round him an' addhressin' thim on th' needs iv th'
workinman. Whiniver I see a man that's niver brought annything
home to his wife iv a Saturdah night but a song an' dance on th'
rights iv labor, I find a free-silver ad-vocate. An' whiniver I see a
man that's ready to have murdher done in th' name iv law an' 'd
rather buy cartridges thin bread, I find th' other kind. It looks to
me like a contist bechune Tom's Lodgin' House an' th' Audjootoroom,
bechune th' alley an' th' boolyvard, bechune thim th' polis looks
afther an' thim they ought to. But what I'd like to know is, where th'
meejum people comes in? Where are th' poor divvles that don't owe
annything an' have nothin' owin' to thim? There must be wan or
two bechune th' bank prisidint an' th' hobo. What're they goin'
to do?"

Mr. McKenna said nothing, but laughed.

"If I had to advise thim in this campaign," said Mr. Dooley, "I'd
give thim what an ol' sign in th' Union dee-poh used to say: 'Lind
no money to sthrangers; bee-ware iv pickpockets.' "

[*EP,* Aug. 15, 1896]

Mr. Dooley heartily enjoys recapitulating the cataclysmic predictions
of goldbugs and silverites alike. "Th' counthry's ruined, annyway you
luk at it," he claims on July 3. "If we get free silver at a ratio iv sixteen
to wan, with goold even money an' lunch twelve to two, th' whole dam
fabric iv th' gov'rmint 'll tumble down." Depositors and European
investors will pull their money out of American banks, and "th' credi-
tor class'll be skinned an' the few people that owes money will be th'
cocks iv th' walk." On the other hand, if free silver loses,

> "Wall sthreet'l have its foot on th' poor an' th' lowly. Th' Prince iv
> Wales 'll be r-runnin' th' whole counthry. Manny a man that today
> is injyin' his constitootinal right to stand off th' constable 'll have to
> pay his debts. An' they'll be wurruk f'r all. An' that's th' worst iv it.
> As far as I can see—an', Jawn, between you an' me, I can see as
> far as anny man through a dale board—th' raysult iv a goold standard
> 'll be that rich an' poor alike 'll be made to wurruk. They'll be no
> escape f'r anny livin' man undher th' sun."   [*EP,* July 3, 1896]

As to counseling which way to vote, Dooley never gets more serious
than his advocacy of the whiskey standard: "It niver fluctuates; an'
that's funny too, seein' that so much iv it goes down. . . . Goold an'
silver fluctuates, up wan day, down another; but whisky stands firm

an' strong, unchangeable as th' skies, immovable as a rock at fifteen or two f'r a quarther" (*EP*, Aug. 1, 1896).

For all their lightheartedness, though, these pieces contain trenchant commentary on the American political scene. For example, Mr. Dooley's contempt for preelection oracles stands up well today against Gallup, Harris, and the CBS computer.

> "That's th' beauty iv iliction statistics—they're not burdened with annything like facts. All a man wants is a nice room in th' back iv a Chinese laundhry an' a lung full iv hop an' he can make a monkey out iv th' la-ad that wrote th' arithmetic. He sees majorities grinnin' through th' transom an' roostin' on th' top iv th' bed an' crawlin' up his leg. Here's wan man says Texas will go raypublican, an' th' on'y states Bryan has sure is Mississippi, Arkansaw an' Hell. Here's another claims Bryan 'll carry New Hampshire an' upper Canada an' that Bill McKinley won't get wan vote in Canton but his own, an' he won't get that if he hears Bryan make wan speech."

He goes on to report a few "straw votes," the results of which are both humorous and acute: "A pool iv Lyman J. Gage [prominent Chicago banker] was taken yistherday. It was conducted on th' Austhralyan system an' it was sthrictly private. It showed $16,000,000 f'r McKinley an' none f'r Bryan. Thursdah Governor Altgeld took a secret ballot iv himself. It showed him almost solid f'r Altgeld an' Bryan." [6] Finally, after all the polls are in, Mr. Dooley remains uncommitted.

> "An' who ar-re ye goin' to vote f'r?" demanded Mr. Hennessy.
> "That's my business," said Mr. Dooley.
> "Anarchist!" roared Mr. McKenna.
> "Co-erced!" hissed Mr. Hennessy.
>   And Mr. Dooley swore because the seltzer wouldn't fizz before they reached the door.   [*EP*, Oct. 3, 1896]

Mr. Dooley also disagrees astutely with Bryan's policy of maximum exposure to the common people. Commenting on the campaign wind-up in Chicago, when the candidate spoke at twenty-four neighborhood halls and social clubs in three days, Dooley declares emphatically that

> "th' more people sees a candidate f'r Prisidint th' less votes he gets. If I was Bryan's manager I'd keep him in a chilled-steel safe an' have him talk in a phonograph. Th' lad Hanna has th' right idee. He makes his inthry stay at home an' on'y those that have carfare or

passes can get a squint at him. Th' rest iv th' counthry can't tell whin he's dhropped part iv his breakfast on his coat front or whether he's gettin' bald on th' back iv his head." [*EP,* Oct. 17, 1896] [7]

Perhaps familiarity did breed contempt in the urban electorate; Cook County went Republican in November by 65,000 votes (*T-H,* Nov. 4, 1896).

Rhetoric was important in 1896 from the beginning, when Bryan's nomination followed hard upon his electrifying "Cross of Gold" speech. Certainly, the surface simplicity of the issue of gold vs. silver lent itself readily to flights of polarizing oratory on both sides. And because he had been observing Chicago politicians and Irish nationalists for years, Dunne was well qualified to expose rhetorical excess on the national level. He had sufficient perspective on the "Cross of Gold" speech, for example, to parody it immediately—in a Bridgeport political vignette in which a young reformer running for alderman declares that "ye shall not, Billy O'Brien, . . . crucify th' voters iv th' Sixth Ward on th' double cross" (*EP,* July 18, 1896). O'Brien's subsequent easy victory through application of the principle that "th' roly-boly [money for bribery] is th' gr-reatest or-rator on earth" provides a further comment on Bryan's chances against McKinley's formidable monetary assets.[8] The following week Mr. Dooley parodies the Bryan speech again in a report of the Populist convention in St. Louis, where the delegates quarrel heatedly over which state song should be used to open the proceedings. When the chairman rules in favor of a song from Oklahoma, a New Mexico delegate rises to assert that "ye shall not press down upon our bleedin' brows this cross iv thorns, . . . Ye shall not crucify th' diligates fr'm th' imperyal Territ'ry iv New Mexico on this cross iv a Mississippi nigger an' Crow Injun fr'm Oklahoma" (*EP,* July 25, 1896).

In early August, Mr. Dooley reports on Bryan's oratorical progression toward Chicago in the language of the American tall tale:

"Is Bryan comin'?" Mr. Dooley asked.
"Sure he is," said Mr. McKenna.
"Thin that explains it," said Mr. Dooley.
"Explains what?"
"Th' heat. What else cud cause it? Th' nearer he comes th' hotter it gets. Willum Joyce tol' me he'd bur-rn up th' counthry an' he's doin' it. Whin he wint on his las' thrip th' cor-rn took fire in th' fields

an' th' stacks was all flamin' like so manny torches. Th' injine r-run out iv fuel an' Bryan had to go for'd an' talk into th' boiler. He whispered tin wurruds an' th' safety-valve was wrenched. Every place he stopped th' fire departmint turned out an' played on th' audjence durin' his speech. He fell into a conversation in th' car with a goal bug an' melted th' brass chandeliers. He did so. Whin he put his head out iv th' window wanst to hail a man he see goin' by th' air was full iv live coals an' a livery stable in Oconto bur-rned up with all on boord. Lately, f'r reasons iv public safety, he's been talkin' through a cake iv ice, but even thin 'tis unsafe to go too near him."

"But I suppose you'll go to hear him?" asks John McKenna. "I'll go, be dad," Dooley replies, "if I have to rint an asbestos coat an' carry a Babcock fire-extinguisher" (*EP*, Aug. 8, 1896).

Throughout the campaign, Mr. Dooley presents the issues in pointed parodies of political speech; not only in the discussions of coinage, but also in more general remarks such as the following, in which the reader is given a choice of poisons:

"'Tis th' importance iv th' sthruggle makes it exciting. 'Tis no mere party question. On wan side are arrayed th' inimies iv th' counthry, thim lads that wud tear down th' immortal sthructure reared up be Washin'ton, Adams, Jackson, Lincoln, Grant and Lazard freres; on th' other side are th' pathrites an' th' bulwarks iv naytional honor. Or, if ye don't take kindly to that, on wan side are th' insidious foes iv pop'lar liberty that are bint on establishin' a monarchy in this counthry, an' on th' other side are th' pure-minded heroes that wud keep intact th' liberties definded by Washin'ton, Adams, Jackson, Lincoln, Grant an' Jake Kern." [*EP,* Oct. 24, 1896]

Inherent in his balancing of these ludicrous excesses is Dunne's conviction that hot air alone changes nothing. Even before the Democratic convention, Mr. Dooley knows that all the talk of revolution is going to resolve itself into equal parts of apathy and self-delusion.

"They'd be no escape fr'm a horrible ol' ruction if it wasn't that they'se sivinty million people in this land iv th' free an' home iv th' brave that don't care anny more f'r th' vital issue thin if 'twas a circus where they was ast to vote f'r th' most beautifullest woman. Gawd help thim; they owe money an' have it owed to thim, and they always will, an' they'll be no betther off wan way or th' other, an' 'twud be a man with th' sowl iv a shrimp that'd deny thim th' pleasure they have encouragin' a dogfight ivry four years—an' thinkin' they're th' dogs."
[*EP,* July 3, 1896]

And at campaign's end, amid mutual declarations of war by the armies
of silver and gold, Dooley remains unruffled and unconvinced.

> " 'It may look like war now,' I says. 'An' it may look like war nex'
> Choosdah night, but Win'sdah mornin',' I says, 'it'll on'y be th' fag
> end iv th' common dhrunk that it is,' I says. 'Ye'll wake up at home
> or in th' polis station,' I says, 'an' wondher where ye got that bad
> taste in ye'er mouth an' why ye'er voice sounds like a man planin' a
> pine knot an' who hit ye, just as ye done befure,' I says. 'Th'
> wurruld'll go on just th' same. Th' starry banners iv freedom'll be tore
> down, th' stock exchange will shuffle up th' ca-ards an' begin playin'
> f'r markers, an' th' arnychists an' th' pathrites together will carry th'
> immortal hod up th' laddher an' there'll not be wan r-red brick or wan
> pound iv mort shy f'r all that th' counthry's been saved an' th'
> govermint at Wash'n'ton still lives.' "   [EP, Oct. 31, 1896]

In his election postmortem piece, Mr. Dooley finds that "th' defeat
iv Humanity be Prosperity" (McKinley's victory) means only the re-
sumption of work, because "Prosperity grabs ivry man be th' neck, an'
sets him shovellin' slag or coke or runnin' up an' down a ladder with
a hod iv mortar. It won't let th' wurruld rest. . . . It goes round like a
polisman givin' th' hot fut to happy people that are snoozin' in th' sun"
(EP, Nov. 7, 1896). He is understandably contemptuous of the general rejoicing in the daily press, which "is run be a lot iv gazabos that
thinks wurruk is th' ambition iv mankind." On the contrary, he reasons, "most iv th' people I know 'd be happiest layin' on a lounge with
a can near by, or stretchin' thimsilves f'r another nap at eight in th'
mornin'." Dooley ends the piece and the election series with a laconic
rejoinder to John McKenna that carries the full weight of Dunne's
ironic perspective:

> "We must all work," said Mr. McKenna sententiously.
> "Yes," said Mr. Dooley, "or be wurruked."

Though the issues take him far afield, Mr. Dooley still makes an
effort in these pieces to balance national events and their relevance in
Bridgeport. The postelection piece just quoted, for example, contains
an apposite memory of political boss Mike McDonald's gambling
house, which Dooley compares to the stock exchange, rejuvenated by
McKinley's election. Moreover, Dooley's continuing concern with the

campaign was plausible because so much of the excitement had centered in Chicago. The Democratic convention had been there, Governor Altgeld played a major role throughout the campaign, and Bryan made his climactic appearances in the city.

Few such local connections existed between Chicago and the Spanish-American War of 1898. The trouble in Cuba had been on America's mind since at least 1895, however, so it was natural for Mr. Dooley to be talking about it too. Where that interest ultimately led him no one could have predicted, least of all Peter Dunne. Like the makers of American foreign policy, he was blind to the implications of involvement with Cuba: for both, it was an unexpectedly decisive step.

Early in 1895, the last in a series of insurrections against Spanish rule broke out in Cuba. By September, every major newspaper in Chicago was at least considering American intervention, so convincing were the stories of Spanish atrocities against the rebelling colony. Even the moderate *Times-Herald* deplored "the perpetuated repetition of government by systematic plunder and massacre in an island country not a hundred miles distant from our own southeastern coast" (Sept. 24, 1895). On September 30, two mass meetings were held in the city, at both of which resolutions were passed recognizing the belligerent rights of Cuba (*T-H*, Sept. 30, Oct. 1, 1895). Thus began the clamor for aid to Cuba that was to mount steadily under the name of jingoism until the declaration of war against Spain in April 1898. During the intervening two and one-half years, Cuba was in the headlines constantly. In New York City, Joseph Pulitzer and William Randolph Hearst started their bitter competition for sensational news, and yellow journalism was born in the harrowing tales of Spanish Governor-General Weyler's merciless "reconcentration" policies. Pressure for war came also from increasingly vocal advocates of American expansion such as Alfred Thayer Mahan and Theodore Roosevelt, and from a Congress sensitive to the pro-Cuban sympathies of larger and larger numbers of constituents.[9]

Before the sinking of the battleship *Maine* at Havana, Mr. Dooley changes his mind several times about what should be America's course of action regarding Cuba. Dunne did not republish these pieces, perhaps because of their inconsistency, but as a group they mirror the confusion that prevailed among even the most thoughtful and best informed Americans. The earliest Dooley response, quoted above to illustrate Dunne's interweaving of Bridgeport and the wider world, warns of the danger of American cockiness toward Spain by means of an analogy with barroom brawling: "A big dhrunk man is th' littlest man there is, an' there are dhrunk min an' dhrunk countries" (*EP*, March 23, 1895). The piece appeared after a Spanish man-of-war had fired upon an American merchant ship, the *Allianca*. The official apology offered by Spain seemed inadequate to the American jingoist press, which used the incident to fuel their campaign for intervention in Cuba (*EP*, March 18, 19, 1895).

Mr. Dooley reverses himself in his next response, delivered during the February 1896 Senate debate over a resolution calling for recognition of the Cuban rebels. Scorning the proliferation of rhetoric on the issue—"this is th' year iv th' big wind"—Dooley regrets that "we're not a fightin' nation, me la-ad. We used to be, but thim days is long past. . . . If gunboats was phonographs an' th' wurruld done its scrappin' be wurrud iv mouth we'd clane off th' face iv th' globe iv all but th' ring-tailed monkeys, an' we'd tire thim out" (*EP*, Feb. 29, 1896). Continuing on this tack in April, Dooley acknowledges America's position as "th' mos' powerful nation on earth," but again doubts whether that power will be brought to bear against Spain. But here his ambivalence comes out, for at the end of the piece he deplores war and cowardice at the same time, in a curious mixture of irony and chauvinism that allows no clear position to emerge:

> "I don't mind havin' a war. I'd as lave as not th' Ar-rchey road r-run knee deep in th' blood iv th' invader. I'd sacrifice anny frind I have on earth rather than see this country overcome or humiliated. But what I kick again is th' suspense. I want to find out, Jawn, are we a nation iv fighters or a nation iv foot-racers?" [*EP*, April 11, 1896]

Mr. Dooley also sometimes minimizes the gravity of the Cuban situation. At one point he postulates that Spanish commander Weyler and rebel leader Maceo are really allies engaged in bamboozling the rest of the world: "They wint to school together an' married sisters. They'se no hard feelin' between thim. Maceo is stirrin' up throuble f'r th' sake iv keepin' his brother-in-law imployed" (*EP*, Nov. 21, 1896). Also in this vein is Dooley's declaration that reports of General

Maceo's death (like those of Mark Twain's) have been greatly exaggerated. The occasion prompts one of Dunne's flights of wild fancy:

> "Iv coorse 'tis a death blow to th' rivolution. Ivrything is a death blow to th' rivolution. Th' frequint obsequies iv McCeo is wan iv th' most frightful features iv th' crool war. His death rate is higher thin th' nineteenth wa-ard's. He has an annual mortality iv twelve in a hundhred. He crosses th' throchay an' dies an' he crosses it back an' dies again. He's perishin' like sheep with th' rot. He's dyin' be th' thousands, stricken at his own fireside or in th' field or down on th' farm. His bones whiten ivry corner iv unhappy China. His silk socks, sad emblem iv th' end iv man, darkens ivry hamlet iv that ill-fated counthry. His undhertaker's bills amount to more thin his salary. He's been waked till there ain't a voice among his frinds that can raise th' keen. It's time f'r him to call a halt an' lave some wan else do th' dyin'." [*EP*, Dec. 12, 1896] [10]

The very next week Mr. Dooley swings back once again to a serious prowar position by complaining that "ye can't make war be means iv r-resolutions," and criticizing the opposition to intervention of the American financial community, who, he says, wish "to presarve an attitude iv beniv'lint neuthrality an' loan money on rhinestones at th' old stand" (*EP*, Dec. 19, 1896). He repeats this indictment of American business in February 1897 in a piece about a Cuban sympathy meeting in Bridgeport, which again cleverly connects the parochial and the worldly. The community's businessmen speak loudly for war at first, but they are frightened away by the threat of financial hardship, and only a handful of poor workingmen, most of them former Fenians, remain to start a campaign fund (*EP*, Feb. 27, 1897).

In the fall of 1897 the jingoist campaign for intervention was boosted by the outré Cisneros affair, in which a Hearst reporter rescued Evangelina Cisneros, the niece of the president of the insurgent Cuban republic, from a Havana prison.[11] Meanwhile, in their defense of President McKinley the Kohlsaat papers had been waging a campaign of their own against yellow journalism and the jingoes, and singling out the *Chicago Tribune* as the worst local offender.[12] Mr. Dooley joins in criticizing the *Tribune* and the other yellow journals in a piece that constitutes yet another reversal of position:

> "Now, if we left it to th' newspapers they'd be no small talk. . . . Yes, I know they have some brave editors in Spain—as gallant a lot

iv la-ads as iver slung a pen. But they're not in the same class with our sojers. Th' columns iv their pa-apers ain't so long. They can't do th' sthrat-ee-gee that a good American editor is brought up on. . . .

"What cud Spain do? Wan good editor cud blow all her hundhred ships into smithereens with a single article on circulation and th' Spanish ar-rmy iv wan hundhred thousan' men'd crumble befure th' gallant char-rge iv wan American hackman. You betcher life."

[*EP*, Oct. 2, 1897] [13]

Ironically, Dunne and Mr. Dooley were at this time only three months away from conversion to the extreme sentiments satirized here.

At this point Dunne's journalistic career took an important turn. From the beginning he had chafed under the restrictions imposed on the editorial staff by Herman Kohlsaat. Ellis reports that Dunne often entertained his friends by mimicking the editorial conferences run by the bakeryman-publisher. Thus, when the *Chicago Journal* changed hands and the new owners offered him the position of managing editor and editorial page chairman, Dunne accepted. Sometime in the winter of 1897–1898 he moved over to the *Journal*, and his last dialect piece for the *Evening Post*, the only home Mr. Dooley had ever known, appeared on January 22, 1898.[14] In it Dooley claims that the last straw for him has been the election to the governorship of Illinois of John R. Tanner:

"I've bore with iverything. I've stud Yerkuss, an' Bill Lorimer and Bath House Jawn an' th' Relief an' Aid Society, an' Schwartzmeister cuttin' th' price iv pints. I've seen all kinds iv onjestice done an' all kinds iv goodness punished. I seen civil service an' I stud that. But I'll not stand Tanner." [15]

Evidently there were no immediate plans to transfer the Dooley pieces to the *Journal*, but at the end of this valediction, Dunne left the door ajar:

"Good-by," said Mr. Hennessy. "Ye'll think betther iv it. I'll see ye again."

"Mebbe," said Mr. Dooley. " 'Tis har-rd f'r me to lave off talkin'. Good-by."

As Mr. Hennessy plodded down the street the philosopher locked the door and turned out the lights of his place, perhaps for the last time.

The *Evening Post* and *Times-Herald* took moderate positions on the Cuban question: Kohlsaat advised faith in President McKinley's caution and unwillingness to sacrifice American lives. The situation was very different, however, at Dunne's new home, the *Journal*. Originally a respectable, conservative organ and one of the oldest newspapers in Chicago, it had been taken over by a group from Detroit who immediately set about turning the paper into a cheap afternoon daily with mass appeal, modeled on the example set by Hearst's *New York Journal* and Pulitzer's *World*.[16] To this end, its editorial page when Dunne joined the staff glowed a bright yellow. Throughout the month of January 1898, there were daily shrill demands for intervention in Cuba, "to end the years of killing and starving, of brutal murder done by wholesale in the attempt to subdue a liberty-loving people" (*Journal*, Jan. 15, 1898). One editorial, "Now Is the Time," claimed that the *Journal* had been favoring armed intervention for "more than a year." Others condemned McKinley's waiting game as "a disgrace to a first-class power," and lamented the continuance of atrocities that were sending "a thrill of horror and disgust to the ends of the civilized world" (Jan. 17, 25, 1898). Furthermore, the paper's Cuban policy was part of a general philosophy of expansion. In stock manifest-destiny terms, *Journal* editorials argued that the Navy should be strengthened and American trade extended, for American connections with other parts of this "new world" were "inescapable." Annexation of Hawaii was advocated simply because the islands lay "in the path of our Chinese trade. . . . Is some outworn political creed to be invoked to help some other country get them?" (Jan. 12, 1898).

In retrospect, the week beginning February 9, 1898, seems almost to have been orchestrated by Hearst and Pulitzer, so perfectly did it bring to a climax the campaign for intervention. First, the New York *World* printed Spanish Minister de Lôme's intercepted private letter, the contents of which were insulting to President McKinley and contemptuous of his December proposals to negotiate a Cuban settlement. The next day brought the official Spanish reply to those proposals—an emphatic, belligerent rejection of American intrusion. Then, on the evening of February 15, the battleship *Maine* blew up and sank in Havana harbor, killing 258 American sailors.[17] To this day, the cause of the explosion is a mystery, but few at the time bothered to question

Assistant Secretary of the Navy Theodore Roosevelt's automatic assertion that "the *Maine* was sunk by an act of dirty treachery on the part of the Spaniards." [18] The *Chicago Journal* contributed to the hue and cry with an editorial, "Strike, Mr. President," calling for "cowards and copperheads to move to the rear" (Feb. 16, 1898). A day later, with no solid evidence in, the *Journal* claimed that "the crime is almost proved. Circumstances indicate the criminal. Unless the president can show some better reason than he has yet advanced, it is time for the American people to take this yellow cur of nations by the throat and shake the life out of it" (Feb. 17, 1898). From this point until the declaration of war on April 25, a steady stream of war-mongering invective poured daily from the *Journal* editorial page.

In fairness to the *Journal*, its reaction was part of a general hysteria that gripped America in the weeks after the *Maine* disaster. More puzzling, though, is Mr. Dooley's immediate enlistment in the ranks of the jingoes. On February 19, four days after the *Maine* blew up, Dunne brought him from his brief retirement with a reaction to the explosion in keeping with the *Journal's* editorial policies but out of character for the historian-philosopher that Chicago had come to know. Abandoning his usual stance as a cool and neutral ironist, Mr. Dooley becomes one more loud, irrational voice expressing cruelly simplified hatred of Spain and anger at President McKinley. These new pieces mark the low point in the Dooley canon, for in them Dunne shatters the persona that he has built up so consistently by using Mr. Dooley to articulate unjustifiable contentions through petty, ignoble rhetorical ploys. Like so many others, Dunne was probably swayed by the damaging events of the preceding week. Also, his new bosses may have exerted pressure on him to bring Mr. Dooley to the service of the war argument. Still, the results are disappointing. We have come to expect so much more from him.

The first piece opens with Mr. Dooley presenting President McKinley's position in a tone of heavy-handed sarcasm:

> "What do I think iv it?" said Martin Dooley, in response to Mr. Hennessy's question. "What do I think iv it? I think me frind McKinley ought to apologize to Spain. 'Tis th' on'y thing he can do. They're a nice frindly nation with a way about thim iv stickin' a knife in th' backs iv thim they don't like, an' 'tis no more thin right

that Willum shud set down an' tell thim how sorry he is th' Maine
was blowed up. . . . Also, he's overflowin' with woe to think iv th'
damp sailors now mussin' up th' beach iv a frindly power an'
thrusts they'll be dumped into a trinch an' nawthin' more said about
it. They're on'y a lot iv poor, foolish Irishmen that wint to sea
because they cudden't find wurruk ashore an' they're better dead."
[*Journal*, Feb. 19, 1898]

Mr. Dooley goes on from there to take a backhanded shot at the
American business community for their opposition to the war, by
telling the excited Hennessy, who is ready to enlist himself, "Ye cud
niver be a rale pathrite. Ye have no stock ticker in ye'er house."
Finally, he relates two offensive anecdotes which bolster his position
with sentimentality and a facile appeal to masculinity. The first recalls
the childhood of a "Bridgeport boy" who is supposed to have died in
the *Maine* explosion, "a wild sort iv a thing though good at hear-rt,
an' th' ol' man was happy whin they took him to th' ol' tub iv a Mitchigan f'r to make a sailor iv him." Dooley concludes that "he died in th'
sarvice iv a lot iv gamblers down east that'd look as cold on his body
as though 'twas a dead fish cast up be th' sea." The second concerns
Doherty, a strong and quiet Irish farmer, who is provoked to fury at a
county fair by the jibes of a smaller man, presented as drunk and vin-
dictive. The other farmers urge Doherty to restrain himself, for a fist
fight would "ruin business" at the fair; but the little man pushes him
too far, and Doherty chases him off down the road. A final exchange
between Dooley and Hennessy points the moral:

"Be hivins," said Mr. Hennessy, "I think Doherty was r-right."
"Mebbe so," said Mr. Dooley; "annyhow, r-right or wrong, he
was a man."

For the next month pieces in this vein appear. The following week
Mr. Dooley explains to the increasingly impatient Hennessy that
America will not fight simply because the Spaniards "haven't insulted
Mark Hanna" or attacked any of our "sacred institutions":

"Th' counthry's good name has been made as common as th' r-road
to th' pawnshop. But that ain't an institution. A ship's been blowed
up an' a lot iv siventeen-dollar-a-month la-ads is floatin' face down-
ward in th' water, but they ain't institutions. A man's come along

an' batted Willum McKinley on th' head, but he ain't an institution, thank th' Lord." [*Journal,* Feb. 26, 1898]

He declares next that all of Bridgeport is solidly in favor of war, excepting only "th' la-ads with stocks an' bonds" and "th' skimpy little clerk men" (*Journal,* March 5, 1898). Recalling Civil War terminology, Dooley inveighs against "a copperhead that's a copperhead just because he's a poor sick soul an' because they'se as much as wan twinty-five in it f'r him, an' because if he stands f'r his counthry some wan is li'ble to get his business away fr'm him" (*Journal,* March 12, 1898). He also scorns President McKinley's statement that a war has to be "holy" to be worth fighting: "It ain't holy f'r to fight whin ye'er nose is pulled an' it ain't holy to fight to save some wan fr'm bein' murdhered an' robbed. Whin is a war holy thin?" Dooley asks. Only, he explains, when "Heidelback, Ickelheimer, an' comp'ny 'll get into throuble with a for'n nation. They'll rayfuse to give th' prince iv Wales his watch back an' th' prince iv Wales 'll go into their hair. Thin ye'll see throuble begin. . . . McKinley'll call out th' throops th' first day" (*Journal,* March 19, 1898). The Dooley position in these weeks even does violence to the verisimilitude of the other familiar Bridgeport characters and props: both Molly Donahue and Father Kelly make speeches in favor of war, and the big turnout at the St. Patrick's Day parade is interpreted as a martial sign (*Journal,* March 19, 26, 1898).

Many Americans, of course, from Theodore Roosevelt on down, shared these views. President McKinley's failure to take sufficient offense at the de Lôme letter and the *Maine* disaster did look like cowardice to the uninformed. Indeed, McKinley's persistent, courageous attempts to achieve a peaceful diplomatic solution of the Cuban crisis amid mounting public and congressional hostility have only recently become known.[19] Nevertheless, about all that can be said for these Dooley pieces is that they parallel the editorial position of the Chicago *Journal* for the same period. Never did the call for war to avenge the *Maine* slip below a full-throated scream. Of the other Chicago dailies, the *Tribune* alone held similarly extreme views; but the *Journal* seemed louder because of its policy of printing all Cuban news in headlines of an inch or more. Most distressing in the *Journal* for these months is the fact that its position on Cuba cannot be separated from the desire of its management to raise circulation. In this they were strikingly successful. Notarized statements gloated weekly on the editorial page, telling of the steady increase in sales—the average daily circulation rose from 91,000 in January to 193,000 in May (*Journal*, June 14, 1898). At the same time, the editors reacted self-righteously to charges of yellow journalism articulated by less belligerent papers such as Kohlsaat's *Times-Herald*. They declared at one point that if it is yellow "to distinguish primary from secondary news," to "speak out when it is more profitable to stay silent," to face this greatest crisis since the Civil War "with courage," to "refuse to abandon national principles," to believe that "the common man is right, and that the market-jobbing, legislature-buying, honor-bargaining Mark Hanna is wrong," and to pity the suffering Cubans, "then the *Journal* is yellow and proud of it." On the other hand, there was "another kind of yellow" also, that of the cowardice of papers "that conceal the truth or print half-truths" (*Journal*, March 4, 1898). This disguising as sheer patriotism of what was at least in part opportunistic pandering to the crowd does not go down well. Unfortunately, Dunne cannot be separated from the policy, for he sacrificed Mr. Dooley to it. These pieces were, however, followed by the series on the war itself, by means of which Mr. Dooley became immediately and justly famous. In a sense, the second group makes retribution for the first.

Mr. Dooley regains his head in April, when the narrow rancor of the pieces that follow the *Maine* tragedy finally dissipates and is replaced by his more customary and justified exposures of humbug and pretense. There is no lightning conversion to an antiwar position, but Dunne returns to sure ground in satirizing first America's military preparations and then the conduct of the war. Mr. Dooley is nearly himself again in a piece that points out President McKinley's inadequacies as a diplomat with an effective analogy—McKinley is to Spanish Premier Sagasta as a country boy is to a city card sharp: "An' th' la-ad fr'm Canton thinks he can pick out th' Jack, an' sometimes he can an' sometimes he can't; but th' end iv it is th' Spanyard has him thrimmed down to his chest protector, an' he'll be goin' back to Canton in a blanket." The American could win, says Dooley, if the game were horseshoes or wrestling, "or chasin' th' greased pig, or in a wan-legged race or th' tug-iv-war," but "whin it comes to di-plomacy, th' Spanyard has him again th' rail" (*Journal*, April 2, 1898). To be sure, Mr.

Dooley is still finding fault with McKinley (and wrongly, as the recent studies suggest), but real humor has blessedly returned to temper the criticism.

The following week, he is even more on target with a portrait of Fitzhugh Lee, the American consul at Havana whose excited messages from Cuba and subsequent florid congressional testimony strongly advocated intervention. Significantly, Mr. Dooley's opinion begins now to contradict that of the *Journal* editorial page, which had been praising Lee as "the man of the hour," and a "gritty" individualist whose "independent manhood" should be emulated by the vacillating Mc-Kinley (*Journal*, April 13, 14, 1898). Mr. Dooley, on the other hand, sees Lee as an impetuous blusterer,

> "a fat ma-an with a head like a football an' a neck big enough to pump blood into his brain an' keep it fr'm starvin'. White-haired an' r-red-faced. Th' kind iv ma-an that can get mad in ivry vein in his body. . . . He hasn't got th' time to be tired an' worrid. He needs food, an' he has it; an' he needs sleep, an' he takes it; an' he needs fightin', an' he gets it. That's Fitz."   [*Journal,* April 9, 1898]

Now, however, despite Mr. Dooley's dawning second thoughts, war was imminent. Hostilities were declared on April 25. The summer campaign that followed was, of course, anticlimactic after its opening engagement—Admiral Dewey's victory at Manila on May 1. The Spanish fleet was destroyed without the loss of a single American life in that action, which a British historian called "a military execution rather than a real contest." [20] News of the "victory" was delayed by a damaged telegraph cable, and the American people waited breathlessly for word from the admiral. Into this breach stepped Mr. Dooley, with a prescient explanation of "Cousin George" Dewey's activities that made his name a household word virtually overnight. Dooley explains that Cousin George cut the cable himself, "so's Mack cudden't chat with him" or suggest "idees iv how to r-run a quiltin' party, an' call it war." Then he proceeded to work:

> "Well, sir, in twenty-eight minyits be th' clock Dewey he had all th' Spanish boats sunk, an' that there harbor lookin' like a Spanish stew. Thin he run down th' bay, an' handed a few warm wans into th' town. He set it on fire, an' thin wint ashore to warm

his poor hands an' feet. It chills th' blood not to have annythin' to do f'r an hour or more."

"Thin why don't he write something?" Mr. Hennessy demanded.

"Write?" echoed Mr. Dooley. "Write? Why shud he write? D'ye think Cousin George ain't got nawthin' to do but to set down with a fountain pen, an' write: 'Dear Mack,—At 8 o'clock I begun a peaceful blockade iv this town. Ye can see th' pieces ivrywhere. I hope ye're injyin' th' same great blessin'. So no more at prisint. Fr'm ye'ers thruly, George Dooley.' He ain't that kind. 'Tis a nice day, an' he's there smokin' a good tin-cint seegar, an' throwin' dice f'r th' dhrinks. He don't care whether we know what he's done or not. I'll bet ye, whin we come to find out about him, we'll hear he's ilicted himself king iv th' F'lipine Islands. Dooley th' Wanst. He'll be settin' up there undher a palm-three with naygurs fannin' him an' a dhrop iv licker in th' hollow iv his arm, an' hootchy-kootchy girls dancin' befure him, an' ivry tin or twinty minyits some wan bringin' a prisoner in. 'Who's this?' says King Dooley. 'A Spanish gin'ral,' says th' copper. 'Give him a typewriter an' set him to wurruk,' says th' king. 'On with th' dance,' he says. An' afther awhile, whin he gits tired iv th' game, he'll write home an' say he's got th' islands; an' he'll turn thim over to th' gover'mint an' go back to his ship, an' Mark Hanna'll organize th' F'lipine Islands Jute an' Cider Comp'ny, an' th' rivolutchinists'll wish they hadn't. That's what'll happen. Mark me wurrud." [*Journal,* May 7, 1898]

This piece contains no link to Bridgeport stronger than the claim of kinship—"Dewey or Dooley, 'tis all th' same. We dhrop a letter here an' there, except th' haitches,—we niver dhrop thim—but we're th' same breed iv fightin' men. Georgy has th' thraits iv th' fam'ly." Otherwise, it is all Mr. Dooley's imaginative recreation of events happening four thousand miles from Archer Avenue. Certainly the amazing popularity of the piece influenced Dunne to allow Dooley to continue to range far afield.[21] Ellis tells us that "Cousin George" was praised from coast to coast and reprinted immediately in "a round hundred papers."[22] From here to syndication was a logical step, soon taken by Dunne and Willis Turner, his fellow *Journal* editor.

The Spanish-American War was at least as natural a subject for Mr. Dooley as the presidential campaign of 1896 had been. Again, Dunne's sensitivity to posturing personalities and inflated rhetoric particularly qualified him to satirize the traveling circus of soldiers, strategists, journalists, and politicians that paraded through the headlines during these months. And to make his job even easier, the Cuban campaign itself was so poorly planned and executed that straight reports of what was going on still read like satire.

Mr. Dooley wasted no time getting started. The week after "Cousin George" appeared, Dunne called on his streak of wild exaggeration to imagine a meeting of the president's wartime Strategy Board as a chaotic all-night checker game on which McKinley drops in to be advised.

> " 'Well, boys,' says he, 'how goes th' battle?' he says. 'Gloryous,' says th' Sthrateejy Board. 'Two more moves, an' we'll be in th' king row.' 'Ah,' says Mack, 'this is too good to be thrue,' he says. 'In but a few brief minyits th' dhrinks'll be on Spain,' he says. 'Have ye anny plans f'r Sampson's fleet?' he says. 'Where is it?' says th' Sthrateejy Board. 'I dinnaw,' says Mack. 'Good,' says th' Sthrateejy Board. 'Where's th' Spanish fleet?' says they. 'Bombardin' Boston, at Cadiz, in San June de Matzoon, sighted near th' gashouse be our special correspondint, copyright, 1898, be Mike O'Toole.' 'A sthrong position,' says th' Sthrateejy Board. 'Undoubtedly, th' fleet is headed south to attack and seize Armour's glue facthory. Ordher Sampson to sail north as fast as he can, an' lay in a supply iv ice. Th' summer's comin' on. Insthruct Schley to put on all steam, an' thin put it off again, an' call us up be telephone. R-rush eighty-three millyon throops an' four mules to Tampa, to Mobile, to Chickenmaha, to Coney Island, to Ireland, to th' divvle, an' r-rush thim back again. Don't r-rush thim.' "   [*Journal*, May 14, 1898]

Prudence restrains me (but barely) from quoting more of this; Dunne was surely enjoying himself, because it goes on for quite a while.

Three weeks later, Mr. Dooley explains the imminent land invasion of Cuba with scarcely less confusion than attended the actual operation:

> "Wan ar-rmy, says ye? Twinty! Las' Choosdah an advance ar-rmy iv wan hundherd an' twinty thousand men landed fr'm th' Gussie, with tin thousand cannons hurlin' projick-tyles weighin' eight hundherd pounds sivinteen miles. Windsdah night a second ar-rmy iv injineers, miners, plumbers, an' lawn tinnis experts, numberin' in all four hundherd an' eighty thousand men, ar-rmed with death-dealin' canned goods, [a reference to the accusations by some soldiers that they were being fed "embalmed beef"] was hurried to Havana to storm th' city.
>
> "Thursdah mornin' three thousand full rigimints iv r-rough r-riders

swum their hor-rses acrost to Matoonzas, an' afther a spirited battle captured th' Rainy Christiny golf links, two up an' hell to play, an' will hold thim again all comers. Th' same aftthernoon th' reg'lar cavalry, con-sistin' iv four hundherd an' eight thousand well-mounted men, was loaded aboord th' tug Lucy J., and departed on their earned iv death amidst th' cheers iv eight millyon sojers left behind at Chickamaha." [*Journal,* June 4, 1898]

These reports have as an additional satiric target the new breed of war correspondent whose bulletins "from the front" were a journalistic innovation of this war. Also in this vein is Mr. Dooley's interpretation of a stampede of American Army mules at the Tampa base camp as "th' first land action iv th' war":

"Th' Alger gyards [named for Secretary of War Russell Alger] . . . bruk fr'm th' corral where they had thim tied up, atin' thistles, an' med a desp'rate charge on th' camp at Tampa. They dayscinded like a whur-rl-wind, dhrivin' th' astonished throops befure thim, an' thin charged back again, completin' their earned iv desthruction. At th' las' account th' brave sojers was climbin' threes an' tillygraft poles, an' a rig'mint iv mules was kickin' th' pink silk linin' out iv th' officers' quarthers. Th' gallant mules was led be a most courageous jackass, an' 'tis undhersthud that me frind Mack will appint him a brigadier-gin-ral jus' as soon as he can find out who his father is." [*Journal,* June 18, 1898]

In this piece, however, Dooley differentiates carefully between the officers and the enlisted men of the army in Cuba. Implying that only jackasses could follow unquestioningly the orders being handed down from Washington, he suggests that the rank and file soldiers be replaced by mules, while "th' officers in th' field at prisint is well qualified f'r command iv th' new ar-rmy," being "as ifficient a lot iv mules as iver exposed their ears." Dooley is critical of American officers because many were rich men's sons, with few real qualifications. He makes this point by imagining an interview between the president and a prospective officer, "Master Willie Dooselbery," who comes to the White House with "his val-lay, his mah an' pah an' th' comity iv th' goluf club." McKinley opens the interview:

" 'Let us begin th' examination,' he says. 'Ar-re ye a good goluf player?' 'I am,' says Willie. 'Thin I appint ye a liftnant. What we need in th' ar-rmy is good goluf players,' he says. 'In our former

war,' he says, 'we had th' misfortune to have men in command that
didn't know th' diff'rence between a goluf stick an' a beecycle; an'
what was th' raysult? We foozled our approach at Bull R-run,' he
says. 'Ar-re ye a mimber iv anny clubs?' he says. 'Four,' says Willie.
'Thin I make ye a major,' he says. 'Where d'ye get ye'er pants?'
he says. 'Fr'm England,' says Willie. 'Gloryous,' says McKinley.
'I make ye a colonel,' he says."   [*Journal*, May 21, 1898]

And so it goes up to generalship, which Willie achieves for having
known the proper uniforms to wear for both day and evening battles.[23]

One of Mr. Dooley's favorite targets is American General Nelson A.
Miles, whose arrival at Tampa, "mounted on a superb specyal ca-ar"
is described with relish: "His uniforms [Miles had in fact designed his
own] ar-re comin' down in specyal steel-protected bullyon trains fr'm
th' mind, where they've been kept f'r a year. He has ordhered out th'
gold resarve f'r to equip his staff, numberin' eight thousan' men, manny
iv whom ar-re clubmen; an', as soon as he can have his pitchers took,
he will cr-rush th' Spanish with wan blow" (*Journal*, June 4, 1898).[24]
When Miles goes off to "invade" Puerto Rico in July, Mr. Dooley is
there to take down his farewell speech to General Shafter in Santiago:

> " ' 'Tis not f'r me to take th' lorls fr'm th' steamin' brow iv a thrue
> hero,' he says [Shafter weighed 300 pounds]. 'I lave ye here,' he
> says, 'f'r to complete th' victhry ye have so nobly begun,' he says.
> 'F'r you,' he says, 'th' wallop in th' eye fr'm th' newspaper rayporther,
> th' r-round robbing, an' th' sunsthroke,' he says. 'F'r me th' hardship
> iv th' battlefield, th' late dinner, th' theayter party, an' th' sickenin'
> polky,' he says. 'Gather,' he says, 'th' fruits iv ye'er bravery,' he says.
> 'Return,' he says, 'to ye'er native land, an' receive anny gratichood
> th' Sicrety iv War can spare fr'm his own fam'ly,' he says. 'F'r me,'
> he says, 'there is no way but f'r to tur-rn me back upon this festive
> scene,' he says, 'an' go where jooty calls me,' he says. 'Ordherly,'
> he says, 'put a bottle on th' ice, an' see that me goold pants that I
> wear with th' pale blue vest with th' di'mon buttons is irned out,' he
> says. An' with a haggard face he walked aboord th' excursion
> steamer, an' wint away."   [*Journal*, Aug. 6, 1898]

Dooley is basically correct in reporting the nature of the opposition
that awaited Miles in San Juan: "He has been in gr-reat purl fr'm a
witherin' fire iv bokays, an' he has met an' overpowered some iv th'
mos' savage orators in Porther Ricky; but, whin I las' heerd iv him, he

had pitched his tents an' ice-cream freezers near the inimy's wall, an' was grajully silencin' thim with proclamations."

By this time, Mr. Dooley's comments on the war were being reprinted all across the nation and had even reached the seat of power in Washington. Dunne's piece on a meeting of McKinley's cabinet had been circulated in that body by Chicagoan Lyman Gage, then serving as secretary of the treasury. The piece was one of Dunne's wilder improvisations on the theme of governmental chaos; the president's contribution consisted, in part, of the announcement that "Sandago de Cuba is not taken, . . . But th' crew iv th' Iowa has taken th' measles, th' crew iv th' New York has taken to dhrink, an' Col. Asthor has taken a morgedge of all th' tinimints in southern Cuba" (*Journal,* June 25, 1898). Ellis quotes a June 1898 letter of reaction to this Dooley piece from Secretary of the Navy John D. Long, who says "I have conferred with the Secretary of War and several others of the Cabinet, and . . . we have come to the conclusion that Dooley is a fictitious name for somebody very near the scene of action and more familiar than any outsider can be with the internal proceedings." By January 1899, the reading of Mr. Dooley's nationally syndicated commentary was a regular feature of the weekly meetings of the cabinet, which, as a Washington reporter wrote Dunne, placed "the philosopher of 'Archey Road' . . . in a position to exert as much influence on public affairs as any salaried member of the administration and doubtless much more than the vast unread editorial literature of the country." [25] Not since Abraham Lincoln read Artemus Ward's "High-Handed Outrage at Utica" to his cabinet before presenting them with the Emancipation Proclamation had an American humorist been taken so seriously.[26]

The Dooley pieces on the conduct of the war were widely appreciated, largely because so many people knew how much of the affair had been a bungled fiasco, eminently worthy of satire. Besides, we had won—easily; it was all wrapped up in four months. So the country enjoyed Mr. Dooley's fresh and funny renderings of what was at best an open secret—that there was a lot that wasn't splendid in the splendid little war.[27] The climate changed, however, as storm clouds gathered over the Philippines. And like just about everyone else, Peter Dunne woke slowly to the significance for American foreign policy of

Dewey's victory and the subsequent American occupation of the islands. One year after his expressions of militant jingoism and his laughter at "Cousin George's" Manila adventure, Mr. Dooley recalls these attitudes with wondering remorse:

> " 'Tis sthrange how I've cam'd down since th' war. . . . Whin I think iv th' gaby I made iv mesilf dancin' ar-round this here bar an' hurooin' whiniver I he-erd iv Rosenfelt's charge again Sandago me blood r-runs cold with shame. I look ar-round me now an' all there is to cheer me is Miles' gallant charge again th' embammed beef an' Alger's gallant charge again Miles an' th' gas company chargin' us all, th' pure an' th' impure alike. . . . Did ye iver set up late at night an' come down in th' mornin' feelin' a taste in ye'er mouth like a closed sthreet car on a r-rainy day? That's th' way I feel. Was I dhrunk durin' th' war?"   [*Journal*, March 18, 1899]

The bartender has a hangover, aggravated by his having arisen to find the goblin of American imperialism peering over the foot of the bed.

Recent studies have suggested that the American involvement in the Philippines came about through a combination of military strategy, happenstance, and lack of foresight, untainted by previous plotting toward a policy of colonial expansion.[28] But even in the absence of premeditated ulterior motives, trouble came swiftly. At first the Filipino insurgents and their leader, Emilio Aguinaldo, welcomed what they thought was American aid in freeing them from Spanish tyranny. But when the terms of the Spanish-American treaty became known, they found out otherwise. Having been "sold" to the United States for $20 million, the Filipinos were forced to proclaim their freedom from yet another tyrant, and in February 1899 came the first battle in a bitter, three-year guerrilla war between the Filipino rebels and their American "liberators." Support for this cause at home in America dwindled fast, for it soon became obvious that the United States had placed itself in the same relative position in the Philippines as had Spain in Cuba. In this context, Mr. Dooley's early enlistment on the side of the anti-imperialists bolstered his growing national reputation for sharp and fair-minded commentary.[29]

Also, his position allies him with many other Irish and Irish-American spokesmen, for whom British rule in Ireland had provided a long-standing precedent for the case against empire. The imperialists often cited England as an example of a properly expanding world power; the Irish saw this analogy with equal vividness but from the other side of the fence. This widespread Irish sentiment has been largely overlooked as an influence on Dunne, but it provides a necessary perspective on his progression from a prowar to an anti-imperialist position.

In Chicago, for example, John Finerty went through the same conversion experience as Dunne. Although *The Citizen* had supported intervention in Cuba, often by means of an analogy with Ireland, Finerty became a vehement opponent of Philippine annexation and President McKinley; [30] in a significant defection for a lifelong Irish Republican, he even supported Bryan's presidential candidacy in 1900. Furthermore, the most consistently sane voice in Chicago journalism on the Spanish issues was that of William Dillon, editor of the archdiocesan weekly, *The New World*. The brother of Irish parliamentary leader John Dillon, he knew the Irish analogy well but refused to apply it in Cuba. Suspicious of "the Cuban fake atrocity volcano," Dillon questioned from the start the assumption of interventionists that a free Cuba would result (March 6, 1897). Even after the *Maine* explosion, he remained calm, suggesting that either side could have set the charge. And during the war itself he reported American victories soberly, with the earnest hope that they were hastening the end of hostilities. The Philippine Insurrection only justified Dillon's worst apprehensions, and his subsequent editorials continued to deplore the hypocrisy of apologists for expansion.[31] Most leading Irish-American papers were also strongly against retention of the Philippines, including Patrick Ford's *Irish World* in New York and James Jeffrey Roche's *Boston Pilot*. And Irish-American political figures, such as New Yorker Bourke Cockran and Boston's Patrick Collins, also figured in the anti-imperialist agitation.[32]

This movement united the American Irish and made them the implausible allies of a group that opposed them on almost every other front—the Anti-Imperialist League. Founded in Boston in November 1898, the League was led by elderly Mugwump reformers (among them E. L. Godkin of *The Nation* and Harvard's Charles Eliot Norton) who had long been against unrestricted immigration and municipal corruption. They were also decidedly biased towards the Anglo-Saxon stock of old-line America (which is to say, themselves) as the best raw material for leadership. Now they were joined with machine politicians and Irish immigrants in the fight against American expansion. Probably the association with the Mugwumps helped to make Irish-American opinion respectable nationally for the first time.[33]

Mr. Dooley first comes to grips with American imperialism in a piece that appeared shortly after the first American troops landed at Manila. Spain had made her initial overture towards peace, offering to give up Cuba if the United States would give back the Philippines, and President McKinley had asked for expressions of opinion from the nation at large. As a representative of unthinking expansion, Hennessy gladly contributes: "I know what I'd do if I was Mack, . . . I'd hist a flag over th' Ph'lippeens, an' I'd take in th' whole lot iv thim." But Mr. Dooley reminds him that " 'tis not more thin two months since ye larned whether they were islands or canned goods. . . . Suppose ye was standin' at th' corner iv State Sthreet an' Archey R-road, wud ye know what car to take to get to th' Ph'lippeens?" Unfortunately for "our poor, tired heads," Dooley continues, the war with Spain has turned out to be more complicated than even he expected:

"Whin I wint into it, I thought all I'd have to do was to set up here behind th' bar with a good tin-cint see-gar in me teeth, an' toss dinnymite bombs into th' hated city iv Havana. But look at me now. Th' war is still goin' on; an' ivry night, whin I'm countin' up the cash, I'm askin' mesilf will I annex Cubia or lave it to the Cubians? Will I take Porther Ricky or put it by? An' what shud I do with the Ph'lippeens? Oh, what shud I do with thim? I can't annex thim because I don't know where they ar-re. I can't let go iv thim because some wan else'll take thim if I do. They are eight thousan' iv thim islands, with a popylation iv wan hundherd millyon naked savages; an' me bedroom's crowded now with me an' th' bed."

And yet, despite the lack of knowledge about the Philippines, everyone but Mr. Dooley knows just what to do with them: "Ye ask anny conducthor on Ar-rchey R-road, an' he'll tell ye. Ye can find out fr'm th' papers; an', if ye really want to know, all ye have to do is to ask a prom'nent citizen who can mow all th' lawn he owns with a safety razor" (*Journal*, July 30, 1898).

A major rationale for retention of the Philippines was the idea that American growth westward was somehow ordained by Providence. Naturally, Mr. Dooley was having none of that, and the appearance of President McKinley in Chicago during the gala Peace Jubilee Week at the conclusion of the war was the occasion of his classic parody of the rhetoric of manifest destiny. The piece echoes McKinley's actual speech, which went, in part, as follows: "My countrymen, the currents of destiny flow through the hearts of the people; who will check them? Who will divert them? Who will stop them? And the movements of men, planned and designed by the Master of Men, will never be interrupted by the American people." With such a model, no wonder Mr. Dooley's version is successful:

"Mack rose up in a perfect hur-cane iv applause, an', says he, 'Gintlemen,' he says, 'an' fellow-heroes,' he says. . . . 'Again,' he says, 'we ar-re a united union,' he says. 'No north,' he says, 'no south, no east,' he says, 'no west. No north east a point east,' he says. 'Th' inimies iv our counthry has been cr-rushed,' he says, 'or is stuck down in Floridy with his rig-mint talkin',' he says, 'his hellish doc-thrines to th' allygators,' he says [William Jennings Bryan and the Third Nebraska Regiment never made it past Tampa, although they were one of the first groups to volunteer for the war]. 'Th' nation is wanst more at peace undher th' gran' goold standard,' he says. 'Now,' he says, 'th' question is what shall we do with th' fruits iv victhry?' he says. (A voice, 'Can thim.') 'Our duty to civilization commands us to be up an' doin',' he says. 'We ar-re bound,' he says, 'to—to re-elize our destiny, whativer it may be,' he says. 'We can not tur-rn back,' he says, 'th' hands iv th' clock that, even as I speak,' he says, 'is r-rushin' through th' hear-rts iv men,' he says, 'dashin' its spray against th' star iv liberty an' hope, an' no north, no south, no east, no west, but a steady purpose to do th' best we can, considerin' all th' circumstances iv the case,' he says. 'I hope I have made th' matther clear to ye,' he says, 'an', with these few remarks,' he says, 'I will tur-rn th' job over to destiny,' he says, 'which is sure to lead us iver on an' on, an' back an' forth, a united an' happy people, livin',' he says, 'undher an administhration that, thanks to our worthy Prisidint an' his cap-ble an' earnest advisers is second to none,' he says."

"What do you think ought to be done with th' fruits iv victhry?" Mr. Hennessy asked.

"Well," said Mr. Dooley, "if 'twas up to me, I'd eat what was r-ripe an' give what wasn't r-ripe to me inimy. An' I guess that's what Mack means."   [*Journal,* Oct. 22, 1898]

Mr. Dooley's uncertainty about the Philippines and manifest destiny again runs counter to the editorial stance of the *Journal,* which strongly favored retention and was willing to argue the point from all possible positions without regard for consistency. One day it preached manifest destiny: "The resourceful Yankee nation, with its recognized genius for justice and government, should not fear the task set for it by destiny in the Philippines" (June 6, 1898). Another day it sanctimoniously laid out the "white man's burden": "There is a primer of civilization, with the small words written large for children to read. It was worth crossing the sea to spread this new gospel. It was worth a war to teach the first step in humanity to a people that for 300 years has been taught nothing but inhumanity" (June 9, 1898). On a third occasion the appeal was to sheer lust for power: "The nation is ready for the race, ready to try its strength in competition with the other powers of the world and to take the place its capacity and its genius shall win for it. . . . In point of wealth, power, and honor, first place in the world is none too good for the American people, and they will press onward until they attain it" (Feb. 15, 1899).

These are the very contradictory ideas, held not only at the *Journal* but all across the country, that Dunne exposed in his summary piece on expansion, which appeared in January 1899, at the height of the Senate debate over ratification of the treaty with Spain and the cession of the Philippines to the United States. He makes his point strictly through control of language. By juxtaposing the rhetorics of racism and moral uplift, Mr. Dooley reveals the latent hypocrisy of the apologists for expansion.

> "Whin we plant what Hogan calls th' starry banner iv Freedom in th' Ph'lippeenes," said Mr. Dooley, "an' give th' sacred blessin' iv liberty to th' poor, downtrodden people iv thim unfortunate isles —dam thim—we'll larn thim a lesson."
>
> "Sure," said Mr. Hennessy, sadly, "we have a thing or two to larn oursilves."
>
> "But it isn't f'r thim to larn us," said Mr. Dooley. " 'Tis not f'r thim wretched an' degraded crathers, without a mind or a shirt iv their own, f'r to give lessons in politeness an' liberty to a nation that mannyfacthers more dhressed beef thin anny other imperyal nation in th' wurruld. We say to thim: 'Naygurs,' we say, 'poor, dissolute uncovered wretches,' says we, 'whin th' crool hand iv Spain forged man'cles f'r ye'er limbs, as Hogan says, who was it crossed th' say an' sthruck off th' come-alongs? We did, by dad, we did. An' now, ye miserable, childish-minded apes, we propose f'r to larn ye th' uses iv liberty. In ivry city in this unfair land we will erect schoolhouses an' packin' houses an' houses iv correction, an' we'll larn ye our

language, because 'tis aisier to larn ye ours thin to larn oursilves ye'ers, an' we'll give ye clothes if ye pay f'r thim, an' if ye don't ye can go without, an' whin ye're hungry ye can go to th' morgue— we mane th' resth'rant—an' ate a good square meal iv army beef. . . . an' whin ye've become edycated an' have all th' blessin's iv civiliza- tion that we don't want, that'll count ye wan. We can't give ye anny votes because we haven't more thin enough to go around now, but we'll threat ye th' way a father shud threat his childher if we have to break ivry bone in ye'er bodies. So come to our arms,' says we." [*Journal*, Jan. 28, 1899]

Dooley later presents this case more succinctly when he attributes the following pithy slogans to expansionist Henry Cabot Lodge: "An open back dure an' a closed fr-ront dure," "Take up th' white man's burden an' hand it to th' coons," and "Hands acrost th' sea an' into some wan's pocket" (*Journal*, March 11, 1899).[34]

The Saturday following the first clash between Filipinos and Ameri- can soldiers, Mr. Dooley again exposes the tragic contradictions inherent in America's policy in the Philippines, with a piece about rebel leader Aguinaldo, whose problem is that he doesn't know when it's time "to come in fr'm playin' ball an' get down to business." He has been a patriot too long.

" 'Tis a good job, whin they'se nawthin' else to do; but 'tis not th' thing to wurruk overtime at. 'Tis a sort iv out-iv-dure spoort that ye shud engage in durin' th' summer vacation; but, whin a man carries it on durin' business hours, people begin to get down on him, an' afther a while they're ready to hang him to get him out iv th' way."

Thinking that "th' boom was still on in th' hero business," Aguinaldo has outlived his usefulness in the cause of making "th' Ph'lippeens indepindint on us f'r support. . . . If he'd come in, ye'd be hearin' that James Haitch Aggynaldoo'd been appointed foorth-class post- masther at Hootchey-Kootchey; but now th' nex' ye know iv him 'll be on th' blotther at th' polis station." And so the Philippine Insurrec- tion begins. Mr. Dooley ends the story with a cynical moral: "Pathri- teism always dies when ye establish a polis foorce" (*Journal*, Feb. 11, 1899).

When the Boer War came into the news in late 1899 and 1900, Dunne again followed his Irish instincts and produced a series of

Dooley pieces that were extremely critical of British-style imperialism.[35] He also dealt with evidences of imperialist land-grabbing on the home front. His piece on the exploitation of the Indians, written during the Chippewa uprising of October 1898, pulls no punches in its indictment of American policy:

> "So, be th' powers, we've started in again to improve th' race; an' if we can get in Gatlin' guns enough befure th' winter's snows, we'll tur-rn thim Chippeways into a cimitry branch iv th' Young Men's Christyan Association. We will so. . . . Th' on'y hope f'r th' Indyun is to put his house on rollers, an' keep a team hitched to it, an', whin he sees a white man, to start f'r th' settin' sun. . . . Th' onward march iv th' white civilization, with morgedges an' other modhern improvements, is slowly but surely, as Hogan says, chasin' him out an' th' last iv him'll be livin' in a divin'-bell somewhere out in th' Pac-ific Ocean." [*Journal,* Oct. 8, 1898]

The Dooley pieces on the Spanish-American War and the Philippine Insurrection constitute the only prose critique of solid literary merit produced in America during the actual crises. (There was also the poetry of William Vaughan Moody: "Ode in Time of Hesitation" was published in May 1900.) The most important resident American writers of the day, William Dean Howells and Mark Twain, were both ostensible anti-imperialists, but neither committed himself creatively until the Philippines was a dead issue. Twain's scathing denunciation of President McKinley, "To the Person Sitting in Darkness," appeared in February 1901, well after the crucial presidential election of 1900, when it could have done some good; and Howells, who disapproved of the war with Spain as well as the Philippine venture, released his powerful antiwar story, "Editha," in January 1905.[36] This is not to say that political relevance measures literary worth, but the uniqueness of Dunne's accomplishment here is remarkable and must be considered in a proper assessment of Mr. Dooley.

Dunne several times rejected the suggestion of his Chicago friends that he bring out a collection, but in the flurry of popular acclaim for his war pieces he relented and agreed to put Mr. Dooley in more permanent form. He contracted with Small, Maynard and Company, a small Boston publishing house with a reputation for care and crafts-manship. To capitalize on the material that had brought him to national attention, Dunne included most of his pieces on the war (nineteen in all) under the heading "Mr. Dooley in War." For the remaining two-thirds of the book, "Mr. Dooley in Peace," he assembled a mixed bag of Dooley pieces, early and late, from the May 4, 1895, portrait of Molly Donahue as "the new woman," to his analysis of the French character of October 29, 1898. The arrangement seems random, and the result is a rough cross-section of Dunne's various types of performance. Included are discussions of politics, both local and national, of customs and pastimes with which a national audience could be expected to identify (Christmas shopping, New Year's resolutions, spectator sports), and of events from the world beyond Bridgeport (the Indian wars, a gold rush in Alaska, Queen Victoria's Diamond Jubilee). Only five pieces are pure Bridgeport social history: that is, vignettes from the daily life of the Chicago Irish, with no external impetus or application. There is little Bridgeport material in part because Dunne was selecting from an incomplete group of clippings that went back only to May 1895.[37] But he also must have had doubts about the suitability of Bridgeport social history for his prospective national audience. He did, however, choose well. Three of the five Bridgeport vignettes included are among his finest: the assimilation tragedy of landlord Ahearn and his shiftless son, the story of Petey Scanlan, Bridgeport altar boy gone wrong, and the eulogy to heroic fireman Mike Clancy.[38]

For this first collection, which appeared in November 1898 as *Mr. Dooley in Peace and in War,* Dunne wrote a brief preface, introducing Mr. Dooley, "the traveller, archaeologist, historian, social observer, saloon-keeper, economist, and philosopher," who, "from the cool heights of life in the Archey Road, uninterrupted by the jarring noises of crickets and cows, . . . observes the passing show, and meditates thereon." The preface was signed "F. P. D.," which was to be the only explicit indication of Dunne's authorship in any of the eight Dooley collections. He must have known that this attempt at anonymity would be ineffectual, but perhaps it was a half-serious gesture toward the separation of Finley Peter Dunne and Mr. Dooley that the world never again allowed him to make.

The American literary world received the book warmly. Reviewers for national magazines understandably tended to see it in national terms, concentrating on the war pieces and comparing Dunne to such

previous providers of humorous perspective in wartime as Lowell's
Hosea Biglow and Charles Farrar Browne's Artemus Ward. Typically
laudatory was Harry Thurston Peck, the respected editor of *The Bookman,* who dubbed Dunne a "real humorist," as opposed to a mere
"funny man"; he listed the qualities of real humor as a true sense of
proportion, discrimination, sympathy, and perspective, joined with
pathos and feeling. Peck praised Dunne's "clear-sighted reasonable-
ness, wrapped up but not concealed by a hundred whimsical exaggera-
tions," and he placed Dunne with "those humorists who have really
made a genuine contribution to permanent literature. We have found
nothing else this season which bears so unmistakably the marks of
freshness, originality, and real genius." [39]

In England, where *Mr. Dooley in Peace and in War* came out in
three separate pirated editions before Small, Maynard could get control, Mr. Dooley was acknowledged as much more than a "funny man."
The *Spectator* review was so enthusiastic that Herbert Small had it
printed up and distributed in America as a promotional device.[40]
While Dunne was visiting London in June 1899, a correspondent for
the Chicago *Journal* described the British response to Mr. Dooley as
follows:

> England doubtless misses a good deal of the humor in Mr. Dunne's
> dialogue, but she finds enough to make her laugh. And she takes
> the whole thing more seriously and treats his achievement as a
> more dignified one than America found it. For America at moments
> almost forgot the real depth of thought and the political sagacity
> which lay behind the satire in sheer delight at the excruciating humor
> of the way in which it was expressed.   [*Journal,* June 5, 1899]

"England finds a tremendous inner significance in the 'Dooley'
papers," the correspondent continued; "in a moment of rashness
Mr. Dunne is reported to have said that sometimes she found considerably more in them than he ever had." Dunne often struck this note of
self-deprecation when referring to Mr. Dooley in the first months and
years of his celebrity. He tended to undervalue the artistic merit of
his dialect performances in Chicago because they had been such a
sideline for him there. The Dooley pieces, for which he was paid
separately at the rate of ten dollars per column, were unrelated to
Dunne's heavy editorial responsibilities. He told an interviewer in
May 1899 that at first he had seen Mr. Dooley as just another Satur-

day feature, "done hurriedly amidst the more serious duty of editorial work, without attempt at polish, and each [piece] rarely consuming more than an hour in the preparation." [41] Moreover, a social acquaintance remembered that Dunne's brilliant conversation in Mary Abbott's intellectual circle was often interrupted by his reluctant announcement that "he had to 'go and write that Dooley rot.' " [42] But Dunne was deceived by his apparently slap-dash method of composition, for it turned out to be the only way that he could write at all. After quitting the *Journal* to work full-time on Mr. Dooley and related projects, he found to his dismay that his literary production was not significantly increased. [43]

Dunne's inability to take Mr. Dooley seriously comes through strongly in his letters to his publisher, Herbert Small, during the preparation of the second collection, *Mr. Dooley in the Hearts of His Countrymen* (1899). So little did Dunne value his creation that he gave Small free rein to "read proof on this whole mass . . . and correct unavoidable inconsistencies. I suspect there are duplicates, also. Cut out anything you wish." A few weeks later he asked

> Wouldn't you like to make some changes? I think "A Winter's Night" [a pure Bridgeport vignette] might well disappear. Also I would like to see the Hobson article toned down. [Mr. Dooley ridiculed the hero's welcome given to Lieutenant Richmond Hobson, a veteran of the Cuban conflict who went on a postwar lecture tour.] I believe I called him a fool and other hard names, which he does not quite deserve. Another point, if in going over the book you see too many "damns" and "hells" cut them out. Too many damns spoil the profane emphasis. [44]

Moreover, Dunne constantly questioned whether the old Dooleys were good enough to be included in the new collection. In March 1899, he wrote Small that "the stuff is pretty rotten in spots. But I persevere." And in April he was "discouraged" at how "thin and flat" the material seemed to him, so much so that "sometimes I doubt my ability to make a book of it." Two weeks later he was bridling at the social radicalism implied in some of the early pieces: "I have piled up my old Dooleys—enough for ten books none of which could be read by a taxpayer. I am quite dashed by the prospect of making something out of the Ms. that will not tip over my little castle." And in the same letter he expressed concern that Mr. Dooley may already be "somewhat Archaic. . . . You recall him, perhaps, as one of the friends of your youth. Now, he is out of favor, alas! like crinoline or whiskers. Is there no way to revive him? The middle west voids him. He irritates the membranes of the national belly." Finally, just before the publication of the second collection, Dunne confided to Small that "I sometimes feel that I ought to have chucked Dooley long ago, and begun on something new." [45]

Despite Dunne's qualms, however, *Mr. Dooley in the Hearts of His Countrymen* was a better book than its predecessor. This time he had chosen from the full Chicago *oeuvre:* "The Irishman Abroad" of November 4, 1893, the earliest piece included, had been only the fifth Dooley piece written. More than half the book dealt with life in Bridgeport, and the pages are alive with some of Dunne's finest character studies. The optimistic slag-shoveler, little Tim Clancy, is there, along with his fellow mill-worker Pat Doherty, the quiet Civil War hero, incited to fiery eloquence on Memorial Day. Also present are Boss Flannagan, who sells out his neighbors for a house on Michigan Avenue; the idle apprentice, Jack Carey, shot dead on Archer Avenue by the police; and old Shaughnessy, who is left in permanent loneliness by the marriage of his last daughter. That Dunne could dismiss the group as "pretty rotten in spots" is proof of the blind spot he had about his own work, especially the Bridgeport pieces. This failure of self-perception probably made the transformation of Mr. Dooley into a disembodied national voice that much easier for Dunne.

With *Peace and War* selling at the brisk rate of ten thousand copies per month, Dunne began to investigate schemes for capitalizing on what he thought would be temporary popularity. In the spring of 1899 he double-sold the right to reprint future Dooley columns: once to *Harper's Weekly* and once to the syndicate of Robert H. Russell, a wealthy New York publisher who became his close friend. He also conceived, and contracted for, a number of alternative literary projects. None of them came to fruition, but their invention alone points to his continuing lack of faith in Mr. Dooley.

To Richard Watson Gilder of *Century* magazine, an early admirer and suitor for his talents, Dunne wrote in December 1898, asking "what you would think of a series of articles—perhaps a story—of Irish-American life. . . . It seems to me the job has not been done with real knowledge of the people. [In that judgment he was certainly correct.] I have something in mind—indistinctly—a study of city politics as well as of character; the two are inseparable in Archey road." A week later he acknowledged Gilder's enthusiastic reply by repeating his "vague conception of what the serial should be," and explaining that he saw it as a way to rejuvenate his flagging creativity: "I fear that Dooley's 'pipe is out.' He keeps on puffing at the ashes after the manner of Archey Road but it is a dhry smoke. I think I ought to get away from him—not too far—at least, put him in the third person." [46] This project never materialized, and for the next four years their correspondence is a sad record of Dunne's false starts and Gilder's increasingly exasperated demands for copy. The contract was finally dissolved in 1904, not one of the planned twelve parts of the serial having been delivered.

Dunne also promised to the *Ladies' Home Journal* a long series of dialect pieces starring Molly Donahue, only four of which appeared (in the issues of December 1899 through March 1900). With the last, the *Journal* printed an apology from Dunne, who claimed ill health and dissatisfaction "with the story as far as it has gone." [47] Three of the four pieces are merely extensions of previous Dooley vignettes about Molly: those concerning her piano, her home vaude-ville show, and her attempt to vote. Apparently Dunne was attempting to act upon his letter to Gilder, for the pieces are all in the third person. And this is really what's wrong with them. Dunne was attempt-ing to work within the established comic convention of the frame narrative, in which a pseudo-serious third-person voice counterpoints the dialect exchanges of the other characters. America's antebellum Southwestern humorists (Harris, Hooper, Longstreet, and others) had used this device to create a perspective of rationality from which to judge their often vicious and sadistic main characters. But Mr. Dooley needs no outside judging perspective; he is used to providing it himself. And so the convention falls flat. The flippant, intrusive third-person voice destroys the sense of compassionate involvement provided by Mr. Dooley as narrator.

Another Chicago journalist, George Ade, went through a similar period of restlessness and abortive experimentation when his "Fables in Slang" became suddenly popular at about the same time as Mr. Dooley. Neither man was sure of the validity of his success, nor of just how talented he really was; both were groping for direction and stability in 1899 while tasting the heady wine of first fame. Ade's confusion comes through in his June 1899 suggestion to his publisher, Victor Lawson, that he be relieved of the six-a-week column in which his "Fables" were appearing. But he was to continue writing them for the rest of his life.[48]

In 1899 Dunne began to act the part of a celebrity. His circle of friends steadily widened to include noted humorists such as John Kendrick Bangs and politicians such as Theodore Roosevelt, who began a long campaign to disarm Mr. Dooley by proffering friendship to his creator. Dunne sailed for Europe on his first voyage in May 1899, after having been feted by the journalists of New York for the second year in a row. In London and Dublin he was wined and dined and praised to the foggy skies, and when he returned to work at the *Journal* on October 1, Chicago had lost its charm. Full-time creative writing and its many rewards beckoned to the thirty-two-year-old Dunne, and New York seemed the right place for both. One year later he moved there; he was never to live in Chicago again.

By this time, though, Mr. Dooley's place of origin no longer mattered, for he had been lifted completely out of the context of Bridgeport, and apotheosized into a national commentator. Since 1898 and the publication of *Mr. Dooley in Peace and in War,* Dunne had been conforming to the demands of syndication by treating only national and international topics. Even here, though, he had to find his own level. One of his abortive projects in 1899 had been a collection of pieces to be titled *Mr. Dooley Abroad,* in which Dooley was supposed to have traveled to Europe and sent back reports on what he found there. This was stretching the character much too far, as the few pieces produced according to the scheme demonstrate all too clearly. The first of these was a five-part series on the trial of Captain Dreyfus at Rennes, France, in which Mr. Dooley appears ludicrously out of character and context, standing before the French court to explain that "I'm here to-day in this degraded counthry to tell ye what's th' matther with ye an' what ye ought to do" (*Journal,* Oct. 15, 1899).[49] Dunne must have seen the incongruity of these pieces, for he soon gave up the project and settled into the position of resident American humorist-philosopher that remained his, unchallenged, for the next fifteen years.

Even at this early date, however, the negative aspects of Mr. Dooley's transformation by celebrity and syndication had registered in Chicago—appropriately, in the Irish community that he was about to leave forever. In *The Citizen* for April 8, 1899, the long-suffering John F. Finerty scored his only palpable hit at Dunne's expense by publishing a doggerel poem, "Dooley's Lamentation." The poet, one "Jonathan Indigo," exhibits the grudge-bearer's memory for embarrassing details in recalling that Dunne had reversed his two given names upon entering the literary life in the 1880s. He also marks well the growing pains of the Dooley persona—all the way back to Jim McGarry's saloon, and he understands the tensions and contradictions inherent in Dunne's attempts to keep himself separate from Mr. Dooley.

> My name is Pether Dooley,
>   My age is thirty-two.
> I'm a native of sweet Archey Road,
>   Not far from Healy's Slough!
> My parents were thrue Irish,
>   Though "Scotch" is now in vogue,
> And they blarney'd all creation
>   With their "pure Roscommon brogue!"
>
> When first I met McNarry,
>   In the year of '92,
> He filled me with philosophy
>   On the banks of Healy's Slough!
> But soon he grew unruly—
>   I made of him some fun—
> So I changed his name to Dooley
>   And mine to Finley Dunne!
>
> How many an hour I rambled
>   'Mid hills of sand and junk!
> How many a time I gamboled
>   'Mid fields of cabbage-skunk.
> 'Twas sweet to watch the sunset,
>   And hear th' bull-frogs mew,
> In those days of happy innocence
>   On the banks of Healy's Slough.
>
> Bad luck to you, McNarry,
>   An' your pure Roscommon brogue!
> You led me into throuble,

You blarneying owld rogue!
Your tongue ran on so clever,
    Your words seemed ever new,
An' you soaked me with philosophy
    On th' banks of Healy's Slough!

But now I have grown famous—
    My works are much in vogue—
An' the English rave in chorus
    Of my "pure Roscommon brogue!"
They've "pirated" my labors—
    Th' ruthless Saxon crew—
I'll abuse them to my neighbors
    On th' banks of Healy's Slough!

Then fare you well, McNarry!
    An' farewell Pether Dunne!
I'm swallowed up in "Dooley"
    An' vanished is my fun!
Oh for th' owld time evenings
    When I heard th' bull-frogs mew,
And watched th' purple sunset
    On th' banks of Healy's Slough!

The author of this poem (and I like to think it was Finerty) certainly knew Dunne's career well, and the final stanza has the added virtue of being sadly prophetic.

Mr. Dooley returned to Bridgeport only once more, in an explicit gesture of farewell. When the flow of the Chicago River was reversed for sanitation purposes in January 1900 upon completion of a drainage canal, Dunne wrote his last unsyndicated piece, "Mr. Dooley's Farewell to the Chicago River," exclusively for the Chicago *Journal* (Jan. 13, 1900). In it Dooley sees the new condition of the river as a sign of eternal flux, and he uses the occasion to evoke the old days, when the river was alive and Bridgeport was a real place as well as a name:

"Man an' boy, I've lived beside th' Chicago river f'r forty year, Hinnissy, an' if they ain't any wan else to stand up f'r it, thin here am I. It niver done naught f'r me but good. Manny's the time I've set on th' bridge smokin' me pipe an' watchin' th' lights iv th' tugs dancin' in it like stars, an' me knowin' all th' captains, be hivins, fr'm th' boss iv th' O. B. Green, with th' fine whistle that sounded like a good keen at a Connockman's fun'ral, to the little Mary Ann

Gray, that had a snow-plow attachment on th' prow f'r to get into th' slip over be th' r-red bridge. I had thim all be name, an' fr'm thim I larned th' news iv th' Boheemyan settlemint down th' crick, where I was not on visitin' terms, fr'm an iliction where we had to use couplin' pins to presarve th' peace. Thim lads will niver sail in anny thin river iv dhrinkin' wather. They wudden't know how to conthrol their tugs. They'd go so fast they cudden't take th' curves at th' lumber yards.

" 'Twas th' prettiest river f'r to look at that ye'll iver see. Ye niver was annything iv a pote, Hinnissy, but if ye cud get down on th' Miller dock some night whin ye an' th' likes iv ye was makin' fireworks in th' blast, an' see th' flames blazin' on th' wather an' th' lights dancin', green at th' sausage facthry, blue at th' soap facthry, yellow at th' tannery, ye'd not thrade it f'r annything but th' Liffey, that's thinner but more powerfuller."

Then, in what seems a conscious litany, Dooley runs through the old familiar names for the last time. He recalls when chemical wastes caused the river to catch fire, and "Chief Swenie come down with thruck nine an' chemical fourteen an' a lot more iv th' best"; and how "me Uncle Mike wint up, that was a gr-reat joker, an', says he, 'Chief,' he says, 'they'se on'y wan way ye can put out that fire.' 'How's that?' says the Chief. 'Tur-rn th' river upside down,' says me Uncle Mike." And to the charge that the old river was unhealthy, Dooley replies, "Did ye iver see a healthier lot iv childher, or more iv thim, than lives along th' river? If ye think 'twas onhealthy, go up some day an' thry a roll with Willum J. O'Brien. He's been here near as long as I have. Or luk at me!" Indeed. Mr. Dooley was surely very much alive in his new role of national sage, but the repudiation of his river with which he ends the piece signals, however unconsciously for Dunne, a very great loss to American letters:

"Now that it's goin' out I'll niver go to th' bridge again. Niver. I feel as though I'd lost an ol' frind an' a sthrong wan. It wasn't so much that I see it ivery day, but I always knew it was there. Night an' day me frind was there!"

7

CONCLUSION

Within the compass of these forty years wherein I have been playing professional humorist before the public, I have had for company seventy-eight other American humorists. Each and every one of the seventy-eight rose in my time, became conspicuous and popular, and by and by vanished. . . .

Why have they perished? Because they were merely humorists. Humorists of the "mere" sort cannot survive. Humor is only a fragrance, a decoration. Often it is merely an odd trick of speech and of spelling, as in the case of Ward and Billings and Nasby and the "Disbanded Volunteer," and presently the fashion passes and the fame along with it. There are those who say a novel should be a work of art solely and you must not preach in it, you must not teach in it. That may be true as regards novels but it is not true as regards humor. Humor must not professedly teach and it must not professedly preach, but it must do both if it would live forever. By forever, I mean thirty years.

SAMUEL L. CLEMENS [1]

I HOPE that the preceding chapters have established that in Mr. Dooley's Chicago years there emerged a coherent body of work, essentially different from his performances after 1900 as a national figure, and worthy of interest on its own. In concluding, I want first to summarize the strengths and limitations of the Dooley form and some of the influences upon its invention. It would be foolish to deny that Dunne was limited by his chosen form: a weekly newspaper column of roughly 750 words is too slight and too time-serving ever to constitute crafted literature of the first rank. The pieces are true sketches, and at the most they provide telling glimpses into character and motive, particular places and times. No synthesis can bring into being what was never there to start with: that is, the coherent, rounded wholeness of fiction. Yet there is more of a realized world in these scattered pieces than Dunne has been given credit for, and its creation in his severely constricted form is a minor miracle of American letters.

The central importance of the milieu of big-city journalism in the genesis of Mr. Dooley was the theme of my opening chapter. In addition, Dunne seems to have borrowed in various ways from three other oral and literary traditions, which have also been mentioned already but need to be brought together now. First, there is the indigenous American tradition of the crackerbox philosopher, or wise fool, the low-caste and unlettered dispenser of wisdom in dialect who was a fixture on the American scene throughout the nineteenth century. Mr. Dooley shares with the Nasbys, Wards, and Downings the stock verbal tricks of the dialect humorist. Also, Dunne's critical commentary on the war against Spain is part of a dialect tradition of realistic/humorous evaluation of American military involvement that includes Lowell's Hosea Biglow, Browne's Artemus Ward, and Locke's Petroleum V. Nasby. Mr. Dooley differs importantly from his predecessors, though, in being both the first immigrant and the first city-dweller to achieve sustained identity in this tradition. Moreover, he is a fully developed character who has been placed in a definite social and geographical context; in this he is unlike the isolated, shadowy figures—little more than disembodied rural voices—of his predecessors. That Mr. Dooley is the first thoroughly localized community member in the American dialect tradition is an element of Dunne's achievement to which I will return.

Second, Dunne seems consciously to make use of the American

tall-tale tradition. His memorable anecdotes from Bridgeport's early, brawling days as a canal port are worthy of Mike Fink, the king of the bargemen: for example, the canalside fist fight between "Con Murphy, th' champine heavyweight iv th' ya-ards" and "th' German blacksmith," which begins at four in the morning and ends after dark, "whin Murphy's backer put a horseshoe on th' big man's fist" (*EP*, Nov. 2, 1895). Throughout his Chicago career, tall-tale hyperbole is one of Mr. Dooley's favorite devices. Among the gems are his description of Chicago air as "so thick with poisonous gases that a wagon loaded with scrap iron wud float at an ilivation iv tin feet" (*EP*, Sept. 4, 1897); and of the "Great Hot Spell," during which "the sthreet-car thracks got so soft they spread all over th' sthreet, an' th' river run dhry," and "th' fire departmint was all down on Mitchigan Avnoo, puttin' out th' lake" (*EP*, Sept. 21, 1895).

Third, Mr. Dooley seems to echo the literary and folk traditions of Ireland. Dunne probably listened to Irish storytellers from his parents' generation, and he may have been influenced by the upsurge of interest in Irish folklore in the 1890s generated by Yeats, Hyde, and Lady Gregory. We know that news of the Irish folk movement reached him in Chicago, because Colonel McNeery spends a column in 1893 explaining to John McKenna that "folk-lore" is "di'lect pothry" (*SP*, July 16, 1893). At least one Dooley piece deals directly with an Irish folk plot—a man's ghost returning to cause trouble for his remarried wife and her new husband. When the ghost of big Tim O'Grady wafts into his old home, "in th' mos' natural way in th' wurruld, kickin' th' dog," he is summarily ejected by his successor, O'Flaherty the tailor, who declares that "I'll make th' ghost iv a ghost out iv ye. I can lick anny dead man that iver lived." The same embarrassing situation occurs in the traditional Irish tale, "Leeam O'Rooney's Burial," which Douglas Hyde translated into English in his seminal collection, *Beside the Fire*, of 1890.[2] Moreover, both stories point the same moral: it is plain bad form to come back after having been decently buried. " 'Tis onplisint iv thim, annyhow, not to say ongrateful," says Mr. Dooley:

> "F'r mesilf, if I was wanst pushed off, an' they'd waked me kindly, an' had a solemn rayqueem high mass f'r me, an' a funeral with Roddey's Hi-bernyan band, an' th' A-ho-aitches, I have too much pride to come back f'r an encore. I wud so, Jawn. Whin a man's

dead, he ought to make th' best iv a bad job, an' not be thrapsin' around, lookin' f'r throuble among his own kind." [*EP,* May 9, 1896]

In Hyde's tale, O'Rooney's wife chides him similarly: "I can't let you in, and it's a great shame, you to be coming back again, after being seven days in your grave. . . . doesn't every person in the parish know that you are dead, and that I buried you decently."

A particular convention of Irish storytelling that Dunne always uses is the repeated interjection of "he says . . . I says . . . he says," by which he is able to control the pace and rhythm of Mr. Dooley's conversation, often for lyrical, humorous, or satiric emphasis. Dunne's ear for the rhythms, contractions, and occasional rolled "r's" of Irish-American common speech is everywhere remarkable. His ability to transfer these tones still living onto the page is central to the perennial freshness of the Dooley pieces; even in the least successful of them, we hear a real human voice.[3]

Actually, Dunne's persistent concern for the spoken language may loosely be labeled "Irish," for, as Oscar Wilde once told Yeats, "We Irish are too poetical to be poets; we are a nation of brilliant failures, but we are the greatest talkers since the Greeks."[4] A major Dooley theme is the abuse of political speech for selfish ends. Mr. Dooley exposes rhetorical excess on every possible political level: in his own Bridgeport precinct, in Chicago municipal affairs, in the camps of the Irish nationalists, in the 1896 presidential campaign, and in the self-justifying speeches of the apologists for American imperialism in Cuba and the Philippines. Moreover, the determined deflation of the high-falutin is one of Dunne's favorite means of cutting through to the deeper duplicity of character whose exposure is at the core of so many Dooley pieces.

Dunne's love of the language and fascination with its potential come through even more in Mr. Dooley's continual verbal playfulness, more sophisticated, by and large, than that of his fellow American practitioners of dialect humor. There are enough ingenious double-entendres and portmanteau words scattered through the Dooley pieces to warrant at least passing comparison with Joyce, the master word-smith. "Jackuse," screams Emile Zola at the trial of Captain Dreyfus, "which is a hell of a mane thing to say to anny man." Admiral Dewey cables home from Manila that "at eight o'clock I begun a peaceful

blockade iv this town. Ye can see th' pieces ivrywhere," while on the
Cuban front "Tiddy Rosenfelt" lays single-handed siege to "Sandago."
And when the smoke clears, and President McKinley asks "What
shall we do with th' fruits iv victhry?", a voice from the audience answers "Can thim." Meanwhile, in Chicago, a city which rose "felix-
like" from the ashes of the 1871 Fire, the river flows backward toward
its "sewerce," the German "Turnd'-ye-mind" meets in Schwartzmeister's back room, and Lake Shore millionaires marry to the strains of
"th' Wagner Palace Weddin' March fr'm 'Long Green,' " after exchanging vows before "Hyman, which is the Jew god iv marredge."

There are, in addition, sustained flights of wit and linguistic inventiveness in pieces such as Mr. Dooley's paradoxical juxtaposition of
the healthful city and the contaminating countryside, or his exposure
of military unpreparedness on President McKinley's Strategy Board.
One of the very best of these, in which Dunne gives free rein to his
verbal imagination, is Mr. Dooley's wild commentary on the use of
"expert testimony" in the trial of Chicagoan Adolph Luetgert, accused
of murdering his wife and mingling her remains with the raw materials
in his sausage factory. To wit: "Did or did not Alphonse Lootgert stick
Mrs. L. into a vat, an' rayjooce her to a quick lunch?" All hell breaks
loose when the court calls in a college professor to give scientific
evidence:

> " 'Profissor,' says th' lawyer f'r the State, 'I put it to ye if a wooden
> vat three hundherd an' sixty feet long, twenty-eight feet deep, an'
> sivinty-five feet wide, an' if three hundherd pounds iv caustic soda
> boiled, an' if the leg iv a guinea pig, an' ye said yestherdah about
> bi-carbonate iv soda, an' if it washes up an' washes over, an' th'
> slimy, slippery stuff, an' if a false tooth or a lock iv hair or a jaw-
> bone or a goluf ball across th' cellar eleven feet nine inches—that
> is, two inches this way an' five gallons that?' 'I agree with ye intirely,'
> says th' profissor. 'I made lab'ratory experiments in an' ir'n basin,
> with bichloride iv gool, which I will call soup-stock, an' coal tar,
> which I will call ir'n filings. I mixed th' two over a hot fire, an'
> left in a cool place to harden. I thin packed it in ice, which I will
> call glue, an' rock-salt, which I will call fried eggs, an' obtained a
> dark, queer solution that is a cure f'r freckles, which I will call
> antimony or doughnuts or annything I blamed please.'
> " 'But,' says th' lawyer f'r th' State, 'measurin' th' vat with gas,—
> an' I lave it to ye whether this is not th' on'y fair test,—an' supposin'
> that two feet acrost is akel to tin feet sideways, an' supposin' that

a thick green an' hard substance, an' I daresay it wud; an' supposin' you may, takin' into account th' measuremints,—twelve be eight,— th' vat bein' wound with twine six inches fr'm th' handle an' a rub iv th' green, thin ar-re not human teeth often found in counthry sausage?' 'In th' winter,' says th' profissor. 'But th' sisymoid bone is sometimes seen in th' fut, sometimes worn as a watch-charm. I took two sisymoid bones, which I will call poker dice, an' shook thim together in a cylinder, which I will call Fido, poored in a can iv milk, which I will call gum arabic, took two pounds iv rough-on-rats, which I rayfuse to call; but th' raysult is th' same.' Question be th' coort: 'Different?' Answer: 'Yis.' Th' coort: 'Th' same.' Be Misther McEwen: 'Whose bones?' Answer: 'Yis.' Be Misther Vincent: 'Will ye go to th' divvle?' Answer: 'It dissolves th' hair.' "

[*EP,* Sept. 11, 1897]

An exercise of such rhapsodic absurdity could only have been given by a man drunk on words, a partner in vice with the likes of Joyce and Flann O'Brien.

This may be stretching for a point, but I see one other affinity with literary modernism in the ironic perspective of the piece in which Mr. Dooley compares the fallen state of modern Greece (currently besieged by Turkey) to the decline of Bridgeport's "fightin' tenth" precinct. "Leonidas an' th' pass iv Thermometer" are compared to Bridgeport's old-time heroes, most of whom "come fr'm th' ancient Hellenic province iv May-o." The glory that was Bridgeport has faded, having given way to an influx of "Polish Jews an' Swedes an' Germans an' Hollanders," and when "a band iv rovin' Bohemians fr'm th' Eighth Ward" swoops down on the precinct, old Mike Riordan, "th' on'y wan iv th' race iv ancient heroes on earth," stands alone against them; and "if it wasn't f'r th' intervintion iv th' powers in th' shape iv th' loot an' a wagon-load iv polismin, th' Bohemians'd have devastated as far as th' ruins iv th' gas-house, which is th' same as that there Acropulist ye talk about" (*EP,* May 8, 1897). The Fisher King of Eliot's *The Waste Land* is a similarly incongruous, ironic figure in a similar urban landscape, complete with gashouse.

Dunne's accomplishment can be measured on its own terms also, in the context of Chicago journalism, for a rival Irish dialect series, "Officer Casey on the City Hall Corner," ran in the *Chicago Times-Herald* for five months in 1895. In this series two Irish patrolmen, Casey and "the Connemara cop," discuss Chicago and Irish affairs, concentrating primarily on politics. There is little to compare between them. The Dooley pieces are invariably shorter and more focused than the Casey columns, which often become rambling catalogs of Chicago political names, most of which have little significance now. Casey's dialect is strained and inconsistent, a mixture of forced Irishisms, incongruous slang terms, and overly formal, uncontracted "ing" forms. Most important, where the Dooley pieces begin solidly rooted in Bridgeport and move easily and naturally into general applicability, the typical Casey piece is a static compendium of flat, provincial, dated gossip, and goes nowhere.[5]

One last strength of the Dooley form that must be mentioned here is Dunne's control of his endings.[6] In the satirical pieces, the ending often constitutes a startling ironic reversal that turns over our perspective on the subject at hand. At its best, the effect is abruptly clarifying, as a window shade in a darkened room flips up to let in a shaft of light. Just when Mr. Dooley appears to have been seduced out of a gloomy contemplation of Bridgeport poverty by thoughts of approaching spring, he concludes that "Th' spring's come on. Th' grass is growin' good; an', if th' Connock man's children back iv th' dumps can't get meat, they can eat hay" (*EP,* April 13, 1895). Similarly, after McKinley's victory in 1896, Dooley overturns John McKenna's sententious moralizing message that "we must all work," by concluding "Yes, . . . or be wurruked" (*EP,* Nov. 7, 1896). Dunne's touch is equally sure in the best of the dark vignettes, which he often ends with haunting images of solitary suffering: Petey Scanlan's mother sitting with her hoodlum son's first communion picture in her lap; or Fireman Mike Clancy's wife waiting at the door for her husband's body; or old Shaughnessy with his elbows on his knees, staring into the fire on his last daughter's wedding night. In these minor-key tragedies we forget the limitations of the Dooley form and respond directly to the flash of common humanity revealed to us.

The Chicago Dooley pieces need, finally, to be examined in terms of Peter Dunne's contributions in three roles: as a historian, as a literary realist, and as a philosopher.

As to historical interest, the value of Dunne's explorations of the circumstances, customs, and attitudes of the Chicago Irish in the 1890s has already been seen. The preceding chapters have been organized to bring together the variously diffused historical materials that Dunne has given us—materials and information available nowhere else. The Chicago Dooley pieces provide a detailed picture of an Irish-American working-class community caught in the throes of assimilation, a picture which contributes to our understanding of nineteenth-century urban and immigrant life. The pieces also provide for the political historian new perspective on the phenomenon of urban boss rule in America, of which Bridgeport in the nineties was a perfect microcosm. In addition, they give us insight into Irish-American nationalism, a curious, tragicomic passion that has been rekindled in our time by the terrors of the crisis in Ulster. And lastly, Mr. Dooley's treatments of the Spanish-American War and the origins of American imperialism reverberate against our latter-day criticisms of foreign policy and unpopular war. In short, Dunne speaks directly to many of our most salient historical interests.

Dunne's importance to American literature needs to be explained more fully. He has not been given his due as a significant contributor to the realistic movement. In the first place, the Chicago Dooley pieces are part of the realistic reaction against genteel strictures of both language and subject matter. Because they were of real literary merit, they constituted weekly exempla all through the middle nineties of the potential for legitimate literature of the common speech and the common lives of American working-class immigrant city-dwellers. William Dean Howells, realism's champion, partially recognized Dunne's contribution in a 1903 review of "Certain of the Chicago School of Fiction," in which he linked Dunne with George Ade, whose "Fables in Slang" were also attempts to salvage for literature the special languages of city streets. Howells, however, missed some of Mr. Dooley's point, for he called on Dunne to shed his persona and "come into the open with a bold, vigorous and incisive satire of our politicians and their methods." [7] To my knowledge, Dunne has not since been called a literary realist. But he does belong in that company, and in a special position that can be defined in terms of two related concepts: place and community.

Eudora Welty has defined "place in fiction" as "the named, identified, concrete, exact and exacting, and therefore credible, gathering-spot of all that has been felt, is about to be experienced, in the novel's progress." She sees "place being brought to life in the round before the reader's eye" as "the readiest and gentlest and most honest and natural way" to begin to do the writer's job of making "the world of appearance . . . *seem* actuality." Welty further remarks on the "mystery" of place, which lies in "the fact that place has a more lasting identity than we have, and we unswervingly tend to attach ourselves to identity." Also, "the magic" lies "partly too in the *name* of the place—since that is what *we* gave it," thereby putting "a kind of poetic claim on its existence. . . . The truth is," she contends, "fiction depends for its life on place. Location is the crossroads of circumstance, the proving ground of 'What happened? Who's here? Who's coming?'—and that is the heart's field." [8]

As surely as Welty and the other Southern writers, Dunne knew instinctively the value of place. He has located Mr. Dooley in Bridgeport by evoking the "identified, concrete, exact and exacting" details of that neighborhood, and by invoking the magic of names. Mr. Dooley defines all movement in relation to the "r-red bridge," which joins Bridgeport to the rest of Chicago. "Archey Road" is a vivid, realized main street—from Dooley's place to Schwartzmeister's "down the way" to the political capital of Bridgeport at Finucane's Hall. Questions of social status hinge on the proximity of one's home to the gashouse and the rolling mills, and every new person to appear in Mr. Dooley's running conversation is given this defining placement. Finally, the waters of that swampy Chicago River run-off, Haley's Slough, provide a meandering backdrop for nearly every scene. Thus, moving the St. Patrick's Day parade downtown to Michigan Avenue is little less than sacrilege, and the irony is only partial in Mr. Dooley's lament at the takeover by newer immigrant groups of Bridgeport's "sacred sites." One must truly belong somewhere to convey the loving sense of place that comes across in the Dooley pieces; and it is a part of Dunne's accomplishment to have created sketches which convey the feeling of the city as a familiar, potentially comfortable, unthreatening place to live.

It is in this perspective of grounded familiarity that Dunne's Chicago work differs most emphatically from that of the two great American pioneers of urban fiction, Stephen Crane and Theodore Dreiser, neither of whom is ever at home in the city. Beginning with *Maggie: A Girl of the Streets,* his 1893 first novel, Crane observes city life as an explorer;

he surveys a strange land for archetypal examples of human fear and suffering. Because he never really lived in the city (except as a bohemian tourist) and because his aim in fiction was "to show that environment is a tremendous thing in the world and frequently shapes lives regardless," Crane cannot present Maggie's New York as a home where real people lead real lives.[9] Either the city remains a static tableau against which Crane works out several acts of his private vision of man as victim of fear and circumstance, or else it comes alive as a malignant force—for example, in the description of Maggie's tenement house as a threatening beast with tenants as devoured victims "stamping about in its bowels."[10] The city is a jungle to Crane, and he imposes this impressionistic, warped perspective on us too; fear, alienation, and helplessness are the only allowable reactions.

The same thing happens in Dreiser's fiction. The Chicago of *Sister Carrie* (1900) is the archetypal city as alien environment. From the beginning to the end of the book, the dominant reaction of downstate villager Carrie Meeber to the city streets is detached fascination— which is to say, they never become familiar to her. Home is the place that Dreiser's American villager leaves behind when moving to the city, and she never finds another. Thus, Carrie's first impression of downtown Chicago as a confusing jumble of "wall-lined mysteries . . . all wonderful, all vast, all far removed" is telling and lasting.[11] She is no closer to New York as she rocks and dreams in a plush apartment above Central Park in the novel's final image. Dreiser's heroine can learn to ignore her sense of the city as an alien organism, by subjugation to mind-dulling routine or, if she is lucky, by escaping into diversion and luxury. But she can never make the city a home. She remains outside.

Both Crane and Dreiser are locked into their private visions of urban man as a stranger in a strange land. Thus, the cities they describe are invariably cold, bleak, and killing to real social life. Community in such settings is impossible.[12] On the other hand, Mr. Dooley's Bridgeport is a real community. The difference is, of course, in point of view: Crane and Dreiser are detached, ironic observers, while Mr. Dooley speaks to us directly, as a committed member of the community he is describing. Crane's admitted purpose in writing *Maggie* was "to show people to people as they seem to me," and both the abstractness of "people" and the impressionism of "me" are revealing.[13] Although the characters of *Maggie* and his related New York City sketches are ostensibly Irish-Americans, Crane makes no attempt to describe them as such; their background meant as little to him as the names of the streets on which they lived, most of which also remain anonymous. But Dunne's purpose was to show Bridgeporters to people as they seem to a fellow Bridgeporter. And so the closest we come to hearing a story like Maggie's is when Mr. Dooley brushes quickly over the moral ruin of old Shaughnessy's first daughter: "She didn't die; but, th' less said, th' sooner mended" (*EP,* March 28, 1896). Instead of the whole story, we get truth to the Dooley persona. To this end, Dunne musters his sense of place and Irish character and his ear for common speech. The result is unique: the literary evocation of a late nineteenth-century urban ethnic neighborhood where the residents have strong attachments to the place and to one another. Mr. Dooley is one of the first characters in American literature for whom the city is a real home.

To be sure, there were other literary attempts to describe the urban Irish in the 1890s. For example, the New York *Sun* printed Richard Harding Davis's "Gallegher" stories about a street-wise newsboy and Edward W. Townsend's "Chimmie Fadden" sketches, which featured a slick young Bowery tough. Both were popular enough to be republished in best-selling collections: *Gallegher: A Newspaper Story* in 1891 and *Chimmie Fadden, Major Max and Other Stories* in 1895. Neither Davis nor Townsend was Irish, however, and neither created convincingly Irish characters or neighborhoods. In fact, one critic dismissed the Fadden series as "a mixture of local color, vaudeville dialect, and Zola naturalism," resulting in "a manufactured thing, no more true to the Bowery of which [Chimmie] was supposed to be a typical specimen than the end-man of a minstrel show is true to Negro character."[14]

There was, though, at least one other American writer in the nineties whose work is comparable to Dunne's—the Russian immigrant Abraham Cahan, whose vignettes of Jewish life in the new world began appearing in the New York *Sun* in 1887. Cahan also wrote as an insider, a member of the culture he describes. Moreover, like the Dooley pieces, his fiction demonstrates that the outside pressures of prejudice and discrimination exerted by the native American majority that created the ghetto in the first place have so strengthened the immigrant group that, paradoxically, the alien city becomes a place where real community is possible. Mr. Dooley may love Bridgeport more because the Irish have been there longer, but Cahan's characters are also at home on the Lower East Side. His stories capture the color and density of ghetto life with a concern for detail and a grudging affection for the city that are wholly absent in Crane and Dreiser, Davis and Townsend. Cahan describes with loving concretion the bursting streets, dance halls, and one-room apartments of the Lower East Side, along with vignettes of daily life—sweatshop jobs in the garment industry, holiday parties, and wedding feasts. And his major theme, available elsewhere in the nineties only in the Dooley pieces, is the painful process of assimilation into American life. In "The Imported Bridegroom" (1898), an arranged marriage backfires on the bride's father when his daughter and her husband both leave the orthodox faith to become freethinkers. "Circumstances," in the same collection, details the break-up of a marriage through pressures of poverty and intellectual starvation in the city. Other stories satirize the pretensions of the Jewish middle class, given, like the Irish, to flaunting the piano in the parlor and affecting American ways, often with ludicrous results. Cahan's first novel, *Yekl: A Tale of the New York Ghetto* (1896), is the story of an "assimilated" garment worker who changes his name to "Jake" and methodically repudiates his European customs. Ashamed of the foreignness of his wife, who has come from Russia to join him after three years' separation, Yekl divorces her and marries an "Americanized" girl of much weaker character. The pained and puzzled tone of Mr. Dooley's tales of community dissolution appears also in Cahan's fiction; most movingly in the attempts of Yekl's frightened and lonely Russian wife to make sense of her situation.[15] Again like Dunne, Cahan turned away from his strongest literary talent after 1900. Throwing himself into New York's *Jewish Daily Forward,* which he edited for fifty years beginning in 1897, Cahan built it into the best Yiddish language newspaper in America. He returned to realistic fiction once more, however, in his great 1917 novel of the Jewish immigrant experience, *The Rise of David Levinsky.*[16]

A more recent direct descendent of Dunne's Irishmen and Cahan's Jews is irrepressible Harlem resident Jesse B. Semple (or "Simple"), whose barroom conversations with his intellectual friend Boyd were reported in the 1950s and 1960s by Langston Hughes. Simple, like Mr. Dooley, is the spokesman for an urban minority group which has suffered from prejudice and has lately begun to climb toward respectability, and his scorn of the black bourgeoisie rivals Dooley's ridicule of the lace-curtain Irish. Moreover, Hughes's Harlem is as colorful and homey a place as Bridgeport or the Lower East Side. In a way, Simple is closer to Mr. Dooley than Cahan is, for Hughes's pieces were also originally newspaper columns, in the *Chicago Defender* and the *New York Post*.[17]

The attitudes toward Dunne and Cahan of their respective immigrant audiences seem to have been similar. In his study of *The Spirit of the Ghetto* (1902), Hutchins Hapgood found that the uptown Jewish bourgeoisie were accusing Cahan of "betraying his race to the Gentiles," just as the middle-class Irish (represented by John Finerty writing in *The Citizen*) condemned Dunne. At the same time, Hapgood found that the Lower East Siders themselves appreciated Cahan's "truthful and sympathetic" portrayal of their lives.[18] What little first-hand evidence there is suggests that the Bridgeport Irish also enjoyed Mr. Dooley. We have, for one thing, the fond memories of James T. Farrell's Paddy Lonigan (quoted earlier), which may have come from the novelist's own father. Also, at the time of Dunne's death in 1936, two local Chicago tributes seem to indicate his popularity among people likely to have patronized Mr. Dooley's shop: there was a memorial mass at St. Bridget's Church on Archer Avenue in Bridgeport, and the girls of St. Patrick's Girls High School laid a wreath at his birth site on West Adams Street.[19] There was, furthermore, a contemporary acknowledgment in the form of an anonymous poem sent to the *Evening Post* in 1895 by an Irishman who was inspired to thank Mr. Dooley in verse for having put his own world into words:

Dooley Darlin'

Yerrah, Dooley darlin', sure 'tis you've the blarneyin',
The scorchin', witty and the tindher tongue.
With McKinna shpakin' you can stop the achin'
Of my poor ould heart, faix it makes me young.

It brings me back to my own Tip'rary—
The fun so rousin', the wit so keen,

So dhroll an' sparklin', so sly an' sooth'rin'
Like a colleen's banther on an Irish green!

. . . .

Ah! there's more than fun, sure, for there's sermons spun, sure,
By you Dooley, darlin', straight from your sowl;
An' 'twixt sayin's witty there are sthrains of pity,
An' scorn as bitther as a Saxon's scowl.

There's been tellin' sthrokes in Dooley's speechin'—
Didn't Pullman squirm at things he said?
And others thank him for thoughts as tindher
As a mother's glances at her baby's bed.

[*EP*, Jan. 26, 1895]

It is also significant that only in Chicago did reviewers of his first collection recognize Dunne's accomplishments as social historian of the Bridgeport Irish. The *Post* called him "the Boswell of the sixth wa-ard" (Dec. 10, 1898), and the *Times-Herald* used the piece about "curly-haired" angel Petey Scanlan's tragic fall to illustrate Dunne's function as the chronicler of a fast disappearing way of life: "Life has surged for decades over the black way of Archey road, from 'the mills' to the 'cabbage gardens,' " the reviewer states, "and Mr. Dooley has watched its comedy and tragedy with keen eye.

Touches of nature, such as this; pictures of life from the circles of the lowly; color taken from the heart, have served and always will serve to make the work of Mr. Dunne in the Dooley papers worthy of permanent preservation. Archey road is rapidly becoming something of the past. The trolley car, the march of modern buildings, the press of commercial activity are destroying the district in which Mr. Dooley and his friends lived. But no iconoclast can lay hands upon what Mr. Dooley has said. He has given his message to all time. [*T-H*, Nov. 20, 1898]

Mr. Dooley's message was not lost on the one writer whose Chicago-based fiction was to have the greatest impact of all on American literature. Although Bridgeport was a world away from the chilling, indifferent Chicago of his imagination, Theodore Dreiser nevertheless declared to George Ade that "as early as 1900, or before, [Ade's *Artie*] passed into my collection of genuine American realism. . . . In fact, I entered it with your *Fables in Slang,* Finley Dunne's *Philosopher Dooley,* Frank Norris' *McTeague* and Hamlin Garland's *Main Traveled Roads. . . .* These were the beginning of my private library of American realism." [20] Dunne should be in everybody's library of realism, for he possessed and acted upon the realist's faith in common life as the stuff of literature. Within the limits of their form, the Chicago Dooley sketches conform to Eudora Welty's definition of fiction as "from the start . . . bound up in the local, the 'real,' the present, the ordinary day-to-day of human experience." Dunne lost his chance for a full career of literary as well as journalistic greatness, but not before giving us Bridgeport and Mr. Dooley. Surely this young Chicago editor's place in American literature was assured from the day in 1893, his own twenty-sixth year, on which he brought to life that sixty-year-old smiling public-house man.

We come now to the placement of Mr. Dooley as a philosopher. John Kelleher has called him "a unique invention: the only mythical philosopher I can think of with a philosophy." [21] And it is true that over the long haul the Chicago Dooley pieces do embody a consistent view of the world—one that, I think, helps to explain two apparently contradictory facts about them: first, that they are still so readable today, and second, that Dunne in effect stopped writing them when he moved on to syndication and New York. The amputation of Mr. Dooley from his life-giving Chicago context was complete by at least 1902, when a survey of "New Humor" for *The Critic* stated that "Mr. Dooley . . . has no place in this list [of humorous creations based on distinctive American character types]. He is not the study of a type,— simply the mouth-piece of his author in the expression of theories on many subjects." [22] Having lost his cultural grounding in Bridgeport, Mr. Dooley still has something to say to us in the later pieces only because of his consistent philosophical stance, which Dunne never abjured. It can be described as a kind of skepticism/relativism, rooted both in the pervasive cultural revolution that Henry May has called "the end of American innocence" and in Dunne's own Irish background.

"American relativism," in May's words, was "a rejection on one ground or another of the mid-nineteenth-century cosmos, the familiar combination of adapted Christianity, science, industrialism, and middle-class mores. In England and America, the revolt was directed particularly against the world of Herbert Spencer, a world of progress *toward* moral perfection." [23] May describes America's turn-of-the-century relativists as fence-straddlers who had rejected the old simplistic certainties of the Victorian world view without stepping out of the mainstream of nineteenth-century American thought, itself predominantly optimistic. William James defines the type: eminently cheerful, he looked both ways at once, "toward skeptical practicality and even materialism, and also toward an acceptance of the promptings of intuition and faith. . . . Moral to the core, with deep idealistic tendencies, devoted to standard culture though impatient of its stuffier tendencies, progressive above all, James was clearly a part of the surviving nineteenth-century American civilization we have described, and he died just before the crucial phase of its disintegration." [24]

Certainly Dunne was affected by the winds of change described here; on the other hand, he really doesn't belong with May's cheerful questioners because Mr. Dooley's philosophy is shot through with prominent dark veins of cynicism, pessimism, and grim fatality. These can be traced to Dunne's position as the child of an already fragmented culture. His roots are in Ireland and in the experience of immigration; which is to say, in a subject nation whose history has been one long lamentation and in an experience of displacement, prejudice, and alienation. In creating Martin Dooley, Dunne was electing to bring in the minority report of the immigrant Irish, rather than allowing himself to be assimilated into the milder skepticism of the dominant American intellectual frame in his time.

Putting Dunne in an Irish philosophical context also helps to explain why the Chicago Dooley pieces demonstrate Eudora Welty's principle of place, so important to the literary achievement of the great Southern writers. As defeated cultures, Ireland and the American South have much in common. C. Vann Woodward has pointed out that the "irony of Southern history" has been its "thoroughly un-American" preoccupation "with guilt, not with innocence, with the reality of evil, not with the dream of perfection." The tragic experiences of slavery, defeat in civil war, and Reconstruction had kept the South "basically pessimistic in its social outlook and its moral philosophy," even "in that most optimistic of centuries in the most optimistic part of the world." What Woodward says of the South is in large part true of Ireland and of the Irish in America: "It had learned to accommodate itself to conditions that it swore it would never accept, and it had learned the taste left in the mouth by the swallowing of one's own words. It had learned to live for long decades in quite un-American poverty, and it had learned the equally un-American lesson of submission." [25] In both cultures the literary preoccupation with place may be a matter of sanity and survival: when everything else is flying apart, the mind and heart can be steadied by concentration on locality, on named, palpable landmarks. Faulkner's having been able to map his mythical county for Malcolm Cowley is of a piece with Joyce's boast that a stranger could negotiate Dublin with a copy of *Ulysses* as guide.

At any rate, Dunne remains most Irish in his consistently dark perspective. Hamlin Garland came close to describing this quality in declaring that "he had the somber temperament of the Celt. I felt in him a sadness of outlook, a fatalistic philosophy which was curiously at variance with his writing." [26] Of course, Garland was speaking of Dunne's later syndicated work; like the rest of Mr. Dooley's audience in the years of celebrity, he never felt the combined pressure of the many Chicago pieces in which Irish background and philosophical skepticism come together so powerfully. Having now felt that pressure, we can grant Dunne his unique position as a philosophical hyphenate: an Irish-American relativist. It only remains for us to go back to Archer Avenue once more, to clarify that position with concrete examples, and to connect it to Dunne's decision to take Mr. Dooley out of Chicago.

Mr. Dooley's philosophy has two basic tenets: first, that human nature and the world are not improving or improvable; and second, that nothing else is certain or simple. In John Kelleher's words, "the complexity of the human spirit was his starting point." [27] The only sure thing, in Mr. Dooley's view, is that a lot of people will always be miserable; otherwise, the world is shifting and relative, a chaos of ill-defined, clashing motives, self-delusions and disillusionments, unpredictable changes of mood, orientation, and desire. His anecdotes pay homage to the myriad ways we can become ensnared by circumstance, one another, and ourselves.

All that keeps Dunne-as-Dooley from the abyss is the attitude he chooses to take in a particular piece toward the bleakly pessimistic truths from which he seldom flinches. Mostly he manages to be funny

—not so much by choice as because humor was in his bones, something he couldn't help producing. This is a mixed blessing, for in some Dooley pieces the defense of dry wit becomes merely a mechanical posture, like the "cast-iron whimsy" (Randall Jarrell's fine phrase) of Robert Frost's late poems, and the result is hollow and superficial laughter. Humor aside then, in the best pieces Dunne had always to decide between two attitudes: tempering compassion and bleak despair, each equally plausible given his view of the world and human possibility. It all depended on how Dunne felt on a given Friday evening as he sat in the editorial offices of the *Evening Post* plotting a column. But whatever his mood, the underlying philosophy stayed the same.

Mr. Dooley attacks the Victorian myth of progress directly in a commemorative discussion of Queen Victoria's Diamond Jubilee. In it, he provides a strong corrective to Herbert Spencer with a bittersweet list of nineteenth-century endeavors and inventions:

"Great happenin's have me an' Queen Victorya seen in these sixty years. Durin' our binificent prisince on earth th' nations have grown r-rich an' prosperous. Great Britain has ixtinded her domain until th' sun niver sets on it. No more do th' original owners iv th' sile, they bein' kept movin' be th' polis. While she was lookin' on in England, I was lookin' on in this counthry. I have seen America spread out fr'm th' Atlantic to th' Pacific, with a branch office iv the Standard Ile Comp'ny in ivry hamlet. I've seen th' shackles dropped fr'm th' slave, so's he cud be lynched in Ohio. I've seen this gr-reat city desthroyed be fire fr'm De Koven Sthreet to th' Lake View pumpin' station, and thin rise felix-like fr'm its ashes, all but th' West Side, which was not burned. . . .

"Oh, what things I've seen in me day an' Victorya's! Think iv that gran' procission iv lithry men—Tinnyson an' Longfellow an' Bill Nye an' Ella Wheeler Wilcox an' Tim Scanlan an'—an' I can't name thim all: they're too manny. An' th' brave gin'rals—Von Molkey an' Bismarck an' U. S. Grant an' gallant Phil Shurdan an' Coxey. Think iv thim durin' me reign. An' th' invintions—th' steaminjine an' th' printin'-press an' th' cotton-gin an' th' gin sour an' th' bicycle an' th' flyin'-machine an' th' nickel-in-th'-slot machine an' th' Croker machine an' th' sody fountain an'—crownin' wur-ruk iv our civilization—th' cash raygisther. What gr-reat advances has science made in my time an' Victorya's! f'r, whin we entered public life, it took three men to watch th' bar-keep, while to-day ye can tell within eight dollars an hour what he's took in.

> "Glory be, whin I look back fr'm this day iv gin-ral rejoicin' in
> me rhinestone jubilee, an' see what changes has taken place an'
> how manny people have died an' how much betther off th' wurruld
> is, I'm proud iv mesilf. War an' pest'lence an' famine have occurred
> in me time, but I count thim light compared with th' binifits that
> have fallen to th' race since I come on th' earth."
>
> [*EP,* June 19, 1897]

Antidotes to optimism are also provided whenever Mr. Dooley discusses poverty, the work ethic, politics, or reform. As we have seen,
he comes closest to despair in describing the plight of the urban poor,
which he believes to be inevitable and irremediable, and in contem-
plating the political process, which he sees as a morass of interwoven
interest groups impossible to unravel without more people being hurt
than helped. At one point he sees poverty as an endless cycle because
"people that can't afford it always have marrid an' always will. . . . an'
they live unhappy iver after, bringin' up a large fam'ly to go an' do
likewise" (*EP,* July 31, 1897). And the classic statement on the tangle
of politics is Dooley's analogy of the crow who is "up in th' three, no
doubt, black an' ugly, stealin' me potatoes an' makin' me life miserable
with his noise, but whin I throw a club at him he's out iv th' way an' it
smashes into a nest full iv eggs that some frind iv mine has been
hatchin' out" (*EP,* April 3, 1897). Another common theme is the
refutation of American rhetorical reverence for work as "th' ambition
iv mankind." Mr. Dooley always argues that, to the contrary, "most iv
th' people I know'd be happiest layin' on a lounge with a can near by,
or stretchin' thimsilves f'r another nap at eight in th' mornin' " (*EP,*
Nov. 7, 1896). "I know th' wur-ruk iv relief is goin' on," he declares
during the poverty crisis of January 1897, "but what th' la-ads need is
th' relief iv wur-ruk" (*EP,* Jan. 30, 1897). Of course there is no
"relief" in sight for the problems of the human condition when they
are stated in such elemental terms. Very few people would choose to
work at the back-breaking jobs by which the majority of Bridgeporters
earned their living. Thus, the reformer's blithe prescription of full
employment as a social panacea never fails to anger Mr. Dooley.
Dunne was, in fact, always skeptical of reformers, and he took pleasure
in exposing their naiveté and their hypocrisy: the former in the cynical
Dooley report of the unequal aldermanic contest between "Onion
League" clubber "Willie Boye" and foxy William J. O'Brien; the latter

in his seeming preference for the straightforward corruption of known boodler Johnny Powers to the machinations of Civic Federation stalwarts who are on the take themselves (*EP*, April 10, 1897; Jan. 15, 1898). Still, Dunne's opposition to "th' wave iv rayform" runs deeper than contempt for its supporters. It is their basic premise that stops him cold: he simply doesn't believe that society can be improved.

Dunne's relativism expresses itself in his refusal to let Mr. Dooley take sides on most issues. Suspicious of the dogmatic statement that does violence to the complexity of experience, he prefers to suspend judgment. (In this respect, his jingoist stance just before the Spanish-American War seems particularly aberrant and wrong-headed.) So it is that Mr. Dooley refuses to place blame for the deaths at one another's hands of a policeman and a young criminal, both Bridgeport natives: " 'It served him right,' said Mr. McKenna. 'Who?' said Mr. Dooley. 'Carey or Clancy?' " (*EP*, Oct. 12, 1895). And in Petey Scanlan's case, he cannot generalize any further than to ask, "Who'll tell what makes wan man a thief an' another man a saint?" (*EP*, June 13, 1896). Moreover, Mr. Dooley seldom takes a stand on election day. Most of the time he is content to expose the venality, hypocrisy, and silliness of all concerned. Notable in this regard is his autumn of nonpartisan commentary during the Bryan-McKinley campaign of 1896.

Mr. Dooley also demonstrates the relativist's abhorrence of simplistic generalization. For example, he criticizes conventional notions of bravery in the piece about jingoist blusterer Fitzhugh Lee, the American consul at Havana:

> "They ain't such a lot iv diff'rence between th' bravest man in the wurruld an' th' cowardliest. Not such a lot. It ain't a question iv morality, Hinnissy. I've knowed men that wint to church ivry Sundah an' holyday reg'lar, an' give to th' poor an' loved their neighbors, an' they wudden't defind their wives against a murderer. An' I've knowed th' worst villyuns on earth that'd die in their thracks to save a stranger's child fr'm injury. 'Tis a question iv how th' blood is pumped." [*Journal*, April 9, 1898]

Similarly, many of the Bridgeport vignettes support Dooley's revisionist idea that "whin ye come to think iv it, th' heroes iv th' wurruld,—an' be thim I mean th' lads that've buckled on th' gloves, an' gone out to do th' best they cud,—they ain't in it with th' quite people nayether you nor me hears tell iv fr'm wan end iv th' year to another" (*EP*,

March 28, 1896). Old Shaughnessy and Mother Clancy (the "Galway woman"), Petey Scanlan's mother and little Tim Clancy the optimist: all are heroic in untraditional ways.

Dunne is most a relativist and skeptic, however, in his treatments of the theme of self-delusion, an important leitmotif in the later Dooley pieces. His own clear-eyed perspective makes him an expert at exposing the tricks we play on ourselves—never more so than in the May 1897 discussion of suicide that initiates the motif:

> "To me suicide is a kind iv play actin'. Th' man that kills himsilf always has th' thought sthrong in his mind that he will be prisint at the ceremonies, lookin' on like a man in th' gallery iv th' Lyceum Theater. It's a sort iv pride with him. He'll be standin' back somewhere an' hearin' th' remarks iv th' people as they come upon th' corpse. 'Poor man, why did he do it?' ' 'Twas a turrible thing, but I suppose he had nawthin' to live f'r.' 'Well, he was a brave man, so he was,' an' there he is lookin' on with a satisfied smile on his face while they carry himsilf tinderly to th' home where his wife is weepin' an' tarin' her hair because she put too much sugar in his coffee that mornin'. If he on'y knew that a man can't be in th' hearse an' march in th' pro-cession too, perhaps he'd think twict befure he jumped wanst." [28]

The theme gets a further turn here, as the illusion itself turns out to be illusory:

> "But mebbe 'tis as well he can't look on. Instead iv people weepin' over him, th' comment he'd hear would be: 'Another blame fool!' And his wife is sure to marry again. Women don't like suicides. If they did they'd be more iv thim. . . .
>
> "I know well a man ain't goin' to r-read his own death notice in bed th' nex' mornin'. They don't deliver the pa-aper in th' place where his ticket is bought f'r. Th' letter he writes will be misspelled annyhow, an' 'tis a thousand to wan th' pitcher th' ray-porter digs up to print'll be a tintype that he had took at th' circus whin he was more or less in th' way iv havin' too much pink lemonade aboord, an' that he thought he'd desthroyed. No, sir; I believe in r-runnin' as far as Halsted sthreet, but niver as far as th' lake." [*EP,* May 29, 1897]

On the following Fourth of July, Dooley undercuts the occasion by claiming that the workers of Bridgeport labor under another delusion: "To-day they're cillybratin' th' declaration iv indepindince that they never heerd tell iv. To-morrah they'll be shovellin' sand or tampin' a thrack with a boss standin' over thim that riprisints all they know iv th' power iv providince" (*EP,* July 3, 1897). And two weeks later he answers reports of a new Alaskan gold rush with a reminiscence about his own youthful view of America as the place "where all ye had to do was to hold ye'er hat an' th' goold guineas'd dhrop into it." "Me experyence with goold minin'," he concludes, "is it's always in th' nex' county. If I was to go to Alaska, they'd tell me iv th' finds in Seeberya."

Never does Dunne allow Mr. Dooley to articulate the hope that men can become less deluded. On the contrary, around this time he begins to accept self-delusion as a necessary condition of life. Consistently his message is that, given our fallen world, we have to get by any way we can. Father Kelly, the compassionate shepherd of the Bridgeport flock, puts it this way in a debate with Dooley on the value of literature:

> " 'Books is f'r thim that can't injye thimsilves in anny other way,' he says. 'If ye're in good health, an' ar-re atin' three squares a day, an' not ayether sad or very much in love with ye'er lot, but just lookin' on an' not carin' a'—he said rush—'not carin' a rush, ye don't need books,' he says. 'But if ye're a down-spirited thing an' want to get away an' can't, ye need books. 'Tis betther to be comfortable at home thin to go to th' circus, an' 'tis betther to go to th' circus thin to r-read anny book. But 'tis betther to r-read a book thin to want to go to th' circus an' not be able to,' he says."

As usual, Mr. Dooley has the last word here, but he is not particularly reassuring: " 'Well,' says I, 'whin I was growin' up, half th' congregation heard mass with their prayer books tur-rned upside down, an' they were as pious as anny. Th' Apostles' Creed niver was as convincin' to me afther I larned to r-read it as it was whin I cudden't read it, but believed it' " (*EP,* Dec. 4, 1897).

Mr. Dooley goes beyond Father Kelly, though, in explaining why he refused to attend the dedication of a new statue downtown. He argues here in favor of willful self-delusion—as preferable to the inevitable disillusionment that follows straight-seeing.

> "If there's annything goin' on I see it in th' pa-apers, an' it reads betther th'n it looks. To me th' Logan monymint is a hundred

miles high an' made iv goold. That's because I niver seed it. If I'd gone with you it'd be no higher than an Injun cigar sign an' built iv ol' melted-down dog tags an' other joolry. Th' crowd was magnificent to read about; if I'd seen it it wud've been just a million sweatin', badly dhressed people, squallin' babies, faintin' women an' a bad smell. Th' sojers were sojerly an' gr-rand, but if I'd seen thim close by I'd 've picked out more thin wan man that'd r-run away fr'm a cow. The bands played beautiful in th' papers, but if I'd been on th' curb with a man with a tall hat standin' in front iv me an' a woman behind me atin' rock candy in me ear all th' bands'd stop playin' befure they come by. So I set here in th' cool shade, playin' solitaire with mesilf an' cheatin' outhrageous, an' whin th' pa-apers come up I bought wan an' enjoyed th' gloryous scene f'r two hours. I heard th' oration; ye didn't. It was grand an' th' man that made it knew more about Shakespeare thin Logan did. But I'll bet ye a hat he was a fat man in a black coat an' swabbed his forehead with a wet towel between sintences.

"Glory be, I've often thought I was lucky not bein' prisint at some iv th' grand occasions I've r-read about. I knowed a man wanst that see th' pope iv Rome an' he become a ragin' pagan. 'Why,' he says, 'he was a little bit iv a thin man that didn't weigh more thin wan hundred pounds,' he says. 'He cudden't carry a bucket iv coal upstairs,' he says."

"He was a liar," said Mr. Hennessy.

"I believe he was," said Mr. Dooley. "But he wint to th' bad just th' same."   [*EP,* July 24, 1897]

The rejection of unembellished truth advocated here does not bode well for the career in realistic fiction that seemed possible to Dunne at this point. Still, in electing not to see as much or as clearly as he could, Mr. Dooley was in fact speaking for his creator. All of these pieces on self-delusion were written in 1897, a year marked by a significant deepening of Dunne's congenital gloom that helps to explain his role change to national humorist. His best pieces in the compassionate vein—such as the stories of Petey Scanlan and Shaughnessy—had been written in 1894 and 1895. In the hard winter of 1896–1897, Dunne began more and more frequently to choose the attitude of despair. Although the leaven of humor remains, there is observable in the Dooley pieces from this point on a definite downhill slide toward cynicism and pessimism.

The tone is set on December 5, 1896, with the story of the death of Mother Clancy, the Galway woman. Then come the powerful poverty

pieces of the January 1897 welfare crisis: the starving Sobieski shot
for stealing coal, Father Kelly's charity toward the parish infidel (with
its questioning of the work ethic), and the Galway tenant's murder
of his landlord, illustrating the imprudence of the Bradley-Martin
masked ball. In March and April, the slide continues with the cynical
four-part series on Mr. Dooley's run for mayor as the tool of "Sthreet
Car Magnum" Yerkes and the boodlers. During the summer, Dooley
discusses suicide, the dedication of the Logan statue, the illusion of
progress in the Victorian era, freedomless workers on the Fourth of
July, and marriage among the poor as a perpetuator of poverty. September brings the rhetorical fireworks of the piece on the Luetgert
trial, which seems, in this context, less a humorous than a shrilly
authentic statement of the world's absurdity. (The piece ends cyni-
cally, as the jury pitches testimony out the window and considers these
questions: "Did Lootgert look as though he'd kill his wife? Did his
wife look as though she ought to be kilt? Isn't it time we wint to
supper?" "An' howiver they answer," Dooley concludes, "they'll be
right, an' it'll make little diff'rence wan way or th' other. Th' German
vote is too large an' ignorant, annyhow.")

This piece is followed by the assessment in similar terms of a current scheme for municipal ownership of "th' sthreet railroads an' th'
gashouses an' th' illicthric lightin' plants an' all." Dooley's answer
here is that "it's on'y a question iv who does th' robbin'. Th' diff'rence
is between pickin' pockets an' usin' a lead pipe." In the new winter
Dooley gives us his last word on the breakdown of the Irish-American
family, the assimilation tragedy of miserly Ahearn and his shiftless son,
as well as Father Kelly's sanctioning of self-delusion through reading.
At last, during the Christmas holidays of 1897, Dunne wrote a bleak
and beautiful three-part meditation on the cycle of suffering in which
Bridgeport and the world seemed to him to be caught. These remarkable pieces, to which I shall return shortly, mark the virtual conclusion
of his five-year Chicago chronicle.

Some of Dunne's best writing is in these 1897 pieces, but the weight
of the pessimistic conclusions to which he was being led had taken
its toll, and he chose to stop mining this dark vein. Upon moving to the
Journal shortly after the turn of the year, Dunne officially ended the
Dooley series with his farewell piece in the *Post* of January 22, 1898.
Having listed some of the dishonest Chicagoans who flourish despite

his diatribes, Mr. Dooley closes up shop over the protests of the still-faithful Hennessy:

> "I've got a right to quit ye, Hinnisy, though ye'er a good man an' so'm I, be th' same token. F'r years an' years I've been standin' behind this counter tellin' ye thruths ye'd hear nowhere else—no not in th' good book or in th' Lives iv th' Saints. Why did I do it? Th' Lord on'y knows. But whin I get talkin' I can't stop anny more thin if I'd started to run down th' span iv th' r-red bridge."

But the piece turns serious and sour when Dooley searches for concrete, positive results attributable to his talking career in Chicago—and finds none.

> "Some iv th' things I've said was wrong an' some was right, an' most iv thim was foolish, but this much I know, I've thried to give it out sthraight. An' what's it come to? What's all th' histhry an' pothry an' philosophy I've give ye an' th' Archey road f'r all these years come to? Nawthin. Th' la-ads I abused ar-re makin' money so fast it threatens to smother thim. Th' wans I stud up f'r is some in jail an' some out iv wurruk."

This is no casual good-bye. Half-way through his thirtieth year, Dunne had despaired of changing the world for the better with his pen. The same date marks the end of his short career as spokesman for the Chicago Irish community.

To my mind, this decision to quit reflects Dunne's identification with the people of Bridgeport. All through 1897 the conviction must have been mounting that his parables of suffering and injustice were falling on deaf ears: in the end, it became too painful for him to write up such stories without real hope of helping the people who served as his models. So Dunne turned his back on the Chicago Irish. Or, to put it another way, Mr. Dooley left home rather than continue to live among neighbors whose troubles he could only observe with impotent anger.

One month later, in February 1898, the declaration of war against Spain provided a convenient vehicle for the return to conversation of the man who had confessed in his farewell piece that " 'tis har-rd f'r me to lave off talkin'." A safe general topic, the war lent itself to brisk, light handling, with little risk of emotional involvement for Dunne. Thus, with the sinking of the battleship *Maine* in Havana harbor, Mr. Dooley returned to the Chicago newspaper scene. Really, though, it was only his ghost—a rootless, disembodied voice, not very different, except for the brogue, from its predecessors in the familiar genre of crackerbarrel dialect humor. The rest of his story is well known. Not surprisingly, the American people outside Chicago soon loved Mr. Dooley—as they had loved Hosea Biglow, Artemus Ward, and the folksy platform image of Mark Twain. That lilting, skeptical voice remained clear and sane and sometimes eloquent, as, for example, in this soliloquy from the Dooley collection of 1910:

"How can I know annything, whin I haven't puzzled out what I am mesilf. I am Dooley, ye say, but ye're on'y a casual obsarver. Ye don't care annything about me details. Ye look at me with a gin'ral eye. Nawthin' that happens to me really hurts ye. Ye say, 'I'll go over to see Dooley,' sometimes, but more often ye say, 'I'll go over to Dooley's.' I'm a house to ye, wan iv a thousand that look like a row iv model wurrukin'men's cottages. I'm a post to hitch ye'er silences to. I'm always about th' same to ye. But to me I'm a millyon Dooleys an' all iv thim sthrangers to ME. I niver know which wan iv thim is comin' in. I'm like a hotel keeper with on'y wan bed an' a millyon guests, who come wan at a time an' tumble each other out. I set up late at night an' pass th' bottle with a gay an' careless Dooley that hasn't a sorrow in th' wurruld, an' suddenly I look up an' see settin' acrost fr'm me a gloomy wretch that fires th' dhrink out iv th' window an' chases me to bed. I'm just gettin' used to him whin another Dooley comes in, a cross, cantankerous, crazy fellow that insists on eatin' breakfast with me. An' so it goes. I know more about mesilf than annybody knows an' I know nawthin'. Though I'd make a map fr'm mem'ry an' gossip iv anny other man, f'r mesilf I'm still uncharted." [29]

In addition, after 1898 a number of things happened to Dunne himself to solidify the new Dooley role as a national spokesman: the move to New York that effectively cut him off from the genius loci of Chicago, embrace of syndication with its confining restrictions of topicality and tactfulness, and the decision to live a high life among men of wealth and ease at whom his satiric powers might well have been directed.

From 1900 until World War I, the syndicated Dooley pieces appeared in newspapers in every major American city, as well as in *Harper's Weekly* and, later on, in *Collier's* and *The American Magazine.* Enormously popular, the pieces were also collected intermittently into books, of which six were published between 1900 and 1919.[30] During these years Dunne was also involved in many other writing and editing projects. He wrote editorials for *Collier's Weekly* for six months in 1902. As a favor to his friend William C. Whitney, who had bought the *New York Morning Telegraph,* Dunne served in 1903 and 1904 as that paper's editor—his last connection with daily journalism. Joining Ida Tarbell, Lincoln Steffens, and Ray Stannard Baker in a take-over of *The American Magazine,* Dunne wrote a lucid, intelligent column of non-dialect commentary, "In the Interpreter's House," between 1906 and 1915. For a time he also wrote monthly essays "From the Bleachers" for his friend H. J. Whigham's *Metropolitan Magazine.* Finally, he returned to his friend Robert Collier and *Collier's Weekly,* where he produced essays and did editorial work from 1913 until late in 1919. Mr. Dooley reappeared twice for syndicated short runs in the early twenties, but World War I marked the virtual end of Dunne's productive writing life, although he lived until 1936.[31]

For most of this time, Dunne lived well in New York City. Many of his friends were businessmen and bankers. He golfed and summered at Southhampton and became a fixture as a dazzling, even legendary, conversationalist at exclusive social clubs. His later life style thus resembled that of Samuel Clemens, about whom Justin Kaplan has remarked that "the code he detested was also, in part, the one he lived by. He wanted to get rich, not just get along." When Clemens gave over his botched financial affairs to the care of Standard Oil corporate wizard H. H. Rogers in 1893, he began paying what Kaplan calls "the price of his becoming a provisional member of the plutocracy, . . . a certain blunting and demoralizing of purpose, a sense of powerlessness and drift. He began to see himself, and everyone else, as driven by self-interest and the compulsion to conform." [32] Dunne seems also to have been disarmed by his associations with plutocrats. At any rate, after he left Chicago he did not again criticize aspects of the American social, political, and economic system by means of powerful anecdotes from the lives of the urban poor. So it was that the early rift between Editor Dunne and Martin Dooley, his disreputable alter ego, was finally resolved to the editor's advantage. All of this is not to deny the value of Mr. Dooley's national commentary. Certainly, America was a better place for the twenty years of laughter and perspective that he provided in the second phase of his career. We ought also to regret and appreciate what was lost, however.

Only one reviewer in Dunne's time understood the extent of this loss. He was Francis Hackett, himself an Irish immigrant to Chicago and a veteran journalist and novelist there and in New York. In a *New Republic* review of *Mr. Dooley on Making a Will* (1919), Hackett regrets that Dunne's considerable gifts have been used "to bring laughs to hold down his job as court jester to the American people— or, more properly, the American bourgeoisie. For it is the bourgeoisie whose limitations this American Juvenal has accepted. . . . Possessing real insight, suggesting real omniscience, he lavishes himself on the patent trivialities and jocularities of the paper-made American world." In declaring that Dunne "spends himself on the facetiae of summer resorts, cards, golf, newspaper fame, newspaper doctors, newspaper Darwinism, newspaper Rockefellers and Carnegies," Hackett complains specifically about the book he is reviewing—the last and thinnest Dooley collection. But even so, his central criticism has wider validity, especially in the context of the Chicago Dooley pieces:

> [Dunne] scores hard and often—on a newspaper target. Only occasionally does he disregard that target and pierce the heart of life.
> Yet it is the heart of life which really invites the genius that Peter Dunne has squandered. Had he given his comic perception free rein, what might he not have done for America? Imagine the release of his real comment on this nation of villagers, in an easier and less arbitrary form than his present form of unconditional humor.

Such, in Hackett's view, were "the penalties of respectability. Mr. Dunne is a true humorist but not sufficiently disreputable." [33]

To measure our loss one more time, let us return now to December 1897 and the three holiday pieces that constitute Dunne's last extended effort as Dooley of Bridgeport. Through the group his mind moves in a steadily widening arc from particular to universal, until, with the ending piece, we have his definitive philosophical statement. "The approach of Christmas," the first piece begins, "is heralded in Archey Road by many of the signs that are known to the less civilized and more prosperous parts of the city. The people look poorer, colder, and more hopeful than at other times." Enter Mr. Dooley—to complain that exchanging gifts in Bridgeport is more painful than pleasant:

> "Ye can't give what ye want. Ivry little boy ixpects a pony at Chris'mas, an' ivry little girl a chain an' locket; an' ivry man thinks he's sure goin' to get th' goold-headed cane he's longed f'r since he come over. But they all fin'lly land on rockin'-horses an' dolls, an' suspindhers that r-run pink flowers into their shirts an' tattoo thim in summer. An' they conceal their grief Chris'mas mornin' an' thry to look pleasant with murdher in their hearts."
>
> [*EP,* Dec. 18, 1897]

So frustrated is Mr. Dooley by this perennial problem, that he goes out of his way to hurt poor Hennessy with an uncharacteristically cutting rejoinder. Having just come back from a successful evening's shopping, Hennessy offers to get his friend whatever he wants for Christmas, "if 'tis within me means." Dooley strings him along for a while, then asks for the Auditorium Building, and Hennessy goes away "with the rocking chair under his arm, the doll in his pocket, and dumb anger in his heart."

A week later, on Christmas Eve, Hennessy has regained his spirits and enters the bar with a cheery "Merry Chris'mas." Once again, Mr. Dooley is uncooperative:

> "But is it a merry Chris'mas all round? I see in th' pa-aper where some wan says Chris'mas dinners has been pro-vided f'r twinty thousan' poor people, but thirty thousan' more is needed. It isn't a merry Chris'mas f'r thim. Nor is it f'r poor Flannigan. 'Tis betther f'r his wife. She died to-day; Father Kelly dhropped in on his way home afther givin' extremunction. His hear-rt was sore with sorrow. Half th' people iv Flannigan's neighborhood has been out iv wurruk f'r a year an' th' sight iv th' sivin fatherless little Doyle childher almost made him cry with pain.
>
> "Do? What can he do? He's spint all th' stole money that he ought to be usin' to buy a warm coat f'r his back, spint it on th' poor, an' he dipt into th' Easther colliction that ought to 've gone to pay inthrest on th' church morgedge. It'll be a smooth talk he'll have to give his grace th' archbishop this year. He was goin' to buy himsilf a Chris'mas prisint iv an altar cloth an' he had to spind th' money buyin' shoes f'r th' little Polackies down be Main sthreet. What can he do?"

From here, Dooley generalizes to the constancy of poverty along the road:

> "What can annywan do, I'd have ye tell me. If ye'd cut up all th' money in th' sixth war-rd in akel parts ye cudden't buy a toy dhrum apiece f'r th' fam'lies iv Bridgeport. It isn't this year or last. 'Tisn't wan day or another. 'Tis th' same ivry year an' ivry day. It's been so iver since I come here an' 'twill be so afther I'm put away an' me frinds have stopped at th' r-road house on th' way back to count up what I owed thim."   [*EP*, Dec. 24, 1897]

Finally, on the following Saturday, Finley Peter Dunne and Mr. Dooley ring in the New Year, 1898, with a meditation on the human condition in the form of a parable of accepted suffering and necessary self-delusion: its central metaphor is fittingly grounded in the common experience of the Irish-American laborer, for whom, in the end, all the Chicago Dooley pieces speak.

> "'Tis a sthrange thing this here New Year's business," said Mr. Dooley. "Here I am to-day, an' 'tis ninety-sivin. I clane up th' glasses, count th' cash an' get ready to close up th' shop f'r th' night. Suddenly I hear a whistle blow on a tug, a bell r-rings an' somewan comes out iv Schwartzmeister's an' fires a revolver. An' I've passed without knowin' it fr'm wan year to another. Gorry, but I feel a lone place in me stomach ivry time I pick up a paper an' see th' number iv th' year changed—an' I ought to be used to it, f'r I've done it manny a time—more thin I want to say. Whin nineteen hundherd comes in I'm goin' to be scared to death, till it turns out like other years, th' same ol' r-run iv good an' bad luck, no money, ol' frinds dyin', new inimies comin' up an' th' rig'lar daily procission walkin' out to Calv'ry an' racin' back. Glory be, I'm afraid fr'm an unknown terror to look into ninety-eight, but if I knew th' things that are sure to happen, no betther an' no worse thin ninety-sivin, barrin' me religion, I'd go down to th' bridge an' fall into th' r-river and break me neck. I wud so."
>
> "All th' years is akel an' th' same," said Mr. Hennessy sententiously. "All th' years an' th' days."
>
> "Thrue f'r ye," said Mr. Dooley, "yet 'tis sthrange how we saw our throubles into reg'lar lenths. We're all like me frind O'Brien that had a conthract on th' dhrainage canal. He thought he was biddin' on soft mud, but he sthruck nawthin' but th' dhrift. But he kept pluggin' away. ''Twill soften later,' he says. Th' ingineers tol' him he was a fool. 'Twas dhrift all th' way through. He rayfused to

listen. He knew he'd come to th' mud th' nex' day or th' nex' an' so he wint on an' on, an' fin'lly he got through an' made a good, clane job iv it. He looked back on his wurruk an' says he: 'I knowed it was dhrift all th' time, but if I'd let mesilf think that what was ahead was as har-rd as what was behind I'd thrun up th' job an' broke me conthract,' he says. 'I niver borry throuble,' he says, 'but I've had to borry money to pay me men.' So it is with us. We've all taken a conthract to dig through th' glacial dhrift. We know it's glacial dhrift to th' ind, but we make oursilves think 'twill come aisy wan iv these days. So we go on, with pick an' shovel, till th' wurruk is done an' we lay it down gladly."

APPENDIX

An Annotated Chronology of Dunne's Dialect Pieces in the *Chicago Evening Post*

1892

December	4	Chicago politician Frank Lawlor visits President Cleveland in Washington.
	11	The first Colonel McNeery piece: the death of Jay Gould.
	18	Comparison: American and British actors.
	25	An old man looks at Christmas.

1893

January	1	New Year's visiting in Bridgeport.
	15	McNeery scorns a charity ball.
	22	On faddism, especially in public school teaching.
February	5	McNeery's natural history. O'Connell and Disraeli.
March	19	Officer Steve Rowan discusses local politics with the statue of Columbus.
May	21	Colonel McNeery at the World's Fair: dazed by the Midway.
June	4	French paintings and the Irish Village at the Fair.
	11	Infanta Eulalia visits the Fair: on democracy.
	18	German Day at the Fair: on Chicago's Germans.
	25	Derby Day: memories of Irish races in the past.
July	2	McNeery and O'Connor on the Ferris wheel.
	9	The wedding of the Duke of York and Princess Mary.
	16	The Fair's Literary Congress.
	23	Poetry and war. The European situation.
	30	A fight at the Fair. A fight in the British Parliament.
August	6	Panic in Chicago: failure of Cudahy packing business.
	13	A meeting of the Fair's Board of Lady Managers.

	10	A new verdict in the Cronin murder case.
	17	St. Patrick's Day in old times.
	24	Not keeping Lent.
April	7	An old style election day in the ward.
	14	The stealing of Hogan's goat.
	21	Coxey's Army and the little priest.
	28	Coxey and spring fever.
May	5	Love affairs in Ireland and Bridgeport.
	12	A brand from the burning: a political biography.
	19	The Dennehy boy back from Notre Dame.
	26	The "Chicago" dinner and Anglo-Saxon supremacy.
June	2	Bridgeport in the Civil War.
	9	The ruling class: marriage cures an anarchist.
	16	The Democratic county convention.
	23	Controlling and inciting riots: mine strikes in Illinois.
	30	Memories of a strike on the Illinois and Michigan Canal.
July	7	The Pullman Strike: lemons and liberty.
	14	The Pullman Strike: the tragedy of the agitator.
	21	An economical romance: two Bridgeport misers marry.
	28	War between Japan and China.
August	4	Japan fires on the British flag: Irish-American support for Japan follows.
	11	Fire Chief Swenie in Bridgeport.
	18	The annual Irish-freedom picnic.
	25	The Pullman Strike: "What does he care?"
September	1	A scandal in the Vanderbilt family.
	8	A scandal in the Astor family.
	15	A political meeting at Finucane's Hall for Billy O'Brien.
	22	The Divided Skirt: Molly Donahue on a bicycle.
October	13	The Russian czar's unenviable job.
	20	Molly Donahue tries to vote.
	27	A victim of the game of politics: a decent man ruined.
November	3	The Cleveland-Hill political dispute.
	10	The Republican election sweep: Cleveland's double-cross of the Irish.
	17	The naming of the Hogan baby.
	24	Poverty and pride in the Callaghan family.

December	1	College football and dissension in Bridgeport.
	8	The courtship of Danny Duggan.
	15	Christmas charity on the road.
	22	Irish county rivalries and employment in Chicago.
	29	A parish fair at St. Honoria's.

1895

January	5	The wave of political reform hits Bridgeport.
	12	A benefit raffle for an ailing bartender.
	19	The French character. Political crisis in France.
	26	Felix's lost chord: courtship in Bridgeport.
February	2	Dooley reviews *Trilby*.
	9	The grip and Irish factionalism.
	16	The wanderers: death on an immigrant ship.
	23	The temperance saloon: a failed enterprise.
March	2	A genealogy lecture in the school hall.
	9	The Gould-Castleanne wedding: American heiresses and European nobility.
	16	Irishmen at the opera: political gossip.
	23	The threat of war against Spain: a Bridgeport parable.
	30	Memories of the O'Reilly-Schultze election.
April	6	Postelection analysis.
	13	The beef trust and the Connock man's children.
	20	The piano in the parlor. Molly Donahue and assimilation.
	27	A gold-silver coinage dispute in the saloon.
May	4	Molly Donahue as the "new woman."
	11	The Nicaragua boundary dispute and the Monroe Doctrine.
	18	The Woman's Bible.
	25	Old age and bicycling.
June	1	The blue and the gray: heroism in Bridgeport.
	8	The optimist: little Tim Clancy the millworker.
	15	The Fenian invasion of Canada recalled.
	22	Hennessy umpires a baseball game.
	29	The British cabinet crisis of 1895.
July	6	A parochial school graduation.
	13	Boyne water and bad blood: the Orange parade.
	20	The Harvey-Horr silver debates in Chicago.
	27	The naming of schools. The assassination of Stambuloff.

August	3	A fishing trip.
	10	Mrs. Mulligan and the Illinois Central Railroad.
	17	The Lutheran flag dispute in Chicago.
	24	The Dooley family reunion.
	31	Heresy at a church fair.
September	7	An immigrant millionaire denies his brother.
	14	The America's Cup and a race in the old canal.
	21	The great hot spell: a tall tale.
	28	The stock-plunge suicide of a Chicago German.
October	5	A Republican primary at Finucane's Hall.
	12	The Idle Apprentice: crime in Bridgeport.
	19	The Venezuela boundary dispute: Monroe vs. Hoolihan doctrine.
	26	Football on the road.
November	2	A canal-side championship fight.
	9	The Duke of Marlborough marries a Vanderbilt.
	16	A school play at St. Patrick's: "The Doomed Markey."
	23	The popularity of firemen.
	30	A blacklisted worker refuses relief.
December	7	The president's message.
	14	Dooley on a jury: contempt for the law.
	21	The Venezuela boundary and the Irish Republic.
	28	The Dynamite Campaign in the Clan na Gael.

1896

January	4	On charity: a lost child.
	11	An Irish-German alliance in Bridgeport.
	18	Ice skating and old age.
	25	European politics: the possibilities of war.
February	1	Rhetoric in Washington: Sen. Tillman attacks President Cleveland.
	8	Hennessy calls a reform meeting on Archer Avenue.
	15	Mr. Dooley attends a city council meeting.
	22	Molly Donahue's home vaudeville show.
	29	Debates in Congress about war against Spain: "the year of the big wind."
March	7	Keeping Lent in Ireland and Chicago.
	14	Henry Irving in *The Merchant of Venice*.
	21	St. Patrick's Day on the old West Side.
	28	Shaughnessy: the quiet man as hero.

April	4	The city council corrupts a decent man.
	11	A barroom analogy for the U.S.-Cuba problems.
May	2	The state Republican convention: city vs. country politics.
	9	The quick and the dead: a ghost story.
	16	A candidate's pillory: McKinley and Billy O'Brien answer questions.
	23	The czar's coronation compared to postelection visiting by aldermen.
	30	The soft spot in a landlord's hard heart.
June	6	Hennessy meets McKenna: a debate about coinage.
	13	On criminals: the story of Petey Scanlan.
	27	The national conventions.
July	3	American apathy: gold vs. silver.
	11	The O'Briens forever: Willum J. and William Jennings.
	18	Oratory in politics: a model campaign for alderman.
	25	The Populist convention in St. Louis.
August	1	Another debate about currency.
	8	A great heat wave: Bryan burning up the country.
	15	Coinage and the forgotten middle class.
	22	Nansen's polar expedition.
	29	The Vanderbilt-Whitney marriage.
September	5	A diplomatic exchange between America and China.
	12	Dooley on the game of golf.
	19	The Tynan plot to blow up Buckingham Palace.
	26	The campaign promises of Bryan and McKinley.
October	3	Election statistics and predictions.
	10	Political parades for gold and silver.
	17	Bryan to Chicago: on exposure to the masses.
	24	Polarizing rhetoric in the presidential campaign.
	31	The campaign: war rhetoric, but change is unlikely.
November	7	Postelection analysis: prosperity defeats humanity.
	14	President McKinley chooses a cabinet.
	21	Complexities of the war in Cuba.
	28	Pilgrims play the first football game.
December	5	Organized charity and the Galway woman.
	12	A church play and the supposed death of Cuban rebel leader Maceo.
	19	The debate about intervention in Cuba.
	26	Bank failures at Christmas time.

1897

January	2	New Year's resolutions: keeping a strong enemy.
	9	Corruption in the city council. Memories of Stephen A. Douglas.
	16	City politics: the career of Billy Lorimer.
	23	Charity and education: an immigrant shot for stealing coal.
	30	Clancy the infidel saved by Father Kelly (from starvation).
February	6	The necessity of modesty among the rich: a tale of the Famine and the Bradley-Martin ball.
	13	After the ball.
	20	Scenes from the Greek-Turkish war.
	27	A Cuban sympathy meeting in Archey Road.
March	6	The presidential inaugural and the race for mayor of Chicago.
	13	The opera *Lohengrin* and the Fitzsimmons-Corbett fight.
	20	The Fitzsimmons-Corbett fight: the power of love.
	27	The campaign of 1897: Dooley for mayor.
April	3	The campaign of 1897: the crow in the tree.
	10	The campaign of 1897: postelection analysis.
	17	The campaign of 1897: an alderman's life.
	24	Complexities of the Greek-Turkish war.
May	1	In the spring a young man's fancy. . . .
	8	The decadence of Greece and the tenth precinct.
	15	A Polacker on the red bridge.
	22	The flight of the wild geese recalled.
	29	Suicide as self-delusion.
June	5	Street-car boodle bills in Springfield.
	12	Popular government and the state legislature.
	19	Progress in the Victorian Era.
	26	Changing attitudes toward the press. Remembering Storey's *Times*.
July	3	Freedom and the Fourth of July.
	10	Education in Ireland and Chicago: on corporal punishment.
	17	Gold-seeking: illusions about America.
	24	The dedication of the Logan statue.
	31	Only the poor marry.
August	7	Images of policemen vs. firemen: Pipeman Shay.

NOTES

Preface

1. These books are Charles Fanning, *Mr. Dooley and the Chicago Irish* (New York: Arno Press, 1976); and Barbara C. Schaaf, *Mr. Dooley's Chicago* (Garden City, N.Y.: Doubleday, 1977). In line with the concerns of the present study, my anthology collects the pieces that illustrate Dunne's delineation of Chicago Irish community life. The Schaaf book accentuates Dunne's political commentary, both local and national.

Chapter 1

1. *Our American Humorists* (New York: Dodd, Mead and Co., 1931), p. 110.
2. My information about Dunne's early life comes from the fine biography by Elmer Ellis, *Mr. Dooley's America: A Life of Finley Peter Dunne* (New York: Alfred A. Knopf, 1941), pp. 3–16. Hereafter cited as Ellis, *Life of Dunne*.
3. For a brilliant treatment of the importance of urban journalism for the writers of the 1890s, see Larzer Ziff, *The American 1890s: Life and Times of a Lost Generation* (New York: Viking Press, 1966), especially pp. 149–53, 161.
4. Robert H. Elias, *Theodore Dreiser: Apostle of Nature* (New York: Alfred A. Knopf, 1949), pp. 26–43.
5. Ziff, *American 1890s*, pp. 185–93, 250–74; Warner Berthoff, *The Ferment of Realism: American Literature, 1884–1919* (New York: Free Press, 1965), pp. 223–35.
6. Lincoln Steffens, *The Shame of the Cities* (1904; reprint ed., New York: Hill and Wang, 1957), p. 192 (the quote is from a reprint of the article on Chicago that first appeared in *McClure's Magazine* for October 1903); Willis J. Abbot, "Chicago Newspapers and Their Makers," *The Review of Reviews* 11 (June 1895): 647; Bessie L. Pierce, *A History of Chicago*, 3 (New York: Alfred A. Knopf, 1957): 409.
7. Pierce, *History of Chicago*, 3: 417; Charles H. Dennis, *Victor Lawson: His Time and His Work* (Chicago: University of Chicago Press, 1935), passim.
8. Ellis (*Life of Dunne*, pp. 20–21) cites as typical these editorials from the *News*:

> The Payne investigation committee of the Ohio legislature was discharged yesterday. That stupendous effort resulted in accomplishing one great good—it furnished work for the printers. The evidence was ordered printed. Within a few months those ponderous volumes will find their way to the papermills and the current of Ohio politics will resume its placid course. [April 23, 1886]
>
> Michael Davitt declined to attend a school opening the other day because the queen was to be toasted. Mr. Davitt would not object, however, to toasting Victoria over a warm hard-coal fire. [Aug. 19, 1887]

9. To a girl who brings him a poem that begins, "And this is the end of all, Ernest; the end of our happy dreams;/A walk to the quiet graveyard where the snowy marble gleams," the horse reporter advises as follows: "You take this poem, . . . and send it to him. Then drop him a line saying the papers have agreed to print it for you. If he doesn't weaken when it comes to having his name mixed up with a lot of graveyards, blighted hopes, broken hearts and a desolate life, I shall miss my guess." *The Lakeside Musings* (Chicago: Rand McNally, 1884), pp. 198–99.

10. Ellis, *Life of Dunne*, pp. 18–21; Dennis, *Victor Lawson*, p. 83; idem, *Eugene Field's Creative Years* (Garden City, N.Y.: Doubleday, Page, 1924), p. 151; Charles D. Mosher, "Mosher's Centennial Historical Album, 1876," manuscript, Chicago Historical Society, vol. 7, "Journalists," p. 33.

11. Bernard Duffey positions Field as a "licensed fun-maker whose liberty went unchecked only so long as it never really threatened the establishment which he amused. And, one might guess, much of his unusual popularity sprang from the ample testimony he provided of his strong basic loyalty. There was the reassuring sentimentality of much of his verse, the dislike of Europe reflected in his communications from London, a concentration of criticism on those who aped Eastern tastes, and a reliance on home bred sense and common prejudice as the source of his satire." *The Chicago Renaissance in American Letters: A Critical History* (Lansing: Michigan State University Press, 1954), pp. 13–14. See also Pierce, *History of Chicago*, 3: 416; Ellis, *Life of Dunne*, pp. 22–24; Eugene Field, *Culture's Garland* (Boston: Ticknor, 1887).

12. Ellis, *Life of Dunne*, p. 28.

13. Ibid., pp. 30–31; Pierce, *History of Chicago*, 3: 413; Abbot, "Chicago Newspapers," pp. 50–52; Henry Justin Smith, *A Gallery of Chicago Editors* (Chicago: *Chicago Daily News*, 1930), pp. 11–13.

14. Undated newspaper clipping, Wallace Rice Scrapbooks, Chicago Historical Society; *Herald*, July 17, 1892; Charles H. Dennis, "Whitechapel Nights," *News*, Aug. 28, 29, 31, 1936; Ellis, *Life of Dunne*, pp. 49–50.

15. Ellis, *Life of Dunne*, p. 50.

16. Ibid., p. 50; Dennis, "Whitechapel Nights," *News*, Aug. 13, 1936; Wallace Rice, "Whitechapel Club Dedicates Its New Clubhouse," *Chicago Inter-Ocean*, March 6, 1892; *EP*, March 13, 1893.

17. Ellis, *Life of Dunne*, pp. 51–52.

18. Ibid., p. 51.

19. Dennis, "Whitechapel Nights," *News*, Aug. 8, 1936.

20. Ellis, *Life of Dunne*, pp. 48–54; Rice, *Chicago Inter-Ocean*, March 5, 1892; Bill Nye, *Herald*, April 5, 1891.

21. Ellis, *Life of Dunne*, pp. 38–40; Abbot, "Chicago Newspapers," pp. 648–50. Founded in 1847, the *Tribune* is today the oldest functioning newspaper in Chicago.

22. *Tribune*, March 23, May 4, March 30, Feb. 23, April 27, 1890; Ellis, *Life of Dunne*, p. 40.

23. *Tribune*, Jan. 5, March 2, April 13, Feb. 4, 1890.

24. Quoted in Bessie L. Pierce, *As Others See Chicago: Impressions of Visitors, 1673–1933* (Chicago: University of Chicago Press, 1933), p. 255.

25. Chicago: R. J. Kittredge Co., 1891.

26. Ellis, *Life of Dunne*, pp. 48–52; John Moses and Joseph Kirkland, *The*

History of Chicago (Chicago and New York: Munsell and Co., 1895), 2: 148; *EP,* April 7, 1894 (obituary for Ben King, who died suddenly at age thirty-four); H. E. Fleming, "Literary Interests of Chicago," *American Journal of Sociology* 11 (Jan. 1906): 517–19.

27. Arthur R. Williams, "The Irishman in American Humor: From 1647 to the Present" (Ph.D. dissertation, Cornell University, 1949), p. 71. See also Walter Blair, *Native American Humor* (San Francisco: Chandler, 1960); and Constance Rourke, *American Humor; A Study of the National Character* (Garden City, N.Y.: Doubleday, 1953).

28. Williams, "The Irishman," pp. 175–81; William Hanchett, *Irish: Charles G. Halpine in Civil War America* (Syracuse: Syracuse University Press, 1970).

29. Williams, "The Irishman," pp. 96–127; E. J. Kahn, Jr., *The Merry Partners: The Age and Stage of Harrigan and Hart* (New York: Random House, 1955); Richard M. Dorson, "Mose, the Far-Famed and World-Renowned," *American Literature* 15 (Nov. 1943): 300.

30. *Native American Humor,* pp. 120–24.

31. Brand Whitlock, *Forty Years of It* (New York and London: Appleton, 1914), p. 46; *EP,* Sept. 10, 1894. At the age of forty-two, Dolan was found wandering the streets of Chicago suffering from acute alcoholism and was committed to a state hospital. Hence this *Post* article.

32. *Chicago Daily Journal,* April 22, 1924; Ellis, *Life of Dunne,* pp. 40–41; Pierce, *History of Chicago,* 3: 408.

33. Clipping from *Trib* magazine for February 1926, in Wallace Rice Scrapbooks, Chicago Historical Society.

34. Ellis, *Life of Dunne,* pp. 43–44; *Herald,* Sept. 7, 1892.

35. Ellis, *Life of Dunne,* pp. 45–46; *Herald,* Oct. 27, 1892.

36. Abbot, "Chicago Newspapers," p. 654; William T. Stead, *If Christ Came to Chicago! A Plea for the Union of All Who Love in the Service of All Who Suffer* (Chicago: Laird and Lee, 1894), p. 318.

37. Abbot, "Chicago Newspapers," p. 654; Pierce, *History of Chicago,* 3: 418; Ellis, *Life of Dunne,* pp. 46, 54–61.

38. In the *Sunday Post*'s inaugural issue there appeared a dialect piece about Chicago politician Frank Lawler's job-hunting visit to newly elected President Grover Cleveland. Ellis attributes it to Dunne and dates the Dooley series from it, but there is evidence against that attribution. The narrator is a nameless patron of Alderman Johnny Powers's saloon, whose speech in describing "Frank's Visit to Grover" is so heavily, clumsily dialect-laden as to appear retrogressive in comparison to the Dolan pieces. The beginning of the piece will illustrate:

> "Gimme a loight, Jawnny," said the little man. "Hov ye hur-rd about Lawluhr? Na-aw! He's been down to see Grover. What th' 'ill! He's as good as Grover anny day. He wint there loike a mon an' knockit at th' dure. Whin th' hoired gurl come he sez: 'Miss, me complimints, Mr. Lawluhr wants to see th' Prisidunt.'"

Ellis was unable to find the Dolan pieces, which may explain his unquestioning assignment of this piece to Dunne, who himself remembered the Jay Gould piece as his first for the *Post.* See Ellis, *Life of Dunne,* p. 65; and Finley Peter Dunne, *Mr. Dooley at His Best* (New York: Scribners, 1938), p. xxiii.

39. Ellis, *Life of Dunne,* pp. 68–71.

40. Ellis, *Life of Dunne,* pp. 65–67; John J. McKenna, "Fond Memories of McGarry's Place," in *Reminiscences of the Chicago Fire on Sunday Evening, October 9, 1871* (Chicago: Clohesey, 1933), pp. 26–32.

41. Hamlin Garland recalls the reaction of his parents and their generation of prairie farmers:

> The wonder and the beauty of it all moved these dwellers of the level lands to tears of joy which was almost as poignant as pain. In addition to its grandeur the scene had for them the transitory quality of an autumn sunset, a splendor which they would never see again.
> Stunned by the majesty of the vision, my mother sat in her chair, visioning it all yet comprehending little of its meaning. . . .
> At last utterly overcome she leaned her head against my arm, closed her eyes and said, "Take me home. I can't stand any more of it."

A Son of the Middle Border (1917; reprint ed., New York: Macmillan, 1941), p. 460.

42. Moses and Kirkland, *History of Chicago,* 2: 489–90.

43. My sources of information about the Fair include the following: William A. Coles and H. H. Reed, eds., *Architecture in America: A Battle of Styles* (New York: Appleton, 1961); Hubert H. Bancroft, *The Book of the Fair* (Chicago and San Francisco: Bancroft, 1893); Ray Ginger, *Altgeld's America, 1890–1905* (Chicago: Quadrangle Books, 1965), pp. 22–25; Pierce, *History of Chicago,* 3: 501–12; Moses and Kirkland, *History of Chicago,* 2: 488–94; *Chicago Tribune, Evening Post, Sunday Post,* May-October 1893. A recent, and definitive, study of the Fair as a watershed cultural event is David F. Burg, *Chicago's White City of 1893* (Lexington: University Press of Kentucky, 1976).

44. *Chicago Journal,* April 22, 1924; H. E. Fleming, "Literary Interests of Chicago," *American Journal of Sociology* 11 (May 1906): 792–93; Dennis, *Victor Lawson,* pp. 164–65; Sidney Kramer, *A History of Stone and Kimball and Herbert S. Stone and Company* (Chicago: N. W. Forgue, 1940), pp. 96–123, 327.

45. One of Dunne's best friends at the station house was Inspector John Shea, with whom he recalled walking "the night streets of Chicago, talking ancient Irish poetry" (Ellis, *Life of Dunne,* p. 17).

46. On the castle issue, Joseph Kirkland remarked that "one can only smile, shake the head, and fall back on the general belief that no one party of that truculent, masterful race is ever too small for it to be divided against itself." The more official of the two exhibits was a replica of Blarney Castle engineered by the Count of Aberdeen, who had served as president of the British-sponsored Irish Industries Association, and his countess. Its rival, a replica of Donegal Castle and environs, was the work of the nationalistic Donegal Industrial Fund, which had been fostering such Irish-oriented activities as the translation of spinning and weaving handbooks into Gaelic. See Joseph Kirkland, *The Story of Chicago,* 2 (Chicago: Dibble, 1894): 209–10; Bancroft, *Book of the Fair,* pp. 144–47, 836–38.

47. *EP,* Oct. 7, 1893. The voice is Mr. Dooley's in this, his first appearance. On Irish Day, see Bancroft, *Book of the Fair,* pp. 895–96. Dunne's dialect pieces had moved to the Saturday *Post* when the Sunday edition folded in late August.

48. Ellis, *Life of Dunne,* pp. 56–57.

49. Dennis, *Eugene Field's Creative Years,* pp. 130–36.

50. The colonel's knowledgeable explanation may reflect Dunne's acquaintance with the new interest in folklore that was important in the Irish Literary Renaissance of the nineties, when Douglas Hyde, Lady Augusta Gregory, Yeats, and John Synge were rediscovering the Gaelic folk tradition and transmuting its materials into fresh artistic forms. Hyde's collection of Irish tales, *Beside the Fire,* appeared in 1890 and was followed by Yeats's *The Celtic Twilight* in 1893. Between 1889 and 1892, Yeats was publicizing Irish myths and folklore in a series of articles for the *Boston Pilot* and the *Providence* (Rhode Island) *Journal;* these have been collected by Horace Reynolds as *Letters to the New Island* (1934; reprint ed., Cambridge, Mass.: Harvard University Press, 1970).

51. Dunne, *Mr. Dooley at His Best,* p. xxiv.

52. *News,* June 8, 1927; Ellis, *Life of Dunne,* pp. 77–80.

53. Ellis, *Life of Dunne,* pp. 53–56; *EP,* April 25, 1915 (Twenty-fifth Anniversary Issue).

54. *Mr. Clemens and Mark Twain* (New York: Simon and Schuster Pocket Books, 1968), p. 7.

55. *American Journal of Sociology* (July 1897), reprinted in Allen F. Davis and Mary Lynn McCree, eds., *Eighty Years at Hull-House* (Chicago: Quadrangle Books, 1969), p. 59. Britisher William T. Stead also praised the saloons for performing social services that the churches and the municipal government were ignoring. Singling out the saloon free-lunch program during the Black Winter of 1893–1894, he declared that "it is one of the gravest questions which confront Chicago how long the saloonkeeper is to be allowed a practical monopoly of ministering to the wants of mankind." *If Christ Came to Chicago,* p. 165. A corroborating recent study is Jon M. Kingsdale, "The 'Poor Man's Club': Social Functions of the Urban Working-Class Saloon," *American Quarterly* 25, no. 4. (Oct. 1973): 472–89.

56. Lord Frederick Cavendish, chief secretary for Ireland, and his undersecretary, T. H. Burke, were knifed to death while walking in Dublin's Phoenix Park in May 1882, by a band of fanatic Irish nationalists. One of these "Invincibles," James Carey, turned state's evidence at their trial in January 1883. In July, Carey was murdered by an avenging nationalist. See P. J. P. Tynan, *The Irish National Invincibles* (New York: Irish National Invincible Publishing Co., 1894), pp. 402–10, 446–64, 487–500.

Chapter 2

1. Finley Peter Dunne, *Observations by Mr. Dooley* (New York: R. H. Russell, 1902), p. 271.

2. For an excellent firsthand account of the suffering and deprivation of Irishmen bound for America see the late chapters of Herman Melville's *Redburn: His First Voyage,* published in 1849 at the height of the Famine emigration. A recent powerful reimagining of the experience appears in Matthew Stanton's self-justifying speech to his wife in Act One of *Hogan's Goat* by William Alfred (New York: Noonday Press, 1966), pp. 13–14.

3. My information on the early years of the Irish in Chicago comes from the following sources: The records and manuscripts of the W. P. A. Federal

Writers' Project for Illinois, stored at the Illinois State Historical Library at Springfield (hereafter cited as FWP), Boxes 68, 87 ("Bridgeport"), and 196 ("The Irish in Chicago"). Also, these special Irish issues and features in the newspapers of Chicago: "The Irish in Illinois," by John T. McEnnis, *News,* May 30–July 2, 1889; "Ancestral Homes of the Chicago Irish," by Edward M. Lahiff, *Tribune,* May 23–June 14, 1909; *Tribune,* March 17, 1907, and March 11, 1962; *Chicago Herald-Examiner,* Nov. 7–9, 1927; *McKinley Park Life,* Jan. 20, 1959. Also, these works: Joseph Hamzik, "Gleanings of Archer Road" (typescript, Chicago Historical Society, 1961); John J. McKenna, *Reminiscences of the Chicago Fire on Sunday Evening, October 9, 1871* (Chicago, Clohesey, 1933); Ruth Piper, "The Irish in Chicago, 1848–71" (M.A. thesis, University of Chicago, 1936); Joseph J. Thompson, "The Irish in Chicago," *Illinois Catholic Historical Review* 2 (April 1920): 458–73, and 3 (Oct. 1920): 146–69; Bessie L. Pierce, *A History of Chicago,* 2 (New York: Alfred A. Knopf, 1940): 6, 13–16.

4. Boston: Small, Maynard and Co., 1898, pp. vii–viii. The near West Side had been losing its respectable character because of contamination by unsavory elements from Chicago's expanding downtown area, and the Irish middle class was moving farther and farther west to escape. Two such moves by the Dunne family—in 1883 and 1886—are registered in *The Lakeside Annual Directory of the City of Chicago* (Chicago: Reuben H. Donnelly, 1883–1900). Today, St. Patrick's Church and School form an island in a sea of factories, warehouses, and expressways, and the far West Side is a black ghetto.

5. *Dubliners* (1916; reprint ed., New York: Viking Press, 1958), pp. 9–18. The classic Irish literary statement on forced vocations is T. C. Murray's *Maurice Harte* (1912), a two-act play about a brilliant divinity student for whom the entire family have struggled and denied themselves for years. Because of their sacrifices to keep him in the seminary, they force Maurice to continue against his will. In Act II he comes home mad, and everything falls apart.

6. John V. Kelleher, "Mr. Dooley and the Same Old World," *Atlantic* 177 (June 1946): 119–20; Dunne, *Mr. Dooley's Philosophy* (New York: R. H. Russell Co., 1900), p. 5.

7. FWP, Box 196; *Chicago Record-Herald,* May 30, 1913.

8. The department-authorized figures for that year showed 1,965 policemen on the payroll, 585 of whom had been born in Ireland. Three-fourths of the department were sons of foreign-born parents, many, of course, from Ireland. *America,* Oct. 2, 1890.

9. In 1894, W. T. Stead, the British reformer, blasted the police force in his controversial book, *If Christ Came to Chicago!* (Chicago: Laird and Lee, 1894), claiming that "the people who run the town are the police," and that the system was "permeated through and through by the influence of politics." "Pull" had wholly replaced "impartial justice," and police perjury for personal gain was widespread and accepted, for "the police are a law unto themselves, and have the very scantiest respect for any law which they can evade without getting themselves into trouble" (pp. 303–11). Also, in the fall and winter of 1894, the *Evening Post,* where Dunne was editorial chairman, gave wholehearted support and a good deal of editorial space to the "war on the police" sponsored by the Chicago Civic Federation, a citizens' lobby made up of the old-line wealth of the city (*EP,* Nov. 10, 19, Dec. 11, 28, 1894).

10. *EP,* Oct. 27, 1894; Nov. 18, 1893; Oct. 19, 1895.

11. Dunne was just finding his voice in this, one of the earliest Dooley pieces, in which a drunken father incurs the wrath of Dooley and John McKenna by sending his young daughter out for beer on a freezing winter night (*EP,* Nov. 25, 1893). See Chapter 3 for a discussion of this piece.

12. Remember also that Dunne experimented with the dialect voice of an Irish policeman; most recently, the Saturday before the first Dooley piece in October 1893. Perhaps, as I suggested in Chapter 1, he rejected this persona because of its vulnerability to criticism in Chicago.

13. Attribution of this unsigned editorial is based on these facts: both the editorial and the Dooley piece deal with exactly the same topic, arrive at the same conclusions, to a point, and appeared on the same day, August 7, 1897. The Dooley piece appeared in the *Evening Post;* the editorial, in the *Times-Herald,* the *Post's* morning affiliate, on whose editorial staff Dunne had been working since mid-1895. Evidence of a similar nature justifies all subsequent attribution of editorials to Dunne.

14. Stead, *If Christ Came to Chicago!,* pp. 28, 304.

15. John Moses and Joseph Kirkland, *The History of Chicago* (Chicago and New York: Munsell and Co., 1895), 1: 281; *EP,* Dec. 5, 1894. Dunne may well have written this editorial; note the reference to Swenie's "green heart" and the adjective "divvlish."

16. Richard M. Dorson, "Mose, the Far-Famed and World-Renowned," *American Literature* 15 (Nov. 1943): 288–300.

17. The "Three medal" was the Tree Medal, given annually to the Chicago fireman who performed the most heroic act in the line of duty.

18. When Marshall Murphy retired in 1894, the *Evening Post* agreed with the city's granting him a life pension as "just reward for his sufferings in the line of duty. His very qualities of courage force him to the rear" (Jan. 10, 1894). He could easily have been Dunne's model for Fireman Shay.

19. Kelleher, "Mr. Dooley and the Same Old World," p. 124. For the analogy with epic heroism I am indebted to Professor Kelleher's article, the finest single piece we have on Dunne and Mr. Dooley.

Chapter 3

1. *A Journey to the Western Islands of Scotland* [1775] (New Haven: Yale University Press, 1971), p. 131.

2. Morton and Lucia White, "The Intellectual versus the City," in Arthur Schlesinger, Jr., and Morton White, eds., *Paths of American Thought* (Boston: Houghton Mifflin, 1963), pp. 254–68.

3. *Atlantic Monthly* 77 (March 1896): 289–301. Merwin was a Harvard-trained Massachusetts lawyer.

4. Carl Wittke, *The Irish in America* (1956; reprint ed., New York: Russell and Russell, 1970), pp. 62–74; Sister M. Sevina Pahorezki, *The Social and Political Activities of William James Onahan* (Washington: Catholic University Press, 1942), pp. 47–48, 87–88, 98. Onahan, a prominent Chicago businessman, was national treasurer of the Colonization Association.

5. Fr. Stephen Byrne, O.P., to William J. Onahan, Jan. 25, 1885, in Pahorezki, *Social and Political Activities,* pp. 105–06.

6. Finley Peter Dunne, *Mr. Dooley in Peace and in War* (Boston: Small, Maynard and Co., 1898), pp. viii, x–xi.

7. A piece of local Bridgeport doggerel from the 1890s (FWP, Box 87, "Bridgeport") corroborates the authenticity of Mr. Dooley's attitude toward the river. Its subject is Haley's (or "Healey's") Slough, a sort of creek, mentioned often by Mr. Dooley, that ran out of the Chicago River diagonally southeast across Archer Avenue. The treatment here is a mixture of realism and humorous bravado that also sometimes characterizes Mr. Dooley's view of city life.

Haley's O'd Slew

I will sing you a ditty
Of our beautiful city,
Of a neat little stream that
Cuts its way through.
Its water is as pure
As the mouth of a sewer
And it's known over Bridgeport
As Haley's O'd Slew.

Old Ireland can boast
Of its beautiful waters,
There's the Boyne and the Shannon
The Black Water, too,
But where is the nation
That can boast of such water
As flows through the channel
Of Haley's O'd Slew?

8. The Luetgert referred to in the second paragraph was one Adolph Luetgert, a German-American sausage manufacturer, convicted of killing his wife and then grinding up her body in his sausage-making apparatus. His trial was a sensation in Chicago in the late nineties. Armour's was one of Chicago's largest packing-houses, situated in the Union Stockyards, just to the south of Bridgeport.

9. FWP, Box 87, "Bridgeport." The area known as Bridgeport today, still heavily Irish-American, is some ten blocks south of Mr. Dooley's Bridgeport, which lay just below the south branch of the Chicago River.

10. Interestingly, this seems to have been a bona fide appointment. A list of the mayor's new appointees for May 1897 includes the assignment of one "W. Punchek" as bridgetender at South Halsted Street, "salary, $3,400" (*Citizen,* May 1, 1897).

11. Sarsfield Hogan is named for Patrick Sarsfield, the seventeenth-century Irish patriot-soldier. C. S. Parnell Hogan was born during the widespread agitation that followed the formation of the Land League in Ireland. He was named for the Irish parliamentary leader, who supported the League publicly in 1879. William Joyce Hogan is named for a Bridgeport political boss.

12. For corroboration in general terms of most of the traits of the new Irish-American middle class particularized by Dunne in these Dooley pieces, see "The Changing Image" in William V. Shannon's fine study, *The American Irish* (New York: Macmillan, 1966), pp. 131–50. Here is Shannon's definition of "lace-curtain Irish" (p. 142); it applies perfectly to the people satirized in the columns we have just been looking at:

It seems impossible to document the origin of the term "lace-curtain," but oral tradition indicates it had come into common usage by the 1890's to denominate those more well-to-do Irish whose rise in the world enabled them to afford, among other prestige symbols, lace curtains on the windows. The radio comic Fred Allen once offered a capsule definition of "lace curtain": "They have fruit in the house when no one's sick." Like similar terms, "lace-curtain Irish," while denoting a certain level of financial achievement, has connotations that go well beyond mere prosperity. It connotes a self-conscious, anxious attempt to create and maintain a certain level and mode of gentility. The Irish of the middle class were trying to live down the opprobrium deriving from the brawling, hard drinking, and raffish manners of the "shanty Irish" of an earlier generation.

13. Donahue's reaction to his daughter's "pants" may not be exaggerated. Earlier that year Alderman "Bathhouse John" Coughlin had introduced to the city council an ordinance banning women bicycle riders "in bloomers, knickerbockers, baseball attire or trousers." The motion failed to pass (*T–H,* May 29, 1894).

14. Apropos of such "lace-curtain" props, Edward Harrigan's last great theatrical success was *Reilly and the Four Hundred,* an 1890 production that satirized the social climbing of the newly rich Irish in America. Its hit song, "Maggie Murphy's Home," declared that "There's an organ in the parlor, to give the house a tone/ And you're welcome every evening at Maggie Murphy's home." Shannon, *American Irish,* p. 143.

15. Francis O'Neill, Chicago police chief and Irish music collector, tells of "Murphy the blind piper" who lived "by the Archer Avenue bridge" and was a favorite of the men of the Deering Street police station. An atrocious piper, Murphy was known to carry "a little black bottle," because of which "he never lacked for hearers." Perhaps Mrs. Donahue is talking about Murphy (though she calls him Crowley) when she lashes out at Slavin and her husband. See Francis O'Neill, *Irish Folk Music: A Fascinating Hobby* (Chicago: Regan Printing House, 1910), p. 210.

16. Dunne expanded a few of these situations into an abortive "Molly Donahue" series for the *Ladies' Home Journal* in December 1899 and the early months of 1900. In one of these pieces the Donahue household splits into two warring camps on a Friday night. In the kitchen are old Donahue, Mr. Dooley, and their friends, singing Irish songs at the top of their lungs, while in the parlor Molly and Mrs. Donahue host a "musicale" around the piano. In another piece, Molly organizes a literary club and holds poetry readings after disagreeing with her father about his assertion that Carleton's *Willy Reilly* is the greatest book ever written, with the possible exception of the Bible. Some of these pieces show promise as fiction, and they do fill out the picture of the generational conflict within the Irish-American family; but Dunne did not warm to the task of turning out an extra thousand words a month, and he abandoned the project after four installments. See *Ladies' Home Journal* 17 (Jan. 1900): 6; 17 (March 1900): 6.

17. New York and London: Macmillan Co., 1904, pp. 327–28. This book was a bombshell; its reception has been compared to that accorded Michael Harrington's *The Other America* sixty years later. See Allen F. Davis and Mary

Lynn McCree, *Eighty Years at Hull-House* (Chicago: Quadrangle Books, 1969), p. 127.

18. Stead, *If Christ Came to Chicago!* (Chicago: Laird and Lee, 1894), pp. 17–24; Jane Addams, *Twenty Years at Hull-House* (1910; reprint ed., New York: New American Library, 1960), p. 21.

19. Stead, *If Christ Came to Chicago!*, p. 142; Addams, *Twenty Years at Hull-House*, pp. 123–24.

20. Stead, *If Christ Came to Chicago!*, p. 139; *EP*, Feb. 3, 1894.

21. The editorial writer, possibly Dunne, is answering a critique of the charity principle by Reverend Jenkin Lloyd Jones, a conservative Chicago minister:

> We have so-called charitable organizations wherein the brain has controlled since the heart shrivelled up in them and died of starvation. We have seen how they have organized on business principles with the result that every dollar received by them is divided into two parts—90 cents for salaries and 10 cents for the funeral expenses of the "case" which they are "investigating" perpetually. We have a Relief and Aid Society engaged in the relief and aid of its officers. . . . We are not in favor of "making paupers" [this had been Rev. Jones's accusation]. Is the Rev. Jones in favor of making funerals?   [*EP,* Dec. 12, 1893]

This point-blank attack, launched without the buffer of the Dooley persona, suggests that the organized relief agencies were a woefully unresponsive lot.

22. Dunne had established his attitude toward Christmas well before he invented Mr. Dooley. The *Tribune* at Christmastime 1889 printed a curious short story, signed "F. P. Dunne," in which a starving mesmerist hypnotizes his young son into thinking he is eating a Christmas turkey, then collapses and dies from the emotional exertion, his face set "in the heart-sickening expression one sees more and more often on human faces as the cities grow" (Dec. 22, 1889). The piece is a typically Whitechapelian combination of social consciousness and the macabre. Again in 1892, Dunne wrote for the *Post* the story of "A Christmas at Home," the hero of which is an escaped convict bent on murdering everyone responsible for his incarceration. He is recaptured on Christmas day after his wife, whom he has previously knifed in the cheek, informs on him. The conclusion is hardly in the Christmas spirit: "They have 7879 in prison again, solitary confinement, bread and water. But he will come out some day, and when he does the woman with a scar on her cheek will have also a scar on her throat. For you can't tamper with the little affectionate outburst of Christmas sentiment from a strong man, you know" (Dec. 25, 1892). After seeing these early disturbing performances by a twenty-two and twenty-four year old, we should be less surprised to find that the blackest, most despairing Dooley pieces come during the Christmas holidays.

23. From "The Fisherman," copyright 1919 by Macmillan Publishing Co., Inc., renewed 1947 by Bertha Georgie Yeats. *The Collected Poems of W. B. Yeats* (New York: Macmillan, 1956), p. 146. Quoted by permission of the publisher.

24. I attribute the editorial to Dunne because it treats the same themes as the Dooley piece and it appeared on the same day. Moreover, there are parallels between the two pieces besides the reference to men picking up coal on the tracks. The editorial counsels that "the man who is so meek in spirit as to accept a stranger's alms deserves unquestioning assistance"; and Mr. Dooley says "Anny man that's so far gone that he'll ask, ought to have."

25. *EP,* Jan. 25, 1897; *T–H,* Jan. 21–25, 1897.

26. *T–H,* Feb. 25, 1897; *New World,* Feb. 28, 1897.

27. The following Saturday, after the ball, Dooley discussed it again, lamenting the reversion of New York society to a savage state, likening the masqueraders to tattooed natives, and remarking that "whin people dhraw f'r to make fools iv thimsilves, . . . they ginrally fill their hands" (*EP,* Feb. 13, 1897).

28. When he included this piece in his first collection, Dunne omitted the reference to first communion, presumably because of possible offense to the clergy. I have replaced the reference because this final reminder of Petey's fall from grace as a "curly-haired angel" adds poignance and coherence.

29. *T–H,* Dec. 10, 1898; Ellis, *Life of Dunne,* p. 82.

30. James T. Farrell, *Studs Lonigan: A Trilogy* (New York: Modern Library, 1938), pp. 16–17.

Chapter 4

1. The speaker is Matthew Stanton, leader of the sixth ward of Brooklyn, in William Alfred's play *Hogan's Goat* (New York: Noonday Press, 1966), pp. 13–14. Reprinted with the permission of Farrar, Straus & Giroux, Inc.

2. William Shannon lists most of these reasons for Irish-American political success, stressing as "advantages other immigrants did not have," a "knowledge of the English language and an acquaintance with the dominant Anglo-American culture." See *The American Irish* (New York: Macmillan, 1966), pp. 60–63. Lawrence J. McCaffrey emphasizes the Irish political experience back in Ireland and declares that Daniel O'Connell was "the first Irish machine boss" because he used "the existing avenues of the British constitutional system" and created "the tactics of modern democratic pressure politics." See McCaffrey, *The Irish Diaspora in America* (Bloomington: Indiana University Press, 1976), p. 138.

3. Shannon points out that the machine was "virtually a parallel system of government. . . . a supplementary structure of power that performed some functions more vital than those of the nominal, legal government" (*American Irish,* p. 62).

4. See Arthur Mann's introduction to William L. Riordan, *Plunkitt of Tammany Hall* (1905; reprint ed., New York: E. P. Dutton, 1963); and Daniel P. Moynihan, "When the Irish Ran New York," *The Reporter,* June 8, 1961, pp. 32–34. *Plunkitt* is a collection of interviews with a real Tammany boss, George Washington Plunkitt, recorded by Riordan of the *New York Evening Post* in 1905, and providing a vivid firsthand account of the operation of the machine.

5. John Paul Bocock, *Forum* 17 (April 1894): 186–95.

6. "The Irish in American Life," *Atlantic* 77 (March 1896): 297.

7. F. Spencer Baldwin, "What Ireland Has Done for America," *New England Magazine* 24 (March 1901): 84.

8. For a description of the A. P. A. "platform," see E. M. Winston, "The Threatening Conflict with Romanism," *Forum* 17 (June 1894): 425–33; and Frederic R. Coudert, "The American Protective Association," *Forum* 17 (July 1894): 513–23.

9. *If Christ Came to Chicago!* (Chicago: Laird and Lee, 1894), pp. 161, 162, 173.

10. Lloyd Wendt and Herman Kogan give an entertaining account of the machinations of first ward aldermen Michael "Hinky Dink" Kenna and "Bathhouse John" Coughlin) in *Bosses of Lusty Chicago* (Bloomington: Indiana University Press, 1967). See also Theodore Dreiser's portraits of these two (as aldermen Tiernan and Kerrigan) in *The Titan,* called by John Berryman "the most effective ward leaders in American literature." *The Titan* (1914; reprint ed., New York: New American Library, 1965), p. 506.

11. *Mr. Dooley at His Best* (New York: Scribners, 1938), p. xxiii.

12. I use the *Herald* again because Dunne was still a political reporter on it at this time and there is a good chance that he wrote some of this material.

13. *Mr. Dooley in Peace and in War* (Boston: Small, Maynard and Co., 1898), p. xii.

14. *EP,* April 3–7, May 5, 11, 12, 1894; *Tribune,* April 4, 1894.

15. On several other occasions Dooley recalls with relish memories of illicit electioneering: "I mind th' time whin we r-rolled up twinty-siven hunderd dimocratic votes in this wan precinct an' th' on'y wans that voted was th' judges iv election an' th' captains. I was a captain thin, Jawn, an' a man iv great inflooence" (*EP,* Nov. 11, 1893). Or again: "I mind whin McInerney was a-runnin' f'r county clark. Th' lads at th' ya-ards set up all night tuckin' tickets into th' box f'r him. They voted all iv Calvary Symmitry an' was makin' inroads on th' potther's-field" (*EP,* June 18, 1893). And on another occasion: "I was captain in me precinct whin we carrid it f'r O'Broyn be more votes than they was min, women, childhern an' goats in th' whole sixth wa-ard" (*EP,* Dec. 9, 1893).

16. Dreiser's books are *The Financier* (1912), *The Titan* (1914), and *The Stoic* (1947). All through the nineties Mr. Dooley took caustic potshots at Yerkes. For example: "But if iver I go out f'r to rob annywan I'll make arrangements with Yerkuss to divide up th' territory an' thin I'll wait till he's out iv town" (*EP,* Sept. 28, 1895). Or again, upon Yerkes's purchase of a Chicago newspaper: "He's a great journalist. All he needs is a bald head an' a few whiskers an' principles to be a second Horace Greeley" (*EP,* Nov. 20, 1897).

17. Earlier in the week, Harlan had charged that Yerkes was taking an active part in the campaign. Yerkes had replied that Harlan was "a fraud and an ass" (*T–H,* March 31, 1897).

18. The results of the mayoral contest were: Harrison, 142,000; Harlan, 66,000; Sears, 57,000; Hesing, 15,000. This constituted a majority of 4,000 for Harrison over his combined opposition. At the first meeting of the new council the notorious Johnny Powers was elected chairman of the all-powerful finance committee, and Bridgeport's Billy O'Brien was chosen to lead the second most lucrative committee, licensing, thus confirming the worst fears of the reform element (*T–H,* April 6–8, 12, 1897).

19. The only "Tom" prominent in Bridgeport politics in the nineties, Reed served as a ward six alderman from 1893 to 1895.

20. For a description of this campaign, see Ray Stannard Baker, "Hull-House and the Ward Boss," *Outlook,* March 26, 1898, pp. 769–71. On Johnny Powers, see the *Tribune* obituary, May 20, 1930, and his sketch in *Prominent Democrats of Illinois* (Chicago: Democrat Publishing Co., 1899), p. 350.

21. Ellis, *Life of Dunne,* p. 100.

22. This January 17 *Journal* editorial may not be Dunne's work; the last Dooley piece in the *Evening Post* appeared on January 22. However, Ellis sug-

gests that Dunne had already moved to the *Journal* before the Dooley pieces stopped appearing in the *Post* (*Life of Dunne*, p. 100). At the least, Dunne was aware of the *Journal's* position when he wrote his dissenting Dooley piece on Powers for the *Post* of January 15. And he certainly contributed to the *Journal's* vociferous campaign against Powers that continued until the April municipal election.

23. I have seen only one biographical sketch of William J. O'Brien, a strange, sometimes contradictory, newspaper piece in the *Chicago Inter-Ocean* of March 23, 1892. According to this article, O'Brien was born and raised in Gloucester, Massachusetts, and spent some years there as a fisherman. He came to Chicago in the 1860s with his mother, who opened "an apple stand on Archer road" in Bridgeport. In the 1870s, he seems to have spent time in Chicago, Gloucester, New Jersey, Boston, and jail, before returning permanently to Chicago around 1876 and opening "a saloon at the corner of Archer avenue and Main street" in Bridgeport. "He has been suspected several times of crime," the article continues, and his personal fortune increased from $10,000 to "between $75,000 and $100,000" in the three years (1889–1892) following his election as sixth ward alderman.

24. No less reluctant to criticize the Irish politician was William Dillon, the judicious editor of the Chicago archdiocesan weekly, *The New World*. He did so at least once, though, fully realizing that "most of our Irish-American subscribers are against us on this issue." Still, his editorial is compelling. Admitting that the Irish have a talent for politics, Dillon sees that skill as

> a curse and a bane to the Irish population of this country [which has] prevented them from occupying anything like the position which they certainly would have occupied had their time and attention been less taken up with the political manipulations of our great cities. How many young men of Irish birth or descent are there in this city today who have been ruined, or are being ruined, physically and mentally, by bumming around after ward bosses, and doing, mainly in saloons, the services by which political jobs are secured, instead of turning their attention to the making of an honest livelihood?
>
> We suppose that, in regard to this matter, our voice will be, for the most part, as the voice of one calling in the wilderness; but that belief will not prevent us from saying, in this as in other matters, what we believe to be right and true.   [Nov. 20, 1897]

25. A list of the worst boodle bills passed in the nineties would include these: the Lake Street Elevated Railroad ordinance of October 1890, which gave Lake Street to Charles T. Yerkes for fifty years (*Tribune,* Oct. 24, 1890); the Cosmopolitan Electric and Ogden Gas franchises of February 1895, after passage of which a mass meeting was held to demand mayoral veto—he signed them both (*EP*, Feb. 25, March 3, 1895); and the Union Loop ordinance of October 1895, which gave Yerkes the contract to construct and run the Loop without paying a penny of legitimate compensation to the city (*EP*, Oct. 8, 1895).

26. Dunne seems to have been reluctant to give the legitimacy of book form to his more radical utterances: he wrote his publisher in 1899 that "I have piled up my old Dooleys—enough for ten books none of which could be read by a taxpayer." Dunne to Herbert Small, April 25, 1899, Dunne Letters, Chicago Historical Society.

27. Ellis has described the reaction to this piece at the *Post:* "When the type-setter ran off his proof of this piece he passed it about the composing room, and later when Dunne stepped into the room for a moment, the typesetters started to drum their sticks on their cases, and then broke into the more customary applause of handclapping. It was painfully embarrassing because it was so un-usual and yet so natural, and Dunne remembered it as one of the great thrills of his life" (*Life of Dunne*, p. 86).

Chapter 5

1. From "September 1913," copyright 1916 by Macmillan Publishing Co., Inc., renewed 1944 by Bertha Georgie Yeats. *The Collected Poems of W. B. Yeats* (New York: Macmillan, 1956), p. 106. Quoted by permission of the publisher.

2. After a calamitous revolt in Ireland in 1848, refugees from internment scattered over Europe, the United States, and Canada. The two most persistent of these latter-day Wild Geese were James Stephens and John O'Mahony, who became friends and fellow dreamers in Paris in the early fifties. After ten years of planning and recouping their energies, they were ready to institutionalize the cause once again. On St. Patrick's Day 1858 in Paris, Stephens launched a new secret society, the Irish Republican (or Revolutionary) Brotherhood—the IRB—with the aim "to make Ireland an independent democratic republic." Later that year, in New York City, O'Mahony founded the American branch, the Fenian Brotherhood. See F. S. L. Lyons, *Ireland Since the Famine* (New York: Scrib-ners, 1971), pp. 111–15; and Carl Wittke, *The Irish in America* (1956; reprint ed., New York: Russell and Russell, 1970), p. 80.

3. The book is still exciting and readable. It has been reprinted with an intro-duction by Oliver Knight (Norman: University of Oklahoma Press, 1961).

4. Charles Ffrench, *Biographical History of the American Irish in Chicago* (Chicago: American Biographical Publishing Co., 1897), pp. 24–35; Alfred T. Andreas, *History of Chicago from the Earliest Period to the Present Time*, 3 (Chicago: A. T. Andreas, 1886): 707–08; *Tribune* (obituary), June 10, 1908.

5. Later attempts in 1870 and 1871 also failed. See Lyons, *Ireland Since the Famine*, pp. 125–26; Wittke, *Irish in America*, pp. 155–60.

6. Dunne wrote this piece in the context of the accelerating revolutionary movement in Cuba. In "Whitechapel Nights," Charles Dennis verified the participation of Bridgeporters in the Fenian raid as follows: "In the early spring of 1866 Gen. O'Neill and other leaders of the movement addressed a meeting at Haley's hall, on Archer Avenue, Chicago. Many of those in attendance wore the blue uniforms which had served them in the civil war. That night there were numerous enlistments in the Fenian army. So crowded was the hall that the floor collapsed." Dennis is also my source for John Finerty's participation in the raid of June 1866 (*News*, Aug. 1, 1936).

7. For background on the Clan, see Lyons, *Ireland Since the Famine*, pp. 151–55; Thomas N. Brown, "The Origins and Character of Irish-American Nationalism," *Review of Politics* 18 (July 1956): 327–58; idem, *Irish-American Nationalism, 1870–1890* (New York and Philadelphia: Lippincott, 1966), passim.

8. Lyons, *Ireland Since the Famine*, pp. 168–69; Brown, *Irish-American Nationalism*, pp. 69–73 and passim; Merlin Bowen, "Irish National Movements in the Nineteenth Century" (typescript, FWP, Box 196), passim. Bowen is my

main source for information on the Dynamite Campaign and for references to the newspaper coverage of the bombings.

9. Bowen, "Irish National Movements," passim; Brown, *Irish-American Nationalism,* p. 22.

10. Sullivan is a fascinating, enigmatic figure whose life and motives are shrouded in mystery. The fullest, but wholly undocumented, treatment of his life is an unpublished, unsigned 370-page manuscript, "The Case of Dr. Cronin," in the Federal Writers' Project for Illinois archives (FWP, Box 290). See also Brown, *Irish-American Nationalism,* passim; John Devoy, *Recollections of an Irish Rebel* (New York: Charles P. Young, 1929), pp. 211, 345–46; idem, *Devoy's Post Bag,* William O'Brien and Desmond Ryan, eds. (Dublin: Fallon Co., 1948–1953), vols. 1 and 2, passim. Born in Canada in 1847, Sullivan had arrived in Chicago by way of a checkered career in Arizona and Detroit. A Republican, he tried to swing the Irish vote for Blaine in 1884 from his position as president of the Irish National League of America. Dunne may have known him personally, for Sullivan's wife, Margaret, a fine political journalist, was Dunne's colleague on the *Times-Herald* in the mid-nineties.

11. Bowen, "Irish National Movements" (unpaginated); *Citizen,* June 7, 1884, Feb. 9, 1884.

12. Finley Peter Dunne, *Mr. Dooley's Philosophy* (New York: R. H. Russell, 1900), p. 258.

13. Brown, "Origins and Character," pp. 337, 357; idem, *Irish-American Nationalism,* p. 23.

14. *New York Times,* Sept. 4, 14–19, 1896; *T-H,* Sept. 14–16, 1896. Tynan's book is *The Irish National Invincibles* (New York: Irish National Invincible Publishing Co., 1894).

15. The "Ah-o-haitches" in Tynan's parade are the Ancient Order of Hibernians, the largest Irish-American fraternal and insurance organization in the nineteenth century, founded in 1836.

16. Tynan was actually arrested under a warrant that had been issued at the time of the Phoenix Park murders, fourteen years earlier.

17. Brown, *Irish-American Nationalism,* pp. 174–76; "The Case of Dr. Cronin," FWP, Box 290, passim; *Devoy's Post Bag,* 2: 307, 308, 310–16.

18. Imprisoned as a Fenian, Devoy had been deported to New York in 1870, where he began a fifty-year career in journalism and agitation for Irish freedom. Thomas N. Brown has called him "the ideologue, the Lenin of Irish-American nationalism." See Brown, *Irish-American Nationalism,* p. xiv; Ellis, *Life of Dunne,* p. 22.

19. Ellis, *Life of Dunne,* pp. 34–38; Philip Dunne, ed., *Mr. Dooley Remembers: The Informal Memoirs of Finley Peter Dunne* (Boston: Little, Brown, 1963), pp. 68–77. Dunne wrote this memoir in the last year of his life, 1936, nearly fifty years after the events. Consequently, it is not entirely reliable. However, I have checked the *Times* and the other major newspapers in Chicago for the days leading up to the arrest and indictment of Daniel Coughlin, with these results. The *Times* did publish the first story connecting the Chicago Police Department with the murder; it did scoop the city with the news of Coughlin's arrest for "guilty knowledge of the crime" in an extra edition at 6 P.M. on Saturday, May 25, 1889; and it did produce the evidence that linked Dan Coughlin to the horse and buggy rented to drive Dr. Cronin to his death

on May 4. Therefore, I conclude that the *Times* had sources of information unavailable to the other papers, and I accept Dunne's explanation of his major role in the case as substantially true.

All of the major papers saw themselves as investigatory agencies, and they contested hotly for pieces of evidence. The *Tribune* asserted its claim by reprinting several times a cartoon depicting a roomful of policemen pouring over the *Tribune* with the caption, "Searching for Clues." The *Times* quotes the *St. Paul Globe:* "If it weren't for its newspapers, Chicago would be without a detective system," and the *Cincinnati Inquirer:* "The only hope of the detection of the murderers of Dr. Cronin rests with the newspaper men of Chicago. They cannot be bought and they cannot be frightened. If the mystery is ever unraveled it will be done by them" (May 28, 1889). In the best contemporary account of the murder, John T. McEnnis declared that "from first to last it was the press that made the case. The police were distanced in the race for news, and surprise after surprise was scored morning after morning in the columns of one journal or the other. It was the reporters of Chicago who uncovered the conspiracy and really wound the chain of evidence about the prisoners in the dock." See McEnnis, *The Clan na Gael and the Murder of Dr. Patrick Henry Cronin* (Chicago: Schulte and Iliff, 1889), pp. 147–48.

20. Brown, *Irish-American Nationalism*, p. 175; *Times*, May 27, June 28, 1889.

21. For more on this fascinating story, see the FWP manuscript, "The Case of Dr. Cronin," or either of the contemporary accounts of the case: Henry M. Hunt, *The Crime of the Century, or, The Assassination of Dr. Patrick Henry Cronin* (Chicago: People's Publishing Co., 1889), and McEnnis, *The Clan na Gael and the Murder of Dr. Cronin*. See also the two articles, "The Murder of Dr. Cronin," by Michael J. Lennon in *The Bell* (Dublin), 18 (April 1952): 20–29, and 18 (May 1952): 92–102. Lennon's study contains the assertion that Finley Peter Dunne "sent money yearly for I. R. B. work to Dublin to Tom Clarke" (p. 26). The last word on all of this business is the recent study by Michael F. Funchion, *Chicago's Irish Nationalists, 1881–1890* (New York: Arno Press, 1976).

22. *Tribune*, Nov. 27–30, 1890; *Herald*, Nov. 26–29, 1890. I begin to follow and quote from the *Chicago Herald* at this point because Dunne quit the *Tribune* and joined the *Herald* sometime in December 1890.

23. The anti-Irish weekly *America* also printed the list of platform guests, which included, besides Dunne, Mayor Dewitt Cregier and most of Chicago's aldermen. *America*'s editor, Slason Thompson, suggested that the list might be useful "in some future investigation . . . to prove how many of Chicago's prominent (?) citizens honored the dishonored and discrowned king of Ireland" (Dec. 4, 1890). The *Tribune* also reported that John Devoy and Mrs. Stewart Parnell (Parnell's mother) were in the audience.

24. Quoted in Brown, *Irish-American Nationalism*, p. 177. See also *Herald*, Oct. 1–3, 1891. Fully a fourth of those in attendance were Chicagoans.

25. *Citizen*, March 15, June 7, Sept. 6, 1890; *Tribune*, Aug. 23, 1890.

26. To be sure, some of the dialect pieces preceding the inception of Mr. Dooley had been less than kind to the Irish. One especially virulent series had appeared in the Chicago-based, anti-immigration periodical *America* in 1888. Ten "Intercepted Letters" from Chicago to County Tipperary create a one-

sided, stereotyped picture of the urban Irishman as a drunken, dishonest political hack. But these were certainly exceptional. See "Intercepted Letters by Patrick O'Sullivan to His Cousin, Michael O'Mara, Tipperary," by Elizabeth Cumings, *America,* May 26–Aug. 11, 1888.

27. The *Post* was owned by John R. Walsh, a native of Ireland and a successful Chicago banker. Finerty's antipathy to the *Post* as a "Democratic" organ may stem from his own Republicanism. The previous literary references are from *The Citizen* of these dates: Jan. 7, 1893; March 8, 1884; Nov. 12, 1887.

28. Brown, *Irish-American Nationalism,* pp. 181–82.

29. Dunne is referring here to men such as Matthew P. Brady, Chicago lawyer and leading nationalist orator, and Alexander Sullivan, who served as head counsel for Charles T. Yerkes's street railway interests in the nineties.

30. Two changes between the *Post* and publication in *Mr. Dooley in the Hearts of His Countrymen* illustrate how Dunne sometimes softened the local and personal bite of his references. "Th' 'ell's own conthroller" may be a reference to the prominent Chicago businessman and former city comptroller, William J. Onahan. In *Hearts* this passage becomes "a great city threasurer." Also, John Finerty's name is omitted in the final form of the piece, although notorious nineteenth-ward alderman Johnny Powers is kept in.

31. Brown continues: "Herein lies the explanation for the curious frailty of the bellicose Fenian Brotherhood and the organizations that succeeded it. As long as they remained close to the warming sun of Irish nationalism they thrived; but when by the very law of their being they came into contact with the divisive realities of American life they inevitably disintegrated." *Irish-American Nationalism,* pp. 40, 41.

32. Born in Liverpool of Irish parents, Brady came to Chicago in 1865. *America* reports that he once refused to serve as "orator of the day" at a rally for presidential candidate Benjamin Harrison because Harrison requested a copy of his speech beforehand, and Brady was "an orator who depends upon the moment's inspiration for the inspiring words . . . and, rather than relinquish his right to deliver a spontaneous effusion, he declined to speak at all" (*America,* Sept. 27, 1888). See also *Prominent Democrats of Illinois* (Chicago: Democrat Publishing Co., 1899), p. 394.

33. Two Fenian leaders had been rescued from a prison van in Manchester, England, in September 1867, and a police guard was accidently shot dead while the van lock was being blown off. Five men were arrested and after a questionable trial three, all Irishmen, were executed. See Lyons, *Ireland Since the Famine,* pp. 126–27.

34. *Citizen,* March 17, 1894. Most of the dailies assumed that Coughlin was guilty, but thought the jury had deliberated honestly and found a "reasonable doubt" about that guilt. The *Tribune* blamed the length of the trial, conjecturing that "even Nero" might have been acquitted after four months of confusing testimony (March 9, 10, 1894).

35. Sister M. Sevina Pahorezki, *The Social and Political Activities of William James Onahan* (Washington, D.C.: Catholic University Press, 1942), p. 49.

36. He goes on to trace the history of the parade. An Irish-American invention, stimulated by the Know-Nothing movement, the parade very early attracted the attention of politicians, who saw "that it was a good thing to mount a

horse or sit in a carriage at the head or in the wake of a big parade." Its
demise began when "Parnell asked the Irish-American societies to give it up in
1880" because it served no purpose in the Home Rule agitation. Now, the editorial concludes, only the politicians are hanging on; but it is to be hoped
that "in another year or two there will be nothing left of the St. Patrick's
Day parade, and Irish citizens will be the greatest gainers by its extinction."
There is an element of wishful thinking in these sentiments to which Dunne
certainly subscribed.

37. Mr. Dooley does not exaggerate the bloody history of July twelfth in
America. There were terrible Orange-Green riots in the American Irish past.
Probably the worst were in New York City in 1870 and 1871. Unfortunately,
today's painful crisis in Ulster makes these events all too easy to envision.

38. F. S. L. Lyons, *The Irish Parliamentary Party, 1890–1910* (London:
Faber and Faber, 1951), passim.

39. Dunne is here describing the 1886 "union of hearts," when Parnell's
Irish party joined with Gladstone's Liberals in an unsuccessful attempt to defeat the Tories, led by Lord Salisbury. The reference to Salisbury's "camp" of
the Clan na Gael is comically farfetched. Mr. Dooley also makes fun of the
British parliamentary game when Lord Rosebery, whom he calls "a young
la-ad that owned race hor-rses—a mere child," is ousted from leadership in
1895 (*EP*, June 29, 1895).

40. At the time, Dunne wrote his publisher that "I might like to engage in
a public controversy on the question of my consideration for the feelings of my
fellow countrymen, but certainly not with Pat Ford or any of that funny
crowd of Turks." Dunne to Herbert Small, Nov. 7, 1899, Dunne Letters,
Chicago Historical Society.

41. From "Easter 1916," copyright 1924 by Macmillan Publishing Co., Inc.,
renewed 1952 by Bertha Georgie Yeats. *The Collected Poems of W. B. Yeats*
(New York: Macmillan, 1956), p. 179. Quoted by permission of the publisher.

Chapter 6

1. *Citizen*, April 8, 1899.

2. Ellis, *Life of Dunne*, pp. 97–98.

3. The coinage of silver as panacea for the depression of 1893–1898 became
the great issue in the campaign of 1896, but it received early and popular treatment in W. H. Harvey's *Coin's Financial School* (Chicago: Coin Publishing Co.,
1894), in which an authority on currency known only as "Coin" instructs the
American people on the advantages of bimetallism. See Harold U. Faulkner,
1890–1900: Politics, Reform and Expansion (New York: Harper and Row,
1959), pp. 187–88.

4. A follow-up piece is Dooley's rollicking report of the actual debate between
"Coin" Harvey and New York Republican Roswell Horr at the prestigious
Illinois Club of Chicago (*EP*, July 20, 1895).

5. Ellis reports that McKenna, in real life an Irish Republican and McKinley
man, "did not permit Mr. Dooley to use him as a foil for his wit, now to be
exercised on a Republican gold-standard paper." Consequently, Dunne was
forced to invent Hennessy to shift the burden from his old friend. Ellis, *Life of
Dunne*, pp. 98, 99.

6. Bryan's campaign fund contained a total of $300,000. McKinley's has been estimated at somewhere between $3.5 and $10 million. Faulkner, *1890–1900,* pp. 203–04.

7. The *Times-Herald* for this date prints Bryan's Chicago itinerary, which included stops at Polish School Hall, Germania Hall, Battery D and Curran's Hall (both in Bridgeport), Pulaski Hall, Bohemian Turner Hall, and St. Paul's School. The contrast is marked between this schedule and McKinley's "front porch" campaign.

8. This piece appeared one week after the Democratic convention. The *Times-Herald* was similarly unmoved by Bryan's famous speech. The editorial analysis classified it as "genuine popular oratory," the result of "natural gifts rather than profound reasoning or even trained power," and containing "a transparent resort to superficial devices" and "meretricious or absurd" comparisons (July 11, 1896).

9. Faulkner, *1890–1900,* pp. 216–28.

10. The piece constitutes another example of Dunne's balancing of Bridgeport and national material, for in it Mr. Dooley moves plausibly from Maceo to a situation from a local parish theatrical production of the play "Pizario." Young Dougherty plays the villain who dies by the sword every night, and "he done it so well," declares Dooley, "that th' people used to shudder whin he come out afther th' show." In addition, "no wan iv th' young ladies 'd walk home with him," and as a result, Dougherty takes to drink.

> "Th' play had been goin' a week whin wan night I seen a bad light in his eye [continues Dooley]. 'Did you have mercy on me,' says Ahern. 'Die, thraitor,' an' he made a swipe at Dougherty. Dougherty give the soord a kick an' says he, 'I'll not die a lick,' he says. 'I'm tired iv dyin', he says. 'It's a bum's job, annyhow,' he says. 'Ye'll have to sind to th' morgue f'r an' undherstudy f'r me,' he says. 'I'm too full iv contintment tonight to seek th' cold embraces iv th' grave,' he says. An' he done a shuffle an' wint off th' stage singing 'A Life on th' Ocean Wave.' "

11. Evangelina Cisneros was charged with complicity in the murder of a Spanish officer who was alleged to have threatened her with rape. Stories of her maltreatment at the hands of her Spanish jailors were rampant. An American committee petitioned Pope Leo XIII, who, in turn, asked Spain's Queen Regent to have Miss Cisneros released. The Spanish command in Cuba refused to let her go, and instead, she was rescued by a Hearst reporter, who climbed to the roof near her cell window and worked loose a bar so that she could pass through the window. Smuggled out of Cuba, she was given jubilant receptions in New York and Washington. Faulkner, *1890–1900,* pp. 226–27.

12. There was truth in the accusation, for *Tribune* publisher Joseph Medill was an early and vociferous supporter of manifest destiny and Cuban intervention. At the height of the Cisneros controversy, a *Times-Herald* editorial conjectured that the *Tribune* might yet "rush single-handed on the foe. We should miss the *Tribune* very much. There is little enough in this weary world of gayety that we should sacrifice the most amusing little cuss in the journalistic menagerie" (Sept. 20, 1897). *Times-Herald* editorials as far back as May 15, 1897 (on "War and War Editors") complain of the *Tribune's* extreme positions and compare Medill's tactics with those of Hearst and Pulitzer.

13. The piece concludes with a comparison between the jingo press of 1897 and the Irish-American press during the Dynamite Campaign of the 1880s,

previously discussed. The editor of the radical nationalist paper *The Explosive* jumps through his front window when confronted with a bogus stick of dynamite. The application to the yellow press is plain: "If we go to war with Spain we don't want to lean too har-rd on th' editors. We may need other assistance."

14. Ellis, *Life of Dunne*, p. 100.

15. Tanner's victory in the 1896 gubernatorial election was mostly due to a reaction against Governor Altgeld's pardon of the Haymarket anarchists and his strong advocacy of free silver coinage at 16 to 1. Tanner was thought to be a tool of Illinois businessmen, and his signing of controversial traction ordinances seems to bear this out.

16. Ellis, *Life of Dunne*, p. 100.

17. John A. S. Grenville and George Berkeley Young, *Politics, Strategy, and American Diplomacy* (New Haven: Yale University Press, 1966), pp. 253–55.

18. Faulkner, *1890–1900*, p. 230.

19. See Grenville and Young, *Politics, Strategy, and American Diplomacy,* pp. 239–66.

20. Faulkner, *1890–1900*, p. 240.

21. Life imitated art on the issue of kinship with the admiral. On August 24, 1898, the *Journal* printed the story of an old man named John Tuhey who wandered into a Chicago police station, claiming to be George Dewey's uncle. He stated for the record that "Dewey's name is Tuhey. The young fellows have changed the spelling of the good old name—the divvils. They ought to be shot."

22. Ellis, *Life of Dunne*, p. 116.

23. Faulkner reports that upon receiving the news of the declaration of war, "Theodore Roosevelt telegraphed to Brooks Brothers for a 'blue cravenette regular Lieutenant-Colonel's uniform without yellow on the collar and with leggings' " (*1890–1900*, p. 235). Dunne is also the probable author of an editorial on the issue, in which he complains that "we are assured of an army officered partly by rich men's sons who have never led anything more desperate than a cotillion or a charge on a cigarette counter. . . . the McKinley administration has been guilty of discharging some of its real or fancied obligations by an indulgence in a form of toadyism that no European nation, except Spain perhaps, would tolerate thirty minutes" (*Journal,* May 24, 1898).

24. A pre-war *Journal* editorial that may have been Dunne's ridicules Miles's gold-laden personal uniform as follows: "He moved through the modest throng like a beautiful, splendid, shining brass-bound trunk going down a crowded railway station platform on a hand truck" (Feb. 3, 1898).

25. Ellis, *Life of Dunne*, pp. 113, 122.

26. James C. Austin, *Artemus Ward* (New Haven: College and University Press, 1964), p. 107. On the other hand, Grenville and Young have determined that McKinley's cabinet was deliberately second-rate, which allowed the president to keep personal control of foreign relations. "His cabinet councils," they find, "were little more than jolly social gatherings" (*Politics, Strategy, and American Diplomacy,* p. 244). Of course, this makes Mr. Dooley's picture of the cabinet meeting all the more plausible and helps to explain Secretary Long's suspicions about his proximity to the action.

27. In 1898 the United States Army numbered 28,000 scattered and ill-trained troops, with no experience other than occasional skirmishes with the Indians. The whole was presided over by lumberman-politician Russell Alger of Michigan,

the easygoing secretary of war, who became the scapegoat for much post-facto criticism of the handling of the war. Actually, no one man could have solved the problem of assimilating, training, and transporting (not to mention feeding, clothing, and housing) the 200,000 men who volunteered to serve in 1898, and Alger's responsibility for the chaos must be shared with the president, Congress, and the army hierarchy (Faulkner, *1890–1900*, pp. 235–38).

28. Grenville and Young, *Politics, Strategy, and American Diplomacy*, pp. 267–96. These findings are disconcerting. We seem to have been led into "deep involvement in the Philippines" by a series of haphazard decisions based on the obscure contingency war plan of Lt. William Kimball, combined with "the exigencies of war and faulty appraisal of Spain's naval strength" (p. 292).

29. Faulkner, *1890–1900*, pp. 251–59. See also Frank Friedel, "Dissent in the Spanish-American War and the Philippine Insurrection," in Samuel Eliot Morison, Frederick Merk, and Frank Friedel, *Dissent in Three American Wars* (Cambridge, Mass.: Harvard University Press, 1970), pp. 65–95.

30. Finerty's editorials deploring the Philippine involvement could have been written about Vietnam. For example: "We have the deepest sympathy for our army . . . and hate to see it bleed, not for the good of mankind, not for the glory of the Republic, but for its unspeakable shame" (April 29, 1899).

31. Throughout the Insurrection Dillon's only hope remained that the bloody guerrilla war would "open the eyes of the people of this country, and enable them to realize the kind of work they have before them if the policy of expansion is adhered to" (Feb. 11, 1899). *The New World* is on microfilm at that newspaper's offices in downtown Chicago. See also James J. Swaner, "Clarion Voice in a Jingo Wilderness: The Chicago *New World* on the Spanish-American War" (M.A. thesis, St. Paul Seminary, St. Paul, Minnesota, 1960).

32. Collins, for one, had gone through the familiar progression. At first in favor of American intervention against Spain as a means of freeing Cuba, he reversed himself so as to oppose American intervention in the Philippines as subjugation of a people "against their will and by brute force." See Michael Curran, *Life of Patrick A. Collins* (Norwood, Mass.: Norwood Press, 1906), p. 151.

33. Certainly Norton must have had mixed feelings about his convergence of opinion with the very group who had driven him out of Cambridge to summer in Ashfield, Massachusetts, where, as he wrote to James Russell Lowell, there was "but one Irish family." Quoted in Kenneth S. Lynn, *William Dean Howells: An American Life* (New York: Harcourt, Brace, Jovanovich, 1971), p. 143. On the anti-imperialists, see Friedel, "Dissent in the Spanish-American War," pp. 78–79; and Robert L. Beisner, *Twelve Against Empire: The Anti-Imperialists, 1898–1900* (New York: McGraw-Hill, 1968), pp. 5–17.

34. In a 1900 letter to Dunne, Theodore Roosevelt, an ardent expansionist, acknowledged the wisdom of "your delicious phrase about 'take up the white man's burden and put it on the coons,' " which, he said, "exactly hit off the weak spot in my own theory; though, mind you, I am by no means willing to give up the theory yet" (Ellis, *Life of Dunne*, p. 147).

35. These appeared in the *Journal* between October 28, 1899, and June 2, 1900—six in all—and were collected in Dunne's third book, *Mr. Dooley's Philosophy* (New York: R. H. Russell, 1900).

36. This is more surprising in the case of Howells, who so often used his

personal experience in his fiction. As early as July 1898, he wrote Henry James that "our war for humanity has unmasked itself as a war for coaling stations, and we are going to keep our booty to punish Spain for putting us to the trouble of using violence in robbing her." This letter is quoted in my main source for this paragraph, Fred Harvey Harrington, "Literary Aspects of American Anti-Imperialism, 1898–1902," *New England Quarterly* 10 (Dec. 1937): 666.

37. Ellis describes the process—Dunne and several friends sat around a table reading and selecting pieces. One of these friends had produced a scattering of the earlier Dooleys, from which the "Peace" selection was made (Ellis, *Life of Dunne,* p. 119).

38. Dunne also found titles for the early pieces: these three were called "On Paternal Duty," "On Criminals," and "On the Popularity of Firemen."

39. *The Bookman* 8 (Feb. 1899): 574–76. Ellis quotes from this and other reviews in *Life of Dunne,* pp. 120–21.

40. Herbert Small to Dunne, March 9, 1899, Dunne Letters, Library of Congress.

41. W. Irving Way, "Mr. Martin Dooley of Chicago," *The Bookman* 9 (May 1899): 217.

42. Mrs. Reginald De Koven, *A Musician and His Wife* (New York and London: Appleton Co., 1926), p. 138.

43. Lincoln Steffens recalled that Dunne "could not master himself. He could not make himself write. I never knew a writer who made such a labor of writing; he seemed to hate it; he certainly ran away from it whenever he could." Steffens remembers that Dunne was incensed when his office wallpaper at *The American Magazine* was changed from a floral pattern to a plain tone, which no longer allowed him to spend his time counting the flowers from floor to ceiling and along the diagonal: "Now, doggone it," said Dunne on this occasion, "now I come in here and I've got to write. There's nothing to count, no sums to multiply; I've just got to sit here doing nothing or—write." *The Autobiography of Lincoln Steffens* (New York: Harcourt, Brace and Co., 1931), pp. 537–38.

44. Dunne to Herbert Small, Aug. 31, Sept. 25, 1899, Dunne Letters, Chicago Historical Society.

45. Dunne to Herbert Small, March 29, April 6, April 25, and undated, 1899, Dunne Letters, Chicago Historical Society.

46. Dec. 12, Dec. 17, 1898, *Century* Collection, New York Public Library.

47. *Ladies' Home Journal* 17 (March 1900): 6.

48. Charles H. Dennis, *Victor Lawson: His Time and His Work* (Chicago: University of Chicago Press, 1935), pp. 384–85.

49. The piece was called "Mr. Dooley's Advice to the Court." See Ellis, *Life of Dunne,* pp. 127–32; Dunne to R. H. Russell [?], Aug. 25, 1899, Dunne Letters, Chicago Historical Society.

Chapter 7

1. *The Autobiography of Mark Twain* (New York: Harper, 1959), p. 273.

2. Reprinted in Vivian Mercier, ed., *Great Irish Short Stories* (New York: Dell, 1964), pp. 58–63.

3. One of the slightest pieces, Dooley and Hennessy on a fishing trip, sticks in my mind simply because their voices are so alive. Here is part of it:

> "Him an' me, Hinnissy th' fool an' me, bought a pole an' some minnies, f'r th' fish does be cannybals in thim parts, an' out we wint undher a sun so near to us that ye cud almost catch it in ye'er hat. Sare a fish had I iver caught but a can iv salmon, but Hinnissy, th' crazy wan, he said we'd be all right, so I set in th' ind iv th' boat an' dhropped th' minny overboard an' waited. Jawn, look at th' back iv me neck. Broiled, be hivins, broiled! I cukked there like a doughnut f'r five hours. 'Have ye a bite?' says I to Hinnissy. 'Not yet,' says he, 'but patience,' he says, 'an' pass th' bottle.' Th' blisters begun comin' out on me poor neck like bubbles in a pot iv stirabout. 'Have ye a bite?' says I. 'None but fr'm th' fly on th' ind iv me nose,' he says. 'Hit it, Martin, if ye love me. Hol' on,' he says. 'Here's wan,' he says, 'Oh, 'tis a whale. Come here,' he says, 'come up, me beauty,' he says. 'Come up, feerocious shark,' he says. 'Now, d'ye stand by, Martin,' he says, 'an' kill him with th' oar,' he says. 'I think be th' weight an' fight iv him 'tis th' sea sarpint I have here.' 'Thin,' says I, 'f'r hivins sake lave him be or tow him ashore,' says I. 'I had a cousin wanst that had his feet bit off be a fish.' But Hinnissy wint on pullin' an' swearin', an' what d'ye think he fetched? A hoopskirt, by gar. 'Twas bad enough f'r me to hook a box iv beer an' a mud turtle, but a hoop-skirt—dear, oh, dear, he was that mad.
>
> " 'What ar-re ye goin' to do with it?' says I. 'Ye can't wear it,' I says, 'an' ye can't ate it,' I says, 'an' ye can't put it in th' poor box,' I says. He didn't bat his eye f'r an hour." [*EP*, Aug. 3, 1895]

4. John Henry Raleigh quotes Wilde's epigram in an article on Eugene O'Neill's Irishness, and then agrees that "the real forte of the Irish is just in talking, and talking in a special way, histrionically: striking a comic pose and exaggerating it into a burlesque." "O'Neill's *Long Day's Journey into Night* and New England Irish Catholicism," *Partisan Review* 26 (Fall 1959): 580.

5. The Casey pieces ran in the *Times-Herald* from April 14 through August 4, 1895. They were revived in the *Evening Post* in January 1906.

6. Henry Seidel Canby remarked on Dunne's "marvelous little satires, each perfectly constructed with a twist at the end as incomparable as the last line of a sonnet." "Mr. Dooley and Mr. Hennessy," *Saturday Review of Literature* 14 (May 9, 1936): 3.

7. "Certain of the Chicago School of Fiction," *North American Review* 176 (May 1903): 734–46.

8. "Place in Fiction," *South Atlantic Quarterly* 55 (Jan. 1956): 57–72.

9. From the inscription to Hamlin Garland's copy of *Maggie*, quoted in Joseph Katz, ed., *The Portable Stephen Crane* (New York: Viking Press, 1969), p. 1.

10. *Portable Stephen Crane*, p. 7. Mr. Dooley would never have observed such a house on Archer Avenue. Here is Crane's full description:

> Eventually they entered into a dark region where, from a careening building, a dozen gruesome doorways gave up loads of babies to the street and the gutter. A wind of early autumn raised yellow dust from cobbles and swirled it against an hundred windows. Long streamers of garments fluttered from fire-escapes. In all unhandy places there were buckets, brooms, rags and bottles. In the street infants played or fought with other infants or sat stupidly in the way of vehicles. Formidable

women, with uncombed hair and disordered dress, gossiped while leaning on railings, or screamed in frantic quarrels. Withered persons, in curious postures of submission to something, sat smoking pipes in obscure corners. A thousand odors of cooking food came forth to the street. The building quivered and creaked from the weight of humanity stamping about in its bowels.

A small ragged girl dragged a red, bawling infant along the crowded ways. He was hanging back, baby-like, bracing his wrinkled, bare legs.

11. *Sister Carrie* (1900; reprint ed., New York: W. W. Norton, 1970), p. 13.

12. Very helpful in developing this sense of Crane's and Dreiser's characters as outsiders in the alien city are Larzer Ziff's Crane chapter in *The American 1890s: Life and Times of a Lost Generation* (New York: Viking Press, 1966), pp. 185–205; and Alfred Kazin's essay on "The Realistic Novel" in Arthur Schlesinger, Jr., and Morton White, eds., *Paths of American Thought* (Boston: Houghton Mifflin, 1963), pp. 238–53.

13. "A Letter from Stephen Crane to Miss Catherine Harris," dated Nov. 12, 1896, quoted in *Portable Stephen Crane, p.* 2.

14. Fred Lewis Pattee, *The New American Literature* (New York: Century, 1930), pp. 60–61. Flashes of realistic description, somewhat undercut by sentimental plotting and character stereotypes, are to be found in two other collections of urban sketches and tales from the 1890s. These are James W. Sullivan, *Tenement Tales of New York* (New York: Henry Holt, 1895); and Brander Matthews, *Vignettes of Manhattan* (New York: Harper, 1894).

15. These stories and the novel are collected in Abraham Cahan, *Yekl and the Imported Bridegroom and Other Stories of the New York Ghetto* (1896, 1898; reprint ed., New York: Dover, 1970).

16. Bernard G. Richards, "Introduction," *Yekl and the Imported Bridegroom,* pp. iii–viii. See also Ronald Sanders, *The Downtown Jews: Portraits of an Immigrant Generation* (New York: Harper and Row, 1969), which is mostly a portrait of Cahan; and Irving Howe, *World of Our Fathers* (New York: Harcourt Brace Jovanovich, 1976), pp. 522–33.

17. See Lawrence E. Mintz, "Langston Hughes's Jesse B. Semple: The Urban Negro as Wise Fool," reprinted from *Satire Newsletter* (Fall 1969) in *The Harbrace College Reader,* Mark Schorer et al., eds., 4th ed. (New York: Harcourt Brace Jovanovich, 1972), pp. 186–99. The most representative of Hughes's own collections is *The Best of Simple* (New York: Hill and Wang, 1961).

18. *The Spirit of the Ghetto* (1902; reprint ed., New York: Schocken Books, 1966), pp. 239–41.

19. *Tribune* (obituary), May 29, 1936; Ellis, *Life of Dunne,* p. 286.

20. *The Letters of Theodore Dreiser,* Robert H. Elias, ed. (Philadelphia: University of Pennsylvania Press, 1959), 3: 949.

21. John V. Kelleher, "Mr. Dooley and the Same Old World," *Atlantic* 177 (June 1946): 119.

22. Burges Johnson, "The New Humor," *The Critic* 40 (June 1902): 531.

23. *The End of American Innocence* (Chicago: Quadrangle Books, 1964), p. 140. Also useful on this aspect of American intellectual history is Eric F. Goldman, who, in *Rendezvous with Destiny* (New York: Random House, 1956), charts the disintegration of "the steel chain of ideas," the links of which included Spencerian Social Darwinism, "the laws of God" in religion, "objective fact" in biology and psychology, and "natural laws" of philosophy,

law, politics, and economics. According to Goldman these ideas were "standard doctrine in thousands of American pulpits, universities, and newspaper offices" in the late nineteenth century. "Always they were unchallengeable Truth, an ideological chain protecting America as it was with iron strength" (pp. 70–71). Goldman pushes the date of the fomenting of the "revolt against absolutes" back into the nineties, by discussing an impressive group of pre-1900 subversives from a variety of disciplines: Edward A Ross in sociology, Richard T. Ely and Thorstein Veblen in economics, Oliver Wendell Holmes, Jr., in law, Walter Rauschenbusch in religion, Franz Boas in anthropology, William James in philosophy.

24. May, *End of American Innocence,* pp. 142, 146.

25. C. Vann Woodward, *The Burden of Southern History,* revised ed. (Baton Rouge: Louisiana State University Press, 1968), pp. 21, 190.

26. Ellis, *Life of Dunne,* p. 103.

27. "Mr. Dooley and the Same Old World," p. 122.

28. This piece was a response to two suicides in Chicago during the previous week. The second was that of a German-American dancing instructor, who shot himself in the head and then fell 140 feet from a thirteenth-floor balcony of the Chamber of Commerce building downtown. A note was found, blaming his wife. *T–H,* Sept. 25, 26, 1897.

29. *Mr. Dooley Says* (New York: Scribners, 1910), pp. 130–31. Always the relativist, Mr. Dooley here is like Herman Melville in the great letter to Hawthorne that ends:

> Lord, when shall we be done growing? As long as we have anything more to do, we have done nothing. So, now, let us add Moby Dick to our blessing, and step from that. Leviathan is not the biggest fish;—I have heard of Krakens.
> This is a long letter, but you are not at all bound to answer it. Possibly, if you do answer it, and direct it to Herman Melville, you will missend it—for the very fingers that now guide this pen are not precisely the same that just took it up and put it on this paper. Lord, when shall we be done changing? Ah! it's a long stage, and no inn in sight, and night coming, and the body cold.

Marked "Pittsfield, Monday afternoon November 1851," this letter is quoted in Perry Miller, ed., *Major Writers of America* (New York: Harcourt Brace and World, 1962), 1: 903–04.

30. The entire Dooley canon is as follows: *Mr. Dooley in Peace and in War* (Boston: Small, Maynard, 1898); *Mr. Dooley in the Hearts of His Countrymen* (Boston: Small, Maynard, 1899); *Mr. Dooley's Philosophy* (New York: R. H. Russell, 1900); *Mr. Dooley's Opinions* (New York: R. H. Russell, 1901); *Observations by Mr. Dooley* (New York: R. H. Russell, 1902); *Dissertations by Mr. Dooley* (London and New York: Harper, 1906); *Mr. Dooley Says* (New York: Scribners, 1910); and *Mr. Dooley on Making a Will and Other Necessary Evils* (New York: Scribners, 1919).

31. For more details about these years see the later chapters of Ellis, *Life of Dunne.*

32. *Mr. Clemens and Mark Twain* (New York: Simon and Schuster Pocket Books, 1968), pp. 103, 378–83.

33. "Mr. Dooley," *New Republic* 20 (Sept. 24, 1919): 235–36.

INDEX